D1602792

EMIGRANTS AND SOCIETY

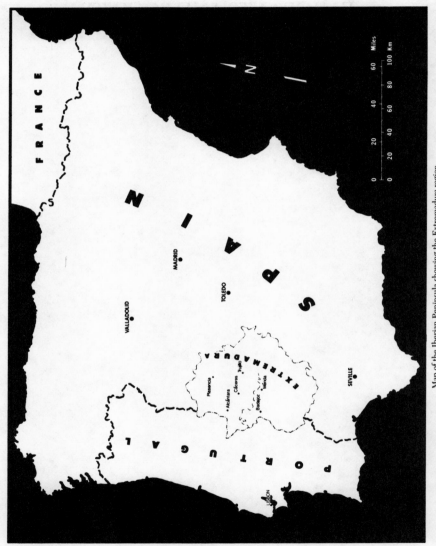

Map of the Iberian Peninsula showing the Extremadura region.

EMIGRANTS AND SOCIETY

Extremadura and America in the Sixteenth Century

IDA ALTMAN

UNIVERSITY OF CALIFORNIA PRESS
BERKELEY   LOS ANGELES   LONDON

The publisher wishes to acknowledge the generous
assistance of The Program for Cultural Cooperation
between Spain's Ministry of Culture and United States
Universities in the publication of this book.

University of California Press
Berkeley and Los Angeles, California

University of California Press, Ltd.
London, England

Library of Congress Cataloging-in-Publication Data

Altman, Ida.

Emigrants and society : Extremadura and America in the
sixteenth century / Ida Altman.
    p.   cm.
  Bibliography: p.
  Includes index.
  ISBN 0-520-06494-1 (alk. paper)
    1. Cáceres Region (Spain)—Emigration and
immigration—History—16th century.   2. Trujillo Region
(Cáceres, Spain)—Emigration and immigration—
History—16th century.   3. Cáceres Region (Spain)—
Social conditions.   4. Trujillo Region (Cáceres, Spain)—
Social conditions.   5. Latin America—Emigration and
immigration—History—16th century.   I. Title.
JV8259.C33A68 1989
325.46′28—dc19   88-38074
                                                      CIP

Printed in the United States of America
1 2 3 4 5 6 7 8 9

Contents

Acknowledgments

Research and writing to a great extent were made possible by funding from the Commission for Educational and Cultural Exchange between Spain and the United States, for dissertation research in 1978–1979 and postdoctoral work in 1985, and from the University of New Orleans in the summers of 1984 and 1987.

I wish to acknowledge a number of people for their contributions to the completion of this book. María Isabel Simó, director of the Archivo Histórico Provincial of Cáceres, Magdalena Galiana Núñez, director of the Archivo Municipal of Trujillo, and Fátima Martín Pedrilla of Cáceres offered crucial assistance in the archives and friendship as well. My thanks also to Carmen Otuerta de Salas of Madrid and Trujillo. I am very grateful to the following: James Lockhart for invaluable suggestions and criticism; Helen Nader, Stuart B. Schwartz, William B. Taylor, and David S. Reher for their comments on the manuscript; Richard L. Kagan and Franklin W. Knight for their encouragement over the years; Scott Mahler of the University of California Press for his support and assistance; Paula Cizmar for copy editing; and Beryl Gauthier for efficient and patient typing of most of the manuscript. Suzanne Shean of the School of Urban and Regional Studies, University of New Orleans, drew the excellent detail map of the region; special thanks also to Dick Jacobs for additional artwork on the maps.

I also thank the many other friends and colleagues who have provided insight and inspiration and especially my family for their support, understanding, and unfailingly sound advice. At its best this volume reflects the efforts and concern of those acknowledged

here; its shortcomings are my responsibility alone. I dedicate the
the book to my parents, whose love and example in so many ways
have made this work possible.

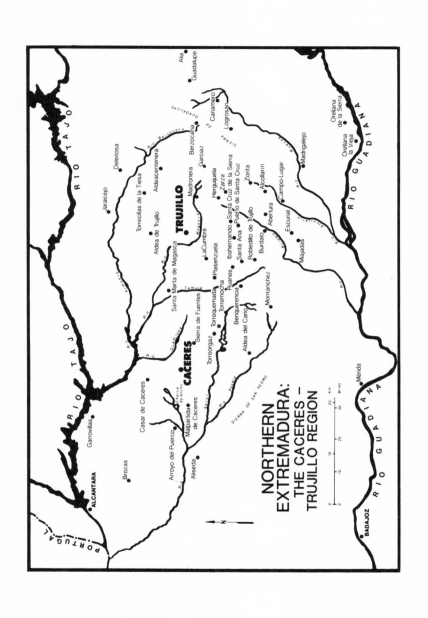

NORTHERN
EXTREMADURA:
THE CACERES –
TRUJILLO REGION

Alia
Guadalupe
Orellana de la Sierra
Orellana la Vieja
Canamero
Logrosán
Madrigalejo
Berzocana
Garciaz
Madroñera
Herguijuela
Zarza
Santa Cruz de la Sierra
Zorita
Alcollarín
Campo-Lugar
Aldeacentenera
Torrecillas de la Tiesa
Deleitosa
TRUJILLO
Aldea de Trujillo
Jaraicejo
Santa Ana
Puerto de Trujillo
Robledillo de Trujillo
Burdalo
Abertura
Escurial
Majadas
La Cumbre
Plasenzuela
Santa Marta de Magasca
Ruanes
Torremocha
Torrequemada
Montanchez
Benquerencia
Sierra de Fuentes
Aldea del Cano
Torreorgaz
CACERES
Casar de Caceres
Malpartida de Caceres
Garrovillas
ALCANTARA
Brozas
Arroyo del Puerco
Aliseda
SIERRA DE SAN PEDRO
Merida
BADAJOZ

RIO TAJO
RIO GUADIANA
RIO BERZOCANA
RIO ALMONTE
RIO GUADALUPE
SIERRA
RIO TAMUJA
RIO MAGASCA
RIO SALOR
RIO GUADILOBA
RIO AYUELA
PORTUGAL

KM
MILES
0   10   20   30
0   10   20

N

Introduction

The purpose of this book is to study the movement of people between Spain and America in the sixteenth century by examining the experiences of emigrants who lived in, left, and sometimes returned to a specific area in southwestern Spain. It is not activities in the Indies that define the emigrant group; in the New World the people in question engaged in a variety of pursuits and achieved both failure and success, notoriety and obscurity, distinction and mediocrity. What the emigrants did have in common were their origins in and connections to the small cities and villages of northeastern Extremadura. They were relatives, friends, and neighbors. They knew or knew about one another, associated closely once they arrived in the New World, kept in touch with people back home, returned home to visit or to stay, and encouraged further emigration from their home towns, thus nurturing the patterns of association based on kinship and common origin that served to define them as a group.

Given the above, the reader will find that the present work differs in its objectives and conclusions from studies of sixteenth-century Spanish emigration which have taken an ostensibly broader and more inclusive approach to the subject or used some aspect of the Spanish American context and experience as the basis for investigation. While such approaches to the subject have yielded important data and insights, they have not allowed a systematic examination of the question of the relationship of local Spanish society to emigration and the Indies enterprise.

As one of the three distinct, if internally heterogeneous, groups

1

that contributed to the formation of Spanish American society—the indigenous peoples of the Americas, the Europeans, and the Africans they brought with them—the Spaniards played a pivotal role in that they were responsible for bringing the three together. Yet in recent years Spaniards have attracted less scholarly attention than Indians or Africans, in large part, no doubt, because of the imbalance that resulted from the earlier historiographical focus on Spanish institutions in the New World. It is also possible that the much greater cultural homogeneity of the Iberian group, compared to the other two, has discouraged more detailed inquiry into the background of Spanish emigrants. The uniformity of Spanish behavior, attitudes, and expectations in the process of transferring Spanish institutions and forms of socioeconomic organization to the New World would seem to suggest that the detailed investigation of Spanish society and culture can reveal little that would be new or unexpected to the student of early Spanish America. Furthermore, certain basic features of Spanish society did change rapidly or even disappear in the New World setting, and this in turn might be seen as further evidence that little is to be gained from an in-depth examination of the nature and organization of Spanish society.

Yet the assumption that early Spanish American social history has only an indirect relationship with the social history of early modern Spain (Castile) can be sustained only as long as the histories of the two are kept separate. If they are brought into direct connection—as can be done most effectively by looking at people rather than institutions—they become inextricably intertwined. If we consider Spanish and Spanish American societies of the sixteenth century as variants within a definable but expanding Hispanic world, then individual career patterns, continuities of socioeconomic organization, and historical developments that originated in Spain in the Middle Ages and carried over to the New World can be seen as part of a coherent line of development. Because of these continuities and the ties between people in Spain and America, the study of emigration as such provides the basis for an examination of socioeconomic patterns and change in the Old and New Worlds. The societies were distinct but closely connected and in some ways interdependent.

Spanish emigration to the New World in the sixteenth century is a vast subject. Doubtless the most important contribution to the field to date has been the compilation of listings of emigrants by year and place of origin for much of the sixteenth century, which has made it possible to delineate the overall regional and demographic patterns of the movement.[1] Scholars also have considered the efforts to legislate and control emigration, the problem of calculating the numbers of legal and illegal emigrants who departed for the Indies, and the intellectual and economic impact of the opening of the New World on Spain and Europe.[2] In addition historians primarily interested in the formation of Spanish American society have studied the background, activities, and careers of individuals or selected groups in the New World. They have shown how the examination of careers that spanned the Atlantic can tell us something about people who emigrated and about social structure in both Spain and the New World. These studies, together with collections of letters principally from nonofficial sources, demonstrate the importance of family and personal ties between people in Spain and Spanish America, of cycles of emigration in which one family member who emigrated would be followed by others—often from the next generation—and of local and regional association in the Indies.[3]

The impact of emigration, return migration, and involvement in the Indies enterprise on local society in Spain is only beginning to receive the attention it merits.[4] Whereas most studies relevant to emigration (with the exception of the biographical or prosopographical works mentioned) have tended to be broad, taking most of Castile as the basic unit of analysis, Spanish society of the period in question was highly localized in its structures and orientation. The strong sense of identification that Spaniards felt with their place of origin meant that most people who returned from the Indies did not establish themselves at court or in the cosmopolitan city of Seville (or did so only temporarily) but rather in their home towns (or if these were very small, perhaps the nearest large town or city of their region). This sense of identification with the locality continued to figure strongly in the New World as well, as emigrants sent home for relatives, visited, and sent back money to invest in properties, chaplaincies, charitable works, and to support family members. It seems clear, therefore, that the study of emigration within the context of a specific locale is potentially one of the most revealing approaches to the subject.[5] Analysis of the position of emigrants and returnees in their home societies not only provides a more concrete basis for studying the transmission and transformation of social structures and cultural attitudes from one side of the Atlantic to the other than can broader and more general analyses, it also can illuminate processes of social change or continuity in Spanish society itself.

The focus of my research on emigration and society is the eastern part of what is called Alta (or northern) Extremadura, specifically the neighboring cities of Cáceres and Trujillo. These two cities or large towns, with populations of around 8000 or 9000 by the mid- to late sixteenth century, were located in a relatively sparsely populated region whose economy hinged on stockraising. Sheep were predominant; one of the three major routes of the northern transhumant sheep herds and the Mesta led directly into the area. Rental of winter pasturage to sheepraisers of Castile and León complemented the local stockraising industry and provided an important source of income for the local nobility, who held much of the region's grazing land. I chose northeastern Extremadura because it produced substantial numbers of emigrants in the sixteenth century but was located well outside the immediate hinterland of Seville. Seville apparently acted as the principal collection point for potential emigrants from much of Castile. By focusing on a region some 250 kilometers (and several days' travel) to the north, I hoped to clarify and delineate the essentially local processes and structures that affected migration.

Emigration from the area studied can be seen as both typical and atypical of Spanish emigration as a whole, as would probably prove to be true for any locality chosen. All the patterns we have come to expect existed there: participation of a broad cross section of social and occupational types, significant impact of family structure and position on determining who would stay at home and who would leave, cycles and traditions of emigration quickly taking shape, and continued contacts and association of people in the Indies both with each other and with people at home. There were certain features, however, of the emigration movement from this part of Extremadura that would make it distinctive within the movement overall. No doubt the most important was the early prominence and participation of such figures as Frey Nicolás de Ovando, early governor of Hispaniola and member of an important noble family of Cáceres, and Francisco Pizarro, conqueror and first governor of Peru, and Pizarro's brothers, natives of Trujillo, who recruited young men from Trujillo and the region in 1529. The crucial role played by such citizens of Cáceres and Trujillo helps account for an early and sustained involvement in the Indies that would not be found, for example, in the nearby city of Plasencia.

The present work represents a revision and expansion of my doctoral thesis on emigration and society in the city of Cáceres in the sixteenth century,[6] and much of that material appears here. I expanded my research in the expectation that additional material on Trujillo and its jurisdiction would provide a more substantial base for drawing conclusions about Extremaduran emigration and return migration than Cáceres alone could afford. Since no other study like the one I did for Cáceres existed, it seemed reasonable to assume that looking at a neighboring city of comparable size and lying within the same rather well-defined region would reveal essentially similar patterns for emigration and its impact on local society. Yet the sources for Trujillo and its towns and villages suggested some notably different developments there. Research on Trujillo brought into sharp focus the strength of local structures and relations and their potential implications for patterns of emigration. The most striking difference found between the two cities with regard to emigration was quantitative. Well over twice as many people emigrated from Trujillo as from Cáceres in the sixteenth century, although Cáceres was actually only slightly smaller in population.[7] In Cáceres, *hidalgos* (members of the privileged class)— especially younger sons—were a substantial element in the emigrant group, relatively few nuclear families emigrated, and the participation of people from the towns of the city's jurisdiction was fairly limited. Trujillo, on the other hand, while it also had many hidalgos among its emigrants, sent numbers of families, groups of young men who probably came from the middling commoner groups (artisan or peasant background), and significant numbers from the villages of its district.

The distinctive patterns in emigration in some ways arose from the notable localism of early modern Spanish society discussed above, and they suggest an important conclusion. Spanish emigration to the New World at one level was a coherent phenomenon characterized by overall similarities in socioeconomic and demographic composition, regional origins, pace, timing, direction, and the legal and actual constraints or incentives that were brought to bear. At another level, Spanish emigration was the aggregate of many smaller movements. These regional and local movements shared many elements and some direct connections in common. But they also stemmed from and reflected a particular configuration of circumstances which was tied to the locality and point of origin as well as to the degree of involvement in and knowledge of the Indies of the people of a particular place. Although emigration from Cáceres to the Indies got going earlier than from Trujillo, probably because of the importance and example of Frey Nicolás de Ovando, the ties between Trujillo and Peru that resulted from the activities of the Pizarros proved to be a powerful and sustaining force. Ultimately the movement from (and back to) Trujillo became a far more substantial and central phenomenon than would be true for Cáceres. Hand in hand with the greater size of the movement to and from the Indies was a much more visible and direct impact on the home society in Trujillo than in Cáceres.

Because of its concern with the relationship between locality and emigration, this study is an examination both of local society and of movement away from and back to the locality. The social structure and mobility patterns that characterized local society assured that emigration to the New World and involvement in the Indies enterprise would be reflected perceptibly in the local scene. Whereas the kinds of sources utilized and the specific nature of my research meant that much of the material gathered on local society would relate directly to emigrants and returnees or their families, use of sources that are in effect neutral as regards emigration (for example, documentation from notarial and municipal archives) has shown that, within the local context, emigrants and returnees functioned much as did everyone else. Furthermore some of the material specifically on emigrants (for example, testimonies found in the Archive of the Indies in Seville) has proven invaluable in illuminating certain sectors of Spanish society, especially members of the humbler groups, which usually do not emerge very clearly. Such sources complement notarial and municipal records, which tend to be more revealing of the upper middle and upper classes of society. The portrait presented here of local society and its relationship to emigration and the Indies is intended to demonstrate the extent to which emigration became an integral part of the local context in the six-teenth century at the same time that it contributed to the formation of new societies in the Indies and the extension of the Hispanic world.

This approach to understanding the relationship between emi-grants and their home society has significant implications for assess-ing the nature of Spanish activity in the Indies and the formation of postconquest societies there. Nearly thirty years after anthropolo-gist George Foster delineated his suggestive theory of the forma-tion of "conquest culture" in Spanish America and its relationship to the diverse culture of Spain itself, we still have scarcely begun to analyze how Spanish forms of socioeconomic organization and cul-ture below the level of governmental and ecclesiastical institutions were transferred to the New World and, in the process, trans-formed. The failure to address that process directly has produced two contradictory but often implicitly accepted models of the rela-tionship between Spanish and Spanish American societies and cul-tures. One holds that early Spanish American society fully repli-cated Spanish society, the other that the dramatically different circumstances of the New World called forth entirely new re-sponses and patterns among Spaniards.[8] Careful consideration of Spanish society and the people who left can demonstrate that the truth lies somewhere in between.

Although it owes historiographical and conceptual debts to other scholarly works, this book represents the first systematic attempt to describe and explain the background and activities of a group of Spanish emigrants of the sixteenth century and simultaneously to make a detailed inquiry into their home society. By using local society as the basic context for analysis of the careers of emigrants, it becomes possible to examine their relationship to a cultural and socioeconomic milieu with a great deal of specificity. Although I have not identified every emigrant from the area studied, most likely I have found the majority; the people who figure here consti-tute the core of the movement between one region in Spain and the New World. This study of emigration from Extremadura, there-fore, can claim a completeness and grounding in the concrete real-ity of local society that no other consideration of Spanish emigration has offered to date.

In the following chapters I attempt to portray society in the

8 *Introduction*

Cáceres-Trujillo region and the relationship of that society to the New World. Chapters 1 through 4 deal with social and economic groups, structures, and relations; they focus primarily on the home society but incorporate much material on emigrants, returnees, and their families. Chapters 5 through 7 treat more specifically the activities of emigrants to the Indies and people who returned home again.

The book's time frame is the sixteenth century, with principal focus on the middle decades of the century, from around 1530 to 1580. Practical rather than theoretical considerations largely determined this choice. The documentation is strongest for that period and is, in fact, sufficiently abundant and complex that a somewhat arbitrary cutoff point had to be adopted. As the initial phase of Spanish efforts in the New World, the sixteenth century still merits much more systematic scholarly attention than it has received. Continuing investigation into the seventeenth century might well reveal that new patterns of connection and interaction between Spain and Spanish America developed to replace or coexist with those identified here for the sixteenth century; that inquiry, however, must remain to be done. At the other end of the time spectrum, the fifteenth century, many uncertainties persist as well and to some degree limit the extent to which we can assess the broadest questions regarding socioeconomic and political changes in local society which arose from involvement in the Indies enterprise. The historiography for the late middle ages in Extremadura is weak[9] and at present does not offer an adequate basis for examining some aspects of long-term development.

A few more comments on historiography and focus should be offered. Long a poor and isolated region, Extremadura has received only sporadic attention from historians. Although recently the situation has begun to improve,[10] the gaps and limitations that characterize the region's historical literature mean that initiating and carrying out research on a particular place and time can be difficult. I did not find for Cáceres the kind of solid local history that scholars of other cities often produced in the nineteenth and earlier twentieth centuries, although the works of Miguel Muñoz de San Pedro (the Count of Canilleros), many of them biographical, shed much light on the fifteenth and sixteenth centuries. But serious students of Cáceres undoubtedly will find themselves piecing together the city's history directly from the documentary evidence for some time to come. Trujillo, on the other hand, has received better treatment. The histories written by Clodoaldo Naranjo Alonso and Juan Tena Fernández—both of whom were directors of Trujillo's municipal archive and incorporated (especially Tena Fernández) a good deal of archival material into their texts—offer an excellent starting point for studying the city.[11] And, of course, the fame and achievements of Francisco Pizarro and his brothers have long attracted attention to Trujillo.

The Pizarros were by far the most famous native sons of Trujillo. Documentation of their activities in Peru especially is vast, and the secondary literature on their lives and impact, already considerable, is still growing.[12] Yet the Pizarros do not occupy center stage in the present study. They might well have done so, but a quite different book would have resulted. Here the reader will find the Pizarros treated much as other emigrants and returnees, as examples of certain trends or patterns. Naturally their greater influence and wealth meant that they frequently played key roles not only in major episodes of the time (the conquest of Peru, the civil wars, Gonzalo Pizarro's rebellion) but in the more prosaic events of everyday life as well. Hernando Pizarro, the legitimate brother and the only one to return to Trujillo, became (despite his years of imprisonment) one of the wealthiest and hence most powerful citizens of Trujillo, exercising considerable influence for many years. But the full story of the family could be told only at the cost of neglecting the many other people and elements that shaped local society and its relation to the Indies. The Pizarros were not Trujillo, even after the conquest of Peru and their spectacular rise in wealth and prominence. Nonetheless, because their activities in Peru had such a great impact on early events and on the experiences of many of their relatives, retainers, and other compatriots there and at home, and because they figure frequently in the following pages, it is worthwhile to review here the main outlines of their careers and involvements.[13]

Francisco Pizarro was born around 1478, the illegitimate son of Captain Gonzalo Pizarro, member of an hidalgo family of middling rank (minor gentry, in other words) which had lands in La Zarza, a village within Trujillo's district. Francisco's mother was Francisca González, the daughter of a farming family; she worked for a time as a servant in a Trujillo convent. At the time of Francisco's birth, his father Gonzalo probably was still in his teens and had not yet begun the military career that would take him to Granada, Navarre, and Italy. Although he used, uncontested, the Pizarro surname and seems to have had contact with his paternal relatives while he was growing up, unlike his younger half-brothers and sisters Francisco did not live in his father's household but instead was raised rather humbly, mostly among relatives on his mother's side. His mother eventually married, and Francisco maintained ties with that side of the family, taking his maternal half-brother Francisco Martín de Alcántara with him to Peru in 1530, where Francisco Martín became perhaps his closest companion.

In 1502 Francisco Pizarro left Spain for Hispaniola in the fleet of appointed governor Frey Nicolás de Ovando, probably either accompanying or intending to join his father's brother Juan Pizarro, known to have been in the Indies. During the next two decades Francisco rose steadily in rank and prominence, moving from Hispaniola to Panama and Nicaragua; by the mid-1520s he was indisputably the most senior and experienced leader in the Isthmian area known as Tierra Firme. Pizarro undertook exploratory expeditions down the coast of modern Peru in the later 1520s and by early 1528 was aware of the existence of a great empire in the area. Late that year he returned to Spain to obtain from the crown the *capitulaciones* (licenses) for the conquest and governorship of Peru. Before leaving again for the Indies in early 1530 he recruited a number of men, especially from Trujillo and that part of Extremadura, for the final expedition to Peru; among his recruits were his paternal half-brothers Hernando, Juan, and Gonzalo.

The climax of that effort was the capture at Cajamarca of the Inca emperor Atahuallpa, who pledged to collect a huge quantity of gold and silver as ransom in exchange for his life. In the summer of 1533 the Spaniards executed Atahuallpa and divided the amassed treasure. One-fifth went to the crown, with the remainder shared among the 168 men present. The Inca treasure was the single largest windfall of all the years of Spanish activity in the Indies to that point, and the men who received shares became wealthy and influential. Many became leading figures and *encomenderos* (holders of *encomiendas*, grants of Indian labor and tribute) in Lima, Cuzco, or other Spanish cities in Peru, or returned to Spain to establish themselves. The

Cajamarca group included fourteen men from Trujillo, one from its town of La Zarza, and two from Cáceres. All of the Pizarro brothers except Hernando, the legitimate son, died in Peru; Hernando returned to Spain, as did the majority of the Trujillo contingent at Cajamarca, and eventually married his brother Francisco's *mestiza* (person of Spanish and Indian parentage) daughter doña Francisca, thus consolidating the family fortune.

This is a skeletal and simplified account of a complex series of events. Cajamarca symbolized but by no means completed the conquest of the Inca empire. The Andean Indians resisted and rebelled; they besieged the Spaniards in Cuzco (the old Inca capital) for more than a year in 1536–1537. Francisco Pizarro's brother Juan died in that conflict. Complicated and deadly rivalries also put their mark on Spanish activities in the early years. Hernando Pizarro was responsible for the execution of Diego de Almagro, the former Pizarro partner turned rival; Hernando left for Spain in 1535, where he was imprisoned (he had returned briefly to Spain after Cajamarca and went back to Peru in 1534). Followers of Almagro's mestizo son don Diego retaliated by assassinating Francisco Pizarro in 1541.

These events left the youngest Pizarro brother, Gonzalo, the sole surviving member of the immediate family still in Peru. Disgruntled over the loss of the governorship bequeathed to him by his brother and supported by most of the big encomenderos, Gonzalo led a rebellion against the viceroy, Blasco Núñez Vela. The viceroy had arrived in Peru in 1544 with royal orders that would have undercut considerably the basis of that key institution of Spanish exploitation of Indian productive capacity, the encomienda. Gonzalo effectively ran Peru for four years but finally lost support with the advent of the royal representative, Licenciado Pedro de la Gasca, sent to restore order in 1547. The end of the rebellion and Gonzalo's execution closed the era of Pizarrist domination in Peru; but this twenty-year period of Pizarro leadership had a decisive impact on the timing and dimensions of emigration from their home town and region and affected patterns of extremeño association and involvement in the Indies for years to come. (The term "extremeños" as used here refers primarily to the people of the Cáceres-Trujillo subregion, unless otherwise noted.)

This study emphasizes the importance of family ties, socioeco-

nomic networks based on common origin, and the loyalty and solidarity these engendered; yet it must be remembered that the generalizations offered here cannot be applied wholesale to people or
developments either in Spain or Spanish America. Individual lives
and events may contradict or subvert almost any rule that can be
formulated. There is strong and consistent evidence for the importance of family relations and local cohesiveness both at home and in
the New World. Yet husbands abandoned wives and parents left
children behind; people sometimes ignored close relatives and instead formed partnerships and enduring friendships with individuals with whom they shared no roots but rather a compelling range
of common experiences and interests. Even what at first glance
looks like regional solidarity in fact could mask more complicated
forces. In light of their ultimate (and profitable) defection, the
support that the cacereño captains gave to Gonzalo Pizarro seems
to have been motivated as much by opportunism as regional loyalty; and a close examination of the almost unanimous participation
of the trujillanos in the rebellion shows that a fair degree of coercion was brought to bear on a number of them. (The terms "cacereños" and "trujillanos" will be used to refer to the people of
Cáceres and Trujillo respectively when it is necessary to distinguish between the two groups.)

Despite the variety and particularity of human behavior, however, the generalities still stand. The basic principles underlying
social structures are not simply products of the historian's retrospec-
tive analysis; these principles emerge in great part from the vocabu-
lary and actions of the people we are discussing. Francisco Pizarro's
favoritism toward his brothers and extremeño compatriots, Gonzalo Pizarro's faith in the strength of the ties of common origin that
he shared with many of his key supporters, Alvaro de Paredes's
letters home to Cáceres that constantly referred to family relations
and obligations, the uncles and aunts who sent for nephews back in
Spain to join them and inherit the fruits of their success in the
Indies—these are not at all abstract; they are a reflection of the
reality of people's lives.

Consideration of emigration from Cáceres and Trujillo shows
that at the most basic level the movement to the New World was
idiosyncratic, conditioned by a variety of circumstances tied to the
locality that could produce rather distinctive patterns and choices.

Despite similarity between the two cities, the emigration movement from Trujillo was much larger and the impact of the Indies much more perceptible and immediate there than in Cáceres. The region as a whole was itself atypical in some ways. The crucial initial role played by the Pizarros in Peru in large part not only accounts for the greater size of the movement from Trujillo but also explains why the movement from the area in certain ways differed from general patterns of Spanish emigration; for both cities Peru overall was by far the favored destination, whereas Mexico actually drew the largest number of emigrants from Spain in every decade but one in the sixteenth century from the time of the conquest. And there is no single good explanation for why Extremadura provided such a remarkable proportion of the leadership in the early years in the Indies.

Yet the idiosyncrasies that characterized emigration from Cáceres or Trujillo fit well within the general trends of the movement. The extremeño emigrant group was not exceptional in its socioeconomic or demographic makeup; it included representatives of a broad cross section of occupational and social groups, single and married adults, men, women, and children. Similarly extremeños, like other emigrants, departed for the New World under a variety of arrangements, recruited officially and privately, as appointed officials or servants, as part of entourages, or at their own initiative. In the New World their distinctiveness lay mainly in their own perception of their common origins and identity and their efforts to preserve those allegiances and associations brought from home.

A last qualifier should be made here. This study does not treat all of modern-day Extremadura or even historical "Alta" Extremadura but rather the subregion formed by the cities of Cáceres and Trujillo and their districts. In the sixteenth century Extremadura did not function as an effective geographical or political unit and was scarcely recognized as such. It should also be noted that Spanish terms are explained in the text and included in a glossary at the end.

I

Local Society in Northern
Extremadura

At one level this book is concerned with matters that are abstract
and general. The formation, perpetuation, and modification of social patterns, the function and implications of mobility, and the
processes of cultural and social transmission or transformation from
Old World to New are subjects that are at least one step removed
from the reality of the day-to-day lives of individuals in specific
localities. When we approach the topic of the movement of people
from Spain across the Atlantic in the sixteenth century, uniformi-
ties of behavior and development become readily apparent. Yet
every Spanish emigrant was from a particular area and part of a
regionally defined movement. Thus a book such as this must go
beyond generalizations and become in large part the tale of real
people, specific places, and the connections that bound them.

The lives of sixteenth-century extremeño emigrants and returnees and their families, friends, and fellow townspeople largely un-
fold in a part of Spain that attracted little notice then or since.
Isolated, rural, and rather poor even today, Extremadura is unfamil-
iar to outsiders and even to many Spaniards. A brief description of
the region and discussion of its history may help set the scene for
the story of Extremadura's people and their role in Spanish expansion to the New World. This chapter will sketch out the underlying
environmental, institutional, and socioeconomic framework that
shaped social structures and relations in the region. We will see
that in the period with which we are concerned local society in

Extremadura was both traditional and dynamic, conservative yet changing.

Of the many and varied regions of modern Spain, Extremadura is the largest, comprising two provinces—Cáceres and Badajoz— that only recently, with some effort, have begun the process of constructing a shared sense of identity. In fact the Extremadura of the past encompassed several regions, defined at least partially geographically. The historical experience of these regions from ancient until quite recent times varied considerably. Badajoz, the southernmost of the two modern provinces, historically was oriented toward Andalusia to the south and more directly affected by its proximity to Portugal to the west than was Cáceres; following the reconquest most of this southern half of Extremadura came under the sway of the powerful military Order of Santiago.

Cáceres to the north, however, was more closely tied to Castile and less homogeneous. This northern province—once known as Alta Extremadura—divides into at least two subregions. In the north lies a green, agriculturally prosperous region that includes the Vera and other valleys of the Sierra de Gredos. Plasencia has long been the main urban center for this area, and Yuste, the monastery to which Charles V retired in the 1550s, is located in the Vera. Appended to this fertile area are the barren and impoverished Hurdes, lying south of Ciudad Rodrigo, reputedly an isolated enclave of morisco settlement. The second, and larger, subregion of Alta Extremadura lies between the Tajo River to the north and the Guadiana (which passes through the city of Badajoz) to the south. It is a dry plateau, hilly and mountainous in parts, generally more suited to stockraising than intensive agriculture. Historical developments in some ways divided even this wide tableland. After the reconquest the western part (including Alcántara, Albuquerque, and Valencia) became the stronghold of another important military order, Alcántara, whereas the eastern part of the province, the Sierra de Guadalupe, was remote, relatively isolated from the rest, and during the late Middle Ages increasingly dominated by the wealthy and royally favored monastery of Guadalupe.

The subregion formed by the cities of Cáceres and Trujillo and their contiguous districts is a coherent geographical entity that for some observers epitomizes the conjunction of environmental and human factors that differentiate Extremadura from the regions to the north and south and imbue it with a distinctive character of its own.[1] This central subregion, less directly influenced by Castile and León than Plasencia and less tied to Andalusia than Badajoz, was above all a pastoral region, with vines and olives cultivated in the hilly and mountainous areas and pigs fattened in the woodlands of the hills. Cáceres and Trujillo, with their dramatic hilltop silhouettes, offer among the finest examples in all of Extremadura of the fortified towns and castles of the Moorish and postreconquest periods and the results of the fifteenth- and sixteenth-century boom in private, public, and ecclesiastic construction.

Despite the physical and cultural homogeneity of the Cáceres-Trujillo subregion, however, historical experience—as almost everywhere in the Iberian peninsula—again generated differences. León claimed Cáceres and Castile Trujillo after the reconquest of the early thirteenth century, although both towns received extensive jurisdictions and similar privileges aimed at encouraging resettlement of the area.[2] Cáceres became part of the diocese of Coria, whereas Trujillo was included in what would be the much wealthier bishopric of Plasencia. And though the original districts of both cities were very large, subsequent readjustments and changes left Trujillo far more populous and wealthy.

The historical differences between the two cities long predated the events of the reconquest. Although the Romans eventually occupied the entire region, Cáceres doubtless was a far more important site of Roman settlement than Trujillo. The Romans fortified the site not long before the beginning of the modern era (probably around 20 B.C.). The principal Roman road crossing the region from Mérida north to Salamanca was the Via Lata, a major military route that the Muslims later called the "Silver Road." This road passed through Cáceres, while Trujillo was on a secondary route that led from Mérida to Toledo.[3] The foundations of Cáceres's walls and at least one of the gates of the old city were Roman in origin, and the city preserved for centuries its lovely Roman statue of Ceres. The Roman origins of Trujillo are not as well established. Possibly its Moorish castle was built on a Roman base. Nonetheless remains found near the city and throughout its jurisdiction attest that Roman settlement existed in the area, if not perhaps precisely at Trujillo's modern site.[4]

Perhaps the most consistent feature of Extremadura's historical experience has been its marginality in the context of peninsular history and development. Certainly people inhabited the region from ancient times; the cave of Maltravièso near the city of Cáceres has Paleolithic paintings, and archeological remains from the Celtiberian period dot the countryside. But the region lacked the mineral resources and rich agricultural potential that so strongly attracted outsiders to other parts of the peninsula, such as the Guadalquivir Valley. The Romans more or less ignored the region until they finally undertook the effective occupation of the whole peninsula. The area of what is today central-southeastern Portugal and Extremadura witnessed a good deal of conflict before Rome subdued it with characteristic thoroughness; Cáceres doubtless originated as a military colony. Similarly the Visigoths took little interest in the region and only incorporated the Cáceres-Trujillo heartland into their kingdom in the sixth century.

In the eighth century the Muslim invaders at first bypassed the region altogether on their way north from Mérida to Toledo and did not reach the area around Cáceres for at least forty years. Even after they did so, like their predecessors they found the region offered no great attractions; and so they made no concerted efforts to colonize there. A diverse population of Berbers, Muladíes (Christian converts to Islam), and Mozarabs (Christians living under Muslim rule) gradually filled the area. The decisive moment for formal Moorish occupation occurred with the arrival of the Almoravids in the early twelfth century, followed by the Almohads. They fortified the towns of Cáceres, Trujillo, Santa Cruz, and Montánchez in face of the southward movement of the Christian reconquest.[5] Coria was reconquered by the Christians in 1079 and then lost; its definitive reoccupation by Alfonso VII in 1143 signaled the beginning of a sustained Christian effort to claim the entire region. Key fortified towns such as Cáceres and Trujillo passed back and forth between Christians and Moors until finally Cáceres was reconquered in 1229 and Trujillo in 1233.[6]

Thus in the early thirteenth century, with the final Christian reconquest, Extremadura—which had never been an independent Christian kingdom nor a center for Islamic civilization and culture— was simply annexed to the crown of Castile-León. Extremadura became a Castilian province, to be settled by people from Castile, León, and Galicia.[7] Reoccupation was slow, in part again because of

the region's relative lack of strong attractions and in part because of
the very magnitude of the reconquest enterprise. The whole Duero
region already had been occupied by settlers from the north, and
once Andalusia had been secured its attractions proved greater than
those of Extremadura; so once again a movement of population partially bypassed the region. These obstacles notwithstanding, probably most of the towns of Alta Extremadura were resettled in the
twelfth and thirteenth centuries. No doubt the majority of the sites
had been inhabited previously, or more or less continuously; preferred locations were on hilltops or sides, beside rivers or springs, or
along already-established routes such as the Silver Road. The locations of many towns and villages at the confluence of rivers (for
example, Plasencia), on hilltops (for example, Cáceres), and adjacent
to castles (Trujillo), and even the names of many settlements—near
Cáceres alone were villages named Torrequemada, Torreorgaz, and
Torremocha—reflected their defensive character.[8]

During the two or three centuries following the reconquest the
region developed steadily if not spectacularly. Merino sheep introduced from North Africa made local stockraising increasingly viable and lucrative, and the incorporation of Extremadura and Andalusia into Castile opened the green winter pastures of the south
to the transhumant stockraisers of the north. A degree of prosperity, the routes of the transhumant herders (cañadas), and Extremadura's location between Castile-León and Andalusia brought
people through and to the region. Cáceres and Trujillo expanded
rapidly beyond their old walls. They became centers for commerce and industry as well as agriculture and supported a growing
religious establishment. Their populations reflected the ethnic and
socioeconomic mix characteristic of much of the Iberian peninsula. By the late fifteenth century both Cáceres and Trujillo had
communities (aljamas) of Moors and Jews. In 1479 Cáceres had
130 Jewish families. Trujillo's Jewish residents had clientage ties
with some of the leading nobles, and important visitors to the city
often lodged in Jewish homes.[9] Not all developments were peace-
ful, however. Factionalism was endemic, and the necessity of
defending oneself from one's neighbors sometimes supplanted the
military exigencies of the reconquest. The Golfines, a family of
strongmen who came originally to fight in the reconquest, settled

down to terrorize and prey on everyone in the region until they finally were brought under control.[10]

Alta Extremadura essentially became a secondary, politically and economically subordinated province of Castile in the centuries after the reconquest. Nonetheless the region took on a certain character and underwent a development of its own that did not derive solely from Castile. Two of the great Spanish religiomilitary orders—Santiago and Alcántara—originated in Alta Extremadura. The Order of Santiago formed in 1170 as the "Congregación de los Fratres de Cáceres" during one of the periods that the Christians held the city, which the Leonese King Ferdinand II gave to the order as their headquarters. The order, known as the Knights of Santiago by the end of the twelfth century, played an important role in the final reconquest, although ultimately the king refused to reinstate them in Cáceres, making it a royal town instead. The Order of Alcántara was founded in 1218 in the west.[11] While the military orders clearly were modeled on other crusading orders such as the Templars, the strength of their dominion over much of Extremadura after the reconquest and the weakness of royal power during the later Middle Ages meant they would become largely autonomous and in some ways distinctively extremeño. While Cáceres and Trujillo themselves came under royal jurisdiction and remained directly tied to the crown (with only brief exceptions), some of the major figures who held positions in the powerful and unruly orders—especially Alcántara—came from leading noble families of the cities.[12] After Ferdinand and Isabella brought the orders under direct royal control, they began to be transformed from extremeño into more nearly Castilian institutions, a source of royal patronage and revenues.

Another institution that arose in Alta Extremadura, the monastery of Nuestra Señora de Guadalupe, also came to have great significance in the larger world of Castile. The story of the appearance of the Virgin Mary in the mountains to a humble shepherd from Cáceres who was searching for a strayed cow and of the subsequent discovery of the dark wooden image of the Virgin buried at the site of the apparition reputedly dates from the first part of the fourteenth century.[13] The shrine constructed there in 1380 became a Jeronymite monastery that the Trastámara kings generously

patronized—to some extent at the expense of Trujillo, which forfeited some of its lands to Guadalupe. The proximity of Trujillo's
jurisdiction to the monastery, and the royal concession of the right
to appoint the notaries of Trujillo and its district purchased by the
monastery in the late fourteenth century, gave rise to numerous
and sometimes quite bitter disputes. But the monastery's position
could not be challenged. With the shift of power and interest toward the center and south, Guadalupe arguably became the most
famous and important Spanish shrine in the fifteenth and sixteenth
centuries. Guadalupe had direct connections with the monasteries
of Yuste and San Lorenzo el Real (El Escorial). Extremeños were
known for their devotion to the Virgin of Guadalupe, which they
carried to the New World.[14]

Given their emphasis on centralizing and stabilizing royal authority, it is hardly surprising that Ferdinand and Isabella went to some
effort to win support among Extremadura's nobles and secure the
region for the crown. They formed strong ties with and liberally
rewarded key figures who came over to their side, simultaneously
assuring their future loyalty and undercutting the power of the
orders and other factions. Captain Diego de Ovando de Cáceres,
Sancho de Paredes (chamberlain of the Catholic Queen), and Luis
de Chaves, el viejo (the first two from Cáceres, the last from
Trujillo) allied themselves to Ferdinand and Isabella. All three
were patriarchs of powerful and wealthy families that for generations maintained their ties to the crown.[15]

Naturally Ferdinand and Isabella did not depend only on personal ties and alliances to consolidate their hold over Extremadura.
During the early years of their reign they visited Cáceres and
Trujillo (and, of course, Guadalupe) individually or together a number of times.[16] During these visits they organized the local militias
under the Santa Hermandad, issued ordinances regulating the composition and election of the city councils, and ordered the demolition, with some very few exceptions in the cases of their favorites
like Captain Diego de Ovando de Cáceres, of the nobles' fortified
towers. All these measures in some sense had as their objective the
diminution of the region's endemic violence and the nobility's independence. Their ordinances directed that seats on the councils be
divided among the cities' principal factions, and the demolition of
towers and incorporation of the militias into the royally controlled

Santa Hermandad also undercut the potential for destructive factional conflict. By the sixteenth century Alta Extremadura had been brought under royal control, and the turbulence of the previous couple of centuries subsided.

In the sixteenth century, then, the period in which people from Extremadura joined the Indies enterprise and provided such a remarkably large proportion of the leadership in the early years of exploration and conquest, Extremadura was very much a province of Castile. The region exported most of its wool, and the wool trade was in the hands of northern merchants. Local clothmakers produced an inferior product that served the local market; the upper classes imported high-quality cloth from Segovia, Valencia, or elsewhere. Northern stockraisers rented Extremadura's winter pastures. And the region, even its cities, offered few opportunities for individuals of ambition. As long as royal power in Castile was weak, perhaps restless and active men found a sufficiently open arena in which to pursue their ambitions in Extremadura. In the sixteenth century, with the demise of the orders and local strongmen, men who aspired to ecclesiastical, bureaucratic, or military careers had to leave cities like Cáceres and Trujillo for the court, or to study in Salamanca or Valladolid, or to fight in Italy or Flanders. They also went to the New World in some numbers. That they were no less attached and loyal to their home towns than were other Spaniards is clear from the number of people who left and returned again or at least maintained strong ties with home; but opportunities at home were limited.

Perhaps there is no single good explanation for why extremeños formed such a significant element (not in absolute numbers, but proportionally to the population and in terms of leadership) in the early years of the conquest and settlement of America. Nonetheless Extremadura's backwardness and marginality in the larger world of Castile and the empire surely played a part; a person who wanted to do something most likely had to leave. As a result in the sixteenth century, when Extremadura became an undeniably secondary and subordinated province of Castile, it also produced some of the most distinguished and famous figures of Castilian and imperial history: Frey Nicolás de Ovando, governor of Hispaniola from 1502–1509; Hernando Cortés from Medellín, conqueror of Mexico; Francisco Pizarro of Trujillo, conqueror of Peru; Fray Jerónimo de

Loaysa of Trujillo, first bishop and archbishop of Lima; Licenciado Juan de Ovando of Cáceres, who ended his active career in the church, university, and government as president of the Council of the Indies; Licenciado don Gaspar Cervantes de Gaete of Trujillo, archbishop of Messina, Salerno, and Tarragona and representative to the Council of Trent; the architect Francisco Becerra who left Trujillo in the 1570s to work in Mexico and Peru; and many others. The possibility that people from a rather backward and unimportant region could enter into the highest academic, ecclesiastic, and governmental circles and participate fully in some of the greatest events and episodes of the period also underlines an important aspect of early modern Spanish society—its permeability and flexibility. If Castile penetrated and subordinated Extremadura, Extremadura for its part proved capable of entering quite successfully into Castilian affairs and undertakings.

The discussion to this point has suggested a number of common historical, geographical, and socioeconomic features that characterized the Cáceres-Trujillo region. The two cities were reconquered within years of each other, came under the direct jurisdiction of the crown, developed along similar institutional lines, and controlled large districts encompassing a number of towns and villages. Their districts bordered on each other, and Cáceres and Trujillo were separated by only about fifty kilometers, which meant that each was closer to the other than to any other important town or city such as Badajoz or Plasencia.

Did this similarity and proximity mean that the area formed by their jurisdictions acted as a region? Viewed externally, in some ways it did; but judged by almost any structural or functional standard, a strong localism prevailed. Such regionalism as existed was largely circumstantial, superficial, or confined to the perceptions of relatively few people. The origins of the name "Extremadura" have been debated; but the fact is that in the sixteenth century generally the only people who used the term were individuals who were living or had lived outside the area. Hernando Pizarro (who had been with his half-brother Francisco Pizarro in Peru and returned to Spain), for example, in 1551 during his confinement in the fortress of Medina del Campo gave his power of attorney to someone in Trujillo to rent out the lands and pastures he owned in Trujillo and its district "and in all of Extremadura."[17] Sometimes the older form of the regional designation appeared in the sixteenth century. The merchant Juan González de Vitoria, who signed over a power of attorney to his son in Peru in 1561, referred to himself as a *vecino* (citizen) of Trujillo "which is in the frontier [extremo] of those kingdoms of Castile."[18] Most people ignored the whole problem of regional designation and specified the location of Cáceres or Trujillo as Castile or Spain.

Such terminological usage, if in itself of interest, does not necessarily shed much light on people's perceptions of their relations to an area and to each other; it is in any case clear that "Extremadura" had not entered into common popular usage. The use of the term "tierra" is more revealing. Usually "tierra" referred to a city and its jurisdiction; essentially the term was synonymous with "término" or district.[19] Hence normally no one living in Trujillo's jurisdiction would claim to be from the same tierra as that of Cáceres or vice versa. When people left the area, however, and especially when they found themselves in circumstances as different as those of the New World, the concept of tierra became more flexible and less precise. In the Indies tierra still retained its original and basic meaning; but in face of the necessity to extend and buttress personal networks and connections, usage became more inclusive. In Peru in 1546 Gonzalo Pizarro wrote to his field marshal Francisco de Carvajal that Antonio de Ulloa of Cáceres was "de mi tierra."[20] Nevertheless, despite the importance of regional ties and identification in the Indies, in the final analysis a fairly strict localism prevailed; cacereños and trujillanos, or even people from towns in Trujillo's district like Zorita, did not maintain the same solidarity with one another as they did with the people of their own tierra, city, or village.

The institutions of the cities, if virtually identical, were almost entirely independent. Such ties as existed outside the district linked local ecclesiastic or governmental institutions to the diocese or order or to the court. The movement of people was mainly local as well. People living within Trujillo's district often moved from one village or town to another, or to the city, or they might marry within the district if they did not marry someone from their own town; but they were far less likely to move (or marry) into Cáceres's district. Because Cáceres's district contained only six towns and villages, a native or resident had fewer possibilities for relocating within the city's jurisdiction; yet it is interesting to note that people from Cáceres or its villages who did move or marry outside the district more likely looked to the towns to the west—Garrovillas, Albuquerque, Brozas—than to Trujillo's district to the east. In fact whatever extralocal association and orientation existed seems to have followed roughly the diocesan divisions; cacereños had more contact with the towns of the diocese of Coria, while trujillanos more frequently formed ties with people from places like Jaraicejo and Deleitosa in the bishopric of Plasencia. Such ties can be seen in the example of Alonso Bravo, a native of the town of Búrdalo (in Trujillo's district) who had become a vecino of Trujillo. In his will of 1584 Bravo said he belonged to *cofradías* (lay religious assocations) in Trujillo, Puerto de Santa Cruz (a village formerly part of Trujillo's district, sold by the crown in the 1550s), and Jaraicejo.[21] The towns themselves had some significant connections. In 1536 Trujillo and Jaraicejo made an agreement providing for mutual rights to pasture on their common lands.[22]

Naturally certain ties connected Trujillo and Cáceres. There was some intermarriage, especially at the level of the nobility, who were in the best position to seek out the most advantageous marital alliances. Juan Cortés, a wealthy returnee to Trujillo who had participated in the division of the treasure of Cajamarca in 1532, married doña María de Ribera, member of a leading noble family of Cáceres who had two brothers who also went to the Indies. Their daughter doña Catalina Cortés in turn married a cacereño noble, Diego de Ulloa.[23] Commoners also intermarried. A couple living in San Miguel de Piura in Peru in 1568 called themselves "natives of the cities of Cáceres and Trujillo."[24] But commoners were most likely to marry within the range of their normal contacts; the architect Francisco Becerra, for example, married a woman from Garciaz, a town in Trujillo's jurisdiction where he worked on the church. Given the economic patterns that tied each city to its own hinterland of towns and countryside, movement and association to a great extent took place within the district.

Economic activities could bring the cities into contact. Merchants often had dealings beyond the immediate locality. By virtue of purchase, marriage, or inheritance, cacereños might hold *censos* (mortgages),[25] *juros* (annuities), rents, or lands in Trujillo or its district, or vice versa. The noble families of one city sometimes sent their daughters to the convents of the other, although they usually placed them locally. And although the cities and towns of the region scarcely participated in the comuneros revolt of the early 1520s, occasionally they formed or joined temporary coalitions. In 1580, for example, a number of towns in Extremadura, including Cáceres, jointly protested a royal edict that recognized the rights of the Mesta (the stockraisers' assocation) to certain cultivated lands.[26] Both Cáceres and Trujillo had markets and annual fairs that could attract people from outside; Trujillo's weekly *mercado franco* (free market), a royal concession dating from the time of Charles V,[27] in particular seems to have served as a regional center for exchange. In January 1578, for example, a *pellejero* (wineskinmaker) from Talavera de la Reina apprenticed his son to another pellejero from Puebla de Guadalupe at the mercado franco. On the same day a vecino of Puerto bought a mare from a man from a village near Sepúlveda.[28]

On the whole most of Cáceres's and Trujillo's significant economic, political, and institutional ties connected them not to each other but to the important centers of trade and capital (Segovia, Burgos, Medina del Campo, Seville), higher learning (Salamanca or Alcalá), or government (the royal court in Valladolid or Madrid, the high court of appeals in Granada) outside the region. This outward, extraregional focus in some ways stemmed directly from the nature of the cities and the homogeneity of the region. In most ways Cáceres and Trujillo were quite similar, hence they had to look elsewhere and not to each other for higher education, financial, legal, or academic expertise, and necessary business connections. Beyond that, the strong sense of identity with the specific point of origin, the awareness of a city's independence and particular history, underlay and strengthened the reality and perception of separateness.

The City and Its District

In the sixteenth century Cáceres and Trujillo were small cities whose populations probably increased steadily over the course of the century. With about 6500 inhabitants at midcentury, Cáceres was somewhat smaller than Trujillo, which possibly had a population of around 8000 at that time.[29] The number of people living in the towns of Cáceres's jurisdiction equaled or slightly exceeded the number of residents in the city proper,[30] and the population of Trujillo's larger district probably outnumbered that of the city. Thus these towns were not very large, and the major cities of Castile easily eclipsed all the extremeño cities in size. In 1561 Burgos and Segovia had populations of around 22,000, Valladolid 33,000, and Toledo 60,000; Seville's population rose to 100,000 or more by the century's close.[31] Nonetheless in a sparsely populated region whose inhabitants were concentrated in relatively few settlements, Cáceres and Trujillo in every sense were important urban centers, regardless of whether they were called "villa" (Cáceres) or "ciudad" (Trujillo).[32] They dominated their districts and served as centers for industry and commerce, political and religious institutions. A *corregidor*, the crown's representative, presided over the city council of each; the councils, controlled by the powerful local nobility, entered into and regulated many aspects of local life, from setting bread and wheat prices to organizing religious processions to recruiting military levies. The cities had a number of parishes, whereas most villages and small towns had but one.

The towns and villages of the countryside varied considerably in location, size, social composition, and their relationship to the cities. The cities' districts included good-sized towns like Santa Cruz de la Sierra (Trujillo), which had 465 *vecinos* (heads of household) and 7 priests in 1560, and Casar de Cáceres, with 788 vecinos and 6 priests in 1555. There also were small places like Orellana de la Sierra (Trujillo) with only 32 vecinos in 1575.[33] The tax assessments reflected the range in size of the towns. In Trujillo's district, for example, the annual sales tax assessment (encabezamiento) for the years 1557–1561 specified 8000 maravedís for Ibahernando, 120,000 for Santa Cruz, and 153,000 for Cañamero; in the same years the assessments for Cáceres's district ranged from 323,000 maravedís for Casar to 40,000 for Aliseda, 15,000 for Sierra de Fuentes, and a mere 4,000 for Zángano, a hamlet of Cáceres.[34]

Towns like Cañamero and Berzocana in Trujillo's district were so large and distant from the city that they probably functioned with considerable independence long before they secured formal exemption from the city's jurisdiction.[35] Self-purchase and a rash of sales of villages to nobles by the crown beginning in the 1550s left Trujillo with only fifteen towns under its jurisdiction in the late sixteenth century; the city still held twice the number of towns controlled by Cáceres but far fewer than the twenty-five or more it once had.[36] Cáceres's district was more stable in the sixteenth century, with its seven towns (Casar, Malpartida, Aliseda, Torrequemada, Torreorgaz, Aldea del Cano, and Sierra de Fuentes) and one hamlet; but the largest, Casar, fought to remove itself from the city's jurisdiction, causing considerable alarm among the members of the city council. Cáceres had lost all its towns north of the Almonte River by the fifteenth century and the sizable town of Arroyo del Puerco in the mid-1400s; in 1559 Torreorgaz was sold as well.[37] While Casar remained subject to Cáceres's jurisdiction, it enjoyed certain privileges that other towns did not. In the early fourteenth century the crown granted the vecinos of Casar a large *ejido* (grazing or common lands) of half a league around the town protected from any future encroachments of private ownership, and the right to water their cattle wherever they wished.[38] In contrast the small village of Sierra de Fuentes had virtually no lands.[39]

Land ownership, tenancy, and use throughout the area also varied considerably. Fundamentally the region's economy was pastoral, and grazing land predominated. Much of this land was under private control; but the cities themselves owned extensive pasture lands, which they rented out, and the cities and the towns of their districts had common lands for grazing cattle and usually woodlands in the *montes* for cutting wood or grazing pigs. Stockraising, the principal economic activity, mainly meant sheep and pigs. Other kinds of livestock—cattle, donkeys, mules, horses—served as work animals for agriculture or transport and do not seem to have been bred locally to any extent. Both city councils stalled in the implementation of a series of royal ordinances regarding the breeding of horses for cavalry, although Trujillo complied sooner and in the 1570s commissioned the construction of a magnificent gate designed by Francisco Becerra to stand at the entrance of the "pasture of the mares."[40]

Much of the soil of the region is calcareous, which made it poorly suited to agriculture for the most part, although the resulting local production of lime, together with abundant high-quality granite, proved a boon for local construction. Because of the region's aridity and poor soils, it often failed to produce sufficient wheat and other grains to feed its residents. The cities frequently had to import grain from other areas to stock the *alhóndigas* (public granaries). Prices for wheat, in terms of nominal reales at least, rose overall in the sixteenth century. In Cáceres (for which information is more complete) the price of a *fanega* (bushel) of wheat more or less doubled in forty years; in 1534 a fanega sold for about 5 reales and in 1577 for 11 reales. But prices could fluctuate sharply at times (see table 1), since conditions for agriculture often were less than ideal. Drought or floods could ruin crops and cause shortages, and two or three bad years in close conjunction could send wheat and bread prices skyrocketing.

Bad weather was not the only problem that affected local agriculture; the untimely arrival of grasshoppers or locusts could have devastating effects on a crop. The spring of 1580 brought a plague of insects to the entire area. On April 18, 1580 the council of Cáceres ordered everyone between the ages of fourteen and seventy to help kill the insects on the following Wednesday. Two days later the council decided that the people should go out the next day, a Saturday, at sunrise, carrying enough food for two days. In April 1583 Trujillo's *regidores* (councilmen) were directed to find a priest "who will curse the locusts and destroy them." Later the same month one of the regidores went to Jaraicejo with a letter for the bishop of Plasencia, asking that he instruct the priest of Garciaz "so that he will come to conjure away the locusts of this land, that the city will pay his salary."[41]

In addition to pastures and grain lands (tierras de pan llevar), several other types of agricultural land were common. *Alcaceres* (barley fields) provided forage, probably for work animals, and as a result often were located near houses or the headquarters of estates. Gardens and orchards (huertas and huertos) produced a variety of fruits and vegetables that supplied the local market. They usually were close to the cities and towns and, since they required irrigation, near sources of water. There also were olive groves (olivares) in the area. Many vecinos kept beehives, which invariably were sold with the land on which they were located (asientos de colmenar).

One of the most commonly owned agricultural properties was the vineyard. Most of the vineyards owned by the vecinos of Cáceres were in Pozo Morisco, northwest of the city, Santa María

TABLE 1   *Wheat and Bread Prices in Caceres, 1534–1580*

Date	Wheat Price/ Fanega	Bread Price/ 2 Lbs.[a]	Other Information[b]
1534	5½ reales 5 reales (sales)		
1535	5 reales (sale)		
Jan. 1537	4–5 reales (sale)		
Nov. 1537	4½ reales (sale)		
Dec. 1538	6 reales 6 mrs. (sale)		
1543	4 reales (sale)		
May 1552	6 reales (alhóndiga)	6 mrs.[c]	
June 1552			Locusts
Sept. 1552		6½ mrs.	
Oct. 1553			"Want . . . for lack of rain . . . little pasture"; buying bread in Arroyo del Puerco or Las Brozas
May 1555	7 reales (alhóndiga)	8 mrs.	
Aug. 1555	8 reales (alhóndiga)		
Aug. 1555	9 reales (alhóndiga)	9 mrs.	
Sept. 1555	9 reales (alhóndiga)	9 mrs.	
Jan. 1556	11 reales (alhóndiga)		
May 1556	13 reales (alhóndiga)		
June 1556			Council buys wheat in Talaván
Jan. 1557	19½ reales (price of wheat bought by council in Talaván)		
1559	5½ reales (sale)		

TABLE 1 *(cont.)*

Nov. 1561	11 reales (sale)		
Jan. 1562	9 reales (sale)		
1569	14 reales (purchase by council)		
Jan. 1569	12 reales (alhóndiga)		
Feb. 1570	14 reales (alhóndiga)		
Feb. 1571			Expect a good harvest; council buys wheat in Avila, Toro
Mar. 1571	21 reales (alhóndiga)	18 mrs.	
Mar. 1571	19 reales (alhóndiga)	16 mrs.	
Oct. 1571	10 reales (alhóndiga)	9 mrs.	
Nov. 1571	11 reales (alhóndiga)	10 mrs.	
May 1574	6 reales (sale)		
Feb. 1575	9½ reales (alhóndiga)		
May 1575			Procession for good weather
July 1575			Send to buy wheat in Mérida; "lack . . . in this city of bread and in all of Extremadura"
Nov. 1575	11 reales (alhóndiga)		
Feb. 1576	11 reales		Ask clergy and monasteries to pray for good weather
Mar. 1576			Procession for good weather
Apr. 1576		11 mrs.	
May 1576		11 mrs.	
June 1576	13½ reales (alhóndiga)	12 mrs.	
Dec. 1576		14 mrs.	
Jan. 1577	11 reales (alhóndiga)	14 mrs.	Instruct bakers to make 40 loaves of bread per fanega; buy wheat from Villanueva, Don Llorente, Monroy, Mérida, Valdelacasa

Feb. 1577			Council asks people to come sell bread
Mar. 1577		16 mrs.	
May 1577	11 reales (sale)		
June 1577	11 reales (purchase by council)	10 mrs.	
Oct. 1577			Council buys wheat in Torremocha
Dec. 1577		11 mrs.	
Jan. 1578		11 mrs.	
May 1578			Council has bought wheat in Andalusia
June 1578			Dry year; buy wheat in Ciudad Rodrigo
Sept. 1578			Give labradores up to 400 fanegas to plant
Sept. 1578		18 mrs.	
Oct. 1578			Procession for good weather
Jan. 1579		18 mrs.	
April 1579		18 mrs.	
July 1579			"Dearth"
July 1579		18 mrs.	"Much hunger and need for bread"
Jan. 1580			Buy 1500 fanegas in La Calçada; procession
Feb. 1580		18 mrs.	
April 1580			"Great want . . . on account of the difficult years"
April 1580		20 mrs.	Bakers told to make 42 loaves from each fanega
April 1580			Locusts in the dehesas

aAll prices for bread are those fixed by the city council.
bFrom city council records (AMC).
cMaravedís

del Prado, near Casar, or Aguas Vivas, in the city's outskirts. Many
of Trujillo's vineyards were in the Sierra de Herguijuela, southeast
of the city. Vecinos of all ranks and occupations owned vineyards,
which of course varied in size and value, and monasteries and
convents owned them as well. In Ibahernando (Trujillo) 109 of 182
vecinos had vineyards, although some were quite small.[42] Vineyards, like orchards, often included small houses for the guard or
caretaker.

Given the varied nature of terrain and agriculture, the landholdings of both hidalgos and commoners characteristically were scattered. Francisco Hortún, a vecino of Robledillo (Trujillo) mentioned the following properties in his will of 1571: a vineyard he
bought in Valdemorales from a vecino of Zarza; two *fanegadas* (a
fanegada was about one and a half acres) of land in Navaredonda,
purchased from an uncle in Trujillo; three, four, and one and a half
fanegadas in places called Malgrado, Cerroduelo, and Cerrogordo;
three fanegadas on the road to Zarza and another three on the road
to Trujillo; and many other small properties, as well as a mill on the
Tamuja River.[43] While it is not possible to identify many of the
places Hortún mentioned, clearly these properties were not contiguous or even necessarily very close to one another, and they
served a variety of purposes.

In the rather arid landscape of the region, sources of water often
determined the patterns of productive activity. Rivers, springs, and
reservoirs provided water for irrigation and for livestock, as well as
for industrial uses, such as milling, washing wool, and clothmaking.
In Cáceres flour mills, tanneries, and dyeing and fulling shops clus-
tered around the Fuente del Rey on the outskirts of the city, and the
same spring irrigated orchards. Several small rivers traverse the
area. The Almonte runs parallel to the Tajo; the Salor and Ayuela
bisect the southern half of Cáceres's district, while the Tamuja and
Guadiloba run through both districts. Trujillo's jurisdiction included
the Búrdalo and the Magasca. Ponds and reservoirs served as places
for watering cattle or washing wool. Two ponds in Cáceres's tierra—
the Berrueco near Malpartida and the Ancho near Arroyo del
Puerco—were *lavaderos* (places for washing wool); and within the
city's *dehesa* (pasture) of Zafra, near the towns of Torreorgaz and
Aldea del Cano, lay the Generala where cattle were watered.[44] In
Trujillo's district the reservoir of San Lázaro served the same pur-

pose and also was used to breed fish (*tencas*). The city had another reservoir, La Albuhera, built in the early 1570s on the road south to La Cumbre and Mérida. Construction took place under the supervision of the stonecutter and architect Francisco Becerra and the *maestro de aguas* Juan García Tripa.[45]

The City Council

Spanish society of this period is often described as corporate. Individuals belonged to a variety of social, religious, economic, and governmental entities and associations which served or sought to express and guarantee collective needs and interests. The secular clergy had their *cabildo* or council, lay people their *cofradías*, which were as much social service or even political as religious organizations, and artisans had their associations to regulate the practice of trades. Hidalgos and commoners were recognized as distinct groups with their own interests and representatives, and the *sesmero* was the representative for the towns of the cities' districts. Of all these local institutions and associations, by far the most powerful was the *ayuntamiento*, the city or town council. The council directly or indirectly affected the functioning of other corporations, supervising (although rarely interfering with) the trade associations, deliberating upon the petitions of the sesmero or the *alcaldes* of the hidalgos or *pecheros* (taxpayers), and at times involving itself in the conduct of religious life. The council entered directly into many aspects of local life—the economy, religion, social welfare and charity, education—largely because of the nature of society itself in which all these spheres overlapped.

A combination of historical factors endowed the ayuntamiento with considerable power. First, despite the fact that the election and composition of the council were controlled locally, the ayuntamiento was a royal institution, established by the *fuero* (set of rights) given the cities after the reconquest. The council represented the intersection of royal and local power and interests. Regulated by royal ordinances, the council implemented royal directives, collecting normal and extraordinary taxes and producing military levies; even the salaries paid to local officials were tied to royal ordinances. The demands and limitations of the monarchy constrained the actions and authority of the council; but at the same time the ayuntamiento's ties to the crown strengthened its hold over local society. Second, the council could exercise power at least in part because of its wealth. Substantial holdings in lands and rents—the *propios* of the city—gave the council the economic means to implement decisions. The council's financial support for a hospital or construction of a new church, for example, could be crucial. Last, the composition of the council, whose members were among the wealthiest and most important local nobles, reinforced the power and prestige of the institution. The council served as a vehicle for the expression of the interests of the nobility, and the nobility dominated local society by virtue of their economic and political power and social position.

The composition of the councils varied somewhat over the course of the sixteenth century, although the basic structure remained the same. The royally appointed corregidor served a term sufficiently short to preclude any substantial involvement in local affairs. He presided over deliberations and could overrule the decisions of the council members. An assistant (*teniente de corregidor*) assumed some of the corregidor's duties and presided in his absence.[46] In the sixteenth century the councils of Cáceres and Trujillo functioned under the ordinances promulgated by Queen Isabella in the 1470s and confirmed by Charles V in the 1520s. The late fifteenth-century ordinances did not differ greatly from earlier ones; basically they revised and standardized some features. The ordinances provided for the election of twelve or thirteen *regidores* (councilmen) from the principal noble families; a regidor could not be a taxpayer or, in Cáceres, a "señor de vasallos."[47] The seats on Trujillo's council were to be divided between the principal rival factions—half for the Altamiranos, half for the allied Bejaranos and Añascos. In theory these were distinct lineages and kinship groups; but in fact by the sixteenth century the Bejaranos had faded from importance, the surname "Añasco" as such had disappeared altogether, and a number of the important families represented on the council cannot be assigned with certainty to one or the other of the original groups.[48] Similarly although it has been suggested that the regimientos of Cáceres's council were divided between Castilians and Leonese, by the sixteenth century the distinctions between the groups doubtless had blurred, and they no longer constituted separate and exclusive categories.

Because Cáceres's council in the sixteenth century was smaller and more stable in its membership than Trujillo's, it is easier to describe how it functioned. The council saw to its day-to-day responsibilities by selecting a sort of rotating executive committee each month of four regidores who took care of routine business. The councils employed a large number of officials, usually on an annual basis, and in Cáceres each regidor was responsible for nominating individuals to fill certain offices. Approval generally came automatically, but occasionally disagreement among the regidores or with the corregidor, either over the nature of an office or the person nominated to fill it, disrupted the proceedings.[49]

The councils employed a range of officials, from doctors and lawyers to chaplains, musicians, constables, guards for the dehesas and montes, and a variety of artisans; they also appointed the alcaldes of the hidalgos and pecheros. The small salaries allotted to many officials suggest that they worked only part-time for the city. The artisans employed by the ayuntamiento included people who made arms and other items for military or ceremonial use. They received annual salaries ranging from 2000 to 6000 maravedís.[50] The councils also employed artisans to take charge of various public works; the *alarife* was responsible for repairs of public buildings, fountains, and streets. A key employee was the *mayordomo*, who administered the city's funds; in Cáceres a merchant usually filled this position and received an annual salary of 30,000 maravedís.[51] Ecclesiastics also worked for the municipality. The ayuntamiento of Cáceres paid a chaplain 8000 maravedís annually to say mass for the council and the prisoners in jail, and Trujillo paid a maestro de capilla 25,000 maravedís a year.[52]

Education was a continual concern of the ayuntamientos, which frequently experienced problems in locating and retaining Latin instructors (*preceptor de gramática*). In 1528 Trujillo's council spent 100,000 maravedís on a house to be used as a grammar school and residence for the preceptor.[53] In 1571 Cáceres's council hired a man from Salamanca at 21,000 maravedís a year and gave him 4 ducados to cover his moving expenses. In the 1570s conflicts arose between Cáceres's preceptor and some of the clergy, such as Bachiller Ojalvo, who also were accepting students. The preceptor, who was supposed to have a monopoly over Latin instruction, threatened to quit if the competition continued. One of the regidores went to the bishop to ask him to order the priests to desist from teaching. But the following year the preceptor complained that students were abandoning his house to study with Alonso Gómez, and the council worried that if they could not enforce the terms of their contract, they would lose their credibility along with their Latin teacher. In 1578 Cáceres's cátedra de gramática was vacant once again; the council advertised in Salamanca, Alcántara, Alcalá, and other places for a teacher to be paid 30,000 maravedís a year. But several months passed before they hired someone from Alcalá, who apparently stayed only a short while; in 1579 a new preceptor, Bachiller Juan Alonso Fernández, who had taught previously in Montánchez, was in the city.[54]

Trujillo might have experienced fewer difficulties in retaining its teachers because it paid them better; salaries there rose steadily from 37,500 maravedís in the 1550s to 75,000 in 1579. Even so, Trujillo's council also at times seems to have become rather desperate in its search for that elusive commodity, a Latin instructor who would come and stay. In January 1558 one of the regidores wrote to Fray Felipe de Meneses (a native of Trujillo and professor at Alcalá) asking him to send a preceptor for at least a year (preferably three), declaring they would accept without conditions or *oposiciones* (the system of competitive examination) whomever he sent.[55]

It is difficult to avoid the conclusion that the cities offered meager attractions in the realm of education and intellectual life. In 1574 Cáceres's council had to make a contract with a bookseller in Salamanca, offering a salary of 6000 maravedís a year to induce him to come to the city for three years "with his books and trade."[56] Toward the end of the century, however, both cities seem to have made some progress in education. From at least 1569 Trujillo employed a primary school teacher, who received 10,000 maravedís a year in 1599, to teach children to "read, write and count."[57] More formal institutions of secondary or higher education took shape in both cities. In 1579 the bishop of Coria decided to establish a seminary in Cáceres, supported in part by the diocese and in part by the city, which was to provide a site for the future school and continue to employ a preceptor. In the early seventeenth century Philip III authorized the creation of a "cátedra en artes y estudios" in Trujillo's convent of the Encarnación.[58]

The ayuntamientos supervised and supported a range of social services, retaining physicians, surgeons, midwives, and sometimes pharmacists on salary. The ayuntamiento was responsible for the quality of medical care dispensed by practitioners and hospitals. In September 1553 Cáceres's council put a stop to the activities of Diego Genio, a barber who had seriously injured several persons while bleeding them because he was getting old and his hands shook.[59] Hospitals, which were more shelters for the sick and homeless than they were places of treatment, usually drew their support from a combination of sources, including the city.[60] During times of crisis (famine, epidemics) the councils dispensed additional funds to the hospitals.

The role of the ayuntamiento in law enforcement does not emerge very clearly from the records. Crime and disorder within the city itself doubtless came within its purview, while the hermandad maintained law and order in the countryside, and royal constables and officials dealt with matters that were not strictly local. The local law enforcement establishment could not have been very large or complex, probably consisting of a few constables, a jailer, and an executioner. While violent crime was not at all uncommon, criminal cases and complaints frequently were settled out of court. The city jail served mainly for short-term internments, as prisoners awaited trial, release, or execution. In 1572, for example, the corregidor of Cáceres, Dr. Espinosa, responding to a royal directive instructing the cities to hand over any prisoners sentenced to the galleys, found that there were none in Cáceres. In fact only one man, an accused thief whose case was still pending, was in jail. A morisco accused of seriously injuring another man by throwing him off a wall had not been arrested because he had taken refuge in the parish church of Santa María. For alleged blasphemies the suspect subsequently had been turned over to the Inquisition in Llerena.[61] Regulation of the marketplace and protection of the use and access to public and municipal resources (pastures, woodlands) doubtless were more important law enforcement activities and concerns of the city council than were prevention and prosecution of personal crimes as such.

Religious Life

Religion played an important and complex role in local society. Ecclesiastical institutions such as parish churches with their secular

clergy, monasteries, and convents formed the core of the local
religious establishment but did not monopolize religious life, which
also depended to a great extent on lay initiative and participation.
The laity organized and supported cofradías, charitable works, and
numerous shrines (hermitas) in the city and countryside. The municipality also was closely intertwined with the religious establishment, not only contributing financially to the establishment and
upkeep of churches, monasteries, and hospitals but also interven-
ing directly in some aspects of religious observance and practice.
Trujillo's council employed someone "who will teach the cate-
chism," and in 1575 the regidores of Cáceres noted a shortage of
preachers (predicadores) in the city, which they thought was affecting the religious instruction of the populace. One regidor suggested that they not contribute to any monastery that failed to
provide a preacher, and the council instructed one of its members
to talk to the guardian of San Francisco to "remedy" the situation
and also to consult with the bishop on the matter.[62]

The councils organized all kinds of processions, responsibility for
which usually devolved upon the regular and secular clergy; cofradías and members of different trades often participated formally
as well. The purpose of the processions could range from celebration of Philip II's victory over the Turks at Lepanto (1571) to religious observances to entreaties for good weather in times of heavy
rain or good health in face of rumored or actual epidemics. The
councils supervised the conduct of fiestas, procuring bulls, and
seeing to the construction of barricades in the plaza for the holidays
that featured bulls. For Corpus Christi the councils would instruct
city residents who lived along the procession's route to hang out
tapestries and "make altars" and hire troupes of players to perform
miracle plays and short farces.[63]

Churches, monasteries, and shrines filled the cities. Cáceres had
four parish churches and Trujillo six, as well as the archpriestal
church of Santa María la Mayor. Both cities were headquarters for
archpriests, a sign of their importance within their dioceses.[64]
Cáceres had two monasteries and two convents and Trujillo two
monasteries and a total of six convents in the sixteenth century.
During the sixteenth century the religious establishment felt the
impact of some of the forces creating changes throughout local
society. Demographic growth and shifts in the distribution of popu-

lation meant that some parishes (like San Martín on Trujillo's plaza) would grow whereas others (like the old church of Vera Cruz) languished. New infusions of wealth funded the construction and elaboration of sacristies, chapels, and hospitals. Francisco de Chaves, a native of Trujillo who died in Arequipa (Peru) in 1570, willed 2000 pesos for the establishment of a *capellanía* (chantry) in Trujillo's church of San Martín and construction of an altar to the Immaculate Conception. Francisco de Godoy, a returnee from Peru to Cáceres, purchased the upper and lower sacristy of the church of Santa María for 600 ducados in 1560 and established a capellanía in the church in his will of 1564, naming one of his sons as chaplain. The church's council had auctioned off the sacristy to raise money for "a very sumptuous and costly altarpiece" they were building.[65]

The patronage of the crown, municipality, and individuals was crucial to religious institutions; the religious establishment was expensive. The monastery of San Francisco in Trujillo owed its establishment to Queen Isabella, who in 1501 instructed the city to donate 50,000 maravedís for the purchase of the site for the church and garden. The monastery's expansion reached a peak in the 1560s, when the council, with royal authorization, donated over 5700 ducados. The ayuntamiento was the patron of the monastery's church and spent some 600 ducados in the 1590s for the construction of the choir loft and other items for a new church that opened in 1600.[66] Given the rapid expansion of the religious establishment in the sixteenth century, it is not surprising that a proposal in 1590 to found a Mercedarian monastery in Trujillo encountered considerable opposition. Members of the city council pointed out that similar petitions from the Jesuits and Franciscan Descalceds had been rejected because the city could not support any more religious houses. The debate carried into the seventeenth century. Finally, in 1602, with the patronage and financial backing of the Pizarro family (don Francisco Pizarro, son of Hernando and doña Francisca Pizarro, became the patron), the Mercedarians secured the council's approval to establish a monastery in Trujillo.[67]

Cofradías were active in the sixteenth century. The exclusively hidalgo cofradía of Espíritu Santo in Trujillo supported the hospital of that name, in part through the rental of pastures.[68] The cofradía de la Caridad, which accepted members from all social classes, began construction of a hospital in Trujillo in 1578. Gonzalo de Sanabria contributed over 1000 ducados to the project, and the ayuntamiento provided 300 ducados in the 1580s. The cofradía of San Lázaro and San Blas supported the shrine and leprosarium of San Lázaro, and the cofradía de Nuestra Señora de la Piedad the shrine of the Virgen de la Piedad built in 1500. Another cofradía of hidalgos, dedicated to San Martín and the annual observance of his saint's day on November 11, included among its statutes the obligation to come to the defense of the city if necessary "to favor justice and everything else for the good, peace and tranquility of the city and its commonwealth."[69] Thus cofradías fulfilled a number of social functions, acting as exclusive associations for people of a similar social background (hidalgos, members of a particular trade) or as vehicles for integrating individuals from a range of social groups and both sexes. The cofradías, which operated independently of the clerical establishment (priests could join but enjoyed no special status), encouraged active lay participation in religious life and charitable institutions while providing social services for their members; cofradías generally made the arrangements for the funeral and burial of members and often assisted the deceased's family as well. Furthermore, since membership fees were fairly low, the cofradías were accessible to people from many levels of society.

The *obras pías* or charitable works founded by individuals took a number of forms, such as dowries for poor or orphaned young women or clothes for the poor. The wealthy archpriest don Juan Pizarro, long a dominant figure in Trujillo's ecclesiastical establishment, is said to have founded numerous charities, providing money for students, dowries for poor women, food and clothing for the poor, care for abandoned children, and ransoms to redeem captives.[70] The specific terms of an obra pía often reflected the personal loyalties and interests of the founder. Francisco de Chaves, who died in Arequipa, in addition to the 2000 pesos he sent to Trujillo for the capellanía—patronage of which he willed to the city—also designated 500 pesos for charitable works. Of the total, 100 pesos were to go to the city's hospitals, 100 to the poor of the parish of San Martín, and 300 to help marry three poor young women, with preference given to the servants of his sister Francisca de Chaves or to relatives.[71]

The Social Order

The society of the sixteenth-century cities of Cáceres and Trujillo and their region had its historical roots in the period following the reconquest. Apart from basic environmental and economic patterns (sites of settlement, the mix of pastoralism and agriculture that formed the economic base of the region), the region's modern history began in the thirteenth century, although development there of course was tied to historical developments earlier and elsewhere in the Iberian peninsula. In a sense, then, society in the sixteenth century was relatively new and in its two hundred to three hundred years of existence had experienced considerable development and change. By 1500 the great military orders had reached the peak of their expansion and power and had begun to feel the effects of the extension of royal authority; the small but thriving Jewish communities had been eliminated, although very likely at least a part remained and continued to play a role in commercial and professional life; and the origins of the wealthy and conservative local nobility could be traced to some time within the preceding couple of centuries. Movement characterized all levels of society; people moved around, into, and out of the region. The fortunes of families rose and fell. Nonetheless sixteenth-century society was fundamentally traditional. The basic way of life and means of making a livelihood changed but little over the centuries. The majority of people worked the land and devoted most of their time and energy to providing themselves and their families with the basic necessities of life. Wealthy nobles employed large numbers of servants and slaves because the maintenance of large households and estates required considerable amounts of human labor.

Society was hierarchical, divided into ranks or orders, conditioned by authority and dependent upon habits of deference. Yet while the gap between wealthy and poor, noble and commoner was wide, it was scarcely unbridgeable. The various groups were bound by socioeconomic relations and even kinship ties; they shared a common environment and collectively formed the "república" or commonwealth. The maintenance of the social order depended to a great extent on the collective recognition of the rights and duties of the many corporations that overlapped and sometimes competed within the hierarchical structure. Social contact, work relations, and residence patterns all fostered a high degree of familiarity among people from all levels of society. This familiarity stemmed at least in part from the relatively small size of the cities and towns; up and down the social ranks people knew of and about one another, saw one another in the plaza or marketplace, belonged to the same cofradías.

Familiarity, common membership in the república, and Christian ideals created a kind of moral equality or classlessness. An individual merited regard and respect by adhering to and exemplifying the ideals and norms of behavior associated with his or her rank and occupation; in historical documents one encounters such standard types as the honorable farmer ("labrador honrado"), the good taxpayers ("los hombres buenos pecheros"), the virtuous or humble poor ("pobres virtuosos" or "avergonzantes"), as well as the brave and generous noble. Certainly one might argue that such epithets were purely formulaic; yet the very fact that they existed as formulas reflects a perception of the social order that ascribed to each group and rank its particular qualities, rights, and duties.

This sense of moral (as opposed to social, economic, or political) equality sheds a different light on the old cliche of ostensible Spanish contempt for manual labor. Manual labor in itself did not engender contempt, although earning one's living by this means was not compatible with the behavior and ideals to which the nobility aspired. But even at the level of hidalgos and nobles there is room for doubt that manual labor was held in universal disdain. The towns and villages of the cities' districts were filled with hidalgo-labradores; and in the suits or petitions for *hidalguía* (noble status) of that period, the question of the performance of manual labor never surfaced, leading one to believe it would not be a stigma in achieving status. And given the nobility's enthusiasm for physical pastimes and the amount of time they spent on their rural estates, it is hard to imagine that nobles did not know a great deal about agricultural routines. The Hinojosas, uncle and nephew in sixteenth-century Trujillo who compiled a chronicle of some of the city's hidalgos, wrote that one of their ancestors, Diego de Hinojosa, el viejo, in his old age cultivated a garden in the country outside the city for reasons of exercise; the observation was in no way negative.[72] The perceived incompatibility of work with privileged status was relative, not absolute.

The adaptability and flexibility of early modern Spanish society are factors that are often overlooked, particularly when viewed from the perspective of contact with the peoples of the New World; yet those qualities made it possible for Spanish society to absorb and integrate change while maintaining its stability and structures intact. Study of the participation in and impact of the Indies enterprise affords an almost ideal vehicle for examining the question of adaptability. The Indies meant, above all, new infusions of wealth. The effects of this wealth could be incremental or largely indirect, as probably was true for Cáceres; but in Trujillo the wealth of the Indies had repercussions that reverberated for years. By the middle of the sixteenth century Trujillo's city council, previously dominated by the noble families, included five returnees from Peru (all of them men who had shared in the division of treasure at Cajamarca in 1532); at least three of these returnees were from middle-level hidalgo families at best, and one—Alonso Ruiz—was not even a native of Trujillo. The wealthy returnees to Trujillo, whose families became perhaps the wealthiest in the city, intermarried, built huge houses, and bought up the villages that the crown put on sale in the 1550s. The kind of wealth the early returnees had at their disposal, the large numbers of trujillanos who followed their successful predecessors to Peru, the connections people in America maintained with people at home, all meant that the impact of the Indies was far from limited. Yet Trujillo's society remained stable; it was flexible enough to absorb the impact of the Indies and retain its structures essentially intact.

The question of adaptability also bears on the conquest and settlement of the New World. The conquest is often pictured in terms of Spanish rigidity and fanaticism, the ethnocentric drive to dominate cultures and societies deemed inferior. Yet the ability to absorb and subsume difference was fundamental to the success of the whole colonial enterprise. Certainly fanaticism and militarism were underlying factors of the reconquista as well, but it must be recalled that the centuries of reconquest produced not only conflict but the unique pattern of *convivencia,* in which Christians, Jews, and Muslims lived in relative tolerance and learned from and influenced one another. The Spaniards who went to the New World were heirs to the traditions of both conquest and convivencia.

II

Nobles and Hidalgos

The nobility in some ways epitomize the problems of delineating the cultural framework of early modern Spanish society. We can learn a great deal about their activities and lives, but the cultural underpinnings often seem alien. The concepts of privilege, rank, lineage, honor, and duty are viewed today as artifacts, in turn picturesque, frivolous, unjust, or hypocritical. Furthermore these concepts are difficult to reconcile with pragmatism, economic dynamism, and social flexibility. Yet all these factors coexisted, as clearly evidenced by the move to the New World—in which the middle and lower ranks of the provincial nobility played a significant part—or the transformation of the Sevillian nobility, who enthusiastically embraced and participated in the commercial expansion of the fifteenth and sixteenth centuries and who intermarried extensively with wealthy merchant and converso families.[1]

Explanation is further complicated by the fact that the period in question was one of rapid change. What could be considered as medieval and modern outlooks apparently existed side by side—uneasily, perhaps, from our point of view, but not necessarily for the people who lived in those times. How, for example, do we reconcile the consistent, if arrogant and unappealing, practicality of Hernando Pizarro—who devoted all his energy and subordinated all concerns to consolidating and maintaining his family's fortune and position—with the misguided heroism (in the medieval sense) of his brother Gonzalo—who to the ill-fated end of his rebellion (and his life) claimed that rather than live forty years he would prefer to live ten and be governor of Peru?[2] Yet whereas it was

Hernando who was the legitimate son and heir of an old if modest hidalgo family, and Gonzalo one of his illegitimate brothers and somewhat of an outsider as a result, in a sense they both were motivated by the same aspiration. Each sought to claim the position he felt was his by right (and for which, therefore, he was entitled to fight), and this guiding principle emerged directly from the ethos of the hidalgo or noble.

Similarly one might ponder the example of Andrés Calderón Puertocarrero, a caballero and heir to an entail who was related to a number of leading nobles of Trujillo. Andrés was willing to ignore his privileged station to the point of calling himself a merchant when he went to Peru in 1562. But when he returned—as will be discussed—his behavior in every sense reflected the attitudes of his rank. A comparison of Dr. Lorenzo Galíndez de Carvajal and his son Diego de Vargas Carvajal offers a similar paradox. The former, a historian, professor at Salamanca, eminent jurist, member of the Council of Castile and finally of the Council of the Indies (1525–1527), was very much the new-style professional bureaucrat and statesman favored by Ferdinand and Isabella. His son Diego de Vargas Carvajal, who inherited the office of Correo Mayor de las Indias that his father had been awarded while serving on the Council of Castile, seems to have epitomized the Trujillo caballero. Diego de Vargas devoted his attention to his estates and family interests and embroiled himself in the local conflicts and rivalries that characterized the late Middle Ages and carried over into the sixteenth century, to the extent that in his will of 1562 he warned his sons against involvement in the *bandos* (factions or parties) of Trujillo. In contrast to his father's lifelong career of service to the crown, Diego's only endeavor along those lines was his brief (but apparently lucrative) tenure as one of the *Comisarios de Perpetuidad* sent to Peru in 1560. These commissioners proved so venal, and complaints against them so strident, that they were ordered back to Spain; but Diego de Carvajal died in Peru before he could return home.[3]

I will not attempt here a detailed analysis of how the concepts of honor and position operated among the provincial nobility—these concepts have been treated elsewhere[4]—nor will I attempt to assess the impact of Renaissance ideas and education[5] and the growing importance and prestige of the monarchy and court. Nonetheless these currents of influence conditioned the thought and behavior of the nobility; ignoring them obscures attitudes and aspirations that in some ways shaped their decisions and responses. Thus when Diego García de Paredes of Cáceres fell out with President Gasca (or perhaps with some of his officers) in Peru, with disastrous consequences for himself, because he felt that the position Gasca had offered him was beneath him,[6] or Alvaro de Paredes wrote to his brother in Cáceres from Mexico in 1590 to say that despite his failure to find a place there he would not return to Spain out of shame ("vergüenza"),[7] these individuals were thinking and acting in terms of ideals and expectations that for them were as real as the more concrete dictates of political and economic reality. The paradoxes and contradictions we perceive in retrospect, however, need not have troubled the sixteenth-century observer. The educated, urbane Diego and Alonso de Hinojosa, uncle and nephew who authored a chronicle of noble lineages of Trujillo in the sixteenth century, insisted on the Hinojosas' relationship to the Cid and praised a certain Hernando Alonso de Hinojosa for avenging the rape of a female cousin ("peleando con el Corajo le mató , muy como varón"); yet they roundly condemned those individuals who sustained the bandos,[8] a judgment that seems notably enlightened for the time and place.

Nobles and Hidalgos: Definitions and Distinctions

Who, or what, were the nobility of sixteenth-century Extremadura? The origins and formation of the Spanish nobility were multiple, complex, and often obscure, and as a result the group set at the top of provincial society by virtue of privilege and inheritance eludes simple categorization. In Castile as a whole in the sixteenth century there were several classes of nobles (grandes, títulos, caballeros, hidalgos) which had their origins in different historical periods and circumstances. The caballeros, for example, to a great extent could be traced back to the heyday of the reconquista (twelfth and thirteenth centuries) and the military services rendered by armed men on horseback, whereas the grandes and títulos were royal creations of a later era. Furthermore a number of juridical distinctions subdivided these groups; an hidalgo might be, for example, "de solar conocido," "de ejecutoria," "de vengar 500 sueldos." But by the early sixteenth century most of these minute legal distinctions had become blurred or largely ignored in practice and probably had lost much meaning even for contemporaries.[9] Basically what remained was a sort of three-tiered division of all those who had fiscal exemptions and other real or honorary privileges. These three groups roughly corresponded to the designations grandes and títulos (at the top), caballeros, and hidalgos. Although Trujillo, more so than Cáceres, was home to a number of "señores de vasallos"—from the fourteenth century, for example, the Orellanas (a branch of the Altamirano family) ruled Orellana la Vieja—both cities lacked representatives of the highest group of Castilian nobility. Certain members of the título class, however, did figure in local society by virtue of their relationships (both of kinship and clientage) with the local nobility and the proximity of their holdings or jurisdictions to the cities. The Duke of Béjar, one of the largest stockraisers of Castile, for example, was influential in the cities. A number of young men from noble families of Cáceres and Trujillo served in his household; Juan de Chaves, descendant of Luis de Chaves, el viejo (friend and ally of Ferdinand and Isabella) and himself an author of a chronicle of his lineage, was said to have been raised there. One cacereño noble, Diego de la Rocha, in his instrument of entail drafted in 1546, called the "conde de Benalcázar, Marqués de Gibraleón, Duque de Béjar que espera ser" his lord and said he was a *criado* (servant, retainer) of that house, from which he had received "good treatment and many favors." In 1570 don Diego Mejía de Ovando, the lord of Don Llorente and Loriana and vecino of Cáceres, sold a censo on his entail to raise 2000 ducados in order to accompany the Duke of Béjar to Genoa.[10]

Broadly speaking, then, the privileged class in Cáceres and Trujillo comprised two more or less distinct groups. One consisted of the wealthy, powerful, and stable noble families. Most of these nobles were caballeros and many held titles. They filled the seats of the city council, maintained large households—residences in the city and estates in the countryside—and intermarried extensively. The other, larger group included all the other individuals and families which lacked titles but held fiscal exemptions that distinguished them from the taxpayers (pecheros) and could claim hi-

dalgo status of some kind. The distinctions between these groups of
course faded at times, since noble families were hierarchies that
included poor and illegitimate relatives whose status differed considerably from that of the principal heir or heirs and direct line; and
also the fortunes of an entire family could change over time.

The terms "noble" and "hidalgo" will be used here not in a
technical or legal sense but rather to distinguish between these
generalized social (really socioeconomic) groupings. The terms noble and nobility will be reserved for the small circle of principal
families that dominated their respective cities and districts, while
the term hidalgo will refer to the privileged group as a whole or will
be used to distinguish between the leading nobles and all others. If
at first glance the distinction seems confusing or nitpicking, its
significance emerges clearly when one compares the wealth and
position of a great (by local standards) noble like Juan de Chaves
(the chronicler)—who in 1558 at the king's request and at considerable personal expense accompanied the queens of Portugal and
Hungary, sisters of Charles V, from Trujillo to Badajoz[11]—with that
of humble hidalgos living in the villages of the countryside who
worked the land with a pair or two of oxen and were hardly distin-
guishable from their fellow labradores.

The hidalgo group was, then, homogeneous neither in wealth
nor in social standing or political influence, all of which usually
went together. Frequent references to suits for hidalguía indicate
the tenuous claim some had to privileged status; hidalgo status
often came down to a question of whether one paid normal taxes or
not, whether an individual (or, perhaps more important, his antecedents) had been included in the padrón (list of taxpayers). Incorporation of an individual who considered himself to be an hidalgo
into the padrón occasioned a number of suits that were taken to the
royal *chancillería* (high court of appeals) in Granada.[12] The testimony collected in the prosecution of these suits demonstrates
clearly, however, that fiscal exemption was only one of the qualities
that defined the hidalgo; possibly proof of such exemption in itself
did not suffice to prove hidalguía. Just as important was evidence
regarding the rank of one's father and grandfather and, perhaps
even more convincing, one's association and relationship with a
lineage that included prominent and recognized nobles.

Hidalguía adhered to a family and lineage, not to an individual as such, and in effect this meant the male line since in this period women scarcely figured.[13] One case that illustrates the kind of evidence that could be brought to bear on the question of hidalguía was that of the brothers Francisco and Martín de Escobar, who initiated a suit in 1588 because they had been included in the padrón of the village of Robledillo (jurisdiction of Trujillo). Juan de Chaves, former regidor of Trujillo (very likely the chronicler), testified that he had talked with the litigants' father, Pedro de Escobar, in the house of Escobar's relative (deudo) Alvaro de Escobar, whom Chaves called a "caballero muy principal." Chaves further testified that the litigants' older brother Gómez Nuño de Escobar, who had gone to the Indies and returned wealthy, had been an intimate of Juan de Escobar (son and heir of the aforementioned Alvaro de Escobar and brother of Fray Diego de Chaves, the confessor of Philip II). When Juan de Escobar's eldest son, Alvaro Rodríguez de Escobar, caballero of Santiago, and his brother went to fight the Alpujarras rebellion, Gómez Nuño de Escobar "gave his relative a beautiful chestnut horse for the journey." Another witness stated that Juan de Escobar had been *padrino* (godfather) at Gómez Nuño de Escobar's wedding and at the baptism of one of his sons. Chaves's testimony, then, offered evidence of close association between the family of the litigants and a much higher-ranking noble lineage. What further proof of their hidalgo status could be needed? Francisco and Martín de Escobar won their suit in Granada, although virtually none of the testimony bore any direct relation to their own status and activities. Francisco went to the Indies, probably at least twice. While this did emerge in testimony, the fact that he did so as a merchant did not.[14]

An even more remarkable instance of what might be regarded as largely circumstantial proof of hidalguía appeared in the suit initiated by Pedro de Sande of Cáceres in 1551 and pursued by his sons in the 1570s. Pedro de Sande's father, Hernando de Sande, was from Lugo in Galicia, where he was considered to be an hidalgo. The main branch of the Sande family came to Cáceres and Plasencia from Galicia in the early fifteenth century, and one of those Sandes—Juan de Sande Carvajal, el viejo—was corregidor of Salamanca, probably in the early years of the sixteenth century (see table 2 for the Sande family). Hernando de Sande participated in a jousting tournament "de señores y caballeros hijosdalgo" in which

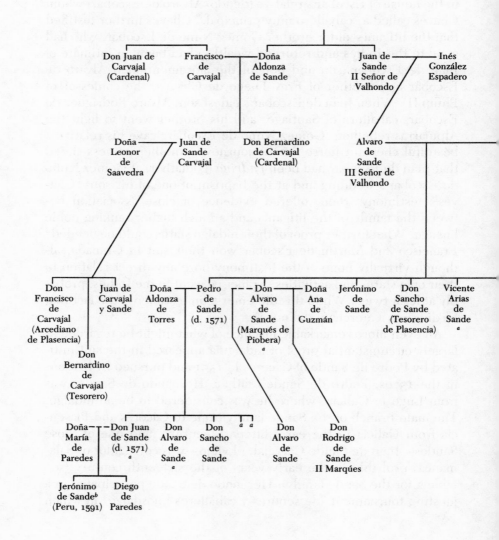

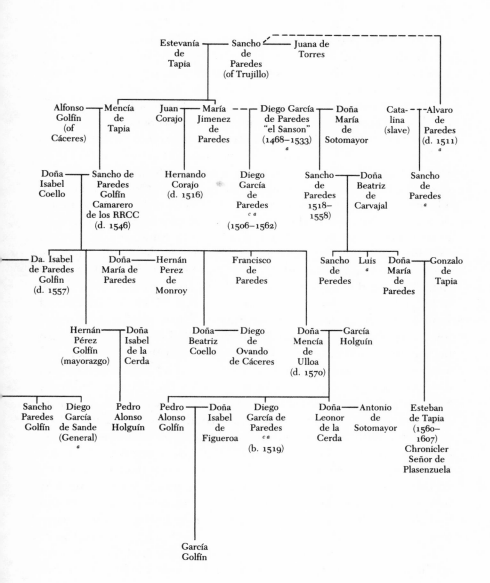

Estevanía de Tapia ——— Sancho de Paredes (of Trujillo) ⟵ - - - Juana de Torres

Alfonso Golfín (of Cáceres) ——— Mencía de Tapia

Juan Corajo ——— María Jimenez de Paredes - - - Diego García de Paredes "el Sanson" (1468–1533) [a]

Doña María de Sotomayor

Cata-lina (slave)

Alvaro de Paredes (d. 1511) [a]

Doña Isabel Coello ——— Sancho de Paredes Golfín Camarero de los RRCC (d. 1546)

Hernando Corajo (d. 1516)

Diego García de Paredes [c a] (1506–1562)

Sancho de Paredes 1518–1558) ——— Doña Beatriz de Carvajal

Sancho de Paredes [a]

Da. Isabel de Paredes Golfín (d. 1557) ——— Doña María de Paredes ——— Hernán Perez de Monroy

Francisco de Paredes

Sancho de Peredes

Luis [a]

Doña María de Paredes ——— Gonzalo de Tapia

Hernán Pérez Golfín (mayorazgo) ——— Doña Isabel de la Cerda

Doña Beatriz Coello ——— Diego de Ovando de Cáceres

Doña Mencía de Ulloa (d. 1570) ——— García Holguín

Sancho Paredes Golfín

Diego García de Sande (General) [a]

Pedro Alonso Holguín

Pedro Alonso Golfín ——— Doña Isabel de Figueroa

Diego García de Paredes [c a] (b. 1519)

Doña Leonor de la Cerda ——— Antonio de Sotomayor

Esteban de Tapia (1560–1607) Chronicler Señor de Plasenzuela

García Golfín

[a]indicates military service
[b]went to the Indies
[c]went to the Indies and returned

he so distinguished himself that he came to the attention of the corregidor Juan de Sande, who on hearing Hernando's name decided he must be a relative of his. He invited Hernando de Sande to his lodgings and was so pleased with him that he insisted that his newly discovered relation send a son to live in his household. Hernando de Sande took his son Pedro de Sande to Cáceres; Pedro remained there and became a vecino.

The testimony amassed to prove the hidalguía of Pedro de Sande and his sons included that of another illustrious Sande, Diego García de Sande, a caballero of Santiago and brother of the famous military officer don Alvaro de Sande (later Marqués de Piobera). He testified in the suit that Pedro's father, Hernando de Sande, was a "justador grande" and that "it was clear that he was related to all who were of the house of Sande." Diego García had taken Pedro de Sande, along with other relatives, with him to Seville when he went there to get married. Diego García de Sande further stated that he had known another son of Hernando de Sande, Juan de Sande, who fought with him in Italy and Sicily and elsewhere, and that this Juan de Sande had received a salary increment in addition to his regular pay that only hidalgos received. Everyone thought of Juan de Sande as don Alvaro de Sande's kinsman; don Alvaro had felt it deeply when Juan de Sande was killed in Turkey, "because he was his relative." Diego García also noted that he himself had another brother named Arias de Sande who had been a captain and died in Italy; Arias was also the name of the litigant Pedro de Sande's paternal grandfather. Proof of the hidalguía of Pedro de Sande's family, therefore, rested on several types of evidence: close association with and recognition as "deudos" by prominent nobles; a relative (Pedro's brother Juan) having had a privilege to which only hidalgos were entitled (the "ventaja" he received as a soldier); and the use of a name associated with the much more prominent line of the family (Arias). Again all the evidence pertained to the male line and the activities of the males of the lineage; women were scarcely mentioned except in relation to the litigants themselves.[15]

It was at this point, when the testimony touched most directly on the litigants, that the case for Pedro de Sande and his sons began to appear less than airtight and that the difference between somewhat tenuous hidalgos and those who were clearly recognized as such becomes more obvious. In Cáceres the litigant Pedro de

Sande married Francisca Picón, the daughter of Francisco Picón, whom witnesses said was an hidalgo and "very rich." In general the testimony emphasized the latter quality; what was undeniable was that Pedro de Sande's wife was not a "doña" at a time (midsixteenth century) when most noble women of substance bore that title. It is also undeniable that, between them, Pedro de Sande and Francisca Picón, hidalgos of middling status, produced a family of upwardly mobile sons whose ambitions and abilities finally brought them at least close to the position to which they aspired. Their son Dr. Francisco de Sande, the most energetic and possibly most capable of the lot, in the last third of the sixteenth century served on *audiencias* (high courts) in Mexico, Guatemala, and Bogotá and briefly as governor of the Philippines (in the 1570s), working tirelessly in the interests of himself and his brothers, one of whom, don Juan de Sande, eventually ended up on the city council of Cáceres. Yet while their mother, Francisca Picón, in her later years at times was called "doña" and at others not, significantly her own son Dr. Sande omitted the doña in referring to her. Similarly his brothers used the title "don" but not consistently, so that the family's claim to the honorific even in the late sixteenth century, when the use of such titles had proliferated, continued to be uncertain.[16]

Clearly, in the latter part of the sixteenth century a successful professional career could go a long way toward elevating the status of an entire family. Like Dr. Francisco de Sande, Licenciado Diego García de Valverde, another cacereño who served on several audiencias in the New World, was the son of a woman who was not a doña. His brother Baltasar de Valverde could not sign his name, and they had a first cousin who was married to a surgeon. But Valverde's wife was a doña, and his son was "don" Francisco de Valverde.[17] A similar process affected Licenciado Diego González Altamirano of Trujillo and his family. He also served on audiencias in the Indies, had relatives who probably were involved in commerce and the lower-ranking professions, and was responsible for his sons' elevation in status. Thus in addition to all the other legal, social, and economic considerations that served to define hidalguía (and foster distinctions between nobles and hidalgos of varying rank and status), in the sixteenth century socioeconomic and political changes generated yet other factors that also came to bear on the determination of hidalguía and status. Inevitably the whole concept

of nobility and hidalguía underwent transformations in the sixteenth century, complicating the task of analyzing and describing
the hidalgo group.[18]

The hidalgos of Cáceres and Trujillo, as suggested, were quite
heterogeneous and really constituted a group only insofar as they
could claim certain privileges in common. More marginal hidalgos
might actively pursue nonnoble trades and occupations or have relatives who did so. One of the more respectable occupations for lower-
ranking hidalgos was that of notary. Among the lower-ranking hidalgos intermarriage with non-hidalgos was common, further blurring
distinctions between individuals at this level. Very likely, however,
as insignificant as the distinction might seem to have been in many
instances, it continued to be recognized. A witness said that the
parents of the first and second wives of Hernando de Encinas, who
petitioned to go to Peru (or Tucumán) in 1591 with his family, were
hidalgos ("estuvieron en posesión de hijosdalgo"), while Encinas's
parents were honorable and prominent people ("en posesión de
gente muy honrada y principal") but obviously not hidalgos.[19] Hidalguía was one's birthright, and being poor or working at a trade or
with the land could not obviate that inherited quality. Thus while it
may seem anomalous that the hidalgo appointed *alférez* (ensign) by
the Cáceres city council was a cloth shearer (*tundidor*), or that the
father of Antonio de Cotrina, an hidalgo who became an entrepreneur in the Indies trade, was a tailor and many of his relatives
dyers, the contemporaries of such individuals apparently perceived
no incongruity.[20]

A large number of middle and lower-ranking hidalgos lived in
the towns and villages outside the cities. Whereas in 1552 Casar de
Cáceres, with over 700 vecinos, claimed to have no hidalgos,[21]
other pueblos had rather large numbers of them. In 1561 nearly 70
of Zorita's 380 vecinos were hidalgos. In 1551 several of them had
obtained a royal provision directing that Trujillo's corregidor allow
the hidalgos of Zorita to hold offices that up until then had been
reserved for labradores; the hidalgos proposed that they be given
half the available positions because of their high proportion among
the town's inhabitants.[22] The pueblo of Zarza, where the estates of
the Pizarro family were located, in 1561 had 10 hidalgos among its
103 vecinos.

These hidalgos of the villages, however, by no means constituted a local aristocracy and did not monopolize wealth or, obviously, political power. Of Zorita's hidalgos 7 were called poor or very poor (1 was a tailor and another a carpenter), and several others had just an ox, or a pair of oxen, or three pigs, or the like. It is difficult to estimate wealth based on the 1561 *vecindario* (census) because the only property listed is livestock, and doubtless some individuals had other sources of income or means of making their living; 4 hidalgos (2 men and 2 women), for example, were described as living well but having no movable property ("tiene bien de comer y no hacienda mueble"). Taking property in livestock as a guide, however, some of the hidalgos probably were among the wealthiest villagers, but some pecheros were their equals. Diego de Trejo, the hidalgo wealthiest in stock, had 300 sheep, 25 oxen and cows, and 40 pigs, and another hidalgo, Pedro de Cacedo, had 250 sheep, 12 oxen and cows, and 60 pigs; but commoner Rodrigo Pérez had 350 sheep, 2 oxen, and 50 pigs. The situation was similar in Zarza, where half the hidalgos were poor and only 3 were called wealthy ("ricos"); but in fact none of them owned as much livestock or land as the well-to-do commoners of the village.[23] In Ibahernando, where the census included a greater variety of properties, the situation was much the same. The town had only a handful of hidalgos among its 180 or so vecinos. The wealthiest of these, Diego de Arévalo, had a house, a vineyard with 800 vines, a horse, ass, 2 pigs, and 80 sheep; but the commoner Rodrigo Gutiérrez had two houses, two vineyards with 1200 vines, 3 oxen, 2 cows, a bull and a calf, 20 pigs, 2 donkeys, and 300 sheep and goats. Another pechero, Francisco de Roda, had a house and nearly 2000 vines in two vineyards, as well as 4 oxen, 250 sheep and goats, 2 pigs, and an ass. Well-to-do commoners far outnumbered hidalgos in Ibahernando.[24]

While the hidalgos of the villages for the most part were a modest bunch, the presence of hidalgos was not limited to these local people, since a number of nobles—who were almost always vecinos of the cities and therefore usually not included in the censuses of the towns—owned houses and estates in and around the villages. Some noble families acquired *señorío* (jurisdiction) over villages in Trujillo's district, a process that accelerated in the sixteenth century and continued into the seventeenth. Around 1558–1559 Alonso Ruiz (returnee from Peru) purchased the village of Madroñera; Diego de Vargas Carvajal (son of Dr. Lorenzo

Galíndez de Carvajal, councillor of the Indies) purchased Puerto de Santa Cruz; Licenciado Juan de Vargas (oidor of the chancillería of Valladolid) bought Plasenzuela with its hamlets Guijo and Avilillos; Pedro Barrantes (another returnee from Peru) acquired La Cumbre; and Alvaro de Loaysa (father of Fray Jerónimo de Loaysa, first archbishop of Lima) became señor of Santa Marta and Diego Pizarro de Hinojosa of Torrecillas.[25] In addition many noble families exercized considerable influence in villages where they owned residences and estates. The Moraga family dominated Aldea del Cano (in Cáceres's district), and in 1561 members of the related Moraga, Vita, and Cano families were living there.[26] The parents of don Juan de Sande (nephew of don Alvaro de Sande) maintained a house in Torrequemada where they lived much of the year. In Trujillo's district the Vargas family was influential in Madrigalejo, where they had built a "casa-fuerte" demolished by orders of Queen Isabella, the Pizarro Carvajals were important in Alcollarín, and the Solís family in Ibahernando.[27] The rich nobles who acquired señorío over villages of course usually already had houses and properties in these places, like the Pizarros in Zarza and Alonso Ruiz in Madroñera.

The Noble Way of Life

Almost all the nobles maintained impressive urban residences that were as much an expression of nobility as the family arms that occupied a prominent position over the entranceway, titles, estates in the countryside, or seats on the city council. No wonder that one of the most noticeable results of the involvement of local people in the Indies was the appearance of new or renovated town houses built by returnees, who probably accounted for most of the major new private construction in the sixteenth century. In Cáceres Francisco de Godoy, who returned from Peru in the 1540s, built his house near the church of Santiago in a largely worker and artisan parish, and don Juan Cano Moctezuma, the son of emigrant Juan Cano and doña Isabel Moctezuma (daughter of the last Mexican emperor), built the "Palacio de Moctezuma" within the walls of the old city. Cristóbal de Ovando Paredes arranged to buy a house in the parish of San Mateo before he even returned from Peru (in the 1580s) and then spent 2400 ducados to renovate it.[28] In Trujillo

Hernando Pizarro built an enormous house on the plaza, as did the wealthy and well-born returnee Juan Pizarro de Orellana. Gonzalo de las Casas, son of the encomendero of New Spain Francisco de las Casas (a cousin of Hernando Cortés), and Licenciado Altamirano, who twice served on the audiencia of Lima, rebuilt or renovated family residences on the plaza of Trujillo as well.

The flurry of construction and renovation of houses in the late fifteenth and sixteenth centuries changed the appearance and residential patterns of the cities. Both Cáceres and Trujillo were walled towns with structures within the walls especially that dated back to the fifteenth or fourteenth centuries, or even earlier; but the facades of most houses were altered in the sixteenth,[29] so it was the architecture of this period rather than of the middle ages that predominated. Furthermore by this time both cities had long since expanded considerably beyond the walls—a process that likely began not long after the reconquest—and the cities' large main plazas lay outside and below the old walls. Still to some extent both conserved the old pattern, with the majority of noble residences located within the walls and the worker and artisan neighborhoods outside. This pattern persisted more strongly in Cáceres, where almost all the residents of the two parishes within the walls, San Mateo and Santa María, were hidalgos or their servants and slaves, or ecclesiastics and professionals. Trujillo's "villa" (as the old walled town was known) was smaller than Cáceres's walled center, bound by the castle and steep slopes on most sides, and it lacked a plaza of any real dimensions—hence the relative attractiveness of the newer part of the city and the monumental plaza for new construction. But the older noble families—the Escobars, Chaves, Altamiranos—had their great houses in the villa, and it was more the newly rich of the sixteenth century who built on and around the plaza.

Regardless of location, a noble's family's *casas principales* were of such importance that, in contrast to movable goods that frequently were auctioned off at the death of the head of the family, houses were retained and passed on to the next generation, usually to the eldest son and often as part of the family entail. In his will of 1579, for example, Licenciado Diego González Altamirano stipulated that the heir to his entail must live in the casas principales on the plaza which he had inherited from his father and rebuilt.[30] Particularly wealthy patriarchs might purchase additional houses to leave to younger sons. The house or palacio and all that it implied symbolized the wealth, status, and continuity of the noble family.

In the city nobles visited and ate in one another's houses. Women might spend the afternoon in the house of a friend, and men strolled and chatted in the plaza or rode about on their horses. The life of the provincial nobles might not have been luxurious or comfortable by today's standards—the huge rooms and dark interiors of many of the noble houses convey more a sense of splendor and wealth than of comfort—but they lived in a style that set them far apart from most commoners. They filled their houses with furniture, wall hangings, rugs, and valuable objects, importing many of these furnishings from elsewhere in Castile or from Europe or more exotic locales such as Asia or America. They took great pride in their clothes, of which they had considerable number and variety, in striking contrast to workers and artisans who might own no more than a change of clothing. Like the furnishings of their houses, the fine cloth of their garments came from all over Spain, or Italy, or Flanders. Women owned and wore costly jewelry of gold, silver, and precious stones; Hernando Pizarro's niece and wife, doña Francisca Pizarro (the mestiza daughter of Francisco Pizarro) owned a fortune in emeralds.[31] And of course the nobles maintained large households and retinues of servants and slaves, who attended them and were outfitted in suitably impressive livery.

While today many of the expenditures and investments of the nobility would be judged uneconomic and seen as a kind of conspicuous consumption, such a perspective is anachronistic because these expenditures were inherent to the role of a noble. A noble had to live nobly, and that implied or required generosity, charity, and impressive personal display, as well as other qualities such as honor, bravery, and military skills. Arms, title, lineage, a great house, an honorable wife and obedient children, advantageous marriage alliances, a seat on the city council, estate in the countryside, entourage of deudos, retainers, and slaves, lavish display in personal dress and for the celebration of important events, fine horses, and livery were all inextricably linked to the noble ideal.

Most of the nobles of Cáceres and Trujillo owned *casas de campo* outside the city, in the countryside or villages, which were not only headquarters for estates but residences where they spent a large percentage or even the majority of their time. In February 1570, for example, the Cáceres city council sent messengers to summon the nobles from the countryside ("todos los caballeros que están en sus aldeas") to a meeting.[32] Two main branches of the Ovando family owned estates and huge country houses that looked like small castles at Arguijuela, about ten kilometers south of Cáceres on the road to Aldea del Cano. Diego de Ovando de Cáceres (grandson of the Captain by the same name who allied with Isabella, for which he was amply rewarded) built a hermitage near his estate at Arguijuela and spent 1000 ducados to construct an altarpiece for the chapel of his house. An inventory of the estate in 1551 included 30 plow oxen, almost 200 pigs, over 300 cows, and nearly 10,000 sheep.[33]

How does one explain the strong liking, or even preference, that many nobles had for their country houses and estates? For the most part the nobles were, perhaps, a rustic lot who enjoyed spending time outdoors and whose entertainments to a great extent were physical. Men liked to hunt and fish, and they had special clothes for such activities and tents and cots for camping that could serve them for military campaigns as well as hunting trips. Young men no doubt devoted much time to training and perfecting their skills at arms and in horsemanship. Women as well as men enjoyed riding horses and mules,[34] and nobles passed the time visiting their estates and friends and family in the countryside and other towns.[35]

The nobles seem to have felt at ease in the countryside and villages where they were surrounded by relatives, old friends, and retainers and were known and deferred to by the people of the towns, with whom they probably had close relations. A vecino of Torrequemada testified in the *información* (testimonial) of don Jerónimo de Sande, one of two illegitimate sons of don Juan de Sande (nephew of don Alvaro de Sande) and doña María de Paredes, a vecina of Torrequemada where Sande's parents had their "casa poblada." He said that everyone had known when doña María was pregnant "because this place Torrequemada is very small and with few people [so] that one knows everything, the bad and the good."[36] Witnesses in Torrequemada knew a great deal not only about don Juan de Sande but about his famous uncle don Alvaro de Sande and a number of other members of that active family (see table 2).

Some nobles took up permanent residence in one or another

town, while remaining vecinos of the city. Juan de Hinojosa de Torres, brother of the famous captain in Peru, Pedro Alonso de Hinojosa, lived full-time in Santa Cruz de la Sierra, and Diego de Torres Hinojosa lived in Torrecillas. Gómez Nuño de Escobar decided to live in Robledillo when he returned from the Indies.[37] Some were more oriented to the life of the country than of the city. Andrés Calderón Puertocarrero's mother-in-law had a country house in Banis Pedro, as did he, where she lived much of the time, attending Sunday mass at the church in Torrecillas. Andrés Calderón's wife had ties with Deleitosa (a small town near their lands at Banis Pedro and close to Trujillo, although not under its jurisdiction), where the couple had married[38] (see table 3 for the family).

Economic Base

Holdings in land and livestock enabled the nobles to live as they did. The nobles of Cáceres and Trujillo controlled a substantial portion of the grazing land in their districts, as well as agricultural and pasture lands located elsewhere. They derived an income from this land in two ways: by renting out pasturage, frequently to stockraisers of the north who annually sent their sheep south for winter pasturage, and by raising their own livestock—sheep first and foremost, for wool and meat, and pigs also. The other principal sources of noble income were redeemable *censos* (mortgages) and *juros*, which yielded an annual increment tied to a specific royal revenue (taxes, customs duties). Both juros and censos meant a fixed annual income in return for advance of a principal. Since they were investments they do not show much about the economic status of those who held them, other than reflecting that the holder had some surplus disposable capital. Sometimes outside circumstances were responsible for such investments. Many returnees and others involved in the Indies had to accept juros from the crown in lieu of the lump sums they brought back or were owed; but since juros for some time had been a typical royal reward for services, and returnees in any case tended to invest their capital in censos and juros, this policy did not necessarily impose any hardship.

Landholding and land use in sixteenth-century Extremadura, as in the rest of Castile, were diverse and complex, and outright ownership of land was not the only determinant of wealth or eco-

TABLE 3 *Relatives of Andrés Calderón Puertocarrero, Noble of Trujillo and Returnee from Peru*

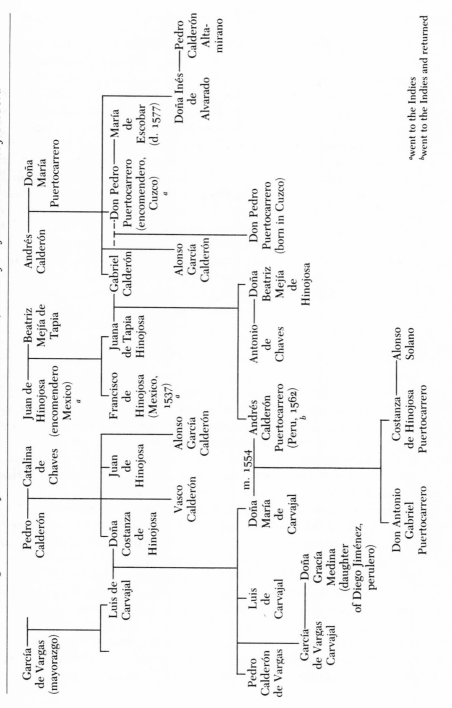

[a] went to the Indies
[b] went to the Indies and returned

nomic viability since there were other means of gaining access. Towns and villages owned common lands in which all vecinos had the right to graze their animals, and landless farmers had access to *tierras baldías* (royal lands) for grazing and cultivation. *Dehesa* was the term generally used for pasture land. Normally the dehesa was enclosed and, although mainly dedicated to grazing, it might include some wooded areas and agricultural land for farming.[39] In addition to common lands cities owned properties (propios) that could be quite substantial. Both Cáceres and Trujillo controlled extensive pasture lands; Trujillo owned thirty-six dehesas known as "caballerías," since they originally were assigned to the caballeros who participated in the reconquest. In the fifteenth century the councils of both cities, dominated by the nobles, tended to favor their friends and relatives in the rental of these dehesas; but with the extension of royal control over the cities in the late fifteenth and early sixteenth century, Ferdinand and Isabella curtailed some of the abuses. In Cáceres the length of rental contracts decreased from five or more years to one or two, and Trujillo was required to give preference in rentals to commoners. People operating on a small scale, however, could not afford the rentals of large dehesas; so groups would rent them collectively, or sometimes the councils of the villages rented dehesas and divided up the land.[40]

The important point with regard to the nobility and their role in the local economy is that, while their holdings were extensive, they did not monopolize grazing or agricultural land; nor in the sixteenth century were they able to use unchecked their institution, the city council, to control and use the properties owned by the cities. This is not to deny, of course, that commoners might have been experiencing real economic difficulties in this period and losing much of their land; in Cáceres's district at least almost all sales of vineyards and agricultural lands in the sixteenth century were to hidalgos or priests.[41] Nevertheless the availability of rentals, either from private individuals or from city councils, and of tierras baldías and common lands meant that one could be a viable and even prosperous stockraiser or labrador while owning little or no land. Juan Pizarro of Cáceres, an hidalgo but not one of the city's principal nobles, in 1559 rented two dehesas, for four and six years, at around 1000 ducados each from nobles of the city, as well as other lands. The fact that he was able to afford these rentals suggests that, despite owning no land himself, he nonetheless was a substantial stockraiser.[42]

Ownership of land often was quite complicated, since generally several people shared title to privately owned dehesas. Frequently the co-owners were related by blood or marriage. Although over generations these ties could become quite distant, the evidence indicates that a dehesa pertained to a family and that custom and even law dictated that possession should be kept within the family. Certainly this was the medieval pattern. The first episode recorded in the Hinojosa chronicle, probably dating from the fifteenth century, relates how the "very honorable and very rich" caballero of Trujillo Pascual Gil de Cervantes was helping to support a nephew who was studying law at Salamanca. When this nephew decided to sell a part of the dehesa of Magasquilla, his uncle offered him a fair price, which the nephew refused to accept. Instead he sold the property to the lord of Orellana la Vieja which, according to the Hinojosas, "he should not have done." The only conceivable explanation for the response this action provoked was that selling part of the dehesa to an outsider went against all custom. When the señor of Orellana (Hernando Alonso de Orellana) sent his squires to take possession, Pascual Gil's criados confronted them and forced them to retreat. In revenge Orellana's retainers killed a son of Pascual Gil de Cervantes who was on his way to the grammar school, setting off a series of murders and acts of vengeance on the part of both families.[43]

By (or during) the sixteenth century the strength of this tradition apparently diminished, and rents were bought and sold in what appears to have been pretty much a free market. Ownership in a dehesa often was expressed in terms of a percentage of the rental income and the price determined accordingly. In December 1558, for example, Gonzalo de Saavedra, a regidor of Cáceres, for the price of 357,000 maravedís sold to his cousin Francisco de Ovando, mayorazgo (that is, the holder of the family entail) a tenth part of a dehesa that rented for 85,000 maravedís per winter; he sold, therefore, 8,500 maravedís of "renta de yerba" for 357,000 maravedís.[44] The price in such sales corresponded to a value figured per 1000 maravedís of rent; for example, a rent of 500 maravedís of renta de yerba which sold at a rate of 25,000 maravedís per *millar* (thousand) would therefore cost 12,500 maravedís. The value of properties varied, of course, but the winter rental was the key element in determining value, since summer rentals were quite low.[45] Rents and dehesas also were among the properties included in noble entails that became increasingly common in the sixteenth century, in which case they became nonnegotiable.

Wills, entails, and inventories convey some notion of the extent of noble properties, which were often quite diverse and scattered over a large area. Hernando Pizarro owned dehesas in Cáceres, Montánchez, and Medellín as well as Trujillo;[46] by virtue of marriages made with nobles from other cities in Extremadura, many nobles of Cáceres and Trujillo held properties in other areas. An example of the variety and extent of noble properties is that of Juan de Hinojosa de Torres (resident of Santa Cruz). He established an entail for his son Pedro de Hinojosa in 1579 that included all or parts of five different dehesas, an orchard with an olive press, estates and houses in Torrecillas and Santa Cruz, an olive grove, orchards and wheat lands ("tierras de pan llevar") in the *ejido* (common or grazing lands) of Santa Cruz, in addition to several houses and an inn in Trujillo and juros in the alcabalas of Ciudad Rodrigo.[47] Another example is that of the huge holdings of the Vargas family which in the sixteenth century passed to doña Beatriz de Vargas, the wife of Diego de Vargas Carvajal who went to Peru in 1560. The entail she inherited included houses, grain lands, and other properties at Balhondo ("todo el asiento de Balhondo"); other grain lands in Puerto de Santa Cruz (señorío of which Diego de Vargas purchased in 1559); houses and estates, including grain land and vineyards, in Madrigalejo; a house and vineyard in Berzocana; orchards and yards in Trujillo (in addition to the main residence there); and parts of twenty-three different dehesas, including one in Medellín.[48]

Many noble estates were, of course, more modest than these; but even much smaller holdings yielded a decent income. Testimony of 1526 revealed that Francisco de las Casas, Cortés's cousin who became an encomendero in New Spain, owned outright in Trujillo one dehesa that rented for 45,000 maravedís, part of another that yielded 14,000 maravedís, and a third dehesa that rented for 50,000 maravedís. Later in the century, of course, these rents would have been higher. Together with his house in Trujillo Las Casas's assets were estimated to be worth 9,000 or 10,000 ducados.[49]

As suggested dehesas and noble estates consisted not only of agricultural or grazing lands but often were diversified and included structures such as houses or mills and small settlements with full-time residents. A complicated legal suit that hinged on the ownership and sale of a dehesa called Magasca in Trujillo's término, on the Magasca River and next to the "berrocal y baldíos" (rocky and uncultivated lands) of the city, included a description of the property which shows plainly it was more than just a pasture. The *heredad* (estate) had houses, yards, and an orchard. One house with a large enclosed yard stood apart, backed by a barley field (alcacer); there also was an alcacer next to a ruined mill and another small one below the road going down to some other mills (which presumably were by the river). Perhaps because of its location on the river and near the city, Magasca might have been a popular spot for trujillanos; almost all the witnesses, including doña María Pacheco, a sixty-year-old widow and relative of the family that had owned the dehesa before its sale, said they knew the property and had been there many times. In 1542 the heredad of Magasca was sold along with a fifth of the pasture of Magasquilla, which bordered on it and rented for 9,000 maravedís, for a substantial 1,446,600 maravedís.[50]

Despite the diversity of noble estates and holdings, for most nobles sheepraising was the most important component of their economic base. While the lack of descriptive material on the size and location of pastures makes it difficult to estimate the scale of local stockraising enterprises, clearly they varied considerably in size from enormous flocks of many thousands to much more modest ones of a few hundred. The Hinojosas wrote that Juan de Chaves had 5000 sheep in one dehesa and 5500 in another, and these flocks represented only part of his holdings in livestock.[51] The most substantial transactions in livestock predictably involved the wealthiest nobles. Diego de Ovando de Cáceres sold 1788 sheep at 10 reales in April 1547 to someone from Medina de Rioseco (an important trading center, although not as important as Medina del Campo). In May 1552 he sold 1867 head at 15 reales to a man from Tordesillas commissioned to buy meat for the royal court; the same man also purchased 1300 head at 8 reales, 1737 yearlings (7½ reales), and 20 rams (at 15 reales).[52] Most transactions, however, involved the sale of several hundred, rather than several thousand, sheep. The presence of buyers from Castile and León who purchased sheep both for meat and for wool production—several men from Burgos bought, among other things, 216 merino yearlings "with their wool" from a noblewoman of Cáceres in 1556—suggests that the extremeño flocks must have enjoyed a reputation for high quality.[53]

The large stockraisers of Extremadura mainly sold their wool to merchants and dealers from Castile, who might come in person to the area to buy wool or send their representatives to do so. Buyers sometimes contracted in advance to purchase wool; for example, in January 1549 Gonzalo Moraga agreed to sell all the wool his sheep produced for the following two years at 450 maravedís per *arroba* (around twenty-five to twenty-six pounds) to a man from Castrojerez. Moraga received an advance of 12,000 maravedís and said he sheared his sheep in mid-April in Aldea del Cano, where the Moraga family had its estates.[54] Stockraisers also made arrangements to transport their wool to buyers and markets, hiring carters to haul their products to cities in Castile. In 1569 Francisco de Ovando, el viejo, hired a man to take fourteen cartloads, each with forty-four arrobas of wool, from his estate at Arguijuela to Segovia or Villacastín.[55] Transactions frequently were completed in Medina del Campo during the annual trade fair of July. As in the sales of livestock, the quantity and type of wool sold varied, as did prices (see table 4).

Despite the preponderance of buyers and merchants from Burgos, Segovia, Villacastín, and other Castilian cities, stockraisers in Extremadura sold wool in a number of markets. Local sales must have been the mainstay of the clothmaking industry, which was of some importance in Cáceres especially. In addition Italians were active buyers in Extremadura. In May 1572 the city council of Cáceres authorized a Genoese, Tomás Sable, to wash all the wool he had bought. They justified their decision saying that "Tomás Sable has made many expenditures here, both in collecting the wool he has bought and for the people he has brought to improve and repair the *lavadero*."[56] In an inventory made at the time of his marriage in 1588 Cristóbal de Ovando Paredes, a wealthy returnee from the Indies, said that he had sent 5,160 arrobas of washed wool, worth 43,000 ducados, to Florence during the years 1584–1587.[57]

Alongside sales of livestock and wool, the rental of pastures to northern stockraisers brought the nobles a significant additional

TABLE 4   *Wool Prices in Sixteenth-Century Cáceres*

Date	Price per Arroba (mrs.)	No. Arrobas Sold	Type of Wool
June 1537	560	20	
1538	832	11	
1544	430	8	Lamb's wool
June 1547	270	54	
Sept. 1548	505	14	
May 1552	750	996	
June 1554	750	186	
June 1557	578	586	
July 1557	375	10	Lamb's wool
July 1558	595	771	
June 1559	697	308	
May 1561	840	811	
May 1569	612	38	
May 1569	442	14½	Lamb's wool
1571	646	77	
June 1572	663	80	
March 1573	697	19	White wool
	782	2½	Black wool
May 1574	816	400	
June 1574	750	18	
May 1578	582	1,505	White wool

Source: Archivo Histórico Provincial de Cáceres.

income. The subject of stockraising in Castile automatically brings to mind the Mesta, the powerful stockraisers' association that regulated the transhumant movement of northern herds to Extremadura and Andalusia and their access to the green winter pastures of the south. But by the middle of the sixteenth century the Mesta had lost considerable ground to local stockraising and agricultural interests. As a result many stockraisers of Castile and León made their own arrangements to rent pastures, frequently for several years at a time and often year-round. The stockraisers who rented pastures in the jurisdictions of Cáceres and Trujillo could come from as far away as Soria, but the majority were from Segovia, Villacastín, Avila, and Piedrahita. In 1578, for example, the mayordomo of don Diego de Vargas Carvajal rented to the foreman (mayoral) of the monastery of Parral in Segovia all or part of several dehesas in Trujillo for a total of 323,500 maravedís for the winter.[58]

The fact that such arrangements in the sixteenth century commonly were made on a private and individual basis does not mean, of course, that the Mesta had become powerless or irrelevant by that time. Both Cáceres and Trujillo had long histories of conflict with and opposition to the organization, which sought to extend its access to all classes of land, and the conflicts continued through the sixteenth century. As late as 1580 the Mesta secured a royal edict ordering the curtailment of cultivation that had been initiated in the past twenty years on certain kinds of land. Twenty-one towns and cities in Extremadura and Andalusia, including Cáceres, protested the directive, which probably was not implemented very successfully.[59] Thus, while by the midsixteenth century the Mesta not only was no longer in the ascendant but in certain ways very much on the defensive, and both the municipalities and their vecinos often succeeded in thwarting the organization by means both legal and otherwise, the Mesta remained a factor to be reckoned with.[60] The Mesta claimed the right to participate in the arbitration of disputes between stockraisers and local landowners. In 1551 some people from the area of Ayllón had rented a dehesa from Señor Martín de Chaves of Trujillo for 100,000 maravedís and twenty-six yards of cloth ("holanda"); Chaves seemingly changed his mind and refused to rent the pasture at the agreed price. The frustrated stockraisers pointed out that there existed an agreement between Trujillo and the council of the Mesta to arbitrate jointly such disputes, but Chaves refused to submit to arbitration.[61]

The last major component of the economic base of nobles and hidalgos was the breeding of pigs, which was important and lucrative. Like sheep, hogs could be raised on a large or small scale, but of the two probably hog raising was more cost effective when conducted on a small scale. Thus while sheepraising tended to be a more exclusively noble, or at least upper class, enterprise, raising pigs could be profitable whether one owned several hundred or just a few. This was particularly true in the tierra of Trujillo, which had extensive *montes* (woodlands) of live oaks which annually provided a rich harvest of acorns (bellota) that nourished and fattened the herds of swine. Since much of this woodland formed part of the city's common lands, vecinos who had little or no land of their own or could not afford to rent pastures with bellota had an important source of sustenance for their pigs.[62] Still it was the wealthy nobles especially (if not exclusively) who raised pigs on a large scale. Pedro Rol de la Cerda, a regidor of Cáceres and member of the wealthy Ovando clan, registered 300 pigs with the city council in August 1553, and tax records of the middle and late sixteenth century show that nobles were the highest contributors to the tax on pigs.[63] Pig breeders of Trujillo sold their swine as far away as the fairs of Toledo and La Mancha.[64]

Nobles and Their Retainers

The economic impact of the nobles and hidalgos on local society of course involved much more than how many sheep or pigs they raised and sold and how much land they had at their disposal for stockraising or rental. Their wealth and control of resources meant that they exercized considerable influence over the economy of the region. In the cities, villages, and countryside the nobles employed large numbers of servants, stewards, agents, shepherds, swineherds, cultivators, and other urban and rural laborers. They also affected people whom they did not employ directly, providing a market for local tradespeople and artisans and hiring temporarily carters and muleteers to transport the products of their estates. Clergymen, professionals, merchants, and other well-to-do entrepreneurs served the nobility as sources of capital and financial and professional expertise in law and medicine.

Because the nobles sat at the apex of socioeconomic hierarchies that included their immediate families and households and extended to encompass large numbers of servants and employees, examination of the relationship between nobles and their retainers sheds light on aspects of patronage and the relations between the nobility and the rest of society. The term most commonly used for a full-time employee, retainer, or servant was "criado," and this designation could refer to individuals who functioned in a variety and range of capacities. Criados were not necessarily closely attached to a household. Cristóbal de Ovando of Cáceres, for example, had criados who were vecinos of Campo Redondo and Malpartida and who probably looked after his properties or herds in those places. "Criado" implied more a relationship (of employee to employer, client to patron) than it did a fixed status. Naturally it was not only hidalgos who had criados; almost any person or family of any substance more than likely would have a criado or two, perhaps a woman who did housekeeping or someone who helped out with the family business. Criados could be tradesmen, artisans, or apprentices, as well as poor or orphaned relatives who might be brought into the household.

As the wealthiest members of society, however, the nobility doubtless employed the largest number of servants and agents of all kinds. Juan de Chaves (the chronicler) reportedly had a squire for each of his dozen horses, in addition to many other servants.[65] While criados might live and function quite independently, many were closely tied to and integrated into noble households, which fostered a quasi-familial relationship between employer and criado. The wills of hidalgos, both male and female, contained numerous bequests to criados—small sums of money in addition to wages owed, or objects of clothing or furniture—and hidalgos often contributed to their servants' dowries as well. Sancho de Figueroa, a returnee to Cáceres from the Indies, left his "muchacho" Alonso 20,000 maravedís and arranged for him to be apprenticed; the ambiguity of the wording, however, suggests that Alonso could have been an illegitimate child. Another cacereño, don Juan de Ulloa Carvajal, archdeacon of Naja, gave 100,000 maravedís to his criado Diego García Machacón on the occasion of his marriage in 1547. He said he gave him the money "because I have raised you and because of the love I have for you," as well as for his services "and so you may live more honorably." This criado's bride brought a dowry that included a slave (valued at 20,000 maravedís) and properties worth 50,000 maravedís she inherited from her father. Given the size of the dowry, the criado must have been a key employee, or possibly even a relative of some sort; relatives certainly served in this capacity. Juan de Carvajal Villalobos gave his niece 70,000 maravedís and a bed as her dowry for the time she had served him.[66]

Given that criados might be integrated into employer households, one would expect that in some cases at least the criado's relationship to an individual or family would be long term and even extend beyond one generation. While there is evidence that service as a criado could be undertaken as a short-term expedient because of lack of other alternatives or as a kind of apprenticeship, fostering an essentially businesslike employer–employee relationship,[67] this kind of arrangement coexisted with a more enduring patron–client type relationship. In testimony of 1549 a seventy-year-old man from Trujillo, Nuño de Ortega, said he had served Martín de Chaves, el viejo, for almost thirty years. A twenty-four-year-old trujillano named Melchor González in 1578 testified that he had been the criado of Bachiller Gaspar González, *clérigo presbítero,* and his siblings for more than eight years and before that had served their parents. In his will of 1578 Hernando Pizarro stipulated that all his criados were to be kept in the household.[68]

One of the best examples of this kind of long-term attachment between criados and their patrons emerged in the testimony presented in support of Diego Hernández de Aguilar, a young widower of twenty-eight, vecino of Trujillo, who in 1579 petitioned for a license to join relatives in Tierra Firme. He planned to take his two younger, unmarried sisters, his three-year-old son, and a criada from Trujillo. Diego had been married to Isabel de Solís, who died in childbirth. According to Juan de Chaves (the chronicler) and other witnesses, the families of both Diego Hernández and his deceased wife were hidalgos, and they and their parents (and even their grandparents) had served the house of Juan de Chaves and his father for more than fifty years. Diego and Isabel were both criados of the family when they married. Mencía Alonso, an eighty-year-old criada who had lived in the household for some seventy years, serving Juan de Chaves's mother, doña Juana de Acuna, said that the parents and grandparents of the pair had served as mayordomos and collected rents ("unos se sirvían de mayordomos y otros le cobraba sus bienes y hacienda y rentas"), while others had served in the household itself. Juan de Chaves and his wife, doña Isabel de Cárdenas, were the padrinos at Diego and Isabel's wedding.[69]

The position of criado encompassed considerable variety. Criados were largely of worker and artisan background but not exclusively so, and they were too heterogeneous to constitute a unified or identifiable class as such. While because of this diversity there could hardly be a typical criado, still the scarce information that we have for certain individuals such as Diego Hernández de Aguilar and his and his wife's family conveys some idea of the activities, responsibilities, and place in society of a criado in a noble household. A Diego García, who wrote his will in 1571, was the criado of the cacereño noble Francisco de Ovando Paredes. García was married to Mari Jiménez, with whom he had three children. Her dowry had included a small amount in cash (6,000 maravedís) and beds and other furnishings, as well as a house in the parish of Santiago which they sold for 10,000 maravedís. At the time of his marriage Diego García had a house he had inherited from his father which he sold for 15,000 maravedís, 10,000 maravedís he had inherited at the death of a sister, and another house that he had bought for 2 ducados in which the family actually lived. Towards the end of his life he occupied a position of some responsibility, but formerly he had worked for Ovando as a shepherd. When his employer went to the royal court in October 1570, he left the keys to his houses in Cáceres and in the country with Diego García. García said he kept accounts during that period, including what he sent to Ovando at court and the cost of food for the servants. He also collected rents and said that he had given account in Madrid for rents collected until August 1571, so evidently he traveled to court on business or to consult with his employer. The picture one derives of García from his will is that of a man of fairly humble circumstances who obviously was literate, somewhat surprising in view of the fact that he was a shepherd at one time. His literacy, of course, would account for the position of responsibility Ovando entrusted to him.[70]

Slaves were far less numerous than criados in sixteenth-century Extremadura but were common enough that they formed a normal rather than a novel component of noble households. A typical noble establishment might have five to ten slaves, including men, women, and children. While there still were a few *morisco* (of Muslim descent) slaves in the sixteenth century, the majority in this period were African by birth or ancestry; Extremadura's proximity to Portugal guaranteed a steady supply of slaves. The status of slaves was quite different from that of criados whose position, as seen, could be flexible and open-ended; an individual could move in and out of the criado category. Slaves, in contrast, had little possibility for the free exercise of choice, especially in a setting like Extremadura which doubtless did not offer trained or skilled slaves the opportunities for earning money on their own that their counterparts in Seville might have. Information on slaves in Cáceres and Trujillo is largely limited to transactions, manumissions, and dispositions in wills, none of which give much indication of their activities, skills, or social ties, either as slaves or after manumission. It seems likely that they functioned mainly as domestic and personal servants and that the majority belonged to noble households, although nonnobles such as members of the clergy or professionals commonly would own a slave or two as well.[71]

Despite the legal and socioeconomic factors that differentiated the status of slave from that of criado, in reality the fact that slaves functioned in households alongside other servants and retainers for extended periods, or might actually be born in the household to which they belonged, meant that their position in some ways was analogous to that of criados. There appears to have been—as was true for criados—considerable variety in the nature and strength of the tie between master (or mistress) and slave, so that treatment of slaves varied greatly, not only among individual slaveholders but even within the same household. The same person who freed one or two slaves in his will, or at least made provisions that certain slaves not be sold outside the family, also might arrange for other slaves to be sold off as part of the estate. For example, Juan de Vita, while omitting any reference to at least three other slaves included in the inventory of his estate, in his will of 1544 made extensive provisions for his slave Juan de Vita (perhaps an illegitimate child related to his household?). Vita stipulated that Juan de Vita must be kept in the family and that he could opt for the household where he was treated best, and he obligated his heirs to care for him in his old age. In a codicil, however, Vita changed his mind and freed Juan de Vita, who in 1550 was living in Cáceres as a free man.[72] Some nobles not only manumitted numbers of slaves but bequeathed them sums of money or personal objects. Ties of affection and intimacy and the birth of illegitimate children to slave women probably accounted for the majority of voluntary manumissions, and most likely many or most of the children freed were mulattoes.[73]

The ties between a noble and his retainers certainly included elements of loyalty and obligation that went beyond the relationship of paid employee to employer or humanized that of slave to master. Recall that it was Pascual Gil de Cervantes's criados who drove off Orellana's retainers when they tried to take possession of the dehesa, and that it was the latter who killed Pascual Gil's son. In a more contemporary example, in one episode of the protracted and occasionally violent enmity between two returnees from Peru, Juan Cortés and Juan de Herrera, both of them regidors of Trujillo in the midsixteenth century, Cortés's criados—apparently at his instigation—attacked and wounded Herrera and his brother, the latter seriously.[74] Nobles generally were held to be accountable for the actions of their criados, the implication being that criados normally would undertake certain actions only with the knowledge and sanction of their patron. A royal letter of pardon issued to the powerful Luis de Chaves in 1476 (for reasons unknown) included not only Chaves's sons and nephews but his criados—and the criados of his criados—as well, for a total of 193 individuals considered to be under his authority.[75] A century later, in October 1576 the regidores of Trujillo's council deliberated about what action to take in regard to a "certain crime that certain criados and a black [slave] of don Rodrigo de Orellana, vecino and regidor, committed." The criados had killed one of the guards of the montes, who were employed by the city. Most of the regidores insisted that some action be taken or no one would be willing to guard the montes. At the time don Rodrigo and one of his criados were already in jail, and the council sent constables to arrest two of his swineherds and a slave.[76]

The loyalty of criados was not, of course, invariable. In August 1573 the *alcalde de la hermandad,* responsible for law enforcement in the countryside, appeared before the council of Cáceres to report that he had taken prisoner a "famous thief" who under torture had named a criado of Antonio Gutiérrez Sanabria as one of the guilty parties in a theft of Sanabria's cattle.[77] But mutual loyalty and trust were the ideal for nobles and their retainers. The Hinojosas described Diego de Hinojosa, el viejo, as being a virtuous and forthright caballero, a good friend to his relatives and friends, and greatly attached to his criados ("por sus criados, erales en gran manera aficionado"). Juan de Chaves was "magnífico con sus deudos y criados y amigos."[78] A noble should be generous and fair, and his retainers loyal.

Noble Ideals and Behavior

Despite the fact that nobles were surrounded by and in constant contact with people from the other orders of society who constituted the majority of the population, these nonnobles to a great extent figured only indirectly in the nobles' world view. Their main points of reference were their peers, families, and lineages. Surely it is no accident that the three sixteenth-century chronicles of Trujillo authored by hidalgos referred by name only to hidalgos and mentioned others only insofar as they formed part of the cast of supporting characters in the episodes recounted. The nobles' concept of history focused on the honor and deeds of their antecedents, since a noble's honor and status were inseparable from and defined by that of his family and lineage.[79] All three of the Trujillo chronicles were essentially genealogies in one form or another. The nobles' view of their place in society and the importance of family and history shaped the institutions characteristic of that group. Entails, the high dowries that formed an essential part of carefully chosen marital alliances, even the importance and prestige of a seat on the city council derived from the ideals and objectives of the nobility.

The noble's relations with both peers and others were judged in terms of ideals associated with his station, which were a product of the amalgam of military and Christian virtues that developed in the Middle Ages throughout Europe. Honesty, charity, generosity, and justice were on a par with physical strength, military skills, horsemanship, and wealth. Juan de Chaves, who received highest praise from the Hinojosas, apparently possessed all these virtues (in their view), as well as grace and authority:

He favors the poor and gives them aid and raises them from the dust; he honors the rich as each deserves and equally esteems and honors the virtuous poor; the bad and haughty, even if they are rich, he persecutes. . . . He works for the good of the commonwealth.

In the same source it can be seen that the ideals for women emerged even more directly from Christian attitudes. Constanza de Hinojosa, mother-in-law of Andrés Calderón Puertocarrero, was "devoted, charitable, prudent, complaisant and quiet." She was temperate and diligent with her household and husband and religious and devoted in her widowhood.[80]

If the ideals of generosity, valor, and justice emerge clearly, other components of the nobles' world view are murkier. This was, after all, a society where the violent feuds and conflicts of the late Middle Ages were still endemic in the sixteenth century, where violence was frequently brutal and treacherous, where "enemistades" seem to have had the same importance and legitimacy as deudos and friendships, and where the natural leaders of society—the nobles—apparently felt free to ignore the law and its representatives as they saw fit.[81] The imprisonment of a regidor of Trujillo, don Rodrigo de Orellana, on suspicion of instigating the murder of a guard of the montes has been mentioned, but this was hardly an isolated or unique occurrence. An astonishing number of regidores, in Trujillo especially, were jailed or placed under house arrest at one time or another. Luis de Chaves, mayorazgo, and Juan de Chaves in 1565 were implicated and arrested in connection with the murder of Licenciado Argüellez, who at the time of his death was serving as a regidor.[82] The bitter conflict between Juan Cortés and Juan de Herrera saw them both in jail at different times. In 1545 the corregidor of Trujillo placed eight regidores under house arrest when, in protest of the monastery of Guadalupe's appointment of notaries for the city and its district, they attempted to instate their own choice. When Juan de Chaves protested the order, the corregidor had him imprisoned in the city's fortress.[83] Regidores of Cáceres also came into conflict with their city's corregidor in January 1571. On a Monday morning by eleven o'clock only one regidor had arrived in the council chambers. Sancho de Paredes and don Diego de Ovando de Cáceres were outside strolling in the *portales* (arcades) of the plaza mayor. When they were summoned and refused to come, the corregidor ordered them arrested and imprisoned in the city hall. He also sent notice to the other regidores, ordering them to appear under threat of a fine of 1000 ducados.[84] Violence and defiance of authority could be found, of course, at all levels of society; but the status and wealth of the nobility often enabled them to evade the legal consequences of such behavior.

The nobles' concept of their rank, their relationship to the rest of society, and of honor fostered a concept of "freedom" that is not easily defined, since it was both an individual and a collective notion. The regidores who protested the monastery of Guadalupe's control of Trujillo's *escribanías* (a royal concession purchased by the monastery in the late fourteenth century) based their objections on the contention that because Trujillo and the monastery had many suits and conflicts over jurisdiction, notaries appointed by the monastery would hardly be impartial and would work against the city's interests. The argument seems fair enough, although of course they hoped to replace the notaries with their own choices, who probably would be no more impartial. Regardless of whether their argument was justified, however, the monastery's right to name the notaries was irrefutable, so that the regidores' campaign to rescind that privilege had to be conducted outside any legal context. They turned to their fellow nobles for support, collecting signatures from the members of the cofradía of La Paz, whose membership consisted mostly of hidalgos. A letter from an unknown source in Trujillo to the prior of the monastery, purporting to inform him of these doings, continually referred to the "pasión" with which the regidores conducted themselves: "so great is the passion that Juan de Chaves and Diego de Vargas and their followers have in this business that even if that house [of Guadalupe] were of Turks it could not be greater." Martín de Chaves was quoted as saying " 'freedom, freedom,' as if he were captive in the land of the Moors."[85] The "freedom" that the regidores and their noble supporters sought to defend in this instance was collective, not individual. The perceived threat to the city translated into a threat to a freedom claimed by the nobility as a group.[86]

The concept of freedom in the individual sense allowed nobles to ignore the entire apparatus of law and officialdom when these conflicted with their own interests or objectives. The case of Andrés Calderón Puertocarrero, caballero and mayorazgo of Trujillo who went to Peru in 1562 (see table 3), is a fine example of the extent to which a noble could flout the law. During his short stint in Peru Andrés Calderón, who was the nephew of the wealthy and respected encomendero of Cuzco don Pedro Puertocarrero (also a native of Trujillo), killed a merchant named Gonzalo de Almonte in Lima. Almonte allegedly had slandered either Andrés Calderón or his mistress. Calderón then fled Peru for Spain before he could be arrested. By 1566 Almonte's mother and sisters in Spain (they were vecinas of Guadalcanal) had discovered that Gonzalo's murderer was back in Trujillo, and they initiated proceedings to have him arrested and tried. The husband of one of the sisters, Licenciado Diego de Puebla, corregidor of the town of Moguer, wrote a brief that included the following observations:

Andrés Calderón goes publicly in the city of Trujillo and its district on horseback, armed with a crossbow, accompanied by many relatives and friends who favor him, against the corregidor's order that no one accompany him . . . under [threat of] a fine of 1,000 ducados . . . and exile. . . . And the worst is that Andrés Calderón boasts that whoever comes to arrest him will have to kill him with a crossbow. And . . . my parties are women and among them a widow and a young orphan, miserable persons whom the law favors, and Andrés Calderón is a man [well] related and favored in that city.

According to the brief, in 1568 Almonte's widow, Isabel García, said that Calderón was living in Trujillo "as if he hasn't committed any crime and because he is a 'mayorazgo' and prominent man," no one had been able to arrest him. Calderón continued to evade arrest, moving between his house in Trujillo and country house in Banis Pedro, or crossing the border into Portugal when the pressure increased. In 1574 he was still at liberty. In that year he finally made an effort to reach an agreement with Almonte's family, authorizing several vecinos of Trujillo in Spain and Peru to settle with one of Almonte's sons in an amount of up to 1000 ducados.[87]

The same Andrés Calderón who in this instance so blatantly placed himself beyond the reach of the law, however, did not hesitate to use the legal system when it suited his own interests. In the 1580s and 1590s he pursued a seemingly interminable suit in Granada over properties in Medellín that his uncle don Pedro Puertocarrero's mestizo son in Peru had inherited and which he claimed.[88] Andrés Calderón's opportunism was as basic to his character as were the ideals of behavior associated with his rank.

The nobles' preference for conducting their private affairs of honor and revenge outside the law prolonged the conflicts and violence of the late Middle Ages; as late as the early seventeenth century Cáceres, Trujillo, and Plasencia were notorious for the continuation of *banderismo*.[89] Hernando Pizarro's son don Francisco stabbed Rodrigo de Orellana, the son of his father's "enemy" Pedro Suárez de Toledo, long-time regidor of Trujillo, in 1571.[90] Earlier in the century García Holguín, the señor of Casa Corchada and chief of the Golfines de Arriba clan of Cáceres (father of the Diego García de Paredes who got into trouble with Licenciado Gasca in Peru) was murdered by Diego Mejía de Ovando in the church of the monastery of San Francisco as a result of a dispute between the two clans over the location of their coats of arms inside the church.[91] Doubtless this violent incident was the culmination of a longstanding feud.

Careers and Mobility

Tales of the bandos, revenge, and local violence conjure up a picture of backward and unenlightened provincial societies, turned in upon themselves and cut off from the currents of change affecting the larger world of Castile in the fifteenth and sixteenth centuries. Yet the provinciality of local extremeño society coexisted with another, perhaps equally important aspect that hinged upon the careers of members of noble and hidalgo families that took them away from home and involved them in the more cosmopolitan academic, bureaucratic, ecclesiastic, and military life of Castile and its empire. Earlier in this chapter mention was made of the successful professional careers of middle-level hidalgos such as Dr. Francisco de Sande of Cáceres and Licenciado Diego González Altamirano of Trujillo; for these men and their families such careers meant a significant elevation in status. But it was not only the middle- and lower-level hidalgos who entered professions and pursued careers that took them away from Cáceres or Trujillo to the universities or the court, to Seville, Italy, Flanders, or the Indies. The noble families of these cities consistently produced important figures in the academic, bureaucratic, ecclesiastic, and military circles of Castile and its empire.

The explanation for this phenomenon lies in several distinct but related considerations. The provincial nobles were the leaders and the wealthiest members of local society. They received at least some education, which would make further study at a university, and all that could imply, more accessible to them than to most. As society's leaders they also were in a natural position to form ties with the court. Captain Diego de Ovando de Cáceres's support of Ferdinand and Isabella paved the way for his son Frey Nicolás de Ovando to become Comendador of Lares of the Order of Alcántara, and Frey Nicolás's continuing ties with Ferdinand—as well as his administrative abilities—led to his appointment as governor of Hispaniola in 1502. Doubtless Dr. Lorenzo Galíndez de Carvajal's long-time professional career and association with the crown was largely responsible for his son Diego's appointment as a Comisario de Perpetuidad for Peru in 1560. Fray Diego de Chaves, eldest son of the prominent Escobar family of Trujillo, served as royal confessor to Philip II's unfortunate son don Carlos and later to Philip himself. Many families had longstanding traditions of service to the crown, either in the bureaucracy or military, or in the Church. The military tradition was particularly strong because such service historically was identified with the nobles' position and role in society.

What underlay and to some extent sustained these traditions of service and career mobility was the structure of the noble family itself. The nobility's emphasis on lineage and preservation of family wealth and position led to an increasing concentration of inherited property in the hands of one or two children. In the sixteenth century the growing number of entails conveyed the largest portion of inheritable estates to one heir per generation, usually (but not invariably) the eldest son. Many noble families, of course, continued to follow the practice of partible inheritance (equal division among all legitimate heirs), and some very wealthy patriarchs might create two or more entails. But it was becoming more and more common for one son to succeed to the entail or largest part of the estate, while only one or two daughters received dowries substantial enough to allow them to marry individuals of comparable wealth and status. While all legitimate children inherited a portion of the parental estate, the creation of entails often impelled noble children who would expect to inherit relatively small legacies to pursue alternative careers. The convents of Cáceres and Trujillo were filled with the daughters of local noble families, and young men went off to study at the university, join religious orders, serve in the military, or, increasingly in the sixteenth century, try their luck in the Indies.

While most nobles and hidalgos probably were functionally literate, levels of education varied considerably. Gómez de Solís, captain and encomendero in Peru from a prominent family of Cáceres, sent a letter in December 1546 to Gonzalo Pizarro in which he said his good friend and fellow cacereño Benito de la Peña actually wrote the letter because his own crude efforts ("estos letrones míos") were unsuitable.[92] In contrast one of Gómez's brothers in Cáceres, Lorenzo de Ulloa Solís, was an ordained priest who managed the family's complicated affairs in Cáceres and Peru for years.

Most extremeños who sought a higher education studied at Salamanca, which is not surprising given the university's proximity to the region and its reputation.[93] A university education did not come cheaply, and most students depended on assistance from their families or other patrons during their years of study. In 1575, for example, Diego de Vargas Figueroa of Cáceres gave his son don Cristóbal de Figueroa Ocampo 250 sheep and 150 lambs to sell in order to buy himself books when he entered the university.[94]

Certain families favored higher education and professional careers. Dr. Nicolás de Ovando, nephew of Frey Nicolás de Ovando and on his mother's side of don Bernardino de Carvajal, canon of the cathedral of Plasencia, spent most of his adult life and career at the court. He served first on the audiencia of Valladolid and from 1550 until his death in 1565 as a member of the royal council of the Military Orders. In his will Ovando left all his law books to his grandson Nicolás de Ovando, who wanted to study in Salamanca or Alcalá.[95] Doubtless the most outstanding member of this family was Licenciado Juan de Ovando, descendant of an illegitimate branch of the family of Captain Diego de Ovando de Cáceres and a cousin of Dr. Nicolás de Ovando. Born in 1514, in his remarkable career Licenciado Juan de Ovando served as a catedrático of the University of Salamanca, canon of the cathedral of Seville, member of the Council of the Inquisition, and eventually sixth president of the Council of the Indies, from 1571 until just before his death in 1575. As president of the Council of the Indies Ovando initiated the codification of laws relating to the government of the Spanish empire. He died before codification was completed, but the ordinance of 1573 represented a first step toward standardization. Ovando also served as financial advisor to the crown. As a public figure, he was renowned for his integrity and competence.[96] Other families also developed traditions of public service and higher education.[97]

The church, especially religious orders, attracted members of the nobility and brought some extremeños into considerable prominence. In addition to the royal confessor, Fray Diego de Chaves, Trujillo produced the cardinal Licenciado don Gaspar Cervantes de

Gaete, who successively served as archbishop of Messina (Sicily), Salerno, and Tarragona, where he died and was buried in 1575, and was a prominent specialist in canon law at the 1562–1563 meeting of the Council of Trent.[98] The first bishop and subsequently first archbishop of Lima was the Dominican Fray Jerónimo de Loaysa, member of a prominent noble family of Trujillo. Another Dominican, Fray Felipe de Meneses of Trujillo, became catedrático of the University of Alcalá de Henares and prior of the convents of Toledo and Segovia. Philip II put him in charge of the reform of the Mercedarian order in Galicia.[99] In Cáceres don Bernardino de Carvajal was a cardinal, and in the late fifteenth and sixteenth centuries several members of the Sande Carvajal clan served as dignitaries of the cathedral of Plasencia.[100] Licenciado Fray Antonio Gutiérrez de Ulloa was Inquisitor of Lima in the 1570s. In addition to these luminaries many other young men of noble families entered orders such as San Juan de los Caballeros or the mendicant orders, which normally took them away from home and sometimes even outside of Spain. Although certainly there were hidalgos in the secular priesthood, and non-hidalgos could enter religious orders, the majority of hidalgos who chose ecclesiastical careers opted for the regular rather than the secular priesthood.[101]

While the church probably accounted for the largest number of hidalgos who sought opportunities away from home—an ecclesiastical career, after all, did offer a lifelong solution to the problem of making one's livelihood—military service might have been nearly as popular. Not only did military service correspond to the traditional role and predilections of the nobles, but it offered greater flexibility in some senses than the church, since entering the military need not be a lifetime commitment. Because so many nobles participated in military campaigns at one time or another—the politics and conflicts of the fifteenth and sixteenth centuries assured there would be many opportunities to bear arms—it is impossible to estimate how many nobles and hidalgos gained at least some military experience at some point.

As was true for the bureaucracy or the church, certain families had a high level of involvement in the military. The patriarch of the Pizarro family, Captain Gonzalo Pizarro, fought in Granada, Italy, and Navarre (in Italy with "el Gran Capitán," Gonzalo Fernández de Córdoba, and with Diego García de Paredes), and his son Hernando accompanied him in the last campaign, as did Juan Cortés, the Pizarro ally who went to Peru and returned to become a regidor of Trujillo. Juan de Chaves ended the brief chronicle of his lineage with a list of his forebearers who died in the service of the crown: Martín de Chaves, older brother of Luis de Chaves, el viejo, died in the battle of Archite; Francisco de Chaves, his great-grandfather, died in "las lomas de Málaga"; Nuño de Chaves, his father's brother, and Francisco de Chaves, his own older brother, both died in Peru; and his brother don Alonso de Sotomayor, who was named captain for the infantry sent to fight the French in 1558, died of illness on the campaign.[102] Captain Martín de Meneses (brother of Fray Felipe de Meneses), who spent over forty years in Peru, claimed his father and three uncles (one of whom died in Florida and another in Mexico) all had served in the military.[103]

Probably the most famous military hero of the epoch was Diego García de Paredes, the "Samson of Extremadura," who had legendary strength, courage, and skill; he was born in 1468 and fought alongside "el Gran Capitán" in Italy. In the early sixteenth century Diego García's illegitimate half-brother Alvaro de Paredes, who died in 1511, accompanied him, as later would Alvaro's own illegitimate son, Sancho de Paredes (see table 2). After numerous campaigns Diego García de Paredes, loyal member of Charles V's entourage, was named "caballero de la espuela dorada" in Bologna in 1530, where he died in 1533. His illegitimate son of the same name, born in Trujillo in 1506 and raised by a cousin, went to the Indies in 1524 but returned to Europe in the 1530s. He spent about ten years fighting in Flanders, Germany, Italy, and Sicily and attained the rank of captain before returning to Trujillo and then leaving for Amazonas with his compatriot Francisco de Orellana. His nephew Luis, oldest son of legitimate half-brother Sancho de Paredes, died fighting in Andalusia.[104]

The participation of the Sande family of Cáceres in the military (see table 2) was perhaps exceptionally high. The outstanding military figure of the family was don Alvaro de Sande. Second son of the third señor of Valhondo and a relative through his grandfather of Diego García de Paredes, don Alvaro was destined for a career in the Church and studied briefly in Salamanca before deciding that his vocation lay elsewhere. In the 1530s he participated in expeditions to Tunis and elsewhere in the Mediterranean and in the 1540s

fought in Flanders and against France, returning subsequently to
Italy. After the Spanish disaster of 1559 at the island of Gelves (off
the Tunisian coast), he was captured by the Turks, taken to Con-
stantinople, and finally ransomed at great cost. Because of his reputation the Turks at first invited Sande to join them. When he
refused, they delayed considerably in arranging the ransom. Ferdinand, the Holy Roman Emperor and grandson of Ferdinand and
Isabella, whom Sande's grandfather Sancho de Paredes Golfín had
served, at the request of his brother Maximilian finally interceded
on Sande's behalf, and the ransom (variously 40,000 or 60,000
escudos) was accepted. Despite the expense and the hiatus in his
career, don Alvaro de Sande returned to active military life in Italy
and the Mediterranean, serving as coronel, field marshal, and captain general, and finally as governor of Milan, where he died in
1573. Philip II granted him señorío of the village of Valdefuentes
and later the title of Marqués de Piobera.[105]

Don Alvaro de Sande was the most famous but not the only
military officer in the family. One of his brothers, Diego García de
Sande, was a general who served in the Mediterranean and a
comendador of Santiago, and another, Arias de Sande, was a captain who died in Italy. Four of his nephews, sons of his brother
Pedro de Sande, joined the military as well. Two of these nephews
died at Gelves and another in Italy. The fourth, don Juan de Sande,
also fought in Italy and served as a captain in the Gelves campaign.
In 1569 the city council of Cáceres made him captain of the two
hundred infantrymen recruited to fight in Granada. He survived
the campaign but died shortly after his return to Cáceres in 1571.[106]
Don Alvaro de Sande's first cousin on his mother's side was another
Diego García de Paredes (they were both grandsons of Sacho de
Paredes Golfín), who fought in Italy under his famous cousin and in
Flanders. He was made a captain before he left the military and
went to Peru in the 1540s. And in the less prominent branch of the
Sande family (those distant relatives who sued to prove their
hidalguía in Granada) at least two sons of that Pedro de Sande had
military careers. Don Juan de Sande served in Italy and Flanders,
and his brother don Bernardino was a captain in the Philippines.[107]

Military service provided an opportunity to earn distinction and
royal favor as well as personal enrichment, but as seen in the case of
don Alvaro de Sande and his relatives, the fortunes of war also

brought death or captivity. For officers and soldiers of some means, the last could mean long periods of imprisonment awaiting payment of ransom money by relatives or charitable organizations at home. Baltasar de Valverde (brother of Licenciado Diego García de Valverde, who served on several audiencias in the New World) thought that his nephew (his first cousin's son) was a captive of the "king of Fez." In his will of 1579 he asked his brother's son to help ransom him because "the lad is very virtuous and very honorable" and deserving of help.[108] Ransoming was a standard feature of the many military campaigns and conflicts of the period. Relatives of Hernando de Monroy, a prisoner in Algiers, sent 200 ducados to Dr. Nicolás de Ovando at the court to negotiate his release. Family and relatives raised 300 ducados toward the ransom of Pedro Alvarez Holguín, who was missing after the Gelves disaster but was finally located in Sicily in 1561.[109]

Like study at the university or entrance into a religious order, military service was a career choice that many noble families willingly supported. The regidor Sancho de Paredes Holguín, for example, gave his brother Jerónimo de la Cerda 75,000 maravedís when he went off to serve in Italy in 1554.[110] While the military was often the career choice of younger or illegitimate sons, this pattern was not invariable. Since military service could be of short duration, and individuals who opted for long-term careers still would be likely to return home periodically between campaigns, the military did not mean a permanent absence and so was not incompatible with marrying and establishing a household. Given the strength of the military tradition, and the possibility of maintaining one's position at home despite periods of absence, conceivably many hidalgos went off to the Indies (especially in the earlier decades of the sixteenth century) in much the same spirit that they, their fathers, or other relatives joined the army. Like the military, going to the Indies meant service to the crown with the expectation of personal distinction and gain and a possibility of returning home.

The careers that hidalgos chose were important not only because they offered a solution to the problem of how to provide for sons whose inheritance was small; these careers also created the basis for a network of contacts that connected nobles in Cáceres and Trujillo with the outside world. The network diminished the provincialism and isolation that threatened to engulf local extremeño society, put the nobles in touch with the wider currents of Castilian life, and provided opportunities to acquire expertise in legal, financial, and commercial matters. Cacereños frequently turned to their compatriots Dr. Nicolás de Ovando or Licenciado Juan de Ovando, and trujillanos to Fray Felipe de Meneses or the royal confessor Fray Diego de Chaves, for assistance and advice. By extending itself geographically—sending its sons or illegitimate or poor relatives away from home—and encompassing a number of different careers, the noble family bolstered its position at home while preserving and protecting the lineage linked to the entailed estate, title, and arms.

Nobles and the *"República"*

Despite the varied and often distinguished careers of nobles who left home, the principal focus of attention for most remained their home towns. There they founded convents, capellanías, and charitable works, belonged to cofradías (some of which limited their membership to hidalgos), and sat on the city council, which enabled them to dabble in many aspects of the city's political, social, religious, and economic life. By law and historical tradition, the nobles monopolized the *regimientos* (seats on the city council), which they retained and passed along within families, even though appointment to the council nominally was the prerogative of the crown. Diego de Vargas Carvajal actually held three regimientos—two in Trujillo, which he left to his sons don Juan and don Diego de Vargas Carvajal, and a third in Salamanca (presumably inherited from his father), which he willed to another son, don Fabian.[111] Nobles who held them considered regimientos as much a part of the family estate as a house, lands, and rents. The practice of passing on city council seats meant that at any time a number of regidores might be related by family ties or marriage. Nonetheless, whereas in Cáceres the occupancy and transfer of regimientos seems to have been fairly conservative and stable, in Trujillo there appears to have existed, or developed in the sixteenth century, something of a free trade in city council seats, which in effect could be rented out. Hernando Pizarro designated one of his regimientos for Francisco Durán and the other for Melchor González (possibly both were returnees from Peru), and don Alvaro de Hinojosa de Torres and his son paid the widow of

García de Vargas Ocampo 40,000 maravedís for five years for a regimiento that her minor son could not occupy.[112] But certainly in Cáceres as well nobles could buy regimientos; the going price in the sixteenth century was around 500 ducados.

The varying practices that affected the disposition or retention of regimientos meant that some nobles spent long periods on the council—in 1571 Sancho de Paredes Holguín said he had been a regidor (of Cáceres) for twenty-five years[113]—while others served perhaps five or ten years, and yet others only briefly. One would expect that individuals who spent longer periods on the council would take a greater interest in the city's affairs. Despite the sale of regimientos and the inheritance practices that kept them within families, nobles who served on the council did fulfill a civic duty that many took quite seriously. Dr. Nicolás de Ovando, after years at the court, willed 12,000 maravedís to the city council of Cáceres "for some payments that were misspent because of my vote while [I] was a regidor."[114]

Conservative and limited as their view of society and their relationship to that society might have been, the nobles nevertheless identified with the "república" and saw themselves as responsible for the common welfare. The nobles on the council sometimes protested the taxes or military levies demanded by the crown, stalled in the implementation of royal directives, or quarreled with the crown's representative (and ultimate authority), the corregidor. Nevertheless, although they doubtless took seriously the obligations of Christian charity, patron-client ties, and their responsibility for protecting the people and república, in fact the nobles' sense of duty to the rest of society ultimately did not serve to protect the less powerful people from economic exploitation and privation. The nobles, especially in their role as city council members, might ponder the proper or just course of action in a given situation; in 1571 Sancho de Paredes, for example, urged that the price of bread be lowered, saying that in all his years as regidor "he has never seen . . . this republic . . . [spend] anything in benefit of the poor in all this time and . . . there have never been such hard times."[115] But they never wavered in their fundamental understanding of their rights and privileges. They saw their obligations to the rest of society as a function of their privileged position, and not the opposite, and this perception negated the possibility of innovation.

III

Commoners, Clergy, and Professionals

The nobles and hidalgos of Cáceres and Trujillo formed a small and in some ways coherent group. The much larger non-hidalgo population encompassed many more occupational and ethnic groups— professionals in law and medicine, clergy, merchants, agriculturalists, tradespeople, urban and rural day laborers, servants, slaves, Portuguese immigrants, moriscos, and paupers. These groups spanned the range from wealth to poverty, some having in common only their non-hidalgo status. Wealthy merchants, successful professionals, and some ecclesiastics might occupy a position quite similar to that of prominent hidalgos by virtue of their wealth, tax-exempt status, and the deference that their callings and social position elicited. The clergy, like the hidalgos, were exempt from most taxes, as were professionals who had attained a doctorate. At the other end of the spectrum, people classified as *pobres* (paupers) usually avoided taxation as well. Thus the taxpayers—the "hombres buenos pecheros"—bore a double burden. As peasants, tradespeople, and laborers, they performed most of the productive work of the city and countryside, and they paid the bulk of the taxes. If the nobility dominated the commonwealth, the workers and peasants— the *pecheros* (taxpayers)—sustained it.

While at times it may seem difficult to penetrate the world view of the nobles, nonetheless by reason of their position in society and their activities we can learn a great deal about how they lived and what they did. Their command of extensive economic resources, their concern for the management of family fortune and affairs, and their entrance into many spheres of public life all left ample record in the documents of the period. For the vast majority of commoners, however, this kind of detailed record simply does not exist. With the exception of some of the more prominent and successful professionals and clergy, information on commoners is scattered and scant indeed. They did not necessarily go before notaries to perform transactions, unless these involved a person of a higher rank (an hidalgo, priest, merchant). Frequently they had little or no property of which to dispose, or what property remained was divided according to custom, so that relatively few commoners made formal wills. Similarly at this level people doubtless made most marriage and dowry arrangements by common consent. A number of commoners emerge in the records only because they decided to leave. Since people who undertook to emigrate legally to the New World often presented lengthy testimony and even letters from relatives who had preceded them in support of their applications, the study of emigrants sheds light on the lives and experiences of common people that otherwise is mostly lacking.

As is true for most traditional or hierarchical societies, one sees the commoners of Extremadura largely in relation to their superiors in rank or wealth. The structure of society and economy in this region was such that to a considerable extent it is possible to discuss the position and activities of the nobility with little reference to the rest of the population. The nobles themselves paid scant attention to the rest, and that only insofar as nonnobles figured in relation to their own interests or objectives. One cannot claim the reverse for the commoners; their lives were much more likely to be affected or shaped in some fashion by the wealthy and powerful.

Nonetheless, it is fundamentally wrong to see the nobility as unilaterally shaping and defining society and economic and social relations.[1] Commoners lived in a world that to some extent they defined for themselves. They were free to move about and organize their own lives. Artisans supervised the conduct and organization of their trades with little outside intervention; they lived together in certain neighborhoods, intermarried, and joined the same cofradías. In the villages, especially, peasants might lead their lives largely without reference to the nobility. Some villages had no hidalgos at all, or only very few (and those not necessarily set apart from the rest by notable wealth), and in some places the commoners retained control over town offices despite the presence of hidalgos.[2] The clergy, of course, functioned with considerable independence, since they often had their own sources of income and significant connections with individuals and institutions based outside local society. While priests often had ties of quasi-dependency with members of the nobility, whom they might serve as chaplains, account keepers, or the like, they had strong links with the commoners as well. Many of them came from the commercial and artisan groups.

None of this is to deny, of course, the crucial role of the nobles in organizing the economy and governing and controlling local society. The social and occupational groups that constituted local society—the various orders or estates—were in constant contact, overlapping, interacting, and affecting one another. The different groups had in common a wide range of social and cultural patterns, not because these were conditioned or imposed by the nobility but rather because they all emerged from and participated in a common society and culture. Many commoners, for example, joined the military as did hidalgos. Physical mobility—with its implications for possible socioeconomic mobility—was just as prevalent and important at this level of society (if not more so) as it was for hidalgos. Furthermore it must be stressed that hardly any of the characteristics or institutions associated with the nobility were the exclusive domain of that group, just as many hidalgos were indistinguishable from commoners in terms of their occupations or social status. Many commoners were literate, and they entered the professions and church as did hidalgos. In their concern for family, commoners again were much like hidalgos, even if they operated on a far more modest scale. Everyone joined cofradías, many of which drew their membership from all levels of society. Perhaps the only institution that the nobles could claim as exclusively theirs was the city council, and in Trujillo there is a strong possibility that even that monopoly had faltered in the sixteenth century. A degree of socioeconomic flexibility and the blurring of distinctions between different groups coexisted with the conservatism and stability that upheld the hierarchical ordering of society. In a sense both social fluidity and conservatism could exist because both were rooted in the common culture that united all groups.[3]

Since the nonnobles were so heterogeneous, in some ways it is easier to discuss various occupational or social groupings separately rather than together. Nonetheless some patterns affected a range of groups. Probably the most important of these patterns was mobility, which could involve nearly everyone. Another factor that affected most commoners, already mentioned, had to do with political power in the broad sense. The commoners were the taxpayers. They provided the bulk of the manpower for military levies, the capital for military requisitions, the quarters for troops. Their direct participation in government usually was limited to village councils and the lower rungs of municipal offices. They were, in other words, subjects. A third point, and one more difficult to discuss adequately because of the scarcity of information, has to do with wealth. Commoners in a number of callings could become "rich." While it might have been easiest for landowners or merchants to accumulate wealth, others could as well. At least three shoemakers in Trujillo were called "rich," as well as an innkeeper who subsequently lost his capital.[4] As would be expected, the reverse was true also; practically anyone could be poor. The following discussion will address these aspects of the lives of the commoners.

Opportunities and Obligations

A high degree of physical mobility characterized the functioning of the local and regional economy. Since the commoners performed most of the actual labor and tasks involved in economic production and exchange, they frequently moved around as part of their normal means of making a livelihood. Shepherds and swineherds moved with their livestock, muleteers and carters hauled materials in and out of the region, stewards and criados tended to the interests of their employers or accompanied them when they traveled, and merchants or their representatives went to trade fairs or other cities in Castile and Andalusia to buy or to complete transactions. The mobility that was inherent to the local economy, though it could bring people into contact with new opportunities they might find attractive, did not result from the need or desire to seek such opportunities. Moving temporarily or permanently to another locale, however, was much more directly related to the search for new opportunities. In the case of extremeños who moved from one village to another, or to Seville, or some other part of Castile, physical mobility likely took on another dimension; these people relocated in the hopes of finding new or better opportunities.

Out-migration from the region is difficult to quantify, but all evidence suggests that it was constant. It is somewhat ironic that because of the special nature of the move to the New World, that kind of migration is better documented than any other; yet the very fact that the possibility of emigration to America was so readily taken up by extremeños in itself is convincing evidence that leaving home to seek opportunities elsewhere was quite normal. Leaving the Indies aside, Seville, as a booming center of commerce and industry, probably was the greatest center of attraction for ex- tremeños in the sixteenth century. People from Cáceres and Tru- jillo living temporarily or permanently in Seville frequently testi- fied in the petitions of people from their home towns who wanted to go to the Indies,[5] and the records indicate that throughout the century people were leaving Extremadura to settle there.[6]

Certainly Seville was not the only destination in Castile that attracted extremeños, and furthermore a good deal of local and regional relocation went on. Francisco Román of Cáceres was a vecino of Valencia de Alcántara in 1574, and Francisco Gutiérrez, a labrador from Cáceres who in 1560 emigrated with his family to New Spain to join his brothers, was living in Albuquerque before his departure.[7] Marriages often involved relocation. For Cáceres it has been estimated that in 30 to 35 percent of marriages of common- ers, one partner was from outside the city; the majority of the outsiders were from nearby towns.[8]

As a result of moves within the area it was not at all uncommon for people to have relatives or property in other towns. In 1558 a vecino of Madroñera testified that his nephew Blas García had been living in a rented house there for about a year, employed by a vecino of Trujillo who paid him to guard his vineyard. Blas García's father had been a vecino of Madroñera, and Blas García was born there, but the family had moved to Abertura (also in Trujillo's district). Thus as a young man Blas García already had lived in two different towns. In another case, when a man named Andres Sánchez was asked whether he was or wanted to be a vecino of Madroñera, he replied no to both questions and said he paid taxes in another village, Herguijuela. In August 1558 he had been living in Madroñera for seven months, having moved his family with the intention of settling there, but apparently things did not work out. He was about to return to Herguijuela and was waiting only for planting season to sow a piece of land he had in Trujillo's commons.[9]

There are many other such examples that suggest that moving from one town to another was not at all unusual and that people often maintained ties with their former place of residence. Alonso Bravo was a native of Búrdalo (in Trujillo's district, today Villamesías) and a vecino of Trujillo when he made his will in 1584. With his wife he owned a house and garden in Búrdalo, in addition to a house in Trujillo; he asked to be buried in the church in Búrdalo. One of the executors of his will was a cousin living in Búrdalo and another was a nephew who lived in Abertura. Alonso Bravo belonged to cofradías in Trujillo, Puerto de Santa Cruz, and Jaraicejo (a town outside Trujillo's jurisdiction but with close ties to it).[10] Economic success may have prompted Bravo to become a citizen of Trujillo, but he retained strong social and economic connections with other towns in the district.

Mobility brought outsiders to Cáceres and Trujillo just as it took local people away from the cities and region. One of the three major routes of the Mesta led directly to the region, and the cities were located on major north–south (Salamanca to Seville) and east–west (Lisbon to Toledo) routes of travel and transport. The existence of inns and records of transactions involving one or more outsiders are evidence that the cities served as stopping-places or destinations for travelers of all sorts.[11] People from elsewhere might decide to take up residence. Whereas in Cáceres at least Portuguese probably were the most numerous immigrants and transients (apart from people from the nearby towns who came to work and live), others came as well, from virtually all over the peninsula. In 1544 a Maestre Pedro, probably a master mason, from Pamplona was living in Cáceres, and in 1569 a vecino of Cáceres originally from Galicia apprenticed himself to a wool carder in Cáceres.[12]

Special jobs and fine craftsmanship in particular might mean bringing in artisans from outside. In 1557 Francisco de Villalobos Carvajal hired someone from Valladolid to make the *retablo* (altarpiece) for the main chapel of the church of Santiago in Cáceres for 3000 ducados; the retablo was to be made from oak and pine from Soria.[13] But the reverse was true as well. The cities had their own master builders and fine craftsmen, and they in turn might go elsewhere to work. Trujillo especially was home to outstanding specialists in construction. In the sixteenth century Sancho de Cabrera worked on the churches of Garciaz, Orellana la Nueva, Jaraicejo, and Saucedilla, and Pedro Hernández on the palacio of don Alvaro de Sande (the military officer) in Valdefuentes. The renowned Francisco Becerra, son and grandson of master *canteros* (stonecutters), in addition to his projects in Trujillo itself, worked on the palacio and parish church of Orellana la Vieja and the sacristy of the church of Valdetorres (jurisdiction of Medellín) before departing for the New World in 1573, where he subsequently worked in New Spain and Peru.[14]

Military service attracted commoners and took them away from home. In sixteenth-century Castile recruitment for the regular army was done on a voluntary basis,[15] and commoners as well as hidalgos from Extremadura served and died in Europe and the Mediterranean.[16] The process by which the crown's frequent military levies were met is not entirely clear, but probably enlistment in these urban militias was voluntary as well. The best evidence of how this kind of recruitment took place comes from the Trujillo city council records of 1580. In March of that year the city's corregidor informed the council that they had to provide 200 infantrymen and 40 horsemen ("caballeros jinetes"). The council divided the levy between the city and the towns under its jurisdiction (40 from Trujillo and its huertas; 24 from Logrosán; 22 each from Berzocana, Garciaz, and Cañamero; 15 from Santa Cruz; 10 each from Escurial and Abertura; and 5 or less from all the others) and directed the towns and villages to send double the number required "of the most healthy and able and diligent." In Trujillo the final group would be chosen.[17]

This method of meeting the military levy suggests that there was little difficulty in finding a sufficient number of volunteers. Probably for many of the laborers of the towns and cities, service in the militia was attractive. The hundred soldiers recruited in Trujillo for the levy of 1558, for example, were to receive 5437½ maravedís for four months, which worked out to about 1½ reales a day. This was the same as the normal daily wage of an unskilled laborer but offered the added advantage of four months of secure employment. Despite the likely attractiveness of militia service for some, how-

ever, there might have been some coercion involved. Martín Jiménez Vaquero, a tailor from Cáceres, hired a substitute to go in his
place to the war in Granada in 1570, and ten years later another
cacereño, Pedro Laso, paid someone 200 reales to serve in his stead
in the Portuguese war.[18]

Discussion of military levies leads to the second point mentioned
in relation to the position of commoners in society. Such levies
were an extraordinary rather than a normal imposition of the
crown, but they came with some regularity in the sixteenth century; there were levies for wars with France or Portugal in either
Cáceres or Trujillo or both in 1542, 1552, 1556, 1558, 1575, and
1580 and in 1569 to put down the rebellion in Granada. Whereas,
as suggested, some enlistees might have welcomed the chance to
earn a regular wage for a time, the cities not only had to pay the
soldiers and officers but usually supplied their weapons as well.
Normally the municipality met these costs out of its own resources
or by taking out loans or censos on its property, but sometimes the
councils collected an additional tax. The taxpayers of Cáceres, for
example, had to cover the 1000 ducados needed to pay the soldiers
sent to Granada in 1569.[19]

Doubtless the necessity of quartering troops constituted an even
greater burden on the people. In February 1575 don Juan de
Avendaño appeared in Cáceres with a royal *cédula* (ordinance) to
recruit 250 soldiers and secure lodging for his troops.[20] In June
1580 vecinos of the city complained bitterly about the behavior and
activities of troops quartered among them, antagonism between
citizens and soldiers having resulted in physical clashes and mutual
accusations. At the same time the council of Trujillo wrote to the
royal confessor, Fray Diego de Chaves, complaining of disturbances caused by soldiers billeted there.[21] Obviously the presence
of troops had a directly disruptive impact on the daily life of the
townspeople. Though taxation was burdensome, it was at least predictable, whereas the demands of troops that might be billeted for
up to two months were far less so.

As might be expected, such extraordinary demands did not fall
equally on all groups. Wealthy and well-to-do commoners were
expected to provide capital rather than personal services in aid of
the realm. For the levy of 1580 the vecinos of Trujillo whose property was worth 2000 ducados had to furnish one horse each; those

with up to 1000 ducados shared between two (or more) the costs of supplying a horse. The vecinos who provided horses were not the principal nobles but rather, for the most part, merchants (seven of the forty-nine were called merchants and at least another ten were from merchant families), well-to-do artisans (a silversmith and candlemaker were included), and landowners.[22]

Wealth and Poverty

The repartimiento among the wealthy or at least well-off vecinos of Trujillo underlines the considerable socioeconomic differentiation that existed among the commoners. Yet it is difficult to identify the "ricos" (rich men) or pinpoint the source of their wealth or their real position in society. In 1578 the regidores of Cáceres disagreed about the appointment of Simón Sánchez, nephew of a prominent cleric named Bachiller Ojalvo, as the alcalde of the pecheros. A regidor who spoke in his favor said "he possesses the necessary qualities to hold the said office and he is a rich man."[23] Sánchez served at least two years as the alcalde, but nothing else is known about him. Some of the early and successful returnees from Peru formed a group of rich commoners which stood out clearly in local society—perhaps too much so; significantly two of the wealthiest of these—Diego de Trujillo and Martín Alonso, both from Trujillo and present at Cajamarca—subsequently returned to Peru.

If few artisans (and perhaps relatively few merchants) became rich, certainly a number of them prospered. Diego García, el viejo, a carpenter of Cáceres, in 1544 was able to endow his daughter with a house in the parish of San Juan, a vineyard, twenty-three fanegadas of land, a pair of oxen, and a bed—a substantial if not dazzling beginning for a newly married couple.[24] The success of artisans distinguished by economic prosperity probably hinged on a combination of factors—patronage, timely investments, and economic diversification. A locksmith named Pedro Alonso, for example, in 1551 said he had had a store in Trujillo in which he had sold barley for many years.[25] Cristóbal García, a pharmacist in Cáceres, was an active entrepreneur who for a while served as the city's mayordomo. In the late 1560s he bought a censo for 500 ducados, and his daughter received a dowry of 1500 ducados when she married Licenciado Gaspar Sánchez in 1578.[26] The two shoemaker brothers who were called "personas ricas" in 1554 were said to own at least 1000 ducados of property; in contrast Lorenzo del Puerto, another shoemaker of Trujillo, who in 1577 petitioned to go to New Spain with his family, said he was poor and that "with this trade I cannot support my house and family in this country since the said trade is of little profit." Witnesses claimed that only shoemakers with substantial capital to invest could survive in the business.[27]

Investments were not, of course, limited to one's own business. While censos and juros were safe investments that appealed especially to the wealthy and well-to-do who wanted to secure their capital, other forms of investment offered greater possibilities for profits, if greater risks as well. People often formed partnerships to rent the collection of tithes or taxes. In Cáceres in 1537, for example, the archdeacon of Plasencia, don Francisco de Carvajal, rented out the collection of that year's tithes for Sierra de Fuentes, Torreorgaz, and Torrequemada to two tailors for 9000 maravedís, those of the parish of San Juan to four men (including a blacksmith and the notary Pedro de Grajos) for 37,750 maravedís, and those of Casar to a lawyer and a merchant (Bachiller Jerónimo de Andrada and Rodrigo López) for 110,000 maravedís.[28]

Commercial investments were probably even more common. In 1579, for example, a vecino of Casar named Alonso Jiménez Garrovillano contributed 100 ducados to a partnership he formed with Jerónimo Carrillo of Cáceres, who put up 200 ducados. Jiménez was to take the money to "the fairs of Salamanca and Ríoseco and Villalón" to buy donkeys and mules to sell in Cáceres. The men agreed to share the profits equally, since Jiménez was contributing his efforts and labor.[29] The majority of commercial investments, however, were less substantial and formal (and therefore more accessible to people with little capital to contribute). Typically two or three individuals or married couples might purchase thirty or forty pigs, or rent jointly an oven or a mill, or the like. But modest investments meant modest profits, and obviously the majority of commoners were not getting rich.

Many artisans, and not only those in the more prestigious trades (such as pharmacists or silversmiths), were literate.[30] Doubtless literacy could enhance their economic possibilitiies and probably contributed to upward economic mobility, especially between generations. The tailor Diego de Monroy's son was Licenciado Antonio de Monroy, who had left Trujillo for New Spain, probably in the 1550s. In 1567 he was said to be flourishing there—"he has everything necessary . . . he sent to say he has mines"—while in Trujillo his father, Diego de Monroy, was "very old and poor." Monroy also had a son-in-law who held a position as a solicitor ("procurador del número") in Trujillo.[31] Francisco Rodríguez, a scribe (escribano) who in 1575 wanted to join his parents in Peru, was the son of a blacksmith; one of his brothers, who accompanied their parents to Peru, was a priest.[32] Upwardly mobile artisans, like wealthy merchants, might adopt some of the customs typically associated with the nobility. The *herrador* (farrier, blacksmith) Hernan Gónzalez of Trujillo left the "tercio y quinto" (third and fifth) of his property to his son Diego González "for the love he has had and services he has done for me," rather than dividing his property equally among his heirs. He also donated all his clothes, except a cape and tunic he gave to one grandson, to the poor.[33]

Some landowners as well were able to improve their economic situation and increase their holdings. Francisco Hortún, a vecino of Robledillo who made his will in January 1571 and was unable to sign his name, inherited a modest amount of property from his father—several pieces of land (including part of a vineyard, an orchard, and some grain land), forty-nine sheep and lambs and a cow, and several bushels of grain and flour. In all his inheritance was worth around 100 ducados. The dowry of his first wife, Francisca Alonso, included a house in Robledillo, two alcaceres, a small garden, an enclosed vineyard and part of another, a cow, and house furnishings. He counted fifty sheep, a few pigs, ten goats, twenty-two bushels of wheat, five fanegadas of land, and a vineyard he sold for 9 ducados as property accumulated during his first marriage. During his second marriage, to Estevanía de Carvajal, he made his most substantial acquisitions: another vineyard, ten and a half fanegadas of land bought from his uncle Gonzalo Becerra, a vecino of Trujillo, and another six from two other men; another piece of land from a nephew Alonso Becerra Hortún; a mill on the Tamuja river near Zarza de Montánchez; and a number of *tinajas* (earthenware jugs) ranging in size from one to fifty arrobas. His second wife inherited 6000 maravedís from her father and some tinajas, including three large ones.[34] Hortún's possessions, which included a total of at least twenty-three fanegadas (around eleven or twelve acres) of grain land as well as other types of land (alcaceres, vineyards), the mill, and some livestock, did not make him one of the "ricos" of his town; nonetheless he figured among the comfortable middle group and, significantly, he had made considerable advances from the starting point of his paternal inheritance.[35]

Alonso Bravo, who moved from Búrdalo to take up residence in Trujillo, was a stockraiser and very well-to-do commoner. In his will of 1584 he disposed of two pair of oxen, a cow, eighty pigs, two mills (one on the Búrdalo river and the other on the Alcollarín, which had two *criaderos* [probably stock farms] nearby), a censo of 5000 maravedís, 160 ducados, and two *cahices* (a cahiz equals twelve fanegas) of wheat, which he variously willed to his wife, nieces and nephews, a cousin, and a sister. He ordered all the rest of his estate (wheat, barley, pigs) to be sold to buy censos and the income used each year to marry one or two orphans or poor women, to be chosen from his lineage or the relatives of his first or second wife. In addition to this *obra pía* (charitable work) he directed that an image he had of the "bien aventurado" San Ildefonso be used to make an altar in the church of Búrdalo where masses were to be said.[36]

From the wills of individuals like Alonso Bravo or the blacksmith Hernán González, it can be seen that the concerns (and possibilities) of successful and well-to-to commoners went far beyond the basic necessities of life. Nonetheless, lacking the protection of the well-established family and kinship networks and resources that many nobles enjoyed, even well-to-do commoners might not have been very far removed from the spectre of want. Only in the codicil to his will did Alonso Bravo decide to give his sister Mari Sánchez 80 ducados, "considering that she is poor." Even knowing how much property an individual or family held, it still is difficult to gauge real economic status. The sons of Juan Muñoz of Trujillo inherited property and goods from their father and grandfather (a vecino of Navalsaz) that totaled about 750 ducados in value and included eighty fanegas of wheat and fifty of barley, ten oxen, three donkeys and a mule, nearly forty cows, and close to sixty pigs. But by the time all debts were settled and expenses met, each of four sons succeeded to little over 20,000 maravedís (about 55 ducados) and a share in a house and piece of land. Juan Muñoz doubtless understood the limitations of his economic situation, since in 1534 he left for Peru, taking three of his sons and a load of merchandise and slaves to sell. He died in Tierra Firme before reaching Peru.[37]

The 1557 census of Trujillo classified vecinos according to four economic categories. At the top were the rich—"los que tienen buena hacienda." Next came the well-to-do, "los que tienen medianamente" (or "los que tienen de comer"). Then there were those with some means—"los que tienen algo"—and last the poor. The first two categories accounted for around a tenth of the 1900 or so vecinos, the people of some means one-third, and the poor nearly 45 percent.[38] While it is clear that there were inaccuracies and shortcomings in this census (it included, for example, only one lawyer and no physicians or priests), the notably high percentage of pobres cannot be ignored. In a much more careful census compiled for the town of Santa Cruz de la Sierra in 1561, of 465 households 163 vecinos (or 35 percent) were counted as poor. The largest number of these, as might be expected, were women; the 51 widows and 27 young single women accounted for nearly half the indigent group. But in addition practically all the laborers were poor (4 or 7 *jornaleros*, 38 of 41 *ganadores*), as were many of the town's artisans—2 of 3 weavers, 2 of 5 masons, 4 of 13 tailors. At the same time in Zorita 73 of 380 vecinos were poor or very poor. Over half of these were women, but nearly a third were male taxpayers, and the poor of Zorita included 3 tailors, a carpenter, a blacksmith, a weaver, and a priest. In contrast, however, Ibahernando in the same year listed only 12 people as poor—some 6.5 percent of the vecinos—and all but one of them were women, mostly widows.[39]

Do these varying percentages of poor mean that the socioeconomic configuration of the towns and villages differed considerably? Probably so, to some extent, but the question of how the authorities defined "pobre" must also be taken into account. In principle at least a person classified as poor not only did not pay taxes but was eligible to receive alms or to beg. Thus, for example, of the 788 vecinos of Casar de Caceres, 53 were called "very poor persons, of whom many beg" ("piden por Dios"). It seems likely that in Casar and Ibahernando the less than 7 percent of vecinos who were classified as poor fell within the legal definition of the term.[40] But in Zorita more than half of the pobres, male and female (including many widows), were listed as "pecheros," taxpayers.

Clearly the term poor, in some cases anyway, was used in the descriptive rather than the legal sense.

However poverty was defined, and however inadequate or ambiguous were the censuses—especially those of the cities—there can be no doubt that the poor were omnipresent and that they led a very marginal existence. Some of the poor of the villages were said to have nothing at all in the way of possessions, not even a house or part of a house, although probably only a very small number were literally homeless. The poor did receive charity, especially during bad times. In March 1558 the clergy of Trujillo presented to the city council a list of 200 paupers "who suffer great necessity and hunger," and the council ordered 400 bushels of wheat distributed to them. But the authorities constantly attempted to control and limit the dispensing of charity. In the same month that they distributed the wheat, the Trujillo council issued instructions for the licensing of paupers to beg; they had to prove illness or need and could not beg at night.[41] Furthermore the city authorities distinguished sharply between their "own" poor and outsiders and transients. The regidores of Trujillo decreed that "pobres forasteros" could stay in the city no more than two days, under threat of a penalty of a hundred lashes. In Cáceres in 1575 the physician Licenciado Ledesma reported that the city's hospitals were overcrowded, and the council had its mayordomo give the hospitals more money to care for the sick. But in November they ordered that the sick who could travel be sent to the neighboring *lugares* (hamlets) at the city's expense. In February 1576 one regidor was asked to appoint someone to remove the healthy poor from the city and provide whatever "beasts that are needed to carry those who cannot walk."[42]

Despite official and religious charity, the poor led a hard and probably mostly unchanging life. In his will of 1580 Juan Martín Alamedo of Cáceres said that when he married his second wife, Juana Pérez la Mejía, he brought no property or money to the marriage; his wife had given him the black suit in which he was wed. At the time he made his will he and his wife still had nothing more than what she brought to the marriage "because they have been very difficult and needy years and times."[43] The assistance of relatives, neighbors, or patrons probably was as crucial to the survival of the poor as was official charity. Crisante de San Pedro, a notary of Trujillo who testified regarding the poverty into which Alonso Blanco, former innkeeper, had fallen, said that from time to time he had given Blanco and his four children things to help them out. Blanco owned only half a house and had entered the service of don Hernando de Chaves as a squire.[44]

Commoners and the Agrarian World

The fact that the economy of Spain (as, indeed, of most of the world) in the sixteenth century was fundamentally agrarian is so generally known that it may seem gratuitous to restate it here. Nonetheless, one cannot consider the lives of Castile's commoners without recognizing that the vast majority of them—and therefore the majority of the Castilian population—owed their livelihood or a substantial part of it to the land. The overwhelmingly agrarian orientation of the economy characterized the smaller towns and villages more strongly than the larger towns and cities, as would be expected. The latter, as centers for governmental and religious institutions, networks of trade and communications, and the principal places of residence for the majority of the nobility, of course encompassed and fostered a much greater diversity of trades and occupations. But agriculturalists certainly were present in the cities as well. On Caleros street in Cáceres, for example, of a total of 60 vecinos counted in 1557, there were 6 gardeners, 3 shepherds, 2 goatherds, and 1 *torero* (probably someone who tended, rather than just fought, bulls). Five others falling within the catchall category of laborer (trabajador) probably worked in either the city or the countryside.[45] Essentially the difference between large towns and small was one of degree rather than kind, since many city dwellers were primarily agriculturalists, and even those with specialized trades and occupations usually owned or rented some land or kept a few animals (chickens, a cow, a donkey or mule) for domestic use and subsistence.

Since the size of a town or village clearly bore a relation to economic specialization, one would expect the smallest places to be most homogeneous, if not necessarily in wealth, at least in the way people made their living. Larger towns like Casar de Cáceres or Santa Cruz de la Sierra could support a number of artisans and some local industry. But in large towns and small villages alike, the largest number of heads of household were labradores. El Campo, in Trujillo's tierra, in 1555 had 97 vecinos, of whom 61 were labradores and 13 *viudas labradoras* (farmer-widows). Of Santa Cruz's 465 households in 1561, 185 were headed by labradores (16 of them women). Most of these labradores were middling to humble. Nearly two-thirds (115) of Santa Cruz's labradores had only one pair of draft animals. Although a peasant might have other kinds of livestock as well, for most labradores the one pair probably represented their principal asset.[46]

The available censuses for the different towns vary greatly in terms of the kind and amount of information they provide on occupations and property held, but it does seem clear that each community encompassed socioeconomic (if not occupational) differentiation. At the top was a small wealthy or well-to-do group, composed usually of both hidalgos and commoners, followed by a larger middle group, and then a large, sometimes larger, poor group made up principally of laborers and widows. In Sierra de Fuentes, with 90 vecinos, the 22 labradores listed as having just one pair of oxen probably formed the bulk of the middle group (25 percent of the vecinos), while for Ibahernando the 28 percent of vecinos who owned vineyards with between 200 and 500 vines probably constituted the equivalent.[47]

If the presence of artisans correlates with the size of towns, the number of laborers in a place does not. One might expect that small places would support few laborers and large towns more; but in fact of Sierra de Fuentes's 90 vecinos 21 were wage laborers, while Casar in 1555 claimed to have only 24 "mozos de soldada," all of them children of vecinos, out of its total of 788 vecinos.[48] Once again the information in some censuses may be misleading. Probably some labradores worked for wages as well as on their account at certain times. Basic unskilled agricultural work paid approximately the same wages as unskilled urban labor. Juan de Figueroa, a priest in Cáceres, paid his criado Diego Gonzáles 1½ reales a day for forty days for harvesting the wheat of Figueroa's brother Sancho de Figueroa in 1549.[49]

In addition to labradores and wage laborers, there were a number of agricultural specialists—shepherds, swineherds, goatherds—who usually contracted their services for a year at a time. An important group of specialists were the *hortelanos* who cultivated the orchards and gardens around the cities. Orchards and gardens were valuable property, since they had to be located near sources of irrigation (rivers, springs, or wells). As a result they changed hands infrequently; more normally they were taken at censo or rented, with rents often paid in an assortment of produce as well as in cash.[50] A number of moriscos who arrived in Extremadura in the 1570s after their expulsion from the Granada region took up their traditional occupation of irrigated gardening there. In 1580 Isabel González gave her huerta in "censo perpetuo" (the equivalent of a long-term lease) to a morisco couple for 9½ ducados a year.[51]

Because of the fertility of the irrigated gardens and the variety of their produce, all of which no doubt was sold on the local market, the municipalities took some interest in their cultivation and maintenance. At the beginning of January 1580 Trujillo's city council ordered a census taken of the city's huertas to find out how many gardeners there were "who really are gardeners and have gardens and wells and provide vegetables and greens." The 108 hortelanos counted included 17 women (presumably mostly widows, since doubtless they were counting heads of household) and 1 mulatto. The largest huertas were those of los Alamos and las Alamedas, with 16 gardeners each.[52] The people of the huertas formed a tightly knit and virtually independent community on the outskirts of the city. Because of stability of ownership or tenancy over generations, the residents were closely connected by ties of marriage and kinship. The testimony of 1559 regarding the situation of Juana Martín, a resident of the huertas whose husband, Francisco Márquez, had been living in Peru for many years, suggests how extensive these kinship ties were. Francisco Márquez himself was a native of Monroy who had moved to Trujillo. He and his wife had married in the church of Santo Domingo, the parish that served the huertas, before he went to Peru (where, incidentally, Márquez continued to practice his "trade of planting and harvesting grain and other vegetables and raising cattle"). The audiencia in Peru had ordered Márquez to send for his wife, but she was too ill to make the journey. In 1559 Márquez's full sister María Alonso was living in the huertas, as was his first cousin Juan Galeras. Another witness was Mari Jiménez, also a resident of the huertas, widow of a first cousin of Márquez's wife Juana Martín.[53]

Artisans, Trades, and Industry

Cáceres and Trujillo had numbers of artisans in a variety of special-ties (the towns and villages of their districts, as seen, had many fewer in either sense); but the most important local industries were clothmaking and construction, and the greatest concentration and variety of artisans were found in the trades related to these enter-prises. Clothmaking and construction were also the two industries that were most nearly self-sufficient in terms of the local economy. Wool and some flax were grown locally and supplied the cloth-makers, who sold most of their cloth locally as well. The construc-tion industry relied on the high-quality granite and lime produced in the area. In the sixteenth century a high level of demand, not only in the private sector—the nobles and wealthy returnees from America—but on the part of the municipalities and various organs of the church as well, fueled a boom in construction. Other trades relied more on materials imported from outside the region. Black-smiths purchased iron at the trade fairs of Castile, and shoemakers and other leatherworkers usually bought hides from suppliers in the more western part of Extremadura (around Albuquerque espe-cially). But clothmakers as well had to look elsewhere, to the Castil-ian trade fairs or suppliers in Seville, for dyes. Furthermore local trades or industries did not have a monopoly over supply or mar-kets. The local cloth produced was of medium to low quality, and local merchants imported and sold substantial quantities of higher-quality cloth from Segovia and Valencia, or even Flanders. Even in the construction industry, the most nearly self-sufficient, artisans and specialists from outside the cities often came to work on particu-lar projects.

In terms of local organization, of course, the different trades did function as monopolies, electing their own *veedores* (inspectors) and examining artisans who wished to establish themselves. The city council generally oversaw the trades by approving the elec-tions of the veedores, ensuring that no artisans set themselves up without the approval of the officials and occasionally hearing and deliberating upon complaints about artisans or the conduct of trades. Otherwise the trades for the most part saw to their own business without outside interference.

Apprenticeships were arranged on an individual basis. While

each trade probably had its guidelines and minimum requirements as to what must be taught, terms of apprenticeships varied not only from one trade to another but even within the same one. The apprentice (or more likely his parent or guardian) might pay the master, or the master might be obligated to provide clothing, room or board, or tools of the trade and new clothing at the end of the term of apprenticeship. The term ranged anywhere from one to five years, depending on the trade; apprenticeship to a tailor might be as short as a year and a half, but it could take three or four years to study to be a pharmacist or a barber. Most apprentices were minors and fairly young, as would be expected, but not necessarily so. In 1544 Juan de la Huerta of Cáceres apprenticed himself for four years to the barber Francisco Durán for 7 ducados. Before the term ended, in 1547, Huerta married, his wife bringing a dowry of 34,000 maravedís, which included two oxen.[54]

Trades and occupations were, to a considerable degree, a "family inheritance," as one historian of Cáceres has suggested.[55] In 1576, for example, Gómez Hernández, barber, son of Martín Hernández, barber, married Ana de Muesas, the daughter of Nicolás Muesas, also a barber.[56] But there was crossover between occupations as well, with fathers not infrequently apprenticing their sons outside their own trade. Still, solidarity within trades (or groups of related trades) manifested itself strongly in marriage choices, living patterns, and carry-over from one generation to the next. Practical reasons underlay this solidarity. Continuity from father to son could minimize investment in tools and equipment or property (a shoemaker's tannery, a blacksmith's forge) and avoid the necessity of arranging a formal apprenticeship. The more successful a business, the more likely it could support a number of family members. The brothers Benito, Martín, Bartolomé, and Francisco Cotrina Delgado were *tintoreros* (fabric dyers), and Pascual López, Martín Alonso Galeano, and Juan Martín Galeano were all "wool carders and brothers."[57] Despite family solidarity, however, because boys usually were apprenticed or trained by their fathers fairly young, an artisan might be established and independent at a rather early age. Melchor González, a locksmith of Trujillo, decided to go to Peru in 1554, taking with him one of his apprentices. He had had his own shop in which three or four artisans worked for four years, although in 1554 he was only twenty-two years old.[58]

The clothmaking industry was small but active, especially in Cáceres. There the range of trades encompassed every stage of the manufacture of cloth and clothing; there were wool carders, fullers, weavers, cloth shearers, dyers, and, of course, numerous tailors (as everywhere). The relatively low price of local cloth compared to imported products indicates that it was not of very fine quality,[59] but some of the local cloth made its way out of the immediate area. Benito Sánchez, a wool carder of Cáceres, in August 1544 made a contract with a man from Badajoz to sell all the "paños berbís como estambrados" (cloth of uncombed and worsted or spun wool) that he could supply until New Year's, at 119 maravedís per yard for worsted and 80 maravedís per yard for berbi. The buyer agreed to arrange to transport the cloth to Badajoz.[60]

Of all the trades and industries, most is known about the construction industry because carpenters, masons, stonecutters, bricklayers, architects, and lime manufacturers usually contracted their services in advance. As a result the records reveal a great deal about the nature and conditions of their work, wages and compensation, and duration of particular projects. Furthermore the construction trades differed from most others in that they frequently involved a substantial use of unskilled labor alongside skilled artisans, whereas in most other trades the artisan probably worked with no more than a handful of apprentices or assistants. One instance has been found where women performed some of the heavy labor in the renovation of the parish church of Herguijuela in the 1560s. They carried stones and tiles on their heads and received only 1 real a day.[61]

A detailed accounting of renovations done on the main house and property of Dr. Nicolás de Ovando in the parish of Santa María in Cáceres in 1559 provides considerable insight into the employment and organization of skilled and unskilled labor. The renovations required the services of a large number of artisans and unskilled workers, called *peones*, employing altogether four stonecutters (three of them brothers), two masons (*albañiles*), and five carpenters, with as many as fourteen laborers assisting the artisans at times. Sancho Carrasco, a priest and former *cura* (parish priest) of Santa María, kept these and all the household accounts of Dr. Ovando, a royal councillor who lived at court in Valladolid or Madrid.[62]

The bulk of the work was the reconstruction of galleries and stairways in Ovando's house. Pero Gómez, master stonecutter, received 43,000 maravedís for building the gallery (*corredor*), stairs, and chimneys. Two other stonecutters (the brothers Hernán López Paniagua and Lorenzo Martín) did some incidental work and earned 2 reales a day. Carpenters and a mason helped complete the work on the corridors. Carrasco paid three carpenters 3600 maravedís for the beams for the arcade, and a mason worked with another carpenter on the ceiling. These two artisans received 2½ reales a day, and seven peones earning 1½ reales a day each assisted them for two days. Three carpenters worked on the other arcade as well.

The renovations used a good deal of semiskilled or unskilled labor. Carrasco paid a man 5 reales to clear the remains of the old corridor where Pero Gómez had taken out the stonework. Starting Monday, April 1, 1559, the work progressed as follows. On Monday and Tuesday two peones earned 1½ reales a day to knock down the corridors and stairway and take out the wood, beams, and planks. Three laborers performed the same work at the same wage on Wednesday and Thursday. Five laborers worked on Friday and Saturday. The following Monday, April 8, fourteen peones were demolishing and cleaning, and the next day thirteen, all receiving the same basic daily wage (1½ reales), did the same. Eight laborers worked on Wednesday. The next day there was no work because it was Holy Thursday, but on Holy Friday eight peones worked after midday, and nine the following day. After Easter work resumed on Wednesday, April 17, with six peones and seven the next day. These laborers probably worked in gangs to perform the heaviest work.

Unskilled laborers were hired for incidental tasks as well. Carrasco paid a man 1½ reales for one day to clear the earth and tiles that had fallen into a neighbor's house during the construction work; a peon who worked at the same job for half a day earned 20 maravedís. A carpenter named Maderuela who worked for six days on the second gallery was assisted by his son, who received a small wage. Carrasco hired a black slave belonging to a neighbor to assist the mason Bartolomé Martín for thirteen days at 1½ reales a day. Later he paid the same slave for four days to clean up and remove stones. A peón received 45 maravedís a day for three days to make the mixture of lime and sand used in building.

Other than Pero Gómez (and the brothers who built the second gallery), none of the artisans employed in these renovations earned a great deal. Their daily earnings exceeded those of the peones by only 1 real, and their employment security was not much greater. All evidence suggests that these wages were standard and hardly varied in the sixteenth century. In 1570 Francisco Becerra received 4 reales a day and the artisans working with him 3 reales for their work on the church of Orellana la Vieja (the parish also paid their lodging, since they came from Trujillo); and Becerra and another stonecutter, Francisco Sánchez, earned 3 reales a day each working on the convent of San Francisco in Trujillo.[63] Master artisans like Francisco Becerra or Pero Gómez of Cáceres had no shortage of work and probably their choice of projects. Becerra in fact took on so many projects during his last years in Trujillo that few were actually completed under his direction before he left for Mexico in 1573. The remarkable entranceway to Trujillo's "dehesa de las yeguas" (pasture for breeding mares) that Becerra designed and initiated was finished in 1576 by three other canteros. The iron grating was fashioned by Santos García, a locksmith who had returned from Peru, where he had gone in 1555 with his half-brother Alonso García, also a blacksmith.[64] But highly skilled individuals whose work was in demand constituted a minority of artisans. The accounts of the renovations on Dr. Ovando's house show clearly that both skilled and unskilled labor was readily available should someone require such services; it was a buyer's market, hence it is no surprise that wages varied little and could be kept low.

The other crafts and trades represented in the region mostly involved the processing of agricultural products and other raw materials for local consumption and use. There were millers, potters, candlemakers and soapmakers, and people who made various kinds of arms. Bakers and cheese vendors were almost always women. People who specialized in transport—muleteers (arrieros, recueros) and carters (carreteros)—were similar to artisans in some ways, also associating closely with one another. They provided essential services that tied Extremadura to the outside world, conveying raw materials and finished products into and out of the towns and cities. They also functioned as trusted messengers, carrying letters and often money as well. Moving over considerable distances, they must have spent a lot of time on the road, although they worked locally as well. The most active muleteers and carters were like

artisans in that they probably worked primarily in their trades
(even if, like other tradesmen, they owned and worked some agricultural property). Mules, the preferred animal for transport, were
expensive, and it seems unlikely that a relatively humble labrador
would invest in these animals unless he planned to use them com-
mercially as much as possible. In sixteenth-century Extremadura
people continued to use oxen rather than mules as the primary
source of animal power for agriculture,[65] and only the wealthier
labradores owned more than one mule.

In addition to all these trades, there were a number of occupations that defy easy categorization, falling somewhere between the
commercial, industrial, and professional sectors. Pharmacists, for
example, were related to the medical profession, but the commercial nature of their business often led to more general entrepreneurial involvements. Barbers performed some surgery, but they were
not identical with surgeons, nor did surgeons—even those with
university degrees—enjoy the status of physicians. Similarly notaries and *procuradores* (solicitors or untitled lawyers) constituted a
part of the legal profession, but they ranked below university-
trained and titled lawyers in status. Even the more purely commercial sector included a range of entrepreneurs, from shopkeepers to
substantial merchants, as will be discussed next. It should be
noted, in any case, that industrial and commercial sectors overlapped considerably, since many artisans were the vendors as well
as the manufacturers of their products.

Merchants and Trade

The merchants of the region maintained a broad network of commercial contacts with other merchants, suppliers, and customers
in Extremadura, Castile, and Andalusia. The majority probably
operated on a fairly small scale in terms of the merchandise they
handled and the amount of capital they had at their disposal. They
were principally retailers who dealt in a variety of items, from
cloth and hides to livestock and iron, although finished cloth of all
kinds probably constituted the core of their trade. Because of the
nature of their activities and their mobility, they frequently acted
as agents and representatives for collecting money or completing
transactions involving other parties, and they also lent money.

The merchants owned houses and shops in the cities, usually on or near the main plaza. Like most vecinos of any means, they frequently owned rural properties and invested in rents, censos, mills, and the like.

The activities of Gonzalo Jiménez, a merchant active in Cáceres in the 1530s, show something of how a successful merchant functioned. In the year 1534 alone he sold wheat, *zumaque* (used in tanning leather), sugar, pigs, an ass, and a calf. In 1538 a vecino of Cáceres owed him 7,204 maravedís for various merchandise purchased in Jiménez's store, and the noble Alonso de Ribera owed Jiménez 29,000 maravedís for loans taken by Ribera and his son. Ribera arranged to repay the money in wheat planted in one of his dehesas in 1540 and 1542. Jiménez belonged to a family of tradespeople and entrepreneurs that produced a number of priests. In 1535 Gonzalo Jiménez bought a vineyard from his nephew Gonzalo Jiménez Solana and another vineyard from Francisco Jiménez Solana, a priest (probably also a relative); both these vineyards were located next to one owned by Jiménez's uncle Francisco Jiménez, also a priest.[66]

Another cacereño merchant, Francisco de Madrid, sometimes called *tendero* (shopkeeper), dealt primarily in cloth in the latter part of the sixteenth century. Madrid had contacts with merchants both within the region and beyond it, but he himself moved around relatively little. He maintained his shop in the city and either sent agents elsewhere to make large purchases or depended on merchants from outside the city to supply his needs. In July 1565, for example, he gave his power of attorney to another cacereño merchant, Antonio Gutiérrez, to buy up to 300,000 maravedís of merchandise at the fair of Medina del Campo, and also empowered two other merchants, Diego Pérez de Herrera and Mateo Ortiz, to do the same. He had frequent dealings with three merchant brothers from Mérida, Hernando de Morales, Tristán de Morales, and Juan López, who were quite active in Cáceres and Trujillo in the 1560s and 1570s. Given the value of Madrid's wholesale transactions, his contacts within the trade networks of Castile must have been fairly extensive. In 1574, for example, he gave his power of attorney to two merchants in Toledo to recover a sum of money which doña Leonor de Guzmán, the wife of don Diego de Mejía (señor of Don Llorente and Loriana) owed him for merchandise; she was at the royal court at the time.[67]

Other merchants did move around quite a bit. Juan Pizarro gave his power of attorney to Diego Pérez, a merchant of Cáceres, in 1562 to buy merchandise in Medina del Campo—"cloth and silks and other things for Sr. Gonzalo de Ulloa . . . up to 400 ducados," give or take thirty.[68] Some merchants apparently served as distributors or wholesalers. In 1562 two men from Ibaren, in Vizcaya, bought 15,000 maravedís of cloth and other items from Mateo Ortiz. They agreed to buy all the merchandise they needed from Ortiz, or at least to go to him first; their purchase price would be equal to cost plus 10 maravedís (presumably 10 maravedís per yard of cloth). If they bought from someone else without Ortiz's consent, they would have to pay him some percentage. They put a mortgage on their merchandise as a guarantee of their part of the bargain.[69]

Local merchants did not have a monopoly over local supply, although they did have a strong hold on it; outsiders like the Morales brothers of Mérida might be active in the area, and of course wool merchants from Castile and elsewhere played an important role in linking the extremeño economy with the rest of Castile. A number of wool carders in Cáceres in the 1570s bought wool from Simón Sable, a Genoese who had formed a partnership with a cacereño merchant, Juan Martín Agudo.[70] Francisco de Madrid bought cloth in 1580 from two Frenchmen who were vecinos of Salamanca,[71] and merchants and dealers from Seville also made their way into the area.[72] As was true for artisans, merchants showed considerable solidarity and often acted jointly, and a successful commercial enterprise frequently was a family business. Juan Pérez, a shopkeeper, was the father-in-law of the merchant Diego Pérez de Herrera.[73] Trade was also a family business in another sense, in that several members of the immediate family all might participate in some capacity. In his will of 1544 the cacereño merchant Diego Martín Sotoval said that if his wife, Benita Jiménez, wished to continue their business "as at present we have it," she and their son Aparicio Martín, a priest, could choose which of the children should work with her. Obviously Benita Jiménez already had an active role in the business, if her husband assumed she would continue to do so in the future, and their cleric son played a part as well.[74]

Most merchants probably lived comfortably, if not on a grand scale. Diego Martín Sotoval left two houses to his sons and some small properties he had inherited from a brother (a priest) and sister—part of a vineyard, an alcacer, some corrals. He and his son Aparicio Martín apparently were patrons of a capellanía, but Martín did not mention who the founder was or what rents it included. Martín also left two beds and 20 ducados to their criada Juana, whom they had raised, if she would serve his widow two more years.[75]

The most successful merchants, or merchant families, of sixteenth-century Trujillo achieved a place in society which went beyond the comfortable but fairly modest position of most local merchants. They secured places on the city council, founded entails, and as time went on identified themselves less and less frequently as merchants. They intermarried with one another and allied themselves with some of the city's most prominent families, especially those other important members of the nouveau riche, the returnees from Peru. In fact a direct or indirect involvement in the Indies might have been of some importance to this group of merchants; but for this realm of their activities—as indeed for many aspects of their lives and careers—there is frustratingly little information.

One of the first of the prominent merchants to emerge in Trujillo in the sixteenth century was Diego del Saz, whose son Luis del Saz was a regidor of Trujillo in the 1560s. Diego del Saz's son-in-law Felipe Díaz was also a merchant (he was one of the individuals required to provide a horse for the military levy of 1580, as was Diego del Saz's grandson Diego del Saz, the son of Francisco del Saz); the three of them frequently undertook transactions and obligations together. Diego del Saz and his son-in-law Felipe Díaz invariably appeared in the records identified as merchants, but Luis del Saz less consistently so, although as late as 1565 he was called a merchant in a power of attorney given to him to collect a debt. The activities of these merchants differed little from the norm, and their success was probably a result mainly of the scale on which they operated. Diego del Saz had customers in the 1540s, 1550s, and 1560s in Cáceres and Benalcázar and suppliers in Segovia and Córdoba, and he and his son seem to have had good relations with Trujillo's nobles. Alvaro de Loaysa owed Diego del Saz 102,215 maravedís in 1561 for merchandise and a loan, and the regidor Cristóbal Pizarro gave Luis del Saz and Felipe Díaz his power of attorney to collect a debt of 184,620 maravedís from vecinos of Pedraza. As a regidor in 1567 Luis del Saz bought part of a dehesa from don Juan de Vargas Carvajal for 240,000 maravedís.[76] One of Diego del Saz's grandsons, Luis del Saz (son of Felipe Díaz) emigrated to Peru in 1592 to join his brother Antonio del Saz, an uncle (his father's brother), and other relatives who had preceded him.[77]

An even more successful merchant family was the Camargos, who intermarried with the Enríquez family; this family also sent sons to the Indies and secured places for themselves on the city council. The patriarch of the family, Luis de Camargo, who had died by 1551, by the end of his life seldom was called a merchant. He had close relations with the Pizarros and their retainers. In 1535 he acted on the part of Inés Rodríguez de Aguilar, the sister of Hernando Pizarro, to purchase part of a dehesa from Juan de Orellana, the señor of Orellana; six years later he himself bought the same piece of land from Inés Rodríguez for the same price, 24 ducados. In 1549 Camargo testified that he had been in touch with Gonzalo Pizarro while he was in Peru and for a year or two had collected juros (159,000 maravedís a year) that Gonzalo held in Mérida. Camargo maintained before royal officials attempting to confiscate all Gonzalo's properties that he had handed the money over to Hernando Pizarro; but he was not released from jail until he had paid off the sum in silver objects and money.[78]

In the next generation, none of Camargo's sons were called merchants, although at least two of them—Juan and Diego—often acted jointly with their father while he was still alive. Among the people required to provide horses in the 1580 levy were Alvaro Pizarro de Camargo, another son of Luis de Camargo, Luis de Camargo, mayorazgo (doubtless a grandson of the first Luis de Camargo), and Juan de Camargo, tesorero, and his cousin Luis de Camargo (also probably grandsons).[79] Two of Luis de Camargo's daughters, Leonor Alvarez and Mayor Alvarez, married two brothers, Vicente Enríquez and Alonso Enríquez.

The line of the family through Vicente Enríquez achieved notable successes. Vicente Enríquez's activities and associations show that he was a merchant. In February 1551 he was a witness along with another merchant, Juan González de Vitoria, to a document executed by Juan de Camargo, who was trying to apprehend a "Turkish" slave, and in 1565 he bought twenty-six oxen from a merchant of Peñaranda. But Enríquez never called himself "merca-der," and in 1569 he was a regidor.[80] One of his sons, Juan de Camargo, was a regidor in Trujillo for the last quarter of the six-teenth century, and Vicente Enríquez created an entail for another son, Vasco Calderón Enríquez. Vasco Calderón's son Licenciado Vicente Enríquez was a *letrado* (lawyer).[81]

Several members of this family also went to the Indies, although whether they functioned there as entrepreneurs or agents for their fathers is not known. One son of the patriarch Luis de Camargo, Alonso de Camargo, went to Santa Marta in 1536. Alonso En-ríquez, son of Vicente Enríquez and Leonor Alvarez de Camargo, emigrated to Chile in 1569, possibly accompanied by his first cousin Vicente Enríquez (son of Alonso Enríquez and Mayor Alva-rez), who died in Chile in 1578 in the city of Concepción. In 1577 an Alvaro de Camargo, son of Diego de Camargo, left Trujillo for New Spain. Another grandson of Luis de Camargo, Juan de Ca-margo, left Trujillo for Peru in 1592 at the age of twenty-five.[82]

A merchant who had connections with the Camargos and with people who went to the Indies was Juan González de Vitoria who, in contrast to the Camargos, virtually always was identified as a merchant. In 1561 Juan González gave his power of attorney to his son Diego González in Peru to collect outstanding debts owed to him by Diego Velázquez (long-time retainer of Hernando Pizarro) or anyone else. Among the witnesses to this document was Andrés Calderón Puertocarrero, the noble of Trujillo who went to Peru the following year as a merchant. Juan González often associated with Juan de Camargo—the two together sold a censo in 1551 to the returnee Diego de Carvajal—and he was either the brother or brother-in-law of the surgeon Juan Alvarez, who emigrated to Peru in the late 1550s, possibly at the same time that Juan González de Vitoria's son Diego went. Juan Alvarez's son Alonso Alvarez de Altamirano, who accompanied his father to Peru as a child, later became a merchant himself. Another indication of Juan González's connection with people involved in the Indies is that in 1561 he was acting as the guardian of don Gonzalo de Hinojosa, the son of Alvaro de Hinojosa and the youngest of the Pizarro sisters, doña Graciana.[83]

Obviously the information on these merchant families is scat-tered and often inconclusive. Since by the 1560s most were trying to downplay their commercial origins and activities and enter into the more genteel ranks of local society, it is difficult to gain a clear picture of their activities. Even less is known, for example, about the Alarcóns, a large family whose names appear frequently in the records. The evidence for their commercial background is entirely circumstantial but fairly convincing. They often associated with the Camargos; six Alarcóns appeared on the 1580 list of vecinos required to furnish horses; and several Alarcóns went to the Indies, one as a merchant in 1557.[84] The most successful merchant families of Trujillo behaved much as did socially ambitious mercantile families elsewhere; they invested in properties and rents, founded entails, got their sons on the city council, and stopped calling themselves merchants. But they stopped short of intermarriage with the local nobility, and not one of them married a woman with the title "doña."

Another unanswered question regarding Trujillo's big merchant families is whether they were converso in origin. It is hard to avoid speculating that at least some were, especially given their connections with physician families (medicine was a profession with strong Jewish and converso associations). Luis de Camargo's son Alvaro married Juana González de Orellana, the daughter of physician Dr. Marcos de Orellana and his wife Isabel Alvarez (who were also the parents of the priest Dr. Felipe Díaz de Orellana). Felipe Díaz, the merchant who married the daughter of merchant Diego del Saz, was the son of a Dr. Gonzalo García Carrasco of Trujillo. A surgeon named Juan de Belvis, who testified when Felipe Díaz's son Luis del Saz emigrated to Peru, said he and Díaz lived next door to each other and visited and talked together frequently. Again, such evidence is inconclusive; but the close association of these merchant and professional families, taken in conjunction with their failure to form marital alliances with hidalgos, certainly suggests a common converso background.[85]

Priests and Professionals

Like the well-to-do merchants and labradores, the clergy and professionals in many senses bridged the gap between noble and commoner. In fact members of either group might themselves be hidalgos; although, as has been noted, members of the nobility who chose ecclesiastical careers showed a marked preference for the regular over the secular branch of the church, and the professions generally had a greater appeal for middle-level hidalgos than for nobles. For all groups, entry into the clergy had much in common with other professional careers. The priesthood required at least some study, not as much as law or medicine, although there were priests in Cáceres and Trujillo who had attained a bachelor's degree or higher; and the priesthood, like the other professions, could be a vehicle for upward mobility.

Both Cáceres and Trujillo had sizable ecclesiastical establishments, with monasteries and convents in addition to the parish churches. Cáceres had four parishes (Santa María and San Mateo within the walls, Santiago and San Juan outside) and Trujillo six (the small, older parishes of Vera Cruz and Santiago in the "villa," to which San Andrés was added in the fifteenth century; San Martín and San Clemente in the newer part of the city; and Santo Domingo, below the castle, serving the huertas), as well as Santa María la Mayor, an archpriestal church. Santa María la Mayor alone had at least six benefices and eight *cantores* (singers) in the sixteenth century.[86] In addition most of the towns and villages of their jurisdictions had their own parish churches, whose priests were sometimes vecinos of the cities.[87] A number of priests served as chaplains for capellanías, and those who had no benefice or capellanía and no private means of support pursued occupations for which their literacy and education equipped them. The priest Sancho Carrasco kept accounts for Dr. Nicolás de Ovando in Cáceres in the 1550s and 1560s, as seen. Bachiller Ojalvo, another priest of Cáceres, was preceptor de gramática for a while in both Cáceres and Trujillo and also taught private students.[88] In contrast to those individuals who left home to join religious orders, secular priests often remained closely involved in family affairs, serving as chaplains for family capellanías or working in the family business, as did Aparicio Martín, the merchant's son.

The secular clergy ranged in background from hidalgos like the vicar Juan de Figueroa or Lorenzo de Ulloa Solís of Cáceres, who were wealthy in their own right by inheritance, to individuals of much humbler beginnings. Probably the majority of priests came from the middle or upper-middle strata of local society, and a number of families produced at least one priest per generation. This pattern has been noted for the families of cacereño merchants Gonzalo Jiménez and Diego Martín Sotoval; the latter had a brother, a son, and a brother-in-law (his wife's brother) who were priests. Juan Sánchez, a priest of Trujillo, was the nephew of Alonso Sánchez, who had been the priest of Vera Cruz.[89]

Thus entrance into the priesthood often was a family tradition, logically passing from uncle to nephew, although the vocation also could pass from father to son, since in the first part of the sixteenth century it was not unusual for priests to have illegitimate children of their own whom they recognized. A prominent priest of Trujillo, an hidalgo named Alvar García de Solís, vicar and *beneficiado* of San Martín, had at least three children. One of them, Cristóbal de Solís, from an early age served in the churches of San Martín and Santa María as a singer and was ordained in Badajoz in 1558. In 1578 he decided to emigrate to Peru to join his brother-in-law Sancho Casco, a priest. Casco had been married to a daughter of Alvar García de Solís and must have joined the priesthood after her death.[90]

Most children of priests, however, probably did not follow their fathers' calling. A shoemaker of Cáceres named Francisco Jiménez in 1562 said he was the "hijo natural" and universal heir of his deceased father, Gonzalo Jiménez, a priest.[91] Illegitimate children of priests were in the same position as all illegitimate offspring, their fortunes tied to the recognition their fathers chose to confer upon them. A vecina of Cáceres named Isabel de Paredes, the wife of the physician Licenciado Salinas, claimed to be the daughter of the vicar Alvaro de Paredes. In 1556 she sued the cofradía de la Cruz, which had inherited Paredes's estate, for a yearly allowance of 40 ducados for herself and her four children. The cofradía maintained that she was not his daughter, but one of the witnesses claimed that Paredes, an hidalgo and caballero, did have Isabel's mother Mari Morena "for his friend" and that he had recognized Isabel de Paredes; furthermore he had brought Isabel to his house and treated her as a daughter. Forty years later the suit remained unresolved.[92]

The exact numbers of clergy in Cáceres and Trujillo are difficult to pinpoint. At least forty-five priests were living in Cáceres in the years in 1534–1537, and so a conservative estimate for the numbers of priests in either city at any time throughout the century might be fifty or sixty.[93] Actual figures notwithstanding, since in any case the secular clergy constituted only a small percentage of the population, the clergy's role in the religious, intellectual, and civic life of local society endowed them with an importance that had little to do with their numbers. In addition to performing the religious duties and other functions of their calling, they taught and served as guardians to minor children and as witnesses to and executors of wills, particularly those of individuals (especially widows and single women) who had few if any close relatives. Furthermore priests were active participants in local economic life, which also enhanced their importance and visibility. They purchased lands and rents and administered capellanías, and as collectors of ecclesiastical and other rents had a solid basis for expanding their personal fortunes.

The clergy, then, was a diverse group but, both individually and collectively, a powerful social and economic force. The will of Antonio Galíndez, a priest of Cáceres, shows something of how one priest lived. A man of obviously comfortable means, almost certainly an hidalgo, he was much involved with his family. A nephew of the vicar Hernando Galíndez, Antonio Galíndez took charge of the rents and estate of the hospital of doña Gracia de Monroy in Plasencia for his uncle. An inventory of Galíndez's estate after his death in 1574 included many books, both secular and religious, in Spanish and Latin. He had established a capellanía in 1572 making a nephew the patron. To a niece who lived in his household with him Galíndez left his bed, an image of San Jerónimo, and 20,000 maravedís. Another nephew, Juan Mogollón de Acosta, had gone to Peru in 1571 to join his parents who had been there for twenty-three years. Galíndez said that he had an understanding with this nephew that "he would send me some portion . . . of money for the quantity that he owes me and [that] I spent in his childhood."[94]

Like the secular clergy, professionals—individuals who had earned a university degree in law or medicine—came mostly from the middle and upper-middle sectors, although possibly a greater percentage of professionals than priests were hidalgos. As was true for the priesthood, some families might produce several professionals (or what might be called semiprofessionals—notaries, procuradores, surgeons). Professionals also were similar to the clergy in that they often diversified their economic pursuits, supplementing the income from professional practice with various investments and business interests.

The city councils employed lawyers, physicians, and surgeons at varying salaries. Cáceres's council contracted in March 1554 with the city's leading physician, Licenciado Bernáldez, to serve as physician for twenty years at an annual salary of 30,000 maravedís. They renewed this contract in 1571, raising his salary to 40,000 maravedís and citing his well-known competence. In 1574 Trujillo's council hired three surgeons for six years at 25,000 maravedís a year and in 1584 contracted with a physician named Bartolomé de Bonilla for four years at 300 ducados (112,500 maravedís) a year, quite a high salary. These salaried physicians provided medical services for the poor and supervised the cities' hospitals, pharmacies, and other medical practitioners, in addition to their own private practices. Similarly the lawyers employed by the city councils might be required to furnish services to the poor in addition to representing the municipality; the Cáceres council appointed Licenciado Lorenzo Delgado letrado at 8000 maravedís in 1570 "provided he help the poor so that their suits do not go undefended."[95] Physicians could be more visible in local society than lawyers, since lawyers frequently worked away from home, tending to the city council's or individuals' interests at court, in the chancillería of Granada, or elsewhere.

Dr. Bernáldez, Cáceres's most prominent physician, epitomized the active entrepreneur-professional. He received his master's and doctoral degrees from the University of Valladolid and appeared before the city council in June 1554 to ask that his name be removed from the tax lists in accordance with the exemption from taxation the doctoral degree conferred. Bernáldez was from a professional family; his father was Licenciado Hernando Bernáldez, a native of Medellín, and his brother Licenciado Bernáldez in 1554 held the position of secretary (*relator*) of the audiencia of Santo Domingo and "teniente de almirante de las Indias." Another brother, Francisco Bernáldez, took his wife and four children to Santo Domingo to join him in 1555. Both these brothers had been vecinos of Plasencia, where their widowed mother was living in 1555.[96]

Dr. Bernáldez owned a number of properties, both rural and urban, in Cáceres and elsewhere: houses on Pintores street, an inn on Camino Llano which he rented out in 1561 for 18 ducados and four hens a year, and a half share of an oven on Pintores which he bought in 1549.[97] In 1546 he bought a house, orchard, vineyard, olive grove, and apiary with sixteen beehives in the Sierra de San Pedro (in Cáceres's district) for 75,000 maravedís and sold the same property (although with only twelve beehives) two years later for 90,000 maravedís. He and his brother Francisco owned land near Plasencia which they rented out for grazing pigs at a rate of 5½ reales (187 mrs.) per pig.[98]

In 1548 Bernáldez formed a company with a merchant named Juan Pérez, by which Bernáldez furnished 400 ducados for Pérez to go to Seville and buy 300 cowhides ("of those which are said to be from the Indies or any others that he sees fit") and then return to sell them in Cáceres. Pérez would earn one-quarter of the profits. Bernáldez had a business that involved cutting and finishing wood, and he also contracted for agricultural work. In 1556 he provided Pedro Carrillo six fanegas of barley to sow in a field he had; Carrillo would cultivate and harvest the crop at his own cost, and they would split the produce.[99]

If Bernáldez's investments were individually modest, together they must have enabled him to live well; their proliferation suggests a man who was ensuring for himself a sound financial future and a comfortable place in society. In 1549 he bought a censo for 78,000 maravedís. In 1556 he acquired a twenty-five-year-old black slave named Isabel for 63½ ducados. He raised his nephew Gonzalo de Sanabria from the age of five, caring for him and teaching him to read and write, and then assisting him to study at the university. Bernáldez's university training, medical practice, and various sources of income allowed him to achieve a lifestyle in some ways similar to that of the nobility. Despite his many economic involvements, however, there is no doubt that he regularly practiced medicine and had an excellent professional reputation. In July 1555 the bishop of Badajoz sent to Cáceres for Bernáldez to come treat him. In 1553 he received a payment of 15 ducados for treating a hand wound.[100]

Professionals as well as priests achieved varying levels of wealth, prestige, and success. A university degree could lead to a position and career away from home. A number of professionals from Extremadura went to the Indies as officials or served in the royal bureaucracy in Castile. Many others, however, remained at home—pursuing practices in law or medicine, employed by the city council, engaging in various commercial activities—either because of personal preference or lack of other options. Similarly, the secular clergy were a prominent and rather heterogeneous group. Many were well established in local society, with holdings in property and rents, a secure position in one of the parishes or a chaplaincy, and a comfortable lifestyle. A number of secular priests nonetheless left home, for the New World or elsewhere. It seems fair to say that, despite the potential for upward mobility that training in the church or in one of the professions might offer, local society could not provide a place for all the individuals who sought such careers.

Ethnic Diversity: Moriscos and Others

Up until 1570 possibly most of the moriscos living in Cáceres and Trujillo were a small number of slaves.[101] That situation changed dramatically at the end of 1570, in the aftermath of the unsuccessful Alpujarras rebellion. This rebellion had begun in 1568 in the region around Granada, and at its conclusion thousands of moriscos were exiled from their homes and sent to towns and cities all over Castile and Extremadura, among them Cáceres and Trujillo. The end of the Granada war also meant the arrival in Extremadura of newly acquired morisco slaves; so in the 1570s the previously very marginal presence of moriscos became much more substantial. Of the more than 50,000 people deported, the orders designated 3,910 individuals for Extremadura—310 to Cáceres, 670 to Trujillo, and 900 to Plasencia—but mortality rates were extremely high. Approximately a third of those sent to Extremadura never reached their destinations, and most of those who did complete the journey arrived sick and destitute.[102] The Cáceres city council attempted to follow royal orders that the moriscos be treated well, although their arrival in the city must have posed serious health problems and strained existing sources for relief. The city's hospitals served as temporary shelters. The council evidently was not altogether certain of the treatment to accorded to the new residents; in the fall of 1571 they wrote to their representative at court, Francisco de Ovando, asking him to find out if there was an order that the "Moors should receive the sacraments."[103] On the whole the response seems to have been fairly humane. In one case a woman and her baby reportedly on the verge of starvation were taken to Mérida where she had relatives.[104]

The moriscos constituted quite a different phenomenon from the travelers, transients, and immigrants who normally came to or through the area. They arrived en masse, and the cities perforce had to allow them to remain; they could not oust the moriscos as they were wont to dispose of other poor transients. The moriscos who survived the illness, poverty, and despair of their exile seem to have entered into local economic life, usually in agricultural occupations or menial positions or as servants, without causing notable disruption. In 1594 there were 290 moriscos living in Cáceres (and an additional 49 in the towns of Aliseda, Sierra de Fuentes, and Casar), and 512 in Trujillo, with half again as many living in eight towns in its district (Santa Cruz had 87, El Puerto 40, Herguijuela 35).

The considerably larger number of moriscos living in Trujillo and its tierra might have meant that they integrated more successfully there and formed significant patronage ties with the city's leading families. The 1594 census recorded as residents of Trujillo a morisco priest, a *beata*, a procurador, and three university graduates: Dr. Vázquez, a thirty-two-year-old physician, and two lawyers, Licenciado Diego Motaça (age forty-five) and Licenciado Gonzalo Pizarro (age fifty).[105] An intriguing suggestion of patronage ties comes from a letter of 1611, written from Algiers after the expulsion by a morisco named Licenciado Molina, to don Jerónimo de Loaysa "caballero of Trujillo." Licenciado Molina referred to "the great favor I have always received from your house" and described their travels and difficulties before arriving in Algiers: "all of us from Trujillo came to this city of Algiers, where there were the others from Extremadura, Mancha and Aragón." He wrote that in Liurna the Italians only wanted them to do agricultural work and "other low occupations."[106]

Former slaves and the mulatto children of slaves contributed another element of ethnic diversity to local society, but these individuals figure so rarely in the documents that it seems likely that they either assimilated fairly easily into local society (recall there was a mulatto living in the huertas in Trujillo), or left Extremadura for other regions. A slave named Diego Martín obtained his freedom in 1558 from Francisco Téllez after the period of twelve years they had agreed upon; Martín was married to a free woman named Toribia Sánchez, and they paid Téllez 15,000 maravedís.[107] The number of people of African origin being so small, race as such seems to have posed little obstacle to assimilation and acceptance.

In his will of 1513 Hernando Corajo named his cousin Sancho de Paredes, illegitimate son of Corajo's uncle Alvaro de Paredes and a black or mulatto slave woman, successor to his entail in default of Diego García de Paredes (the military hero) and his legitimate heirs.[108] A barber of Cáceres named Francisco Martín bought his ten-year-old mulatto son from the executor of don Francisco de Carvajal's estate; and a criado of Juan de Perero who had a child by one of Perero's slaves raised the boy in his home and secured his freedom from Perero's daughter when his son reached the age of sixteen.[109] Acceptance need not mean that race as such was ignored; in fact it was invariably noted. One of the criadas from Trujillo who accompanied Licenciado Diego González Altamirano to Peru in 1569 was Francisca Alvarez "de color negra"; Antón de Vargas, mail carrier ("correo de a pie") and vecino of Trujillo, was "moreno de color."[110] But race and former slave status do not seem to have imposed any real stigma in a society where so many people were humble and poor.

Conclusion

The towns and villages of Extremadura encompassed a large number and variety of social and occupational groupings. This variety resulted in extremes of wealth and poverty and considerable differences in the way people lived, in their status in local society, and in their possibilities for change or advancement. Socioeconomic differentiation characterized not only the cities but most of the smaller towns of the countryside as well. The majority of people lived in poverty or just above the threshold of poverty. Irregular employment, sudden fluctuations in food prices, bad weather and crop failures, new or increased taxes, or other kinds of impositions (such as the billeting of troops), all could constitute real hardships for the many people whose main concern was not advancement but simple survival from one year to the next. For most of the sixteenth century, an unskilled laborer in Extremadura earned an average of 1½ reales (51 maravedís) a day. An inventory of the household of Dr. Nicolás de Ovando, made on his death in 1565, showed that food for two of his pages, a servant of his nephew, and a black slave came to 3 reales a day—in other words, about 25 maravedís per person per day.[111] A laborer's daily earnings, then, provided a little more than twice what it cost for one person to eat. A worker who was married and had a family, therefore, at least at times must have faced severe financial strains and even real deprivation, even assuming that he and his family were able to supplement their income or diet by practicing some agriculture, keeping a few animals, or the like.

Despite the great variation in the way people lived, however, the hierarchical and corporate structure of local society did serve to integrate individuals into groups and groups into the larger society. Strong ties of kinship, marriage, friendship, and common interest fostered coherence within such socioeconomic groups as the nobles, merchants, artisans of a particular trade, or gardeners, whereas clientage, employment, economic interdependence, and sometimes kinship ties bound the different groups together. Furthermore local society had some flexibility and fluidity, even if the possibilities for social and economic mobility were fairly limited. Members of the middle and upper-middle sectors of society—merchants, the better-off tradesmen, well-to-do labradores, lower-level hidalgos—were the most likely candidates for upward mobility. These groups produced the most active entrepreneurs, the individuals who invested in collecting tithes and taxes, and many priests, professionals, and bureaucrats. On the whole, however, upward mobility probably was the exception rather than the rule, especially if one wished to stay at home. The increasing appeal of emigration to the New World, particularly after the first generation or so when people at home were becoming aware of opportunities the Indies offered, perhaps does not require very complex explanations. Certainly there is ample evidence that people were accustomed to leaving home for short or extended periods and seeking opportunities elsewhere.

IV

Family, Kinship, and Society

A broad and varied range of social and occupational groups participated in local society in Alta Extremadura. In exploring the position, resources, and interaction of these different groups, a picture emerges suggesting the crucial role of family and kinship relationships and strategies in the structure and functioning of local society. Family and kinship networks to a great extent provided the basis for the organization of social relations and the allocation of economic resources in early modern society. An individual's position in the family, the family's position in society, and the existence of larger kinship networks encompassing the individual and family in many ways defined the individual's position and expectations from birth to death. And decisions made within the family with regard to marriages, occupations, distribution and management of resources not only patterned the lives of individuals but also collectively shaped the nature and ordering of society itself. Family and society were distinct but inseparable.

Virtually every stage of the formation and maintenance of the family reflected socioeconomic, legal, and individual considerations as well as demographic realities. The marriage of a couple, for example, usually involved an agreement between two families (or the heads of the families or households concerned) on the dowry. The marriage contract reflected the social and economic status of both bride and groom, and it probably usually was tied to the new couple's prospects for establishing an independent household. These prospects depended both on their own resources (generally meaning the man's income and occupation and whatever property either held) and the contributions made by either or both families. While age at marriage certainly had important demographic implications, especially for the number of children a couple might have, age as such appears to have been a less important consideration than the ability to establish an independent household. A marriage reflected not only economic and legal factors but social and even political ones as well, as seen particularly in the marriage alliances of the nobility.

A variety of decisions and considerations thus entered into the establishment of a new family with the marriage of a couple, and marriage itself was but one aspect of family life. Occupational and career choices for children; the position of women; the disposition of property in dowries, donations, wills, and entails; the complexities of family and household structure that resulted from remarriage; the existence of illegitimate children; the inclusion in the household of poor and illegitimate relatives (or even nonrelatives); the kinship network of which families formed a part; family solidarity; as well as the possibility of family conflict, scandal, and even violence all hinged on and generated a similar variety of considerations that both because of their impact on the individual and their wider implications for the structure and functioning of society merit examination.

This chapter will examine the family as a social and economic unit more specifically than was possible in the two preceding chapters— even though, as seen, one can hardly describe the lives of hidalgos or commoners without constant reference to family position, marriage, wills, and the like. Specific focus on the different components of family life, however, unavoidably tends to fragment choices, values, and obligations that usually were closely related and interdependent. By looking at the experiences of one person we can see the importance and centrality of family and kinship in an individual's life and career and the connection between the various concerns related to family.

Alvaro de Paredes: An Extremeño in Mexico

Alvaro de Paredes Espadero, a cacereño from a distinguished hidalgo family, left Cáceres for New Spain, probably in the mid- to late 1580s. He doubtless was a younger son of Licenciado Gonzalo

Martínez Espadero and doña Estevanía de Paredes. He probably was fairly young when he emigrated, perhaps in his early twenties, although he had already earned his bachelor's degree in law by the time he left Spain. After his arrival in New Spain he served for a time as the *alcalde mayor* (chief magistrate) of Colima, but soon afterwards took up residence in Mexico City. He did not use the title "bachiller," nor did he seek a position as a letrado until 1608, when he asked his brother in Cáceres to send his university degree, which he had left behind, probably for safekeeping. From Mexico Alvaro de Paredes maintained a long-term correspondence with his brother Licenciado Gutiérrez Espadero in Cáceres; this brother probably was the oldest son and principal heir who became the effective head of the family on their father's death in the late 1580s. Alvaro also had a sister in Cáceres with whom he stayed in touch (although none of these letters have survived). She at one time asked him for financial assistance and on another occasion sent Alvaro several cartons of law books he had requested.

Alvaro's family was prominent in Cáceres. Family members sat on the city council, and the family had a strong affinity for the legal profession. As seen, Alvaro's father and brother were letrados, as was Alvaro himself, and their relative Licenciado Alonso Martínez Espadero sat on the Council of the Indies. Apparently Alvaro had done well when he first got to Mexico just on the strength of that family connection. He wrote in February 1590, soon after Licenciado Espadero's death, that "although he did nothing for me, his shadow reached here and with it I was able to maintain myself and because of it I was favored." All that changed drastically with his illustrious relative's death. As long as he could capitalize on his name, Alvaro had hoped to make a good marriage; but after Espadero's death, the prospects looked bleak indeed.[1]

In 1590 Alvaro had to resort to borrowing 1000 pesos from a friend, don Antonio de Saavedra, who was on his way back to Spain; he asked his brother to repay Saavedra from the inheritance owed him from their father. Remaining in Mexico, Alvaro disposed of the property or income he had in Cáceres in various ways over time. After his father's death he assigned the income from his paternal inheritance to his mother, and after her death at least partially to his sister. Only in 1609 did he give his power of attorney to a pair of men on their way from Mexico to Spain to collect from his brother the legacy from his parents. He delayed all those years in spite of the fact that—according to his own statements at least— he was often in severe financial straits.

But the year 1590 also brought Alvaro a stroke of good fortune; he married doña Beatriz de Sotomayor, the sister and ward of the *relator* (secretary) of the audiencia, Licenciado Estevan de Porres, himself a widower with one son. Alvaro wrote of his brother-in-law that "although he knows well of my poverty, he wanted my company, and he could have married his sister to wealthy men of quality, and knowing who our parents are, he thought it better to do it with me." His brother-in-law provided a dowry of 8000 pesos and other things, possibly including some land. The next year Alvaro wrote glowingly of his wife: "I am so happy in her company as I never thought I'd be in all my life." He must have talked at length to his wife about his family in Cáceres. "From what I've told doña Beatriz about my lady doña Isabel [his brother's wife?], she is so fond of her that I think she wouldn't mind going to Castile just to see her." The couple did not make such a trip but instead, during the next decade—by 1602—had six children. By 1604, however, two of them, Jerónimo and Beatriz, had died, as well as a mulatto named Juanillo "who was like a son because he was born in the house and raised my sons." By 1606 two more children had arrived, and the couple by then had four sons and two daughters.

That year Alvaro wrote with pride of the progress his son Gonzalillo was making in his study of grammar and Latin verse. Gonzalo must have been his oldest son and a teenager by that time. Alvaro's cherished hope was that he would be able to send Gonzalillo to study in Salamanca—law, of course. His brother in Cáceres told him that it would cost at least 400 escudos a year for Gonzalo to live and study at Salamanca, and in 1608 Alvaro despaired of being able to afford the expense. He did, however, ask his brother to have twelve *reposteros de armas* (wall hangings) made in Salamanca with the arms of his own and his wife's family, so that his children would not forget their origins and lineage. He told him to cover the costs from the legacy from his mother.

From 1606 on yet another familial relationship figured in Alvaro's letters home. In that year he mentioned that "our brother Juan Tejado of the company of Jesus" was due to arrive in Mexico. Juan Tejado, apparently not a blood relative, had been raised from an early age by Alvaro de Paredes's father, who apprenticed Tejado in 1579 for a year and a half to a shoemaker, paying 10 ducados and two bushels of wheat.[2] The relationship between the boys who had grown up together endured throughout their adult lives. Tejado also wrote letters from Mexico to Paredes's brother Licenciado Gutíerrez Espadero, and he referred to the "brotherhood that there is between" himself and Alvaro.

It is impossible to read the letters from Alvaro de Paredes to his brother without being struck by the high proportion of their content which relates quite directly to family concerns and affairs. Certainly to a large degree this can be explained by the very nature of the correspondence; Paredes and his brother did not have complex legal or financial matters to discuss, so family news logically would play a large part in their letters. Nonetheless Alvaro's descriptions of developments regarding his marriage and family, his continued concern for the family left behind in Cáceres, his maintenance of the childhood tie with his adoptive brother, Juan Tejado, all reveal him to have been an individual for whom family and all its ramifications—personal relationships, extended kinship networks, status—were central and vital. And there is no reason to think that Alvaro was in any way unusual in this respect; in fact the familial relations and concerns that emerge from his letters are notable more for their typicality than the reverse. His references to Licenciado Espadero on the Council of the Indies, for example, indicate not only his awareness of a wide network of kinship ties but also the standard expectation that such ties would generate opportunities and resources.

Alvaro's marriage, while it clearly brought him personal happiness and satisfaction, doubtless resulted from more pragmatic motivations. By his own statement he had been hoping for a lucrative match (even before he became engaged to doña Beatriz); he could hardly have done better under the circumstances. His marriage brought him useful connections in high governmental circles in Mexico and ties to a prestigious family (the Sotomayors), as well as a decent dowry. For his part, his brother-in-law apparently was eager to form an alliance with such a distinguished letrado family as the Espaderos (recall Alvaro's statement that his brother-in-law was mindful of "who our parents are"). In face of such considerations, personal feelings surely took second place. After marriage also

Alvaro and doña Beatriz's family developed along standard lines. Eight children were born in fifteen years, somewhat higher than the normal birthrate for the time (two of the children did not survive childhood), and the three children's names mentioned— Gonzalo, Jerónimo, and Beatriz—were all traditional in the family (the first two from the Espadero line, and Beatriz from the maternal side). The repetition of given names in families was conventional, especially among nobles and hidalgos. Alvaro followed family tradition in his desire to send his oldest son to study law, and he wanted his children to be aware of their distinguished paternal and maternal lineages.

The connections that Alvaro actively maintained with his family in Cáceres also reflected the ties of loyalty, obligation, and affection that withstood separation over time and distance; as will be seen, the strength of such connections often imbued the movement to the New World with a distinctive character. In Mexico Alvaro talked about his family, wrote many letters, and assisted his mother and sister financially despite his own economic difficulties. He maintained his ties with his adoptive brother. The relationship between Alvaro and Juan Tejado underscores yet another aspect of Spanish family and household structure—its ability to encompass individuals of varying ranks (note that Alvaro said that the mulatto boy who died "was like a son"). The flexibility of the family made it possible for a status-conscious man like Paredes to call someone who had been apprenticed as a shoemaker his brother. Certainly he would not have thought that they were social equals; but because Alvaro's father adopted Tejado, the two did belong to the same family.

Family, Household, and Kinship

The details of Alvaro de Paredes's family and kinship relations suggest, among other things, that the family was a complex entity that functioned in different ways and on different levels. The family was a legal and economic institution that distributed property and income, but this function was mediated by the positive (or negative) feelings family members had for one another (recall Alvaro's delay in collecting the parental legacies owed him in order to assist his mother and sister). The nuclear family of parents and children stood in relation to the larger network of kin, which varied in its relevance to the individual or family over time. And the family formed the nucleus for a household. Although the two were not identical, the familial norms of affection, loyalty, and duty often extended to include nonfamily members raised in or closely associ- ated with the household so that, like the kinship network, the household also could broaden the scope of familial relations.

In face of such complexity it is perhaps best to begin with the most basic unit, the nuclear family. Despite the existence of large households and the importance of kin, as has been suggested, mar- riage usually implied that a couple should establish their own house- hold, which meant separate living quarters of some kind, no matter how modest.[3] The frequent inclusion in dowry agreements (as will be discussed), especially among commoners, of such items as beds and linens, as well as houses, underlines the importance of estab- lishing a household. A newly married couple living with the par- ents of one spouse or the other for very long probably was excep- tional.[4] The true multigenerational (or multiple family) household was a rarity, except where a widowed parent might live with a married child and his or her family.[5]

Couples normally married for the first time while in their early to mid-twenties. A demographic study of the city of Cáceres in the sixteenth century has shown that the average age at marriage for women was twenty and for men twenty-four,[6] but of course there could be considerable variation in the age at which individuals married and in the difference in age between husband and wife. Teenage marriages for women were fairly common in all social groups.[7] In 1575 Cristóbal Hernández Tripa was thirty, his wife Teresa González twenty-five, and their oldest son eight years old, so Teresa probably was sixteen or seventeen years old when they married.[8] However, men in the process of establishing themselves or relocating might have delayed marriage. Licenciado Diego Gon- zález Altamirano was ten years older than his wife doña Leonor; their first son was born when he was about thirty-five and she twenty-five, so he probably did not marry until his early thirties.[9] Alonso Delvás, a trujillano emigrant, married a woman in Seville, where he lived for a while before going to New Granada. Witnesses described her as being "already older . . . She couldn't give birth unless it were by great chance."[10] Presumably Delvás himself was also middle-aged when he married.

Remarriage, of course, also led to greater discrepancies in age. A thirty-year-old trujillano named Juan de Tapia petitioned to go to Peru in 1579 with his wife Isabel García, who was forty-five, and their sons aged six and eight years.[11] Possibly this was Isabel García's first marriage, but at the least the case was rather unusual. The reverse situation was more typical; it was far more common for men who lost their wives to remarry, and they usually chose relatively young women. Hernando de Encinas at the age of fifty petitioned to go to Peru in 1591 with his second wife, Felipa de Corolla, age thirty-six; they had an infant and a four-and-a-half-year-old and also took with them Encinas's fifteen-year-old son from his first marriage.[12] Juan de Muesas left Cáceres for Peru in 1579 with his wife and family. At the time he was forty-four and his third wife, Jimena González, was thirty. They were accompanied by the twenty-year-old son and three daughters aged eighteen, seventeen, and thirteen from Muesas's previous marriages, and the three children of his current marriage, ranging in age from two to eight.[13]

Early age at marriage for women could mean the birth of children over wide intervals. In 1579, for example, two sons of the trujillano returnee from Peru, Pedro Barrantes, and his wife, doña Juana de Paredes, left for Peru. The older son, Alvaro de Paredes Loaysa, a priest, was thirty-six years old and his younger brother, Alonso Barrantes, was a boy of twelve.[14] These ages were plausible if their mother married in her mid-teens. Generally birth rates were fairly high, with an average interval between births of one to two years; but high mortality rates, the death of either spouse, and probably an increase in the length of intervals between births as parents aged limited family size.[15]

Birth rates in noble families were somewhat higher than among commoners. Wealthy nobles were likely to be healthier (because of better diet and housing), marry young wives, and use wet nurses, avoiding the relative infertility caused by lactation.[16] The division of the legacy of doña Beatriz de Paredes after her death in 1560 involved eleven living heirs, most of them minors; however, two sons died soon thereafter.[17] A list of births and baptisms for the family of one of doña Beatriz's sons, Cristóbal de Ovando Paredes (a returnee from the Indies) and his wife, doña Leonor de Godoy, who married at age fifteen, recorded the births of nine children between June 1589 and October 1602 (another son, not included in

the document, was born in 1605). The shortest interval between
the births listed was twelve months and the longest twenty-nine. A
girl born on 26 March 1592 died the same night; a son born in 1596
died within a week; and the daughter born in October 1602 died
three months later.[18] A woman's age at marriage and the age at
which she stopped conceiving set the limits for childbearing; the
late thirties to forty was considered to be the age of menopause.
Licenciado Altamirano's wife doña Leonor de Torres could not
leave for Peru with her husband in 1569 because, at the age of
forty, she was seven months pregnant.[19] Frequent and rapid remarriage, especially among hidalgos, also helped account for the large
size of some families. A noble who lost his (or her) spouse was likely
to remarry quickly and produce more children.

Households often extended beyond the nuclear family to include
other relatives (including illegitimate ones) and nonrelatives. Large
households characterized the nobility in particular because they
could afford such establishments. At the age of nearly forty in 1549,
Inés Alonso Ramiro testified that she had lived almost thirty years
in the house of her "uncle" Cosme de Chaves; her father Diego
García de Chaves and Cosme were first cousins.[20] Because of the
number of children that Captain Gonzalo Pizarro (father of Francisco, Hernando, Gonzalo, and Juan Pizarro) fathered both inside
and outside of marriage, the Pizarro household in Trujillo at times
must have been quite large. Captain Gonzalo recognized and
raised his illegitimate sons Gonzalo and Juan. The latter had siblings on the side of their mother, María de Aguilar, who had married Bartolomé de Soto. Letters from one of these maternal siblings, Blas de Soto (who was with Gonzalo Pizarro in Peru) to his
sister Isabel de Soto indicate that Isabel also had been brought into
the Pizarro household and raised in part by the Pizarros' sister Inés
Rodríguez de Aguilar. Isabel de Soto married a Pizarro retainer and
returnee from Peru, Diego de Carvajal.[21]

Household structure and the kinship network to some extent
might have tempered the importance or centrality of the nuclear
family, although probably this was more often the case for the upper
and upper-middle groups than for working people—peasants, artisans, and laborers—for whom the nuclear family usually was the
crucial economic unit.[22] Yet even among working people the nuclear
family usually existed in relation to other kinds of connections, not

only those of common residence, occupation, or membership in cofradías but of kinship as well. Examples of siblings who all worked in the same or related trades demonstrate the importance of economic associations and productive units based on family and close kinship ties. The architect Francisco Becerra worked with his father and his first cousin (son of his father's brother) on several projects.[23]

Families, households, and kin groups were hierarchies under patriarchal authority. The position of the patriarch could be filled by the oldest or wealthiest adult (father or even grandfather) or oldest sibling. Usually the family patriarch was male, but women could occupy that position quite effectively and successfully. Consider the case of Inés Rodriguez de Aguilar. After the death of her father, Captain Gonzalo Pizarro, and in face of the absence (and subsequent death) of her brothers Francisco, Juan, and Gonzalo, as well as Hernando Pizarro's long-term imprisonment after he returned to Spain, Inés, who apparently never married, became the effective head of the Pizarrro household in Trujillo. She accompanied her brother Hernando to Seville when he left for the Indies in 1534. When a man named Pablo Vicencio who had come from Peru (where he seems to have known her brother Gonzalo) went to Trujillo in 1547, he visited Inés to ask if she wished to send anything to Peru when he returned. Inés doubtless was recognized as the head of household in the 1530s and 1540s. In her will of 1551 doña Graciana Pizarro (youngest daughter of Captain Gonzalo Pizarro) called Inés Rodríguez "mi señora" and made her one of her executors.[24]

Certainly it was unusual for an unmarried woman to remain at home and become the dominant figure that Inés Rodríguez undoubtedly was. Widows more commonly could attain such positions if they avoided remarriage, and if their children were still fairly young and they sought and obtained legal guardianship. Isabel Corvacho, a vecina of Cáceres widowed by her husband Bartolomé Pizarro by 1552, was a middle-level hidalga who showed remarkable flair and success in managing her own and her family's economic affairs. In the 1550s, 1560s, and 1570s, she bought rents and properties in and around Cáceres and Trujillo. In 1579 she donated her goods and property to her three sons, but reserved 90,000 maravedís of rents for herself each year and retained the right to dispose of up to 1000 ducados in her will.[25] But probably only the most enterprising and determined women were able (and permitted) to take up the position of matriarch. Francisca Picón, the widow of Pedro de Sande and mother of Dr. Francisco de Sande and several other sons, in certain ways was ideally placed to assume such a role, since her sons spent years away from Cáceres in Mexico, the Philippines, or elsewhere in the Indies or Europe; but there can be little doubt that Dr. Sande effectively assumed the position of family patriarch.[26]

A strong patriarch, especially a long-lived one, could wield considerable power by the virtue of the property he controlled, his rank, and his authority over the lineage. The great-great grandfather of the chronicler Juan de Chaves, "Luis de Chaves, mi señor, el viejo, died in [14]92, the year in which the Jews were thrown out of Castile and Granada was conquered, at the age of 90." Luis de Chaves was a powerful man, an ally of Ferdinand and Isabella and friend of the Jewish community in Trujillo, who married doña María de Sotomayor, the daughter of Gutierre de Sotomayor, master of Alcántara, and sister of the first count of Belalcázar, don Alonso de Sotomayor. A royal letter of pardon that Chaves received in 1476 underscored his position. It listed 193 people, including his two sons and two nephews, as well as his criados and the criados of his retainers.[27]

The patriarch served as the custodian of the wealth and status of the lineage. Property in land, houses, and rents was considered to belong to a family and lineage rather than an individual as such, but the person who controlled its disposition occupied a powerful position. Given the importance of inherited property to the nobility, and the fact that children did not legally come of age until twenty-five years, a patriarch could long overshadow his progeny; until the age of twenty-five children had to obtain parental permission for most legal acts and transactions.[28] Martín de Chaves, el viejo, entirely eclipsed his son Tadeo de Chaves. The complicated relations in this family emerged in the course of testimony regarding ownership of the dehesa of Magasca. Doña Isabel de Chaves was supposed to inherit this estate from her mother, Inés Alonso Ramiro (Inés Alonso was the mother of at least two of Martín de Chaves's children, although they apparently did not marry). The confusion over the ownership of the dehesa arose from the fact that Tadeo de Chaves, doña Isabel's brother, had asked for the usufruct of the estate because "he was poor and had no other property with which to sustain himself" until his father Martín de Chaves died. Tadeo must have had some legacy from his mother, but his sister probably inherited the largest share. Tadeo died before his father, and his son Martín de Chaves, el mozo (who departed for Peru in 1534 with Hernando Pizarro), became heir to the bulk of the estate of his grandfather Martín de Chaves, whom he called "mi señor."[29]

The case of Tadeo de Chaves, who had to turn to his sister because his father was unwilling to relinquish control of any of his estate, was not necessarily typical. Custom, affection, or duty usually tempered the authority and power of the head of the family, and most fathers provided some kind of income for their sons or made outright donations, especially when they married (which apparently Tadeo's father had not done), sometimes of a sizable portion of the estate. Such donations in fact represented a part of the inheritance and would be deducted when the final division of property was made.

The family patriarch not only wielded economic and legal power but was often directly responsible for the care and well-being of other family members. This aspect of the patriarchal family emerges in cases where both parents died and the oldest sibling (usually but not always male) became the head of household. Such situations can be seen in connection with the move to the Indies. The priest Bachiller Gaspar González took three of his siblings—a twenty-three-year-old brother and sisters aged thirty-two and twenty-nine—and the orphaned daughter of another brother to Peru when he left Trujillo in 1579, as well as a criada from Orellana and a criado from La Cumbre.[30] Ana González de Cuevas, the daughter of a notary, obtained a license to go to New Spain in 1575 with her brother Hernando de Cuevas, a priest. Witnesses said she had lived with her brother since their parents had died.[31] In both these cases a brother assumed responsibility for his siblings and kept them with him when he relocated. One might imagine that a similar situation accounted for the presence in Peru of the mother and two sisters of Fray Alonso Montenegro of Trujillo, who was prior of Santo Domingo of Quito in the late 1540s. One of his sisters, doña Isabel de Aguilar, married an encomendero of Quito.[32]

How was the kinship network defined? In the case of commoners (and probably lower-level hidalgos as well), less concerned with lineage and property, the effective kinship network possibly did not extend much beyond a fairly small circle of relatives—uncles and aunts, first and sometimes second cousins (or first cousins once removed). Nobles and hidalgos were aware of and kept close track of a wider range of kinship ties, sometimes up to the fourth degree;[33] but beyond the second degree people tended to forget the precise nature of the relationship and remembered only that one existed. Generations of intermarriage between hidalgo families multiplied and complicated kinship ties. In 1573 don Francisco de Torres and his uncle Pedro Rol de la Cerda of Cáceres sought a dispensation at court for Torres to marry doña Luisa de la Peña, Pedro Rol's daughter. Torres stated that "on the one side we are first cousins and on the other we are second cousins."[34] Doña Juana de Acuna of Trujillo married Luis de Chaves, her "nephew" (actually her first cousin once removed), the grandson of Luis de Chaves, el viejo. Nonetheless, while the majority of nobles in Extremadura married women from the same city, marriages between close blood relations (first or second cousins) were not very common. Certain families, however, did form multiple marital alliances (for example, siblings marrying siblings).[35]

Not surprisingly, hidalgo men especially placed a strong emphasis on the male line and agnatic kin, in keeping with patriarchalism and entails that favored males. Wills and other legal documents, transactions, and even letters all contain many more references to agnatic kin than to cognates. But orientation to the male line was not a hard and fast rule; if the female side was more important, it could overshadow or at least rival the male line in importance. Francisco de Saavedra, whose mother, doña Leonor de Orellana, was the only child of Francisco de Ovando, el viejo, by his third wife, created an entail in 1528 with his wife for their son Gonzalo de Saavedra. The entail included lands and houses in Malpartida and a house within the walls of the old city of Cáceres. Saavedra and his wife, doña Marina Gutiérrez de Carvajal, stipulated that in default of their son and his descendants and of Saavedra's brothers' sons, the entail would go to Saavedra's cousins on his *mother's* side—Francisco, Cosme, and Cristóbal de Ovando; in their default the entail would go to whoever succeeded to the entail of his uncle Francisco de Ovando, el rico.[36]

A number of conventions helped to maintain and reinforce the ties of kinship and recognition of a common lineage. Certain names were traditional in families, as mentioned in connection with Al-varo de Paredes. Naming patterns often meant that in generation after generation the firstborn son and heir bore the same name, as seen in the series of individuals named Diego de Ovando de Cáceres who succeeded Captain Diego de Ovando de Cáceres, or the Francisco de Ovandos who followed Francisco de Ovando, el viejo, the brother of Captain Diego de Ovando.[37] Another common practice was to alternate in the name chosen for the oldest son, naming a son for his grandfather rather than his father (the Ribera family of Cáceres, for example, alternated between Alvaro and Alonso). More broadly speaking certain names in conjunction with surnames might appear generation after generation or in different branches of a family, such as Diego García de Paredes and Sancho de Paredes (Golfín) (see table 2). The first sons in the direct male line were not the only ones who received these names, and illustrious names from the maternal line were likely to be used as well. One of the brothers of the chronicler Juan de Chaves was don Alonso de Sotomayor, who died of an illness contracted during the 1558 campaign against the French. Their mother, doña Juana de Acuna, was the granddaughter of doña María de Sotomayor and hence the great-niece of don Alonso de Sotomayor, first count of Belalcáçar.[38] Gómez de Solís, a captain and encomendero in Peru, was the great-grandnephew of Gómez de Solis, a fifteenth-century master of Alcántara from Cáceres. His mother, doña Juana de Solís, was from a Trujillo family (she married in Cáceres); she was the granddaughter of another doña Juana de Solís who was the sister of the master of Alcántara.[39] The naming of women reflected a similar process of repeating the names of important ancestors.

It might be argued that the purpose of the name given to a child was to underscore the child's relationship to the lineage and kin group rather than his or her individuality; hence two children in the same family might receive the same name. Two sons of Diego de Vargas Carvajal and doña Beatriz de Vargas were named don Diego (both survived to adulthood); Lorenzo de Ulloa, an early settler of Trujillo, Peru, was joined there by his younger brother of the same name. One Trujillo family with eight children included three daughters named María, aged nine, eight, and seven years in 1591.[40] The designation of names and their utilization was flexible. The terms of entails sometimes specified that the successor take on a new name, and individuals at times voluntarily changed all or part of their names. Men and women entering religious orders frequently did so. Hernán Pérez Rubio from Trujillo called himself Juan Rubio, his brother's name, when he went to live in Popayán in New Granada, even though his brother was still alive.[41] People ascending the socioeconomic ladder might add or drop a surname; successful returnees from the Indies sometimes did this. Thus Francisco Rodríguez, a notary who went to Peru with his wife in 1575, styled himself Francisco Rodríguez Godoy on his return to Trujillo several years later.[42] Women's surnames were even less fixed than men's; sometimes a feminized form of the surname—for example, "la Solana" or "la Ramira"—was appended.

Another practice that had the effect of drawing kinship ties closer was that of using equivalent terms for more distant relatives, as has been observed. The children of first or even second cousins usually were called nephew or niece. Such designations generally (although not always) followed generational lines. Thus in 1544 twenty-three-year-old Francisco de Villalobos testified that he was the "uncle" of a minor, Diego de Figueroa, because his father and Diego's were second cousins.[43] In reality they were third cousins, but probably the difference in age and fairly close relations between the two families put Francisco de Villalobos in the position of "uncle" to Diego de Figueroa. It was also common to call a brother-in-law ("cuñado") brother ("hermano").

Probably most significant for the vitality and cohesiveness of kinship and marriage networks was that they provided a framework for a wide range of legal and socioeconomic functions—choosing godparents; appointing guardians for minor children; buying and selling censos, lands, and rents; lending and borrowing money; passing along important positions such as seats on the city council; perpetuating traditional professions, occupations, and callings (such as the priesthood or legal profession); choosing executors for estates; and assigning powers of attorney for specific purposes or to take charge of an individual's affairs. Naturally these transactions took place outside the network of relationship as well; but they frequently were realized within it, and probably that was most people's preference.

One can see how this preference operated in the transactions of several related families—the Vegas, Vitas, Canos, and Moragas (see table 5). The Vegas and Vitas were first cousins, and the Vitas

TABLE 5 *The Cano, Vita, and Moraga Families of Cáceres*

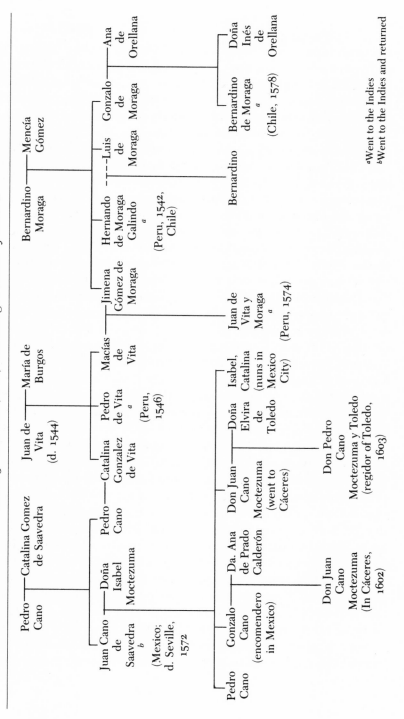

aWent to the Indies
bWent to the Indies and returned

married members of the Cano and Moraga families. Diego Pérez de Vega made his will in 1547, naming Pedro Cano (the husband of Diego Pérez's first cousin, Catalina González, a member of the Vita family) his executor. In his will he said that his legacy should be used to establish a capellanía if his brother Andrés Vega did not return from the Indies, and he named his first cousin Macías de Vita (the brother of Catalina González) the patron. Pedro Cano also had a brother Juan Cano who had gone to the Indies; Pedro looked after Juan's affairs, and they made some joint investments. Juan Cano was an associate of Cortés who married doña Isabel Moctezuma (daughter of the Aztec emperor) in Mexico. He bought lands from the wife of Macías de Vita (his brother's brother-in-law), doña Jimena Gómez de Moraga, and from her brother Gonzalo Moraga in the 1550s. Two of Macías de Vita's Moraga brothers-in-law assigned him responsibility for the patrimony left in Cáceres by a third brother, Hernando de Moraga, who went to Peru.

Of this group of connected families, the Moragas were the wealthiest and most important, at least in the first half of the sixteenth century. Members of the family sat on the city council of Cáceres, and they held extensive properties around the village of Aldea del Cano (in Cáceres's district). The 1561 census of Aldea del Cano included Macías de Vita, Gonzalo Moraga, and Pedro Cano, so the three brothers-in-law maintained residences near one another (although they were all actually vecinos of Cáceres).[44] Because of this close contact and collaboration, it is not surprising that members of all these families went to the Indies. In addition to those already mentioned (Andrés Vega, Juan Cano, and Hernando Moraga), Pedro de Vita and Juan de Vita y Moraga, respectively the brother and son of Macías de Vita, went to Peru in 1546 and 1574, and Bernardino de Moraga, a nephew of Hernando de Moraga, went to Chile in 1578.[45] Of all those who emigrated doubtless the most successful was Juan Cano, who eventually returned to live in Seville. One of his sons left Mexico for Cáceres, where his father had accumulated considerable wealth in rents and properties, married into a high-ranking noble family, and built the so-called Palacio de Moctezuma in the parish of Santa María in the old city.

A final aspect of kinship networks that merits mention is that they linked individuals (and families) who did not necessarily live in the same town or city, or even the same region. The geographical separation of relatives, of course, was one product of the move to the New World; but it should be borne in mind that the separation of family members and kinsmen resulting from emigration across the Atlantic had longstanding precedents in early modern society. Marriage patterns and the forms of mobility discussed in connection with both hidalgos and commoners meant that one's relatives might be distributed over a wide area. The presence or absence of such kinship ties might have had implications for the existence of a sense of regional cohesion or identity, as opposed to one that was strictly local. People living in towns such as Santa Cruz or Zorita in Trujillo's jurisdiction who had relatives in the city, for example, might have felt more strongly and directly tied to Trujillo than those who lacked such personal connections; this in turn might have been significant when such individuals found themselves in a very different environment, such as Peru, where local or regional identification took on a new meaning.

If it is possible to establish some sense of how kinship networks were defined and what were the socioeconomic and legal parameters of family and kinship relationships, can we also form a notion of the personal and emotional side of these relationships? Affirmations of loyalty and love for family members appear frequently in the documents and letters of the period. Regardless of whether duty and loyalty can be equated with the modern concept of love, many people formed undeniably strong attachments to family members. Use of the word "love" (amor) reflected an important emotional bond. In his will of 1534, made on the eve of his departure for Peru, Martín de Chaves left 50,000 maravedís to his brother Juan Ramiro, should he come from the Indies without enough capital, "so that he can live according to who he is. . . . because of the kinship [deudo] and love I have for him." He left the same amount to his brother Francisco de Chaves, also "por el amor que le tengo."[46] In 1602 in Peru Juan de Vera de Mendoza donated 800 ducados to his nephews to help support them in their studies "because of the great love he had for his siblings" (the parents of his nephews).[47] While high mortality rates at times could have engendered a certain transitoriness in family relations, they also might have strengthened the feelings of love and loyalty that surviving family members had for one another. The letters of Andrés and Antonio Pérez from Puebla de los Angeles in New Spain in the 1550s to their brother Francisco Gutiérrez in Cáceres inviting him to join them stressed that he was the last of their stock ("nuestra generación") still living.[48] Expressions of concern and affection for family and relatives appear constantly in letters from emigrants in the Indies (as seen in those of Alvaro de Paredes) to their siblings, parents, aunts, uncles, or children. There is no reason to believe that such expressions were purely formulaic or that emigrants were at all unusual in having or expressing such feelings.

The bond between siblings possibly was the strongest, but there is also evidence of concern on the part of children for parents (especially mothers), parents for children, husbands for wives, and vice versa. For example, in 1567, after their father's death, Alonso Delvás wrote from Victoria in New Granada urging his brother Francisco Delvás to emigrate with his family and their sister; he sent 50 pesos, to "do what is obligated for the lady our mother and our sister until I provide more." The next year he wrote saying that their mother should not worry "because I will provide for her as long as I live."[49] Bequests in wills often included siblings, parents, nieces, nephews, and cousins, in addition to children. These again surely reflected personal feelings of affection or obligation since they were entirely discretionary. Hernando Corajo, who in his will of 1513 made his uncle Diego García de Paredes ("el Sansón") his universal heir, made bequests to the sons and daughter of his nephew Juan Corajo but explicitly barred Juan Corajo himself from inheriting anything; so there can be little doubt that personal preferences and sentiments must have figured. Alonso Bravo of Trujillo, who left a number of things to his wife, also bequeathed her 50 ducados "for the love and union and good fraternity we have had."[50]

As the example of Hernando Corajo suggests, feelings for family members need not all have been positive. The legal, socioeconomic, and customary framework that defined family relations might have acted to minimize conflict, at least within the nuclear family itself, since this framework served to define the expectations and obligations of each family member. Thus a younger son in a hidalgo family whose estate was entailed, for example, would know from an early age that he probably could expect only a limited inheritance, that he must seek an alternative career, and that he might never marry. Open conflict between siblings seems to have been relatively rare, although it did occur occasionally. Doña María de Alvarado in 1554 sought to prevent her brother, Juan de Hinojosa de Torres, from sending his representative to Peru to look into the inheritance of their deceased sibling, Captain Pedro Alonso de Hinojosa. Juan de Hinojosa quite reasonably pointed out that until they found out if their brother had left a will and whether he had made some provision for his illegitimate children, there would be no way of knowing if any of his family in Trujillo stood to gain from his legacy. Yet the fact that Juan de Hinojosa planned to send a representative on his own without involving his sister suggests that her anxieties were not unfounded.[51]

Cousins were more likely to become embroiled in disputes than were siblings. In the 1550s Pedro Calderón de Vargas tried to claim the rich Vargas entail to which his cousin, doña Beatriz de Vargas, wife of Diego de Vargas Carvajal, had succeeded.[52] Andrés Calderón Puertocarrero sued for lands in Medellín that the mestizo son of his uncle don Pedro Puertocarrero, an encomendero of Cuzco, had inherited.[53] Cousins were more likely to become enmeshed in such conflicts because at this level of family relationships the legal complexities and loopholes of inheritance might leave some room to maneuver, whereas among siblings usually the terms of inheritance were clear-cut and incontestable. In the arena of more distant relations, a powerful and influential individual might succeed in imposing his will and bypassing legal safeguards. In Cáceres in the 1540s a lengthy suit pitted Pedro de Paredes, illegitimate son of Alvaro de Paredes Becerra, against his first cousins (his father's nieces). Their father, Alvaro's brother, had taken over the estate worth some 20,000 ducados after Alvaro de Paredes Becerra's death. An illegitimate child ("hijo natural") who had been recognized was legally entitled to two-twelfths of the father's estate if no other provision was made. Pedro de Paredes's cousins alleged that he was not their uncle's son and that he had not acknowledged him as such; but the court in Granada held that they had failed to prove their case and ordered them to pay Paredes his share.[54]

Women and orphaned children with property probably were especially vulnerable to exploitation if they lacked the protection of someone genuinely committed to their best interests. In his will of 1534 Martín de Chaves specifically repudiated a transaction he was

said to have made under the tutelage of Gonzalo de Torres (probably a cousin): "If I did it, which I deny, it was because I was a child
and did not know what I was doing . . . and was led to it and
deceived and I did it against my will."[55] Doña Mencía de Ulloa, the
widow of García Holguín, in her will of 1570 complained that in
1562 she had signed certain instruments in favor of her nephews
Sancho de Paredes Golfín and Pedro Alonso Golfín. She said that
they had "told me that they were for my benefit and advantage . . .
and I, as a woman and their aunt and very poor and more than 70 or
80 years old, believed them and trusted them and in effect they
tricked me." She said that they pressured her into executing documents without her understanding what they were, and she revoked
them in her will "because I am told by lawyers and theologians that
I could not do it in prejudice of myself and of the legacies of my
children and grandchildren.[56]

Intergenerational conflict and disputes over property were common. Under rare circumstances a parent actually could disinherit a
child. Juan Carrasco, an innkeeper of Trujillo, in 1551 left his inn
and the "third and fifth" of his goods to his sons Pedro and Gaspar
Carrasco, but said that Juan, the son of his first wife, should inherit
nothing. According to Carrasco, his son Juan had been very "un-
grateful and disobedient," married against his will, tried to attack
him with a sword, and injured someone else.[57] More commonly a
parent might reduce the discretionary portion of an heir's legacy.
Cristóbal de Ovando de Paredes, one of the wealthiest and most
successful returnees to Cáceres from the Indies in the late sixteenth century, lived long enough to become estranged from his
eldest son, don Cosme. Cristóbal de Ovando had succeeded to the
entail of his father and grandfather (Francisco de Ovando, el rico)
after two older brothers died without heirs. In 1602 he made a will
in which he created a new entail; the original family entail was to go
to don Cosme de Ovando and the new one to his second son, don
Rodrigo de Godoy. But in a codicil of 1618 (by which time he
probably was in his late seventies) Cristóbal changed the terms of
succession radically, making don Rodrigo heir to the family entail
and his third son, don Francisco, heir to the new entail, virtually
cutting don Cosme off from any substantial parental inheritance. In
1635 don Cosme was still trying to claim one of the entails.[58]

Certainly property was not at the root of all family conflicts. Leverage over property could be used as punishment, and thus property as such might come into play only in the late stages of conflict. Personality clashes could wreak havoc in domestic situations, as occurred in the disastrous marriage in 1517 of the military hero Diego García de Paredes to doña María de Sotomayor, daughter of the lord of Orellana, Rodrigo de Orellana. The marriage lasted long enough for doña María to conceive their only child, Sancho de Paredes; but before the year was out, she had fled her husband's house, taking refuge first in the convent of the Coria in Trujillo and then later in her brother's house in Orellana.[59] The couple never lived together again, and Diego García spent most of the remaining years of his life outside Spain. The *Crónicas trujillanas*, especially the Hinojosa manuscript, recount a number of tales of family violence and scandal—jealous husbands who killed their wives, an argument between cousins that ended in bloodshed and the murderer's escape to "la India de Portugal"—but most of these stories belong to an earlier period. On the whole it seems likely that violence most often was directed toward nonrelatives (or distant ones) rather than close family members.

Discussion to this point mainly has focused on the structure and dynamics of the family and kinship network as units. Within these units the experience of individuals could differ notably. Two groups in particular—women and illegitimate children—occupied a position in the family (and society) that often was ambivalent and difficult. Because of the distinct and sometimes problematic nature of their position, they will be considered separately.

Women

A good deal already has been said or implied about the position of women in the family and society. Whereas within the family, particularly in the noble family, women sometimes were at a disadvantage with respect to the inheritance of property (especially in the case of entails, unless there were no male heirs), in terms of the larger society women had much the same legal rights as men. Women, like men, reached the age of majority at twenty-five, at which point they could in their own right conduct a full range of

legal transactions—buying, selling, and otherwise disposing of
property, arranging dowries for daughters, drawing up wills—if
they were single; if married, they had to obtain their husbands'
consent. A woman retained the right to control and dispose of her
dowry, and she was legally entitled to one-half of the economic
gains ("bienes multiplicados") made during her marriage. Hidalgo
women, and probably others as well, often received basic schooling
and knew how to read and write. As seen, they could become the
effective heads of household.

Women at all levels of society could be active economically. In the
working groups they made a vital contribution to the domestic economy, both inside and outside the household. They not only shared
the work of their husbands but also entered directly into occupations. Virtually all the bakers and cheese vendors were women, as
were many candlemakers and innkeepers and, of course, midwives.
The censuses of the towns almost always included women who were
farmers. Girls and women entered domestic service as servants,
housekeepers, and nurses; like men they might stay in service a
relatively short time or remain in that situation virtually all their
lives. Women with occupations who were married operated their
businesses quite independently of their husbands. The 1571 will of
Catalina Hernández la Rentera, wife of Francisco Sánchez Madaleno
and vecina of Cáceres, shows that she was fully responsible for her
bread-baking business. The will detailed a number of transactions
that were still pending, mainly money advanced or lent outright.
She left her daughter 12,000 maravedís and three beds.[60]

Upper class women did not, of course, pursue trades. Most
upper class women who did not marry entered convents, usually
local ones. The dowries families paid to convents might not have
been standardized, but certainly they were well below the dowries
provided for daughters who married. In addition to the dowry
families had to guarantee an annual income for daughters who
professed; 1000 maravedís a year probably was the minimum.[61]
The convents provided what the nobility saw as a suitable alternative to marriage for daughters for whom they could not afford marriage dowries or for illegitimate daughters who perhaps did not fit
in elsewhere. Cristóbal de Ovando Paredes placed his *mestiza*
daughter, doña Beatriz de Ovando, whom he brought back from
the Indies, in the convent of Santa María de Jesús.[62] Underage

women who had no close family with whom they could live also might be placed temporarily in a convent.[63]

While charitable donations might provide the wherewithal for a small number of women from the humbler classes to enter these convents, they were above all the province of noble women. The names of some of the women in the cacereño convent of San Pablo in 1556, for example, read almost like a register of the leading noble and hidalgo families: doña Ana de Ovando, abbess; María Gutiérrez de Ulloa, vicar; Beatriz de Figueroa, purveyor; Isabel de Paredes, doorkeeper; doña Catalina Enríquez, sacristan; and Francisca de la Rocha, Lucía López de la Rocha, Mayor de Orellana, doña Teresa de Monroy, doña María de Mendoza, doña María de Ovando, and Elvira de Paredes, nuns.[64] Women led a mostly comfortable and not necessarily very isolated life in the convents. The rules that the bishop of Coria sought to institute as a result of the visit he made to San Pablo and Santa María de Jesús in Cáceres in 1588 (no visitors unless a nun was sick, no personal servants, no visits outside except in the case of grave illness of a family member) surely reflected practices that were common at one time.[65] Given the large numbers of hidalgo women who entered the local convents, many must have been living alongside their sisters, cousins, or aunts. And, as often has been suggested, the religious life could afford a woman with intellectual or administrative ambitions or abilities a good arena in which to exercise them.

So far, then, the picture of the position of women in society does not appear especially bleak. They had legal rights and protections, important economic roles, and some possibilities for exercising real authority in the household or convent. But it will be recalled that almost invariably the majority of the paupers in the towns and cities were widows and single women. Certainly not all widows were poor; but the frequency with which they were listed as poor and having little or no property in the censuses suggests that the customary and legal mechanisms that governed family property and inheritance might have failed to provide consistently and adequately for older women. One woman included in the 1561 padrón of Zorita, described as "viuda dueña pobre," was the mother of an hidalgo said to have 12 oxen and cows, 250 sheep, and 30 pigs, quite substantial holdings in livestock.[66] If she was poor, clearly her son was not. If a husband failed to ensure that his wife would have at least the usufruct of his property after he died, she might end up with very little indeed. Nonetheless, since frustratingly little is known about the significance of the classification "pobre," one cannot reach definitive conclusions about the economic status of many of the women designated as such.

Widows were not the only women whose position could be marginal. Upper-class women who did not marry could enter convents or perhaps live in the household of parents or siblings; but what became of the other women who did not marry, could not afford to become nuns, and had no male relatives to support them? If they could not enter service and had no trade, they had few recourses. One girl living in Ibahernando in 1561 was an orphan who owned only a small house with the roof partly fallen in. The census of Santa Cruz for the same year included a young woman who was "moza muy pobre vive de por si."[67] It is not surprising that the opportunities offered by the Indies might have been very attractive for single women who could find the means to get there. The sisters María, Catalina, and Marina Solano (ages forty, thirty, and twenty-eight years) left Trujillo for the Indies in 1563. Inés Gonzalez, a thirty-year-old single woman, left Trujillo in 1579 as the criada of the widower Diego Hernández de Aguilar, who was taking his two unmarried sisters and a three-year-old son to Tierra Firme. Lucía Alonso testified that Inés González had lived in her house since her mother died and had worked; now she had "sold the little she had to go to the Indies."[68] There are many similar examples of women emigrating as servants or accompanying brothers or uncles to the New World. In a society where many people were economically vulnerable, widowed and single women were especially so. The laws and customs that regulated the control and disposition of property at times might have failed to protect many women from privation and made them second-class citizens of society. The attractions of emigration might well have outweighed the risks for many single women who understood the precariousness of their position.

Illegitimate Children

Illegitimate children were no rarity in this society, but their position often was uncertain, dependent on the recognition and acceptance accorded by their fathers or other relatives. Some families seem to have incorporated illegitimate children as a matter of course. Diego García de Paredes ("el Sansón") grew up with an older, illegitimate half-brother, Alvaro de Paredes, who accompanied him on his first trip to Italy. Both Diego and Alvaro had illegitimate sons of their own. Diego García de Paredes, born in 1506 and named for his father, during his active career made three trips to the New World and fought in Europe as well; Sancho de Paredes was Alvaro's son by a slave woman who belonged to his nephew, Hernando Corajo. The latter raised both of them; Corajo named his illegitimate cousin, Sancho de Paredes, successor to his entail in default of his uncle, Diego García, and his legitimate descendants and also freed Sancho in his will, since technically he was his slave.[69] Captain Gonzalo Pizarro, as noted, brought most of his illegitimate children into his household, with the exception of Francisco Pizarro.[70]

Possibly in the latter part of the fifteenth century and early years of the sixteenth local society was still sufficiently fluid even at the highest levels that integration of illegitimate children into the main line of the family was common.[71] The children of such respected trujillanos as Martín de Chaves, el viejo, and Gómez Nuño de Escobar were illegitimate but were the principal heirs, married well, and apparently were fully accepted into hidalgo society. During the sixteenth century, with the increasing consolidation and institutionalization of families and estates that resulted from the growing number of entails, incorporation of illegitimate children became less common. Nevertheless the tradition of having children outside marriage remained strong in the sixteenth century among all groups. Hidalgos might have one or two children by the same woman (usually, although not invariably, from the lower classes) before they married and established their legitimate family and household. Normally they made some provision for the children and sometimes the mother, and occasionally they brought the children into the household. This well-entrenched pattern proved to be ideally suited to the needs and circumstances of emigrants in the New World. During their early years in the Indies men would form liaisons with Indian (or sometimes black) women and father mestizo children, whom they often raised themselves, even after they married. When Andrés Pérez wrote to his brother Francisco Gutiérrez in Cáceres in 1559, he mentioned three legitimate children and three illegitimate ones. His eldest illegitimate daughter, whom he named for his mother, was already married (he named another for an aunt); the oldest of his legitimate children, Francisco, was 10.[72] Since he probably arrived in Mexico in the mid-1530s, Andrés likely spent the first ten years or so there living with an Indian mistress who bore his three older children; only subsequently did he marry.

Perhaps the most striking aspect of the experience of illegitimate children was the variation in the treatment accorded to them. With the exception of the legal requirement that one-sixth of a man's estate go to illegitimate children whom he had recognized, treatment of such children otherwise varied according to the individual. While there are many cases that show concern on the part of parents for their illegitimate offspring, it must also be borne in mind that the documents reflect precisely those instances where parents made provisions for the care and support of children; the records are mostly silent as to the rest. Francisco de Ovando, el rico, who left substantial entails to each of his three sons, designated 50,000 maravedís for his bastard son Antonio when he died, quite a meager sum, given his means.[73] The rather high birthrates among slave women,[74] when considered in conjunction with the fairly modest rates of manumission, would suggest that many fathers did not trouble themselves to any great degree about their illegitimate offspring (although it might be argued that a child born to a slave would be raised in the household and therefore receive a certain amount of care).

Illegitimate children of hidalgos no doubt fared best when there were no legitimate heirs. Don Diego de Ovando de Cáceres, who died without legitimate heirs, made careful plans for the education and future of his illegitimate son and daughter. In 1574 he arranged for his son Hernando de Ovando to learn to read and board for a year with Bachiller Ojalvo, a priest. At his death don Diego placed him under the tutelage of his brother (and heir), don Francisco de Torres, and left him 300 ducados to go to the Indies or join the military. Don Diego's daughter, doña Teresa Rol, was to learn how to read and then enter the convent of Santa Clara in Trujillo.[75] Don Juan de Sande, member of the Sande family so active in the military, who fought in the Granada campaign but died soon after his return to Cáceres, made his illegitimate sons, Diego de Paredes and Jerónimo de Sande, his heirs. At the time of his death he was still a bachelor, and the boys' mother, doña María de Paredes, was an hidalgo. The boys were brought up in Sande's parents' home (probably in Torre-quemada).[76] Another cacereño, Diego de la Rocha, had to change the terms of the entail he founded in 1527 in which he named his son Juan de la Rocha, comendador of Santiago, his heir. In 1549 he made Diego de la Rocha, the illegitimate son of his deceased son Fabián de la Rocha, the successor, as he was the sole surviving heir in the direct line; his son Juan had been missing and presumed dead in Italy for years. The amended entail, however, stipulated that thereafter only legitimate children could inherit.[77]

While it is impossible to guess the status of most illegitimate children, certainly it was not unusual for parents to concern themselves with their upbringing. The attention paid to these children might have stemmed in part from the custom of making at least minimal provision for all children; it also might have represented a kind of hedge against the possibility of running out of heirs altogether, as in the case of Diego de la Rocha. In 1578 Juan de la Peña asked to be named guardian of his four-year-old illegitimate daughter, doña María de la Cerda. Her mother had died, and in any case the child had been raised in his home. Alvaro Sánchez de Ulloa in 1561 was named tutor of a one-year-old illegitimate son.[78] Noble fathers who raised or at least recognized illegitimate children for the most part probably expected them to join the middling ranks of hidalgos. Alvaro de Aldana Ulloa gave his "hijo natural" Gonzalo de Aldana lands and a vineyard in Sierra de Fuentes, 250 ducados in cash, and a pair of oxen when he married in 1577 on the condition that Gonzalo not ask for anything else from his estate beyond this. Aldana's marriage reflected his respectable but modest status. His bride's family pledged a dowry of 400 ducados and said that she "will go dressed in holiday clothes for her wedding, in accordance with her rank."[79]

For commoners illegitimate children might not have posed the same problems of social status, but they too had to decide how to treat them in terms of upbringing and inheritance of property. Jerónimo Cotrina of Cáceres simply recognized his two "hijos naturales" along with his two legitimate sons in his will of 1557.[80] Nuño Gutiérrez, a pharmacist of Trujillo, however, in 1551, together with his wife, made complicated arrangements on behalf of his "bastard daughter" María reminiscent of those sometimes made by the nobility.[81] Thus, commoners were just as likely as nobles to show concern for their illegitimate children. In 1557 a barber named Francisco Martín bought his ten-year-old mulatto son from the executor of don Francisco de Carvajal's estate. A criado of Juan de Perero who had a child by one of Perero's slaves raised the boy in his home and secured his freedom from Perero's daughter, as Perero had promised he might do when his son reached the age of sixteen.[82]

Discussion of the treatment and experiences of illegitimate children raises again the question of the position of women. Who were the mothers of these children and what happened to them? They probably fell into two very broad categories—women who formed stable (if often short-term) liaisons (for example, doña María de Paredes who had two children by don Juan de Sande), and those who did not, including (sometimes but not always) slave women, but mainly prostitutes. The sisters Isabel García la Castra and Isabel García la Cuaca, who had between them five children when they decided to go to Mexico in 1578 to join their half-brother, probably belonged to the latter category.[83] Such women must have expected and received little or nothing in the way of assistance for themselves or their children from the children's fathers. For women of the first group, especially if the man were noble, possibly fairly well-understood rules governed the relationship between a man and his mistress. She would not have expected marriage to result from such a liaison, but most likely hoped for some provision for her support and possibly assistance in her marriage. A noble of Cáceres, Diego Cano de la Rocha, who decided to get married in 1568, made arrangements to end his relationship with Ana Sánchez. She was the mother of his two illegitimate children and might have been pregnant with a third in 1568. At that time he said he would provide her with a house and thirty fanegas of wheat but only on the condition that she would live "well and honorably" and have nothing to do with any man unless she married, which in fact she did two years later.[84] Women with illegitimate children often went on to marry; Francisco Pizarro and his half-brothers Gonzalo and Juan (who were full brothers) all had legitimate maternal half-brothers.

The status and position of illegitimate children, especially those born to parents of very different rank as the result of liaisons between hidalgos and women who were commoners, servants, or slaves, was uncertain. As neither completely noble nor common, they did not automatically fit in anywhere in the existing social hierarchy, and hence were likely to be marginalized—consider the aforementioned case of Gonzalo de Aldana, whose father provided him the means to become a prosperous but modest hidalgo-labrador in one of Cáceres's villages. The priesthood offered a suitable career for some illegitimate sons, just as the convent was appropriate for daughters. One of the sons of the influential priest Alvar García de Solís of Trujillo, Cristóbal de Solis, virtually grew up in the clerical life.[85] Alonso Pizarro's father, Juan Pizarro, a wealthy hidalgo and stockraiser of Caceres, supported him while he studied for the priesthood and promised him a bed, rents, and other things he would need after he was ordained in return for the time Alonso had served in the household of Juan Pizarro and his wife.[86]

Departure for the Indies was another option available to illegitimate children whose position and prospects at home were uncertain. Francisco Pizarro spent years in Tierra Firme before conquering Peru and returned to Spain only once, to secure the royal capitulaciones for the conquest and to recruit his brothers and other men. Diego García de Paredes, the illegitimate son of the military hero of the same name, must have found his position in Trujillo problematic despite recognition by his father, especially after the birth of his legitimate half-brother. Paredes's career reflected the contradictions between his abilities and social background, on the one hand, and his insecure position at home on the other. By the age of twenty he had left Trujillo for the Indies, spending time in Tierra Firme and Peru before returning to Spain in the 1530s. Soon after his return he joined the military and fought in France, Flanders, Germany, Italy, and Sicily, attaining the rank of captain, returning to Trujillo only to leave again in 1544 with Francisco de Orellana's expedition to the Amazon. Active in the area of Venezuela for some fifteen years, he went back to Spain again in 1562 and then departed within the year as the appointed governor of Popayán. He was killed by Indians on the Venezuelan coast before he could take his post.[87] While doubtless Diego García de Paredes benefited from family connections despite his illegitimacy, he could hardly have achieved such distinction if he had stayed at home.

Inheritance

The basic pattern of inheritance in central and southern Spain was equal division of property among heirs, male and female. A number of practices sanctioned by law, however, in fact often modified the system of partible inheritance. Either parent could set aside one-third of the inheritance for one child, who also received one-fifth of the remaining two-thirds; this was the "tercio y quinto."[88] Among the nobility the tercio y quinto became the basis for entails that became increasingly common in the sixteenth century; but in fact anyone could opt for this mode of inheritance rather than equal division. Children who entered religious orders received a smaller inheritance than other heirs, and they frequently renounced any further claim to their parents' legacy when they joined the order. Other individuals also might renounce their inheritance in favor of their siblings.[89]

These aspects of the system of inheritance are reasonably clear, but others are more problematic. A woman retained her dowry and therefore was free to dispose of it in her will (she might in fact have promised or donated part or all before her death, possibly as part of a dowry agreement for a daughter). She also was entitled to half of the "bienes multiplicados" or economic gains made during her marriage; but whether she could dispose of this property, or whether it was considered part of the inheritance to be divided equally among heirs after her husband's death (that is, she would have the usufruct of such property until her own death, but then could not dispose of it herself) is not entirely clear. The wills of commoners often designated the spouse as a coequal heir along with the children, or even the principal or only heir.[90] García López de Aviles, whose eldest son, Pedro Lopez de Aviles, received the tercio y quinto of his estate and married Isabel Ruiz, the daughter of the returnee from Peru Alonso Ruiz, assigned his wife the usufruct of his property for her lifetime if she did not remarry.[91] Nobles usually made few provisions for wives, beyond perhaps the furnishings and usufruct of the house or the income from rents during her lifetime, since a woman had her dowry and whatever other property she inherited from her parents.[92]

Although property was conveyed in different ways and at different times (through donations, dowries, wills, entails), all property "counted" in the final reckoning of inheritance. A woman might receive her entire inheritance as her dowry, or a man might receive the bulk of his when he married; but ultimately the legacy took into account all earlier donations. Gonzalo de Olmos, a returnee from the Indies, in his will of 1574 divided his legacy equally among five sons and three daughters (the only exception was a daughter in the convent of San Pedro). He said that the 100,000 maravedís of censos that he gave to his son don Juan de Olmos when he married should be deducted from his share.[93] Three of Gonzalo de Olmos's sons were in the Indies at the time the division of property was made, but physical absence in no way altered an heir's rights to a share in the legacy. Francisco Pavón, a wool carder, and his wife, Isabel Martín la Corneja, executed a joint will in 1574 in which they stated that their son Juan de Cáceres had left for the Indies more than twenty-six years before. They had heard news of his death but did not know if he had left any legal heirs. They instructed that their legacy be divided among their other children but that an appropriate portion should be paid if a legitimate heir of Juan de Cáceres appeared in Cáceres bearing the required proofs of identity, taking into account the 24 ducados they once had given Juan de Cáceres to buy a horse.[94]

Mandatory partition of property generally made wills unnecessary, unless an individual wished to make special bequests or otherwise depart from the basic pattern of equal division among heirs. Members of the upper and upper-middle classes—above all, wealthy hidalgos—were most likely to go before notaries to draw up wills and entails; they held the largest amounts of property and often made complicated arrangements for disposing of it. Therefore we can examine in some detail their inheritance practices.

Entails proliferated in the sixteenth century, reflecting the consolidation of wealth among upper class families and the desire to preserve and perpetuate the family estate (and hence the family's status). The entail often was linked to a surname, coat of arms, and title; when a number of noble families of Trujillo acquired señorío over villages formerly under Trujillo's jurisdiction, these villages also entered into the family entail. Both men and women could establish entails, those of the latter reflecting greater variation. Direct descent in the legitimate male line was the universally favored formula for the entails of fathers and the eldest son was usually favored. Entails generally barred inheritance by illegitimate or adoptive children, but daughters usually received preference over other relatives.

The entails established by women were likely to designate a younger son or a daughter, since the oldest son presumably stood to inherit his father's entail. Doña Francisca de Mendoza, the wife of Diego de Ovando de Cáceres (son of Captain Diego de Ovando de Cáceres) founded an entail in 1539 in favor of her youngest son, Juan de Vera y Mendoza. Doña Isabel de la Peña created an entail in 1575 for her second daughter; but if this daughter married someone who held an entail, doña Isabel's legacy would go to her second son or other daughter.[95] Here again, then, the desire to make an equitable provision for as many children as possible figured. Women's disposition of property in wills and entails often complemented or supplemented the disposition made by their husbands, reflecting a coordinated strategy for the distribution of property and wealth to the next generation. Women sometimes joined their legacies or entails with those of their husbands, at least if they stayed in the direct line; if the husband's entail passed outside the direct line, however, they frequently named their own relatives as subsequent potential heirs.[96]

Despite the many conventional and formulaic elements that characterized the entails of men especially, in one sense their hallmark was their individuality; the founder could make his own determinations with regard to succession, and entails could incorporate a number of particular provisions along with the standard ones.[97] The eldest son was not always the principal or most favored heir. Francisco de Solís of Cáceres wanted to leave his entail to his emigrant son Gómez de Solís rather than to his eldest, although Gómez ultimately turned it down and stayed in Peru.[98] Francisco de Ovando, el rico, established entails for each of his three sons, rather than just favoring the oldest, in effect creating three new branches of the family.[99]

Entails sometimes included the conditions under which heirs might succeed or how they were to be chosen. Diego de la Rocha (whose heir was his illegitimate grandson) said that any woman inheriting the entail must marry someone from the Rocha lineage and retain the name and arms. Mandatory changes of name as well as designated spouses could form part of the conditions for succession. Diego de la Rocha required his grandson to marry doña Mencía de Carvajal, whose family pledged a dowry of 4000 ducados.[100] Hernando Corajo, on the other hand, suggested that if his illegitimate cousin Sancho de Paredes succeeded to his legacy, he might marry his nephew's daughter, María Jiménez, if she wished; but he stressed that this was a request, not a requirement.[101] Children did not necessarily do what their elders suggested, even when the stakes were high. In her will of 1575 Catalina Alvarez de Toro said that she and her husband had created an entail that her eldest grandson would have inherited had he married her niece doña Mencía de los Nidos. Since he did not, her grandson Diego de la Rocha would succeed if he changed his name to "Rodrigo de Toro de los Nidos."[102]

Many instruments of entail specified detailed lists of successors in default of the direct male line, but others were more abbreviated, sometimes directing the establishment of a capellanía or some charitable foundation if there was no one in the direct line or among close relatives who could inherit. Diego de la Rocha, for example, instructed that if his son or grandson or their descendants were unable to succeed, the entailed property should be used to found a convent of the order of Santa Clara (under the Franciscan order). His house on Pintores street was to be used for the convent itself, and he made provisions for some poor women of Cáceres to receive food, clothing, and medical care and to enter the convent without paying a dowry.[103]

Entails, along with the conditions for inheritance sometimes laid down in wills, often restricted the choices an individual had in disposing of property. The entail held by Dr. Nicolás de Ovando, which he had inherited from his father and included his house in the parish of Santa María, a country house, and lands in Zamarrillas and Torreorgaz and other properties, went to his nephew Hernando, since he apparently had no legitimate children of his own. If Hernando could not succeed, then the entail would go to his niece, or to whoever inherited the estate of his grandfather, Captain Diego de Ovando. Dr. Ovando left to his daughter, doña María de Ovando (doubtless illegitimate) only a silver dish; he apologized to her and her husband, Dr. Carrillo, saying "I beg [them] . . . to forgive me for not being able to do for them what I would like, because my estate is entailed." To his grandson, Nicolás de Ovando,

who wanted to study in Salamanca or Alcalá, he left all his law
books.[104]

Dowries

Dowries fulfilled a dual role in family relations and strategies. On
the one hand the value of the dowry related directly to the whole
question of the division and conveyance of property discussed
above, whereas on the other the dowry played an important part in
creating or maintaining alliances between families, whether for
economic, social, or political reasons (most likely some combination). The bride's family's decision regarding distribution of property and its economic means together determined the dowry's
value and composition, but the marital alliance formed as a conse-
quence could generate new means and resources. The dowry agreement marked the intersection between property considerations
and the formation of a new family and household, two distinct but
related aspects of family life. A marriage could represent the culmination of some complicated negotiations and considerations, as
seen in the example of don Francisco Altamirano, the oldest son
and principal heir of Licenciado Altamirano. In June 1580, soon
after his father's death, don Francisco gave his power of attorney to
one of his brothers to arrange his marriage to doña Leonor de
Montoya of the Villa de los Santos. Within a year, however, don
Francisco was married not to her but to doña Francisca de Silva
Puertocarrero, who gave her husband license to sell some lands she
had near Villanueva de Bancarrota in 1581.[105]

As was true for wills and entails, dowries among the nobility
involved much higher sums and more complicated arrangements
than those of most commoners. The dowries of the nobility frequently included rents, properties, and jewelry, although there
was a tendency during the sixteenth century increasingly to express
the amounts in lump sums (which still might be met in various
ways). When Cosme de Ovando Paredes married doña Isabel de
Cárdenas in the late 1570s, she brought a dowry of 5000 ducados in
juros, agricultural land, trousseau, furniture, and cash, guaranteed
by her brother and his wife since her parents were dead. Families
generally did not pay the dowry all at once but rather in a series of
installments over several years. In 1577 Cosme de Ovando Paredes

had received about 2400 ducados of his wife's dowry; in 1580 he received another sum of around 550 ducados plus a female slave.[106]

Despite the great discrepancy in size between noble dowries and those of more modest hidalgos, middle-class, or working people, there were nonetheless elements in common. The dowry or marriage agreement normally included house furnishings and a trousseau. Pedro Calderón de Vargas testified that before his sister doña María de Carvajal married Andrés Calderón Puertocarrero, they went to Toledo to buy the trousseau that his mother gave to his sister. In 1591 Andrés Calderón himself authorized his future son-in-law Alonso Solano to collect 100 ducados in rents to buy bed linens, and the two men went together to Trujillo's weekly mercado franco and spent 230 ducados on a bed and other items.[107]

Another feature common to dowry agreements at all levels of society was that they often were made by a woman's family or household rather than just her parents. Siblings, uncles, even cousins contributed part or all of the dowry in many instances, even if one or both parents were still alive (although more likely if the father were deceased). In 1573 doña Teresa Rol's siblings—don Diego de Ovando de Cáceres, don Francisco de Torres, and doña Beatriz de la Peña—were paying off the dowry of 2300 ducados that had been pledged for her marriage to Juan de Carvajal Ulloa in 1561.[108] Isabel González's daughter Catalina received a dowry of 1000 ducados, 590 from her mother and 410 from her returnee brother Antonio Cotrina. In addition her mother gave her various pieces of jewelry, cloth, and clothing, and Antonio gave her a green satin skirt worth 80 ducados. In 1575 three brothers in Cáceres who were wool carders gave their sister a house in the parish of Santiago with a small yard and three beds as her dowry.[109] A criada's employer often provided all or part of her or her daughter's dowry, which probably was considered a basic part of the terms of employment. Isabel Durán, who made her will in Cáceres in 1571, served Diego de Cáceres and his wife doña Francisca de Torres for eighteen years (and their daughter doña Jerónima for two). They had given her 50 ducados when her daughter married, although her basic compensation was around 4 ducados a year (in addition to clothing and other necessities).[110]

Dowries among the nobility tended to rise in value over the sixteenth century. Don Francisco de Torres, who became heir to the entail founded by Captain Diego de Ovando de Cáceres when his brother don Diego died in 1575, was promised a dowry of 9000 ducados when he married a woman from Mérida in 1576, whereas his paternal grandmother had brought a dowry of 1600 ducados in rents, houses, and cash inherited from an uncle.[111] Some of the most notable sums of the later sixteenth century involved the families of returnees from Peru. Returnee Juan Pizarro de Orellana pledged 6000 ducados for the marriage of his daughter doña Catalina de Orellana to Juan Barrantes, son and principal heir of returnee Pedro Barrantes. His granddaughter, doña Estevanía de Orellana (daughter of Hernando de Orellana), brought lands valued at 5000 ducados (inherited from her mother, doña Mencía de Tapia) and an additional 19,000 ducados when she married Francisco Pizarro, son of Hernando Pizarro and doña Francisca Pizarro, in 1586.[112] The dowry often was identical with the women's anticipated inheritance. When returnee Sancho de Figueroa married doña Francisca de Ulloa in 1548, her dowry included the following: half of her father, Hernando de Ulloa's, estate at La Cervera, which consisted of a house, farm lands, barley fields, and corrals; half of a vineyard and half of his pastures in Pozo Morisco; one-third of an oven; half of whatever had belonged to doña Francisca's mother, Catalina de la Rocha, and after Hernando de Ulloa's death, half of the goods of his estate.[113] Sancho de Figueroa died quite soon after the marriage; but not surprisingly doña Francisca, with so substantial a dowry, remarried quickly.[114]

The dowries of the more middling hidalgo families of course were much lower. Baltasar de Valverde's wife brought a dowry of 500 ducados (Valverde was the brother of Licenciado García de Valverde, who served on several audiencias in the Indies). Pedro de Grajos, a notary of Cáceres, endowed one daughter (who married Alonso de Solís, who succeeded his father-in-law as notary) with 350 ducados and another with 500; one of Grajos's sons and two of his sons-in-law contributed to the latter.[115] The dowries given to daughters of the well-to-do upper strata of commoners fell within a similar range. Hernando Genio, a barber, acquired a dowry of 400 ducados when he married in 1574, and Cristóbal García, a pharmacist and active entrepreneur of Cáceres, endowed his daughter with 1500 ducados when she married Licenciado Gaspar Sánchez.[116] Descending the socioeconomic scale, dowries became more modest yet, although the crucial elements of establishing a new household—furnishings, a house, a piece of land, or a work animal—continued to figure.

Conclusion

Examination of the institutions that governed the distribution of property—wills, dowries, entails—reveals a number of practices that characterized groups at all levels of society: the tradition of equal division among heirs, the use of dowries to effect alliances and help provide the means for establishing new households, evidence that property distribution and economic decision making concerned the entire family and not just the head of household. The basic demographic features that shaped family life—age at marriage, birth rates, illegitimacy—also prevailed throughout society. At the same time, however, much evidence suggests that noble families were modifying some of these basic customs and patterns with some distinct socioeconomic and demographic repercussions, and possibly these distinctive practices of the nobility were becoming more common in the sixteenth century. The establishment of entails and provision of high dowries for daughters fostered a situation where a family might produce only one substantial heir—that is, one son who inherited the bulk of the estate and thus could marry well and establish his own noble household—and formed one other important marital alliance via the daughter who received a high dowry.[117] This pattern of inheritance, though far from universal or invariable, certainly contributed to the consolidation of noble estates and fortunes, but also resulted in notable rates of celibacy as many children (male and female) of the nobility entered religious orders or otherwise failed to marry and produce legitimate heirs.

At the same time, that group's inheritance practices also freed a number of young men to pursue careers that took them away from home and generated new connections and opportunities that benefited both these sons and their families. Emigration to the Indies, whether temporary or permanent, not only proved attractive for these young men but could transform their prospects in life dramatically, since the new resources and rather distinct social milieu of the New World often enabled them to marry and establish households there or when they returned home. The possibilities offered by the Indies might not have had quite the same impact on the lives of commoners (that is, of allowing them to avoid celibacy imposed by socioeconomic constraints); but the presence of many single men and women of the middle- and working classes among the emigrant group suggests that for them as well the closely intertwined economic and demographic aspects of family life played a part in the decision to emigrate.

V

The Movement to the New World

The people who left Extremadura for the Indies in the sixteenth century represented nearly all ranks of society and a variety of occupations. They included distinguished officials and high ecclesiastics, secular priests and notaries hoping to find positions, artisans planning to establish themselves with their trades, people responding to the urging of relatives who had gone before them, and young men and women employed as servants. Emigrants were married and single, adults and children, and traveled in combinations of all kinds: cousins, siblings, friends and acquaintances, uncles and nephews, parents and children, employers and servants, unrelated individuals recruited for out-of-the-way destinations such as Florida and the Philippines. Emigrants left under varying circumstances as well. Some had their journeys paid by relatives, others borrowed money or sold virtually all their belongings to finance the move, or traveled as employees or as part of the entourage of a wealthy individual or an official. Some took capital or merchandise to help make their start in the New World, but others were utterly dependent on the assistance of relatives they expected to join to establish themselves. They traveled to a number of destinations, a choice that seldom was random but in any case not necessarily final. Choice of destinations changed over time and was conditioned by circumstances both at home and in the Indies; hence not surprisingly an examination of destinations, as of most other aspects of migration, reveals some differences between the neighboring cities of Cáceres and Trujillo.

Discussion of the composition, choices, and activities of the emigrant group requires both quantitative and qualitative analysis of the information available. Motivation, individual preferences and capabilities or limitations, or the personal arrangements made by departing emigrants cannot be quantified; yet they reveal much about both the context from which emigrants emerged and the life they expected to find in the New World and so are essential to the study of the movement from Spain to the Indies. Quantitative analysis, on the other hand, can illuminate some of the overall patterns in choices, arrangements, and the social or demographic composition of the movement, thereby providing a basis and framework for other kinds of nonquantifiable considerations. It must be borne in mind, however, that data collected on localities such as Cáceres and Trujillo in the sixteenth century are often far from complete and must be viewed in many instances as suggestive rather than definitive.

Logically, discussion of emigration from Extremadura would begin with an effort to convey some notion of the size of the movement. Records show that some 410 individuals from Cáceres emigrated to the New World in the sixteenth century and 921—more than twice as many—left Trujillo in the same period.[1] In addition, 25 people left the villages of Cáceres's jurisdiction and 160 the villages around Trujillo.[2] These figures are doubtless low—the gaps in the passengers lists in Seville alone would so indicate—but one can only speculate about just how low they are or what a reasonable estimate of the actual numbers would be.[3] The volume of emigration from Cáceres probably reached at least 500 and from Trujillo well over 1000.

Even though the figures must be assumed to be somewhat low, they provide a notion of the scope and volume of the movement, which likely was small enough not to cause any real alarm or disruption at home but large enough to be known and noticeable to almost everyone in these modestly sized cities. Furthermore the impression made by departures for the New World often was a function not so much of numbers alone as of other factors. After visiting the court and securing the *capitulaciones* (charters, titles) for the exploration and conquest of Peru, Francisco Pizarro returned in 1529 to his home town of Trujillo to recruit young men for the venture. The story is that on a Sunday morning he attended mass in the parish church of San Andrés, following which he stood under a tree in the courtyard, had the capitulaciones read aloud, and invited all who were interested to join him in the enterprise.[4] It is well known that a number of young men from Trujillo, including his four half-brothers, as well as others from Cáceres and the surrounding villages responded to his call. Recruitment efforts, which were public and sometimes conducted in a quasi-military fashion, the departure of important officials of the government or church, the concentration of departures in certain years or periods, such as the group of twenty-two men from Cáceres who left for Santo Domingo in 1535 (by which time Mexico had surpassed the Caribbean as the principal destination for emigrants),[5] and the fact that the distribution of emigrants was not necessarily random or equal in all sectors of society all worked to place emigration in the public limelight and endow it with a visibility that consideration of numbers alone might not convey. Last, the visibility of emigration in a sense was guaranteed by the nature of local society itself. If mobility and leaving home to seek opportunities were accepted as normal, likewise the structure of family and society presupposed the possibility (if not the likelihood) that departing or absent individuals would return. Since emigrants retained their place at home in some senses, people were much aware of the fact that they had left. In information compiled to verify the 1558 census of Madroñera, a small village near Trujillo, a man named Diego de Valencia testified that "he has a nephew who is in the Indies that he doesn't know if he's dead or alive and that he is an hidalgo and that he is the son of Cristóbal de Valencia, deceased, and that he has a mother in this place."[6]

The gross figures for the cities and villages also bring to mind another point, the greater size of the movement from Trujillo and its district compared to that from Cáceres. Leaving aside the villages, the city of Trujillo itself was somewhat larger than Cáceres, but only by perhaps 10 or 12 percent. Clearly population base alone cannot account for the striking difference in volume, and other factors and influences must have come into play. The larger size of the Trujillo emigrant group not only was rooted in certain differences but creates others in turn. The data base is larger, and therefore may provide a more reliable basis for analysis; at the least, the representativeness of the Trujillo group seems more reliable than is the case for Cáceres. A larger movement in itself may have fostered greater complexity and variety, so that such differences as the higher proportion of hidalgos in the Cáceres group, the larger percentage of people emigrating in family groups from Trujillo, and the apparently greater participation of people from the pueblos of Trujillo's jurisdiction than those of Cáceres's ultimately may be tied closely to the considerably greater size of the movement from Trujillo.

Destinations

Analysis of the initial destinations chosen by people leaving Spain (see tables 6 and 7) yields some interesting results, although certain factors limit the use and interpretation of this data. For some departing emigrants the information on destination is missing; for other individuals it is only known that they were in the Indies at some time, not where they went or when. Still others, in their determination to secure a license for the Indies, would state their willingness to go, for example, to New Spain, New Granada, or anywhere in the Indies.[7] Though this last kind of case was exceptional, far more common and relevant to the concerns here was the practice of moving on from the initial destination to another area that offered greater attractions. Virtually everyone from Cáceres and Trujillo who went to Cuba in the second decade of the sixteenth century went on to participate in the conquest of Mexico—hardly surprising, especially given that Hernando Cortés was also an extremeño. He was from Medellín, a town not far south of the southern limits of the jurisdiction of Trujillo, where he in fact had relatives. Santo Domingo and Tierra Firme, important destinations for the first generation of emigrants, continued to draw substantial numbers in the 1530s; but again probably many of these people moved on to Peru. Similarly, up until about the middle of the century New Granada served many as a stepping-stone to Peru, and not until the 1550s and 1560s did the region begin to take on some independence from Peru and attract people from Extremadura in its own right. The appointment of two men from Trujillo to the governorship of Popayán in the 1560s—Diego García de Paredes, who was killed by Indians on the Venezuelan coast before he could take office, and two years later (in 1565) don Alvaro de

TABLE 6 *Initial Destinations of Emigrants by Decade, Cáceres*

Destination	To 1510	1511–1520	1521–1530	1531–1540	1541–1550	1551–1560	1561–1570	1571–1580	1581–1590	1591–1600	Date Unknown	Total
Peru				31	16	23	20	27	1	3	13	134
New Spain			7	16	2	3	9	5	1	1	4	48
Santo Domingo	5	4		27			4	1				41
New Granada		1	2	3		12	3	1		1	5	28
Philippines								24				24
Tierra Firme		1		9	1		1		1		1	14
Chile				2	1	3	2	5			1	14
Cuba		11										11
Florida				3			7					10
Guatemala/Honduras			2	2		1		1			3	9
Veragua				5								5
Venezuela				2								2
Puerto Rico	2											2
Isla Margarita						2						2

TABLE 7   *Initial Destinations of Emigrants by Decade, Trujillo*

Destination	To 1510	1511–1520	1521–1530	1531–1540	1541–1550	1551–1560	1561–1570	1571–1580	1581–1590	1591–1600	Date Unknown	Total
Peru			18	67	25	72	44	79	26	76	29	436
New Spain		1	20	26	1	11	26	113	5		4	207
New Granada			1	24		7	37	3	1		4	77
Tierra Firme		1	2	17	9	3	13	6			1	52
Santo Domingo	2	4		15	1		1				4	27
Río de la Plata			1	6	1	1	2	2			4	17
Chile						2	2	6	3		1	14
Cuba		7		2								9
Guatemala/Honduras			2	4				1			1	8
Nicaragua			3									3
Puerto Rico			1	1								2
Florida				2								2
Venezuela			1							1		2

Mendoza—probably helps account for the nearly forty people from Trujillo who went to New Granada in that decade. Last, the destinations used here are intended to give a sense of regional movement and preference, but they do not show exactly where extremeños settled in the New World. In Peru they might establish themselves in Lima, Cuzco, Arequipa, Charcas, Quito, or elsewhere, in New Granada in Santa Marta, Cartagena, or Popayán. Even Mexico, despite the high degree of centralization of settlement in and around the great capital city, offered other foci of attraction such as Puebla de los Angeles. The small number of people who went to Yucatan (mainly with Francisco de Montejo in 1527) are included here in the figures for New Spain, but in fact Yucatan was conquered and settled quite separately from central New Spain.[8]

Given all these qualifiers, what does analysis of intended destinations reveal? The patterns of destination from both Cáceres and Trujillo changed over time, away from the Caribbean and toward the mainland centers of New Spain and Peru, which is to be expected and accords with the findings for the movement from Spain as a whole. Of particular interest here, however, were early events that had a significant impact on choices of destination, since these early events and choices set in motion patterns and cycles that would affect emigration for years to come. The first of these was the appointment of Frey Nicolás de Ovando, Comendador de Lares of the Order of Alcántara and member of a leading cacereño family close to the crown, as the governor of Hispaniola. Appointed in 1501, Ovando left Spain the following year accompanied by a huge expedition of some 2500 people.[9] The group included Francisco Pizarro, and Cortés would have figured in it as well had not a last-minute accident and injury forced him to delay his departure. Ovando governed Hispaniola for seven years, during which time he contributed considerably to the consolidation of royal rule and the growth of royal revenues from the island. He returned to Spain in 1509, shortly before his death. The departure and sojourn in the very recently discovered New World of such a prestigious figure as Ovando influenced cacereños to move in some numbers to the Indies at an early time; it is notable that, despite the overall much higher rate of emigration from Trujillo, in the first two decades of the sixteenth century emigrants from Cáceres outnumbered those from Trujillo almost two to one.

For Trujillo the decisive moment came more than two decades later, when Francisco Pizarro returned to Spain and his home town to recruit. In the decade 1521–1530 emigration from Trujillo to Peru equaled that to New Spain, despite the fact that only in the last year (1529–1530) of that decade did the Peruvian enterprise first directly involve people still in Spain, whereas Mexico had been conquered and opened for Spanish settlement and exploitation by 1521 or so. After 1530 in every decade Peru was far and away the greatest center of attraction for people from both cities, the only exception being the 1570s when nearly 120 people set off for New Spain from Trujillo. Even so, although Peru was the principal destination overall for emigrants from both cities, only a third of the cacereños went first to Peru while nearly half of the Trujillo people went there directly. But people whose first destination was Santo Domingo, New Granada, or Tierra Firme often moved on to Peru, so probably well over half of all emigrants from the region ended up there at some time.

Clearly it requires little explanation that returnees from America to sixteenth-century Extremadura were called "peruleros."[10] Pizarro's recruitment campaign, his position of leadership during the conquest and the years immediately following, and the strong favoritism he and his brothers accorded to relatives and friends from Trujillo and its region guaranteed that Peru would be the favored destination of emigrants. Connections linking Peru to Trujillo and Cáceres were established immediately and maintained through the continued recruitment of family members by people already in Peru and the forging of a perception that identified Peru with the Indies enterprise itself. Potential emigrants from Trujillo especially tended to use "Peru" synonymously with "las Indias," leading to such anomalies as one person's stated intention of going to "la ciudad de Mexico que es en los reinos del Peru que llama la Nueva España" ("the city of Mexico which is in the kingdoms of Peru called New Spain"), or a reference to "un perulero vecino de Mexico."[11] While the volume of emigrants to Peru subsided noticeably during the 1540s, the turbulent decade of Gonzalo Pizarro's rebellion, it picked up immediately thereafter despite the suspicions harbored by licensing officials in Seville who for a while questioned potential emigrants from Trujillo as to whether they were related to the Pizarros.[12]

Summarizing choice of initial destinations by decades in some cases disguises specific movements, such as the departure of the 22 cacereños for Santo Domingo in 1535 already mentioned, while it draws attention to others, such as the nearly 25 people who left Cáceres for the Philippines in the 1570s or the unprecedented 120 or so people who went to New Spain from Trujillo in the same decade. Movements to specific destinations that can be pinpointed in time raise the question of recruitment and organization of emigration. Probably the most notable single year was 1540, when a total of 58 men and 2 women appeared in the passenger lists headed for Tierra Firme, Nombre de Dios, Santo Domingo, or no specified destination (the dates of departure and order of the listing, however, make it clear that the last were associated with the people going to Tierra Firme and Santo Domingo and no doubt they were going there as well). Of the group, 38 men and 2 women were from Trujillo, 14 from its towns, and 6 from Cáceres.[13] In 1544 another 10 men from Trujillo and 2 from Cáceres set off for Nombre de Dios, all but one of them on the same boat.[14] Even if it is not possible in many cases to determine why or how such groups formed and moved together, their very existence suggests that to a great extent emigration was a collective rather than an individual phenomenon.

Organization and Recruitment

Discussion of destinations leads quite directly, then, to the question of organization. How did people move to the New World? Was the movement largely the result of personal initiative and decisions? Did formal or official recruitment play a major part? The evidence suggests that organization of emigration in fact took place on both these levels, sometimes in combination and sometimes not. A young man in Trujillo or one of its towns in 1540, for example, might hear that some appointed official was looking for people to accompany him to the Indies, in this case perhaps preferably young men. His brother would decide to go with him. A couple of close friends also were thinking about going, and they all would end up going together. In such cases, which obviously occurred time and again, the context in which a given individual emigrated existed at two levels. One was personal, in that the young man would travel to the Indies with a sibling or friends. The other might be called formal, in that the actual means and the organization of the move hinged on external factors.

In other words, while the motivation for emigrating might be personal, the way someone went did not necessarily depend on personal ties and possibilities but might have been linked to other circumstances. Both these organizing principles are important in terms of understanding the overall nature of the movement. Juan Gutiérrez de Ulloa of Cáceres in 1577 journeyed to Peru where his brother, Licenciado Fray Antonio Gutiérrez de Ulloa, was inquisitor of Lima, and doubtless he went to join him. He traveled, however, as a criado.[15] Thus at one level personal ties and connections—the desire to join his brother—motivated him to emigrate, though the actual means by which he did so were the arrangements he made to serve as a criado. An even clearer example might be the case of two young men from Trujillo, Juan de Plasencia, a twenty-five-year-old carpenter, and his twenty-two-year-old brother Bartolomé Rodrí-guez. In Trujillo they petitioned jointly in 1576 for a license to go to the Indies. Both went to the same place—New Spain—but as criados of different men.[16] Thus Bartolomé Rodríguez emigrated with his brother, but he traveled as a criado. External or formal arrangements often enabled an individual to make an intended move, but they did not necessarily motivate the move or determine the personal circumstances that also might come into play.

The departure for Peru in 1555 of a number of people from Cáceres and Trujillo, many of whom were attached directly or indi-rectly to the entourage of the new viceroy, the Marqués de Cañete, shows on a larger scale how these different modes of emigration coexisted. The group that went to Peru that year included eighteen people from Trujillo and seven from Cáceres. At least four of the Trujillo men officially formed a part of the viceroy's entourage, and one woman traveled as the servant of an oidor of the audiencia of Lima, Dr. Gregorio de Cuenca. There was one merchant's factor and six working artisans (a shoemaker, two tailors, two locksmiths, and a blacksmith), of whom two were half-brothers. Among the group also were a woman named Costanza Rodríguez, described as "moza y hermosa," and her two sons, accompanied by two of her brothers. She was going to join her husband, Diego de Trujillo, a wealthy veteran of Cajamarca who had returned to Trujillo in 1535 but left again for Peru in 1546.[17] Probably the most prominent member of the Cáceres-Trujillo group was a man from a branch of the Ovando family who took three criados from Cáceres, one of whom was his first cousin. Another was a more distant relative, whose two older brothers had preceded him to Peru.[18]

What emerges, then, is the picture of a group of individuals, of whom many had personal ties that bore on their decision to emigrate and the way they did so. Two brothers departed together, a woman accompanied by her sons and brothers went to join her husband, a young man traveled as the criado of an older relative, another went to join his brothers. These personal arrangements and motivations were subsumed under the more general organization of the viceroy's entourage. The departure of the viceroy in 1555 perhaps accounted for the timing of the group's departure and served as a catalyst for some members of the Cáceres-Trujillo group to emigrate; the large number of artisans in the group suggests that some effort was made to attract working artisans. But to view this group solely in the context of the viceroy's entourage is to obscure some other circumstances and relationships that were just as significant.

Tables 8 and 9 are designed to convey some notion of how extremeños went to the Indies. Again, as in the data for destinations, these categories and figures are not definitive or comprehensive but are intended to show the variety of arrangements by which emigrants traveled and to give a sense of change over time. There are limitations to the approach, precisely because of the dual aspect of organization suggested above. Since the categories (with the exception of the last, which shows how many individuals went to join relatives) are mutually exclusive, they cannot account for individuals who left under more than one kind of arrangement, such as two married couples from Cáceres recruited to go to Florida in 1563. In addition, people who belonged to some of the larger groupings, such as the 1535 contingent to Santo Domingo or the 1540 group to Tierra Firme and elsewhere, have been counted as individuals traveling alone because there is no basis other than surmise or intuition for categorizing them as recruits, although they probably were.

Despite these problems the scheme still shows clearly that the majority of emigrants did not travel alone, especially after around 1540, but were accompanied by family or relatives, friends, ser-

TABLE 8 Modes of Travel for Emigrants, Cáceres

	To 1510	1511–1520	1521–1530	1531–1540	1541–1550	1551–1560	1561–1570	1571–1580	1581–1590	1591–1600
Alone	3	36	7	60	2	7	8	1		1
As merchant/factor	2		9	6		1	2			
Recruited							7(2)[a]	5		
As criado	1	1		1	5	13	14	16	1	1
With spouse				2(1)		5(2)	2	2(1)		
With children (with or without spouse)				4(2)		4(2)		6(3)		
With parents			5	5(3)		5	3(2)	12(7)		
With other relative(s)					3(2)	6		6(2)		4(1)
With other person	1	1	3	3	5	4		5	1	
Joining relatives		2			4	6	3	12		

[a] Number in ( ) indicates the number of women in the total figure.

TABLE 9 Modes of Travel for Emigrants, Trujillo

	To 1510	1511–1520	1521–1530	1531–1540	1541–1550	1551–1560	1561–1570	1571–1580	1581–1590	1591–1600
Alone	1	15	30	105(4)[a]	9	13	14(1)	10(1)	1	3(1)
As merchant/factor	1	1	16	9	4	7	4			
Recruited				1		1		3		
As criado			2(1)			26(3)[b]	24(3)	19(7)		6(1)
With spouse						6(3)	2(1)	8(4)	3(1)	4(2)
With children (with or without spouse)				5(2)		9(3)	20(8)	48(24)	11(5)	16(9)
With parents			1	11(4)		12(4)	26(7)	47(18)	1	44(23)
With other relative(s)			11	14		6(2)	11(7)	21(15)	3	4(2)
With other person			4	8	1	2	8	10	2	
Joining relatives			3	6		8(4)	8	27(7)	9(2)	2

[a] Number in ( ) indicates the number of women in the total figure.
[b] Includes one married couple.

vants, or slaves, or were themselves employed as servants, formed part of an entourage, or were recruited for some expedition. Emigrants who might in fact have made the journey alone often intended to join relatives already in the New World. Others, whose arrangements for the journey are not known, once in the Indies associated so closely with relatives or other extremeños that we could reasonably assume that they had either traveled together or expected to join each other. Some individuals who appeared in the passenger lists by themselves, such as a woman with the title "doña," never would have traveled alone. All these factors negate the image of the lone venturer setting off for the unknown. Such individuals no doubt existed, but after 1540 they were a minority among emigrants.

The figures in the tables show that women began to take their place among emigrants after 1530 and became a substantial presence after 1550, mostly traveling with spouses and families or other relatives, or as criadas. The increasing number of family units moving to the Indies went hand-in-hand with the growing numbers of women, as would be expected. A total of 56 families, accounting for 253 people or 27 percent of the entire group, left Trujillo, most of them after 1550; 13 families with 56 people, or about 14 percent of the total group, left Cáceres, a notably smaller percentage. Despite the smaller proportion of families in the Cáceres group, however, from both cities the volume of emigration of families was sufficiently large to constitute a significant element in the demographic composition of the movement, giving further weight to the argument that relatively few emigrants, especially after midcentury, were unattached individuals.

Exactly why the number of families leaving Cáceres was proportionately a good bit lower cannot be determined, of course. Perhaps the best explanation is the one offered at the beginning of the chapter, that the greater size of the Trujillo group in itself generated significant differences. The larger volume of emigration would have a kind of snowball effect, encouraging more people to consider such a major undertaking as uprooting and moving an entire family. The larger number of emigrants who had preceded the trujillanos also meant an increased likelihood that they would have relatives or friends in the Indies to help them make a new start. At least fifteen of the Trujillo families intended to join relatives—

parents, siblings, an aunt, uncle, or cousin—and one accompanied
the wife's father back to Mexico where he had already been living
for a number of years. Furthermore a fairly large number—almost
a fifth—of the heads of family were artisans, and Licenciado Diego
Gonzalez Altamirano went to Peru to serve on the audiencia; so it
appears that many of the families from the start anticipated a reasonably secure future at the end of the journey, based on assistance
from relatives or the possibility of establishing a trade. Less is
known of the Cáceres group, which included two farmers among
the heads of family and Licenciado Diego García de Valverde, who
went to New Granada in 1557 to serve as *fiscal* (treasurer) of the
audiencia, accompanied by his wife, son, nephew, sister, and possibly a brother, as well as five criados, two of them from Cáceres.[19]

It should be becoming clear that the recruitment of emigrants
took a number of forms, from the personal recruitment of individuals and families by relatives already in the Indies, to the more
formal employment of criados by a potential emigrant, or to organized, official or semiofficial efforts to attract individuals to relatively unknown destinations. Some movements, like the group that
accompanied the viceroy to Peru in 1555, comprised more than one
of these elements. Table 10 summarizes information about the
large group that went to New Spain from Trujillo in the 1570s. The
table actually begins with 1568 because the departure for New
Spain in that year of Gonzalo de las Casas, the wealthy son of the
encomendero of Yanhuitlan (southeast of Mexico City), probably
was a key event. His father, Francisco de las Casas, was a cousin of
Cortés who was present in Mexico from at least 1523, returning to
visit Spain for a year in 1526. Gonzalo became his heir in 1536, at
which time he might have been living in Mexico. When he left
Trujillo in 1568 he took with him three sons by two different
women.[20]

In what sense was Gonzalo's move significant? As did other
prominent individuals, he probably directly and indirectly attracted his fellow townspeople to follow. He served as *fiador* (guarantor) for the carpenter Andrés Hernández, who went to Mexico in
1580 with his wife and children, an apprentice, and his nephew
Alonso Sánchez, also a carpenter.[21] He also might have been responsible for persuading the famous Trujillo master stonecutter
and architect, Francisco Becerra, who had worked on las Casas's

TABLE 10 *Emigrants from Trujillo to New Spain, 1568–1580*

Date	Name	Occupation	Accompanied by	Relation-ship	Accompanying	Joining	No. in Party[a]
1568	Gonzalo de las Casas	encomendero	Don Francisco Don Andrés Pedro Suárez	son son son			4
1568	Francisco de Robledo		wife, children, criada				4
1571	Gracia Hernández		two daughters (natives of Medellín)				1
1573	Toribia Alonso		Juan	son			2
1573	Francisco Becerra	master stone-cutter, architect	Juana González de Vergara (from Garciaz)	wife	Licenciado Alonso Granero de Avalos, Inquisitor of Mexico (from Plasencia)		1
1573	Martín Casillas	stonecutter			Francisco Becerra		1
1573	Alonso Pablos	stonecutter			Francisco Becerra		
1573	Diego Martín	barber	Isabel García Juan de Ribera Alonso	wife son son			3
1574	Diego de Nodera (refused license?)	master stonecutter	Mari Sánchez apprentice criada	wife			2

Year	Head	Occupation	Member	Relationship	Note	Count
1574	Hernando de Cuevas	priest	Ana González de Cuevas	sister		3
			María González	criada		
1574	Catalina de Cuevas		Gaspar de Contreras	son	Juan de Contreras (husband) (son)	8
			Juan de Contreras	son		
			Alonso de Cuevas	son		
			Diego	son		
			Antonia	daughter		
			Estefanía	daughter		
			Isabel de Olmos	criada		
1574	Hernán González	blacksmith (*herrador*)	Leonor Gómez	wife	Francisco Gómez (Leonor's uncle)	3
				son		
1574	Andrés Hernández	blacksmith (*herrero*)	Teresa Alvarez	wife		4
			María Rodríguez	sister		
			Catalina González	criada		
1574	Francisco Jiménez	shoemaker	Inés García	wife		6
			Isabel	daughter		
			Teresa	daughter		
			Juana González	sister-in-law		
			apprentice			
1574	Catalina de Carvajal	criada				1

TABLE 10 (cont.)

Date	Name	Occupation	Accompanied by	Relationship	Accompanying	Joining	No. in Party[a]
1575	Cristóbal Hernández Tripa		Teresa González Pedro Hernández Tripa Hernando Bejarano Alvaro Rodríguez Chacón Ana	wife son son son daughter	Alvaro Rodríguez Chacón (father-in-law)		6
1575	Hernán González		Mari Hernández children	wife	Cristóbal Hernández Tripa (brother)		4
1575	Alvaro Rodríguez Chacón (returning)	merchant	Cristóbal Martín Luis González Alvaro Chacón	son son son			4
1575	Hernando González	blacksmith (herrador)	Teresa González Elvira Antonia Juan Delvas	wife daughter daughter son			5
1575	Alonso Ramiro	tailor	Inés García Alonso Francisco Pedro	wife son son son			5

Date	Name	Occupation	Relatives / companions		Associated person
1576	Pedro Alonso				
1576	Juan de Belvis		wife and children		
			criada		
1576	Juan de Plasencia	carpenter, criado	(Bartolomé Rodríguez, brother)		Alberto de Orozco
1576	Bartolomé Rodríguez	criado	(Juan de Plasencia)		Diego Ortiz de Anda (of Medinaceli)
1576	Gómez de Ocaña	criado			Don Rodrigo de Vivero
1576	Alonso González	criado			
1577	Juan Ramiro	priest			Alonso Ramiro (brother; to Mexico, 1575)
1577	Isabel García		Inés	daughter	Alonso de Girona (husband)
			María	daughter	
			Isabel	daughter	
			Hernán García	brother	
			Juana Rodríguez	criada	
1577	Bach. Alvar García Calderón	priest	Francisco Díaz (from Jaraicejo, nephew of Isabel García, above)		
1577	Lorenzo del Puerto	shoemaker	Francisca de Gironda	wife	
			María	daughter	

TABLE 10 (cont.)

Date	Name	Occupation	Accompanied by	Relation-ship	Accompanying	Joining	No. in Party[a]
1577	Cristóbal Rodrí-guez		Inés González Juana María González	wife daughter sister-in-law			4
1578	Juan Rubio		Juana González 5 children	wife		Alonso González, priest (brother of Juana González; to Mexico, 1576)	7
1578	Alonso Blanco	former inn-keeper	3 daughters son			Martín Blanco, priest (relative, from Cabeza del Buey)	5
1578	Isabel García la Castra		Isabel García la Cuaca five children	sister		Francisco García (their half-brother)	7
1578	Fabían Hernández (received license but did not go)		wife children				
1580	Andrés Hernán-dez	carpenter	wife children apprentice Alonso Sánchez, carpenter	nephew			5

[a] Number in party from Trujillo

house on the plaza in Trujillo, to leave Spain for Mexico. Once established in Mexico, las Casas had called for Spanish artisans to come to work on the convent of Yanhuitlan. Becerra, in turn, in 1573 either took with him or attracted soon after two young men (Alonso Pablos and Martín Casillas) who had been his apprentices in Trujillo.[22] He might also have been partly responsible for the apparently thwarted attempt of Diego de Nodera, another master stonecutter, to obtain a license for the same destination the following year; certainly Nodera and Becerra knew each other and had worked together in Trujillo.[23]

Another pivotal event in this decade was the return to Trujillo of Alvaro Rodríguez Chacón. He first went to Mexico around 1550 (perhaps a little earlier), leaving behind his children by his first wife, who had died. In New Spain he had remarried; he was "casado y arraigado." He returned in late 1574, according to his statement and that of other witnesses, for the sole purpose of taking back his children "por estar pobres y sin remedio." His arrival in Trujillo also set off a kind of chain reaction. He obtained permission to take back his three sons, along with two servants. His daughter Teresa González had married and had four children of her own, and she and her family all decided to go. Her husband, Cristóbal Hernández Tripa, explained that his father-in-law would pay their passage because he was rich. Last, Cristóbal Hernández's brother Hernán González, also apparently at loose ends and with few means of his own, asked permission for him and his family to accompany his brother, claiming that the latter was in a position to help them. González was married to a woman from Plasencia, where they had lived after their marriage with her parents, later moving to Trujillo and living with his parents. Witnesses described them as being poor and without property or goods of any kind.[24]

The group that moved to New Spain in the 1570s, then, is of interest because it is possible to see how different forms of recruitment functioned and often reinforced each other. Alonso González, a priest who went to Mexico in 1576, almost immediately sent home for his sister and her husband and children, authorizing them to collect the 42 ducados a man in Trujillo owed him to help defray their passage. In his letters, one of which he sent with a criado of Gonzalo de las Casas, he told them that although New Spain was not quite what it had been, anyone willing to work could earn a

living. A witness for the *información* (testimonial) of his brother-in-
law in Trujillo in 1578 said that he had heard González had a
capellanía and was doing fairly well ("medianamente") even though
he had only been there a short time. Juan Rubio and his wife said
they were extremely poor and that their total worth was no more
than 60 ducados. They made a living by selling wine for a innkeeper, receiving 1 real per pitcher, and their older children
helped out by hauling firewood.[25]

In contrast to the informal mechanisms that operated to attract
people from Trujillo to New Spain in the 1570s, official recruitment
and organization must have been responsible for the eighteen
young men from Trujillo and its pueblos who went to Santa Marta
in 1536.[26] The group included one pair of brothers, and many
among them went on to Peru. Lucas Vázquez de Ayllón apparently
recruited people in the region for his expedition to Florida in 1563,
attracting seven cacereños (two married couples), a man from Casar
de Cáceres, and two from Berzocana.[27] The recruitment of a number of people from Cáceres and nearby towns to go to the Philippines in 1578 is of much interest because it is the only case for the
region in which the process by which official or formal recruitment
took place is known in some detail.

In 1578 the king appointed don Gonzalo Ronquillo de Peñalosa
captain-general and governor of the Philippines, in which post he
succeeded a cacereño, Dr. Francisco de Sande, whose governorship had begun in 1575. Despite its brevity, Sande's tenure in that
office was significant, because the islands had already attracted
several cacereños before the recruitment effort of 1578. This precedent surely encouraged some people to respond.[28] In July 1578
Ronquillo de Peñalosa received royal authorization to take at his
own cost 600 men, 200 of them married, from Spain to the Philippines, via Panama. He was told not to bother obtaining informaciones for these people in order to speed the process of gather-
ing recruits. The following month he named Señor Agustín de
Arceo of Segovia captain, charged with finding recruits and accompanying them to the Philippines. The language used was military,
although the royal cédula explicitly prohibited Ronquillo from assuming the privileges of a military recruiter; he was not to request
or demand lodging, play military instruments, or raise a flag. Arceo
was to "go with said company of people raised in this way . . . to

serve His Majesty in populating the said islands . . . and accompany [them] until they embark from the port of San Lúcar de Barrameda." He was authorized to name whatever officials he might need before arriving at San Lúcar and then "to designate the persons who seem most suitable as ensign [*alférez*] and sergeants for the said company."[29]

Calling himself "captain-elect to raise . . . people in this villa and Trujillo and Badajoz and Plasencia and their jurisdictions and other parts of their district for the Philippines," Augustín de Arceo in turn signed a power of attorney in Cáceres in October 1578 naming Benito Sánchez of Arroyo del Puerco (a town formerly in Cáceres's termino) as his sergeant. Sánchez was authorized to recruit and register people and make the appropriate agreements. The following month Arceo, saying he wished to leave Cáceres in order to proceed with the expedition and with those "soldiers" already registered in Cáceres and other places, gave power of attorney to a vecino of Cáceres to complete the arrangements for those whose licenses were not yet in order. The actual terms of the contracts were not specified; but since all the men included in the register of the Casa de Contratación were listed as carrying arms of some sort, presumably the recruits agreed to provide their own arms in return for their passage and probably some guarantee of support or assistance once they reached their destination.[30]

The expedition as a whole included some 233 single and 56 married men, the majority of whom came from the central and western regions of the peninsula—Castile, la Mancha, and Extremadura. There were 8 men from Cáceres proper, half of them married, 5 from Caesar de Cáceres, and 1 each from Sierra de Fuentes, Aldea del Cano, and Casas de Don Antonio (a village near Cáceres, although not under its jurisdiction), forming a fairly sizable local contingent within the total group.[31] The cacereños included a pair of brothers, and three of the married couples had children. Most of the men on the expedition, including the cacereños, were in their twenties. For the married men especially emphasis seems to have been placed on attracting people with skills, and twenty-three different occupations were represented. The 4 married men from Cáceres were farmers, the most common occupation among the group as a whole.

Responding to an organized recruitment campaign for some

little-known destination no doubt was a much riskier proposition than setting off for the more secure centers of Spanish settlement, and one wonders what promises or expectations persuaded people to join some of these ventures. In the case of the 1578 Philippines expedition, at least one ship went down soon after departure, and it is not known if the cacereños ever reached their destination. Two brothers who set off for "la China" in 1575 did not even survive the trip across Mexico.[32]

Another risky undertaking was Francisco de Orellana's 1545 expedition to explore the Amazon river. Despite its ultimate (if qualified) success—a small group did complete the journey downriver and reached Isla Margarita off the Venezuela coast—the venture was in most senses a disaster from the outset. Orellana, a relative of the Pizarros, had been in the Indies for perhaps fifteen years before joining Gonzalo Pizarro's expedition to "la Canela" in 1541. The chronicler of that expedition, Fray Gaspar de Carvajal, also from Trujillo, credited Orellana with exceptional linguistic abilities; he was able to learn and understand Indian languages with ease.[33] Trying to find food, Orellana separated from Pizarro, got lost, and could not get back to the main expeditionary party. He arrived in Cubagua in September 1542, and by mid-May of 1543 was at the court in Valladolid in Spain, where after some months he got the capitulacion for the discovery of "Nueva Andalucía."

From the start Orellana experienced difficulties in organizing and financing the expedition. His stepfather, Cosme de Chaves, came to his aid by selling 30,000 maravedís in rents (juros or censos) to raise 1100 ducados for him, but this hardly sufficed.[34] Despite shortcomings in preparations, Orellana, accompanied by his wife, Ana de Ayala (whom he had married in Seville), Diego García de Paredes, and others from Trujillo and elsewhere, set out in 1545; but the group had to linger five months in the Canaries and Cabo Verde islands, where nearly a hundred people died and another fifty stayed behind. They also lost the ship carrying the brigantine they planned to use on the river itself. Once they got there, many more died of hunger on the river, and Orellana himself died in November 1546. Only twenty-five men, including Diego García de Paredes, and Orellana's widow, who lived on into the 1570s in Panama, reached Isla Margarita.[35] Extremeños considering ventures to exotic and unknown places could reflect upon the remarkable success of the Pizarros and their followers, as well as the deprivations and disappointments of Orellana's expedition to the Amazon.

Financing the Move

To this point discussion of emigration has indicated the variety of contexts in which extremeños emigrated and some of the factors that operated to attract them to one destination or another—the presence of relatives or acquaintances who had preceded them, the departure of officials or prominent individuals for certain places, and formal recruitment. It has also pointed to some of the ways emigrants financed their passage. The terms on which they left, the financial and personal arrangements made before departure, and the type and amount of assistance emigrants received naturally varied considerably, but all emigrants faced the same problem: how to pay for the journey. Certainly the costs were far from negligible. The price of passage alone to Veracruz (New Spain) or Nombre de Dios (Panama) rose from around 7 to 9 ducados in 1536, to twice that by midcentury, to 18 to 22 ducados in 1580. The additional cost of provisions could increase expenses by 35 to 50 percent; so by 1580 the total cost of the journey per adult passenger was somewhere between 30 and 40 ducados (11,250 to 15,000 maravedís). Purchase of cabin space meant another additional expense. In 1555 a cabin for four adults, two children, and their baggage on a ship to Nombre de Dios cost 80 ducados (30,000 maravedís).[36]

How, then, did emigrants finance the journey? Those who had something to sell often did so, or if necessary and possible, they borrowed money. Young hidalgo men might sell off rents or borrow from their siblings, whereas commoners, with more limited means at their disposal, might sell part of a house or vineyard or the like.[37] Many people left in debt to relatives or acquaintances, but most were confident they would soon be able to make good on these loans. Cristóbal de Ovando Paredes, member of a noble family who later became one of the wealthiest returnees in Cáceres, left for Peru in 1560 owing an older brother a fairly substantial 152,958 maravedís (over 400 ducados).[38] Antonio de Cotrina received 100 ducados from his mother at the time he first went to the Indies in

1557 as a criado of Licenciado García de Valverde. Clearly the investment paid off, because on a subsequent trip to the New World Cotrina took his brother Juan with him at his own expense, as well as a servant.[39] Yet another returnee to Cáceres, Tomás Casco, said he had received 15,000 maravedís and other assistance from Elvira Cotrina which enabled him to make his trip in 1540. He repaid the debt and gave her a portion of the profits of his sojourn.[40]

Relatives in the New World not only sent back money for the journey but often made all the arrangements for the trip. The two brothers of Francisco Gutiérrez, a farmer from Cáceres who had moved to Albuquerque, sent money for the passage for Gutiérrez and his family to join them in Puebla de los Angeles; they also arranged for him to purchase a black slave for the family's service and sent instructions for obtaining a license in Seville.[41] Juan Carrasco, a native of Zorita (in Trujillo's jurisdiction) living in Peru, gave his power of attorney to Francisco Calderón de Tapia, who was leaving Peru in 1581 for a visit to Spain, to bring back his wife and children. Francisco Calderón, originally from Trujillo, brought back his own children as well.[42] Antonio Gutiérrez Bejarano and his wife, Mari Rodríguez, from Cáceres and Trujillo, who were living in the port of Paita near San Miguel de Piura in Peru, in 1568 sent 42 ducados to three men in Seville, asking one to bring their two daughters to Peru. Their daughters, aged seventeen and nineteen, had been living in Seville with their maternal grandmother since their parents' departure fifteen years or so previously. One of them had married, and her husband decided to accompany them to Peru.[43] Examples of these kinds of arrangements abound in the documents.

Some emigrants were fortunate enough to have sufficient means at their disposal not only to finance the journey but to provide themselves with at least a modest stake as well. A member of one of Cáceres's noble families, Alonso de Torres, was a minor when in 1561 he decided to emigrate, stating that his "aim and desire always has been to go to the Indies and seek my fortune and gain with which better to serve God, our Lord, and his Majesty." He secured his father's permission to go and his consent to release the portion of the inheritance owed him from his mother. Torres received his legacy of 350 ducados from his father, 100 of which he invested in several types of cloth.[44] Rodrigo Bravo, who first went to Peru in 1555 as a criado of the viceroy, applied for a license to return to Peru in 1571 asking to take 800 ducados free of duty "because he is taking them in cloth and merchandise and other things."[45] Again, the documents furnish other such examples.

As has been suggested before, service as a criado was a common way to finance the journey. Virtually every emigrant of any means at all took along at least one criado, and many took more than one. Important officials in particular took numbers of them. Diego de Vargas Carvajal, appointed "Comisario de Perpetuidad" to gather information about encomiendas in Peru in 1560, took with him ten criados from Trujillo, among them a pair of brothers and a married couple with a child, and one from Madrigalejo (one of Trujillo's towns), in addition to seven other criados from Plasencia, Ledesma, Las Brozas, Benavente, Córdoba, and Salamanca. Two of his sons also went with him.[46] Licenciado Antonio Gutiérrez de Ulloa, the inquisitor of Lima, took six criados from Cáceres—one of them a priest, who was accompanied by his nephew—and two others to Peru in 1570.[47] Once there, the inquisitor and his brother Juan Gutiérrez de Ulloa, who had joined him, sent back to Cáceres for Juan del Valle. According to Valle's father, the boy's mother "grew up in the house and service of Licenciado Antonio Gutiérrez de Ulloa . . . and said Juan [his son] served Juan Gutiérrez de Ulloa, brother of the inquisitor." In 1578 Juan del Valle said they had sent for him "to favor me."[48]

Unfortunately there is little evidence on the kinds of arrangements made between servants and their employers, since these were surely made informally. Usually it is impossible to know whether a criado had been in the service of his employer previously or not.[49] In the only real contract between an employer and a criado found, Diego Martín Barquero of Cáceres agreed to accompany cacereño Martín de Figueroa to "las Indias de Petumel" and then to serve him for two months after their arrival. Figueroa agreed to pay his servant's passage and provide him food and drink, and in return Diego Martín would serve him in whatever was necessary and "be willing and honest."[50] Figueroa's stipulation that his criado serve him for two months once they got to the Indies is perhaps telling. It is unlikely that many of the people who went to the New World as servants retained that status for long with so many opportunities at hand. While patterns of deference hardly disappeared once people had crossed the Atlantic, the circumstances in which emigrants found themselves often modified the patron—client relationship considerably. A cacereño named Alvaro de Cáceres, a leading citizen of Puebla de los Angeles and successful entrepreneur involved in the cacao trade with Guatemala and Soconusco, accompanied a Señor Francisco de Ovando (also from Cáceres) on his first trip to New Spain. While clearly Alvaro de Cáceres soon ceased to be primarily Ovando's criado, their connection endured even as it changed. In testimony of 1573 witnesses stated that Ovando had stayed in Cáceres's house in Puebla before departing for the "tierra nueva" and that Cáceres had provided his patron with clothing and other necessities.[51]

Preparations for Departure

After figuring out how to finance their passage to the New World, most emigrants had to make other preparations before leaving, such as arranging for the care of children left behind, the administration of properties, or the payment or collection of rents or debts owed or due to them. Before leaving they signed over their powers of attorney, often to relatives but frequently to friends or *procuradores de causas* (solicitors) to handle their affairs. Some emigrants assigned their power of attorney (poder) to more than one individual, and might continue to do so after establishing themselves in America, so that poderes proliferated almost to the point of chaos. A cacereño named Jerónimo Holguín, who was in Peru in the 1550s, 1560s, and 1570s, had at least seven different men handling his affairs in Cáceres, with one at times straightening out business mismanaged by another.[52]

As was true for many other aspects of the move to America, arrangements emigrants made could take the form of legal contracts and transactions executed before notaries, or they might be made through informal agreements with relatives or friends. Seldom did extremeños execute wills before departing, although they might formalize certain provisions for inheritance before they left—transfers of property, specification of who would receive what portion of an estate, or the like. Juan Gómez of Trujillo, who lived in the huertas of las Alamedas, gave his brother power of attorney so that he could enjoy any income from his property in the huertas while he was away and inherit his property if he failed to return.[53] In another instance don Jerónimo de Ocampo in 1575 decided to prepare a will before leaving for the "conquest" of the Philippines. He directed that, in the event of his death, rents should be bought from the "estate which I acquire and earn in the Indies" to pay for a weekly mass to be recited in the family chapel in the monastery of San Francisco. He also said his father had given him everything he needed for the journey, and he made his parents his heirs. Member of a noble family, Ocampo was one of many younger sons hoping to find his place outside Cáceres and Spain.[54]

One of the most detailed sets of instructions for the management of property and children was left by Gonzalo de Valencia, a vecino of Trujillo who owned property in Madroñera. When he and his wife left for Peru in 1551 they decided not to take their children. He placed their son in the care of his brother Amaro de Torres and his wife, and his daughter joined the household of Alonso Ruiz, the returnee from Peru who acquired the señorío of Madroñera a few years later. Valencia authorized his brothers Alonso de Valencia and Amaro de Torres to rent out his house and yard in Madroñera and to collect a censo of 5000 maravedís, to be used to feed and care for his children after settling a debt he owed to a Trujillo merchant. Another house he owned in Madroñera, next to his father's, he designated for his brother Alonso de Valencia's use, provided he did not turn it into a stable and that he let Amaro de Torres stay there when he came to Madroñera to harvest his wheat.[55]

It was not at all unusual for parents to leave children behind, especially young ones, or they might take only their older children. They would place children with relatives or in a noble household, perhaps in the hopes that, once established, they would be able to send for them, as did the couple living in Paita who sent for their two daughters in Seville. Regardless of the intentions of their parents, however, such children could have a difficult time, since in effect they became orphans, often wholly dependent on the generosity of relatives or the service they provided to the households that accepted them for their survival. Felipe Rodríguez, a silversmith, and his wife went to Peru, probably in the 1550s, leaving their son Rodrigo Alonso de Boroa in Trujillo. He asked for a license to join his father in 1570, saying his father was wealthy and had sent for him via a merchant (Baltasar Díaz, a native of Albuquerque) who was returning to Peru. Witnesses described Rodrigo Alonso as "very poor and needy, alone and abandoned."[56] Andrés Gómez, a tailor married to a woman from Madroñera who asked to go to Peru in 1577, said that when his parents went to Peru (again, probably in the 1550s), they left him "en poder de un caballero que se llamaba Diego López de Ribadeneyra" because he was too young to go. He apparently had had little contact with his parents since that time and did not know if his father was living.[57]

Other parents, of course, continued to show concern for their children. Inés Alonso Cervera, who left several young children in Trujillo and in the 1570s was a wealthy widow living in Lima, sent for her son, García de Escobar, and his family and urged her daughters to come as well. In a letter of 1578 she said she had sent 700 reales for Escobar and one of his sisters in the last fleet and was sending another 40 ducados for them. She had left one or more of her daughters with her aunt and worried that this aunt would do little to help them: "I understand that she is fed up with doing things for me, because I've seen from experience that since I've been here, I haven't had one word from her, and by your [her son's] letters I've seen how little she did for my daughter Juana Gutiérrez." The recipient of these letters, her son, in 1578 petitioned to go to Peru with his family and possibly one of his unmarried sisters, and another sister also planned to go with her husband, who stated that he had never received a dowry and his mother-in-law was rich.[58] Another emigrant, Pedro Alonso Carrasco, a native of Zorita and long-time resident of Cuzco, arranged for his daughter to marry his nephew but apparently never sent the dowry, although he often had sent money and letters to his daughter and son in Zorita in the past. In 1567 his son-in-law asked to go to Peru to collect the promised dowry of 5000 pesos.[59]

Not only children but women as well could be left "desamparada" by absent husbands. A pharmacist from Cáceres named Juan de Ervás apparently made no provision for his family when he went to the Indies. His brother Francisco Alvarez, a vecino of Llerena, had 6000 maravedís that Ervás had left to cover a debt. In 1569 a notary of Cáceres asked Alvarez to give the money to Ervás's wife, Elvira Baez, "to maintain her and her children because of their great need." The notary said that if Juan de Ervás returned and decided that the money should not have gone to his family, he himself would repay it. Elvira Baez's son, Fray Hernando de Ervás, seems to have taken his family's welfare more to heart; he sent his mother 870 ducados from Lima in 1575.[60]

Social Composition and Family

The stories of some potential emigrants or of the families they left behind, told by themselves or by people who knew them, raise the question of the social and economic status of the people who left. Were emigrants broadly representative of their home society? Did certain factors tied to social and economic organization and structures make it more likely that some people would leave and others stay? The discussion of society and emigration in Extremadura to this point certainly indicates a positive response to these questions; nonetheless it is worthwhile to consider specifically how the information on emigrants supports such conclusions.

Virtually all the literature on sixteenth-century Spanish emigration and on the formation of society in Spanish America points to the fact that Spaniards from many ranks of society and a wide range of occupational groupings went to the Indies almost from the very beginning. It was only at the extremes of the socioeconomic spectrum—the highest-ranking and wealthiest nobles, or the paupers at the bottom of society—that participation was very limited. The study of emigration from Cáceres and Trujillo substantiates this picture. The absence of extremes, however, should not be taken to mean that neither hidalgos nor people who were in genuine economic difficulty went to the New World. But in a sense the wide and varied spectrum that ranged from the younger son of a noble family to the artisan struggling against poverty who might be fortunate enough to have a relative in the Indies to help him out constituted the middle classes of Spanish society and the source of the great majority of emigrants to the New World. At the very extremes, the wealthy nobles did not need to leave, and the true paupers were so marginal they had no possibility of leaving. Those who found the means to emigrate and did so were all united in one respect: they were looking for a chance to better their condition in life, and they had some possibility of doing so, whether because of position, connections, skills, or simply being in the right place at the right time.

They were united in another sense as well. They were, for the most part, working men and women, and even the hidalgos among them were used to a life of physical activity. Given their experience and the life to which they were accustomed, they were prepared to withstand the discomforts, dangers, and tedium of a major relocation to a degree that in retrospect appears rather astonishing.

Hidalgos not only were present in some numbers among the emigrants, but they often played a leadership role, taking entourages of family and retainers and acting as centers of attraction for other emigrants to follow, as did Gonzalo de las Casas when he went to New Spain to succeed to his father's encomienda in 1568. A number of hidalgos actually went to the Indies as officials of the state or church, and an official royal appointment naturally reinforced and enhanced their authority and prestige and role as patrons. The representation of hidalgos in the emigrant group overall was substantial. From Trujillo at least 12 percent and Cáceres nearly 22 percent of the emigrants were hidalgos, and possibly around 10 percent of the emigrants from Trujillo's pueblos were also. These figures include only those people whose hidalguía can be established clearly from the documentation.[61]

The difference in representation of hidalgos in the Cáceres and Trujillo groups to some extent may reflect the rather distinct structure and composition of the two cities. Cáceres had a high percentage of hidalgos among its population compared to other extremeño cities, perhaps as high as 17 percent.[62] While Trujillo shared Cáceres's reputation of being home to many nobles and hidalgos, there exists a general and not exactly quantifiable impression that Trujillo's nobles on the whole (not taken individually) were not quite so noble (that is, wealthy and powerful) as those of Cáceres.[63] While this last suggestion certainly could be disputed, the early and enthusiastic participation of members of some of Cáceres's most prominent noble families in the Indies is undeniable and no doubt set an important precedent. The role of Frey Nicolás de Ovando, governor of Hispaniola from 1502–1509, has already been mentioned. If the cacereños did not produce a leader comparable to Francisco Pizarro, the Trujillo group on the other hand could not offer anything that compared to a trio like Francisco de Godoy, Lorenzo de Aldana, and Perálvarez Holguín—three first cousins from important families of Cáceres, all of whom were in Peru in the

1530s and 1540s and participated in the civil wars—or others such as Antonio de Ulloa, Gómez de Solís, and Hernando de Moraga. The Pizarros were hidalgos but not nearly of the same rank; only one daughter—the youngest—of Captain Gonzalo Pizarro (the patriarch of the family) was addressed as doña, whereas all the cacereño hidalgos just mentioned were sons of women who used the title and belonged to families that traditionally held seats on the city council. Gonzalo Pizarro's references in his letters to Lorenzo de Aldana especially and to other nobles from Cáceres express a certain deference, and he seems to have taken pride in being associated with individuals of their status.[64] Since the early noble emigrants from Cáceres to the Indies attracted or by their example encouraged family members to follow them, the contribution of noble families to the emigration movement was notable throughout the sixteenth century.[65] The participation of the Trujillo nobility seems to have begun later and never reached the same levels, although certainly there were families such as the Loaysas whose involvement in Peru was comparable to that of cacereño families.

Consideration of hidalgo participation leads to the question of the relevance of family structure and position within the family to the decision to emigrate. The standard image of younger sons going off to the Indies corresponds to the realities of the noble family, which increasingly emphasized preservation of family fortune and titles in the direct male line. The corollary to this strategy was the assumption that other sons would seek other careers, and these often took them away from home. Emigration to America soon came to figure significantly among the options available to younger sons, and this was true as well for illegitimate children who also usually found only limited opportunities at home. In his will of 1575 don Diego de Ovando de Cáceres, who had no legitimate children, placed his illegitimate son Hernando de Ovando under the guardianship of his (don Diego's) brother and heir, don Francisco de Torres. Don Francisco de Torres was to administer Hernando's legacy of 300 ducados, which his father said he must use to travel to the Indies, go to war in the king's service, or establish himself in the house of some nobleman, and for no other purpose.[66] Francisco Pizarro and Diego García de Paredes (son of the famous military hero of the same name) are two of the best-known illegitimate sons who left Trujillo hoping to find better opportunities in the New World, and the list of younger sons of hidalgo families of both cities who did the same is long indeed. Fray Jerónimo de Loaysa, the first bishop and archbishop of Lima, was himself a younger son in one of Trujillo's noble families.

While inheritance and family position played an important part in determining who among the hidalgo group might emigrate, nonetheless the classic formula of second (and younger) sons going off to seek their fortunes cannot explain everything about the emigration of hidalgos. Personal preferences and decisions often played a part and mitigated what otherwise might appear to be a kind of socioeconomic determinism. Surely some people with no strong economic impetus for leaving responded to the appeal of adventure (especially in the early years) and the successes of friends or relatives who had gone before them. Hernando de Moraga Galindo from Cáceres was reputed to have left behind considerable wealth, but supposedly for reasons having to do with some personal involvement he preferred to remain in the Indies.[67] Gómez de Solís, captain in the civil wars and a wealthy encomendero in Peru, clearly had little interest in returning to Cáceres either. His father tried to lure him back home, bypassing his eldest son to promise Gómez the family entail established in 1555 should he return and purchasing a seat on the city council for him. But eventually both Gómez and his younger brother Juan de Hinojosa, also in Peru, renounced all claims to the family legacy in favor of their older brother.[68] Hernando Pizarro, the only legitimate son of his father, Captain Gonzalo Pizarro, set off for Peru with his illegitimate half-brothers, guessing quite correctly, as events proved, that the family's future lay outside Trujillo and across the Atlantic.

Just as economic motivation cannot be reduced to a question of who inherited and who did not (Francisco de Godoy, who returned very wealthy from Peru in the 1540s, also inherited his father's entail), neither can social position in itself explain the decisions made by individuals. Andrés Calderón Puertocarrero, a noble and mayorazgo, apparently called himself a merchant when he went off to Peru in 1562. Subsequent testimony regarding a murder he committed in Peru indicates that he might have lost or squandered much of his inheritance;[69] therefore, in his case, economic motivations probably overrode social conventions that held that direct involvement in commerce was antithetical to noble status.

Neither do considerations of inheritance and position in the family necessarily account for hidalgo families that as a unit might have been losing the struggle to maintain their economic and social position. Such a situation might have propelled a number of children to leave home, as happened in quite a few instances in Cáceres, where virtually entire generations set off for the New World. In one family five siblings—Hernando Alonso, Gonzalo, Jerónimo, and doña Mencía de los Nidos, and their sister, doña Juana Copete de Sotomayor—all emigrated to Peru in the 1520s, 1530s, and 1540s. Lorenzo de Ulloa, an early settler and encomendero of Trujillo (Peru) and member of a branch of the Ovando family, had three brothers and a sister follow him to Peru.[70] These families and others like them surely were experiencing economic strains. Pedro de Ovando de Saavedra, whose two sons died en route to the Philippines in the 1570s, frankly declared his poverty in his 1577 will, saying he had had many children and very little wealth.[71] Perhaps the only comparable example the Trujillo group offers of large numbers of siblings from an hidalgo family emigrating is that of the Pizarros; but given Francisco's royal authorization and position of leadership, their case was hardly typical.

The prospect of impoverishment or the uncertainty occasioned by the death of one or both parents might have influenced orphans or sons who had recently lost their fathers to emigrate; conversely the death of one or both parents also could provide, through their legacy, the necessary means to finance passage overseas. Bernardino de Moraga, a minor and orphan in 1572, went to Chile in 1578.[72] Both parents of Martín de Chaves had died by the time he left for Peru in 1534 (at which time he might still have been a minor), as had his grandfather, Martín de Chaves, the family patriarch. Two of Chaves's brothers had already left Trujillo by the time he went to Peru, and at least one was in the Indies.[73] The parents of cacereño Miguel Criado Figueroa were also both deceased when he asked for permission to join his brother in Peru in 1578.[74] Another young man from Cáceres named Juan de Vita y Moraga was twenty years old and an orphan in 1574 when he presented an información describing himself as "pobre e hidalgo." He intended to join a maternal uncle in Peru whom he had heard was "very rich and old" and was called "Galindo."[75] He failed to mention his father's brother Pedro de Vita, who had gone to Peru in the 1540s

but possibly was no longer living. Pedro de Vita himself had left
Cáceres in 1546, two years after his own father's death.[76]

Hidalgos facing possible impoverishment or at least economic
strains who decided to emigrate had their counterparts at the other
end of the spectrum of people who left Extremadura for America.
While it probably is true that the most poverty-stricken and marginal people could not have emigrated, it is clear that some emigrants were suffering real economic stress, even allowing for the
standard tendency to exaggerate the severity of economic circumstances. Some examples of what appears to have been genuine
economic hardship have been mentioned already, such as that of
the sister and brother-in-law of Alonso González, the priest who
went to Mexico in 1578; the family subsisted by reselling wine and
delivering firewood. Two sisters in Trujillo named Isabel García la
Castra and Isabel García la Cuaca, who described themselves as
poor spinsters, in 1578 asked to go to New Spain with the five
young children they had between them to join relatives. One witness testified that because they were so poor and already too old to
serve anyone, the only way they could get by would be by running
an inn or tavern or employing themselves in some disreputable
fashion. They had a half-brother, Francisco García, who had gone
to New Spain ten or twelve years before and sent them money
regularly.[77]

A drastic change in economic circumstances led Alonso Blanco,
also a vecino of Trujillo, to ask permission to go to New Spain the
same year with his four children "because of having been a rich and
prominent man . . . and having come to great poverty and need."
Witnesses affirmed that he had been rich ("ha sido hombre rico
y . . . ha tenido muy buena hacienda") and had owned a good
posada (inn), which he had lost six years previously. Blanco had
acted as guarantor for some vecinos of Trujillo who purchased royal
rents. They took off, leaving Blanco to pay. Since he could not, he
was imprisoned and 1400 ducados worth of his property sold, leaving him very poor and forcing him into the service of don Hernando
de Chaves, whom he served as squire for three years. The relative
Blanco planned to join in New Spain was a priest named Martín
Blanco (a vecino of Cabeza del Buey) who had come through
Trujillo about ten years before and said mass in Blanco's house.
Ironically at that time Alonso had given the priest the money he

needed to go to the Indies. Blanco sold his only remaining property, part of a house, to pay for the trip to America.[78]

For other prospective emigrants poverty probably did not make such a sudden and dramatic appearance. There can be no doubt that a substantial sector of the population lived close to the threshold of poverty much of the time, even if they had skills or some property in land or livestock. Andrés Gómez, the tailor whose parents had left him in the household of a nobleman when they went to Peru, was said to be so poor that he had to sew for other artisans to earn his living.[79] Witnesses said that Lorenzo del Puerto, a shoemaker who wanted to take his wife and family to New Spain in 1577, was very poor and slowly losing what little he had because he lacked the necessary capital to invest in his business; without such capital, one witness said, one "dies of hunger."[80] Juan Díaz of Garciaz, the son of a letrado, Bachiller Juan Díaz, in 1584 asked for a license to go to Peru for four years to live with his brother Alvar Sánchez, who was rich and had sent for him. Juan Díaz said he needed the money to support his father, who was poor, and to help marry his sisters.[81]

Still, it must be remembered that people's perceptions of economic threat and poverty could be relative, depending on their own expectations and past experience. Inés de Cabañas, a wealthy native of Trujillo living in Lima in the 1560s and 1570s, wrote to her brother Sancho de Cabañas asking him to come to Peru in 1574, saying it grieved her to hear that he had been forced into service ("me pesó mucho en saber que sirvía a nadie"). Sancho de Cabañas said he was very poor and his only income was 10,000 maravedís yearly which he received from a caballero in Trujillo, which did not suffice to support him, his wife, and child.[82] Baltasar Alvarez, who wanted to go to Peru in 1570 to live with his uncle Diego de Trujillo (the encomendero of Cuzco who had been at Cajamarca) said he was so poor that he "has served in the house of Diego del Saz, merchant."[83] One might suggest that having any kind of steady income or position at all would place individuals like Sancho de Cabañas or Baltasar Alvarez far ahead of those whose livelihood was even less predictable, yet they saw themselves as being in need. Although the majority of potential emigrants provided little or no detail about their economic status or condition, it seems likely that many of them were people who barely managed to keep themselves from poverty and that they saw the move to America as a chance to improve their situation substantially. While some exaggeration probably was involved, it is no coincidence that so many letters from America contained references to misery and economic frustration back home in Spain.

In terms of the hidalgo-commoner distinction, the composition of the emigrant group roughly reflected their distribution in the home society. Beyond that the group differed from local society in general mainly in the ways one would expect, given the nature of the undertaking. Single young men were heavily represented, especially in the earlier decades of the sixteenth century. This is well in keeping with the presumption that young people not yet fully established with household or occupation would be most likely to consider moving as well as a reflection of the relative uncertainty of life in the Indies in the earlier years. With the consolidation of Spanish rule and settlement, the Indies began to attract more women and families by the second half of the century.

The emigrant group also substantiates common-sense perceptions of the circumstances that might motivate some people to emigrate and others not. While members of leading noble families certainly went to America, they seldom did so as family units. The noble who was in a position to marry well and establish a household almost by definition was wealthy or at least had good prospects, in which case he had no motivation to leave. Certainly there were exceptions, especially if there were some strong attraction, as in the case of Gonzalo de las Casas or Francisco de Orellana (of Orellana la Vieja), who went with his wife, doña María de Mendoza from Seville, and children to Peru in 1565 to join his father. His father had been part of the group that went to Santa Marta in 1536 and had been in Peru almost thirty years. Only a few years before, his aunt (his father's sister) and her husband also had gone to Peru, taking their daughter and a criado who probably was a relative.[84] Yet for the most part, with the exception of officials such as Licenciado Diego González Altamirano of Trujillo or Licenciado Diego García de Valverde from Cáceres, the hidalgos among the heads of family who emigrated were from the middle or lower levels of that group, and probably most were relatively poor.

One point that holds for hidalgos and commoners alike is that family ties and considerations were of crucial importance in conveying people to the New World, determining where they would go and when, so much so that the role of family in emigration should be emphasized yet again. Cycles and traditions of emigration developed and operated because of these family ties and strategies. We have seen that when Francisco de Orellana went to Peru in the 1560s he went to join his father and followed his uncle and aunt by a few years. Discussion of emigration has touched on many instances of relatives who emigrated together or went to join others who had preceded them. In addition returnees from the Indies often directly and indirectly encouraged members of the younger generation to go.

The degree of involvement of some families in the Indies could be remarkably high, as in the case of the Castro family of Trujillo. Francisco González de Castro went to the New World as part of the group of young men from Trujillo and elsewhere who left in 1540. In the 1560s he was royal treasurer in Santa Marta and had sent for his nephew Juan de Castro, a pharmacist, to join him since he had never married and had no heirs of his own. Juan de Castro departed for Cartagena in 1569, as did his uncle Pedro de Castro, who left Trujillo with his wife and three children. This was Pedro's second trip, since he had previously been with his brother Francisco in Santa Marta. Two other brothers, Diego González de Castro and Juan de Castro, also were in New Granada. Juan de Castro went there as a merchant in 1555, and Diego probably lived in Popayán, where he returned in 1574. A witness in Trujillo in 1566 said that Francisco's three brothers (Diego, Juan, and Pedro) lived in the interior and one of them had a repartimiento de indios. Subsequently, in 1578, yet another nephew, Alonso de Castro, went to Santa Marta as the criado of the newly appointed bishop.[85] Between the two generations, then, ten members of the family went to Santa Marta and New Granada. A first cousin named Juan de San Juan, a tailor, also was there; he took his wife and son to New Granada in 1555 (the same year Juan de Castro went), but had returned to Trujillo by 1568.[86] This was a family of tradesmen and artisans; one brother of Francisco González de Castro who stayed in Trujillo was a *cerero* (waxmaker), and his brothers-in-law included a tailor, pharmacist, and silversmith. They were upwardly mobile and saw opportunities in the Indies they could not find at home. There were a number of other families, in Cáceres as well,

such as the Ovandos and the Sandes (whose stories are told elsewhere)[87] or the Vitas and Moragas, mentioned earlier, that formed
similarly strong ties to the Indies.

Family obviously played a crucial role in emigration from beginning to end. Family fortunes or position within the family helped
determine who might emigrate or when, and assistance from family
and relatives either at home or in the Indies often enabled emigrants to make the journey. Once in America, emigrants again
often received crucial assistance from relatives already established
there. Finally, the recruitment of relatives at home by people who
were in the Indies or had returned to Spain fostered cycles of
emigration which worked to forge and maintain ties between Cáceres and Trujillo and people and places in the New World. The
sense of familiarity that resulted from these multiple and continued
connections encouraged continuing emigration.

People at home in Extremadura came to know about Peru or
Mexico and people and events there not through vague reports or
the very few printed and published descriptions available but as a
result of continued contacts maintained through letters, visits, and
information and messages brought back by returnees, merchants,
and other individuals who moved back and forth with some frequency. In June 1570 Vasco de la Llave, a vecino of Trujillo,
described a conversation he had during a trip to Seville in January
of that year in which he talked to Bartolomé Díaz, a merchant
from Albuquerque recently returned from Peru. He had asked
Díaz about "people from this city [Trujillo] who are in those
parts."[88] Witnesses in Trujillo especially constantly stated that
they knew of people and events in Peru or elsewhere from people
who had come from there or from letters they or others had
received from emigrants.

In order to understand the way emigration developed in the
sixteenth century it is essential to take into account the rather rapid
formation of networks and connections which usually were tied to
family and place of origin and served to provide a familiar or
semifamiliar context in which people moved from Extremadura to
the New World. While networks and cycles of emigration often
hinged on family relationships, they certainly were not confined to
these. Cristóbal de Solís, a priest ordained in 1558 who was the
illegitimate son of Alvar García de Solís, a prominent priest in

Trujillo serving as vicar and *beneficiado* of the church of San Martín, decided to go to Peru in 1577. He stated that he had there "priests [who are] close relatives and intimate friends of mine." He mentioned two priests, Sancho Casco and Juan Casco, living in Cuzco and Lima, who were his relatives. The first was his brother-in-law, having been married to Solís's now deceased sister. He also said that trujillano Bachiller Gonzalo de Torres, provisor and vicar of Popayán, was a close friend of his father.[89]

Seville, Extremeños, and Emigration

Seville played an important part in the formation and maintenance of networks. Emigrants from Cáceres and Trujillo, after all, took only the first step when they left their home towns; they departed for the Indies from Seville, a booming city of some 100,000 people that for some extremeños might have seemed as much a world apart from their towns and villages as would the Indies themselves. In Seville potential emigrants had to deal with the licensing authorities at the Casa de Contratación if they meant to depart legally, and everyone had to arrange passage on a ship for themselves and anyone who accompanied them, as well as the purchase of provisions, space for baggage, or sleeping accommodations. All of this usually meant a stay in Seville of some duration before departure for the Indies. During this time emigrants would have to make fairly complicated arrangements that doubtless could prove confusing and costly if one did not know exactly what to do and how to avoid falling into the hands of some of the less than scrupulous people who dealt in the business of securing licenses or passage on outward bound ships. Although people in the Indies sometimes assisted relatives about to make the journey by sending detailed instructions or directing them to a friend or merchant in Seville who would help them, of considerable importance were the people from Cáceres and Trujillo who at any given time would be living in Seville, either temporarily or permanently. These people from home probably served as important contacts for emigrants, assisting them in making their arrangements, attending to their business as well as that of people at home in Extremadura, and dealing with the Casa de Contratacíon, through which all money and goods sent back to Spain had to pass.

Despite the distance that separated Seville from Cáceres and Trujillo, many people traveled there on business for themselves or others, often in connection with people and affairs of the Indies, although not necessarily.[90] A number of extremeños, including people who later went to or returned from the Indies, took up residence in Seville for short periods or permanently. Alonso Delvás, who went to New Granada in the 1550s, lived in Seville for a while before he left Spain. Witnesses from Trujillo testified that they had been in his house there and that he had married in Seville.[91] In 1551 Pedro Barrantes, returnee from Peru and regidor of Trujillo, authorized one of his criados to sell houses he owned in Seville.[92] Antón de Andrada, younger son of a cacereño noble family that held the title "señor de Espadero," went twice to the Indies and evidently lived in Seville before and between his trips. He first went to Florida in 1563. On his second departure, in 1576 to New Spain, he took with him an illegitimate son by a Sevillian woman who must have been born shortly before he went to Florida, as well as his wife, also from Seville, two children, and other relatives.[93]

Some returnees, such as Antonio Cotrina who started out as a criado of Licenciado García de Valverde and became an entrepreneur in the Indies trade, and Juan Cano, a cacereño who married one of the daughters of the Aztec emperor Moctezuma and became a wealthy encomendero, established themselves in Seville rather than in Cáceres once they were back in Spain. A merchant named Francisco Sánchez de Melo, a vecino of Seville active in the Indies trade, was a trujillano by origin. He had a niece in Trujillo, Ana de Melo, and in 1557 and 1559 respectively the brothers Pedro and Baltasar de Melo, who must have been his relatives, went to Peru and Tierra Firme as his factors. Pedro de Melo, who returned to Spain in 1575, decided to live in Seville also. As a vecino of Seville he donated a censo to Ana de Melo, niece of Francisco Sánchez de Melo, in the 1580s. Diego de Trujillo, the encomendero of Cuzco, in a letter of 1564 mentioned that Francisco Sánchez de Melo was coming with a load of merchandise, and the following year two vecinos of Trujillo authorized Diego de Melo (possibly Ana de Melo's father) and a criado of Francisco Sánchez de Melo to collect a debt from a man in Seville.[94] Men like Antonio Cotrina and Francisco Sánchez de Melo, as well as others who perhaps had never been to the Indies but were involved in the affairs of those who were, or still others who were living in Seville for other reasons, all served as key contacts both for people at home in Extremadura and people in the Indies.

Given the distance, the volume of movement between Alta Extremadura and Seville may seem surprising, but the presence of numbers of cacereños and trujillanos who were available to serve as witnesses for emigrants' petitions for licenses makes it clear that traveling to Seville and spending time there were commonplace. Another returnee who took up residence in Seville, Luis García Polido, in 1562 was pursuing a suit for hidalguía. Most of the witnesses in Cáceres testified that they had been in Seville, including a wool carder who claimed to be 101 years old, an hidalgo, and a labrador; the latter two said they had been to Seville several times.[95] Merchants and arrieros, naturally, moved back and forth between Extremadura and Seville frequently, and they often collected money from the Casa de Contratación or elsewhere for extremeños. In 1578 Juan Barrantes (son of returnee Pedro Barrantes and his wife doña Juana de Paredes), doña María de Ribera (widow of Juan Cortés, another returnee who had been at Cajamarca), and Licenciado Diego González Altamirano all gave their power of attorney to an arriero of Trujillo, Andrés de Illescas, to collect rents in juros they held in Seville.[96]

Since it was a center for trade, business, and industry, as well as the hub of the Indies enterprise, Seville exercized considerable attraction for extremeños, offering possibilities for employment and upward mobility. Because people traveled there frequently and at times took up residence while still maintaining contacts with people in their home towns, potential emigrants from Extremadura could look to acquaintances or relatives who were in Seville or at least knew the city for advice and assistance. As a result emigrants moved through the various stages of the emigration process in a familiar or partially familiar context, guided and supported by a network that connected people in Extremadura, Seville, and the Indies. Surely this network, which was developing by the middle of the sixteenth century, became an important element in the process by which people emigrated. It facilitated the move to America and thereby perhaps encouraged more people to emigrate, since, along with the assistance of family and relatives, the existence of such a network tended to diminish uncertainty and the sense of risk.

Despite the number and variety of personal and informal arrangements and connections that affected and facilitated emigration and the relative unimportance of official organization overall, the movement of people to the Indies did not, of course, take place in the absence of legal restrictions or structure. The Spanish crown was, in theory at least, quite concerned about who would be permitted to go to the Indies and under what circumstances. Legislation was designed to exclude what were judged undesirable elements—moriscos, gypsies, conversos—and the desire to monitor the quality and condition of emigrants brought into existence the rather cumbersome process that regulated emigration.[97] Potential emigrants who wished to comply with the legal requirements had to present evidence that they were not among the undesirables and also that, once in the Indies, they would not be a burden but rather productive members of society. It was for this reason—certainly a benefit to future historians—that emigrants presented often lengthy testimony regarding their background and what they planned to do in the Indies (establish themselves in a trade, join relatives, and so on). Letters from relatives in the Indies sometimes accompanied and buttressed this testimony.

The multitude of legislation certainly was not enforced to the letter. As seen in the case of the recruitment campaign for the Philippines, the officials themselves felt free to ignore requirements as they deemed appropriate. But the laws constituted an ideal framework that in principle governed emigration and could be brought to bear in particular cases, especially where the posting of bonds (*fianzas*) was involved. Merchants, married men leaving wives behind, individuals going to the Indies on short-term business all could be required to post bond against their promised return. García Ramiro of Trujillo posted a fianza of 100,000 maravedís when he went to Peru in 1555. He planned to collect the estate left by his brother Juan Ramiro and return in three years. Diego Hernández also took out a license to go to Peru for three years in 1567, under a bond of 200,000 maravedís, to collect the estate of his father who had died in Cuzco.[98]

Conclusion

Clearly the movement of people to the Indies was a complex and varied phenomenon. The term "emigration" is modern and perhaps anachronistic; certainly it did not exist in the sixteenth century.

Since there was no special term for going to the Indies, it is questionable whether a general concept of emigration existed. Obviously many people went to America with the intention of settling and remaining there, while others set out with short-term objectives and clear intentions of returning, although in the end they did not necessarily do so. Some who expected to remain might have changed their minds, and yet others probably had no fixed intentions when they departed. There was change over time; as society in the New World stabilized and consolidated, it offered increasingly attractive prospects for permanent settlement. Yet in many cases even those emigrants who obviously had settled down and made new lives in America retained not only strong attachments to home but the lingering, if unrealistic, expectation or desire that they would some time return. It was not uncommon for individuals sending for or writing to relatives to express a wish to return to visit while acknowledging the impossibility of traveling so far at a relatively advanced age.[99] The ambivalence of many people who established themselves in America but continued to look "homeward" to Spain, and their attachment to home and to relatives and acquaintances from home also in the Indies, are reflected in the experiences of extremeños in the Indies.

VI

Extremeños in the New World

Just as the people of Cáceres and Trujillo who went to the Indies in the sixteenth century came from virtually every rank and grouping of society, their activities and experiences there reflected the full range of possibilities and opportunities offered by the New World. They became wealthy encomenderos and high officials, stockraisers and farmers, merchants and artisans, agents and retainers. Extremeños participated in and often were central and decisive figures in some of the most dramatic and important events and episodes of the early years of exploration, conquest, and settlement. Francisco Pizarro and his brothers, friends, and retainers undertook the conquest of Peru; men like Juan Cano of Cáceres and Francisco de las Casas of Trujillo were with Cortés in Mexico; Gonzalo Pizarro and Francisco de Orellana explored the Amazon; Diego García de Paredes (son of the extremeño hero) led the party that captured the "tyrant" Lope de Aguirre in Venezuela.

Extremeños went not only to the centers of the new empire, Mexico and Peru, but to its periphery as well. They accompanied Hernando de Soto and later Lucas de Ayllón to Florida, Cabeza de Vaca to the Río de la Plata, Pedro de Alvarado to Guatemala, García de Lerma to Santa Marta. They upheld law and order and the crown, and they defied royal authority. Frey Nicolás de Ovando, governor of the island of Hispaniola from 1502 to 1509, played a key role in stabilizing and consolidating royal government there and increasing royal revenues; Gonzalo Pizarro and his followers usurped royal authority and ran Peru for nearly three years in the 1540s. People from Extremadura authored chronicles; Fray Gaspar de Carvajal wrote an account of Gonzalo Pizarro's expedition to "la Canela" (in which he participated), while late in life Diego de Trujillo dictated a simple and abbreviated history of the early years in Peru. Men like Hernando de Aldana (of Cáceres) and Francisco de Orellana reportedly had unusual linguistic abilities and quickly learned Indian languages.

Naturally for every individual whose name and deeds were famous at the time and in some cases ever since, there were dozens of men and women whose experiences and achievements (or failures) did not attract much attention then or now. Yet the differences between the much larger, lesser-known group and the great leaders and high officials of church and state were more of degree than of kind. At all levels extremeños in the New World did much the same things. They sought advantage and opportunity and diversified economically. They associated closely with relatives, friends, and acquaintances from home. They maintained their connections with home, sending money and recruiting family members to join them. They considered returning home to Spain and often did so temporarily or permanently.

Nor were there any real, lasting differences between extremeños and emigrants from other parts of Spain. The contingent from the Trujillo-Cáceres region stood out clearly in the early years of conquest and settlement in Peru because of their connections with the Pizarros and the favoritism they enjoyed as a result. But this era lasted barely a generation. The failure of Gonzalo Pizarro's rebellion and the subsequent restitution of royal authority in Peru marked the demise of the power and prestige of the Pizarrist contingent, especially the people from Trujillo. In fact it has been shown that even from the beginning the Pizarros' circle of extremeño recruits and associates never was a closed one, since they could not provide all the expertise and experience needed for the range of administrative, financial, and other tasks at hand.[1] Within a short time, then, extremeños became virtually indistinguishable from other Spanish emigrants in the New World in terms of their activities and possibilities, although new arrivals still benefited from a well-established network of connections. Furthermore the perception of a separate and coherent identity long outlasted the eclipse of any special claim to prominence, and this perception continued to affect choices and expectations.

Their common origins, kinship, and patron–client relations, as well as shared experiences and interests, bound the extremeños in the Indies. Not only did they form a fairly integrated group from the socioeconomic point of view, virtually all these people were part of an extensive network of acquaintance and relationship. The significance of identification with point of origin and the emphasis placed on family and kinship ties hardly disappeared in the Indies; if anything, that context in certain ways probably underscored the importance of these relationships, since they served as crucial points of reference in a world that was new and different. An apt illustration of these ties appears in Pedro Cieza de Léon's description of the encounter between Lorenzo de Aldana (a noble of Cáceres) and Hernando Pizarro, when Aldana arrived as Diego de Almagro's representative:

Capt. Hernando Pizarro took Capt. Lorenzo de Aldana aside, and throwing his arms around his neck, he spoke to him fondly [asking that] he tell him of the *adelantado*'s intentions, since he did not doubt the friendship that would oblige Aldana to tell the truth, since their fathers were so close and they were from the same country ("de una patria").[2]

During his years in Peru Lorenzo de Aldana was constantly in the company of his noble friends and relatives from Cáceres and Trujillo, and he participated actively (with most of his kinsmen and friends) in Gonzalo Pizarro's rebellion, though ultimately deserting Pizarro and emerging with a valuable encomienda in Charcas. Despite his family connections, however, in his will of 1562 Aldana left houses, lands, and slaves to Diego Hurtado, neither a relative nor a cacereño, whom he called "my friend and brother who has been in my house and company." Although Aldana apparently had no legitimate heirs of his own—he had a mestiza daughter whom he married to another encomendero of Charcas—at the time of his death his nephew Lorenzo de Aldana was in Peru; his nephew in fact witnessed the will.[3] Family and kinship ties were not, then, the only significant ones. As Aldana's will reflects, a parallel set of relationships often emerged from the context and experiences of the Indies. Friendships, partnerships, and long-term associations need not have competed with family ties but often, in fact, complemented them. The existence of lifelong friendships that were based on trust and common experience and viewed as quasi-familial (note that Aldana called Hurtado his "brother"), together with the importance of family and kinship, reflect the combination of old and new patterns that influenced the choices and behavior of people in the New World.

This chapter examines who went to the Indies and what they did there, emphasizing in particular how the activities and choices of extremeños continued to reflect their orientation toward family and kin and the bonds of common origin. As suggested, the people from Cáceres and Trujillo over time at one level became all but indistinguishable from other emigrants in terms of their objectives and actions; yet at another level they continued (or at least tried to continue) to function in a context that was shaped by their own particular set of priorities and interests, which to an extent remained rooted in the family and social network and relations of their home towns thousands of miles away. In their preference for associating with family and kin and with people who shared their local or regional origins the extremeños, again, were hardly unique. The appearance of similar patterns among a number of groups (Basques, Asturians, Andalusians) present in the Indies is further evidence that extremeños behaved much as did other emigrants in the New World.[4]

Background and Activities

Despite a rather heavy showing of hidalgos and a discernible lack of business talent in the early years, extremeños in the long run probably entered into nearly every sphere of life in the New World. Naturally people who became encomenderos, successful merchants or entrepreneurs, served as officials, or participated in some of the key episodes of the early years (such as the division of treasure at Cajamarca or Gonzalo Pizarro's rebellion) are better documented than the more modest individuals who set up artisan shops, worked as stewards or employees of encomenderos or entrepreneurs, or the like. Women especially seldom emerge other than as wives, sisters, or nieces, although they sometimes played crucial roles in family and estate affairs. But studies of early Spanish American society have demonstrated convincingly that all these individuals—from the

wealthiest and most powerful to the most humble—played vital
roles in the formation of society in the New World, and hence in the
broadest sense all were important.

Who were the extremeños who went to the New World? Chapter 5 showed that anywhere from a tenth to a fifth (or more) of the
emigrants from Trujillo, Cáceres, and their jurisdictions were hidalgos, who thus constituted a significant element in the emigrant
group as a whole. In Extremadura the hidalgo group encompassed
considerable variety of rank and socioeconomic status; nonetheless
certain features characterized most of the noble and hidalgo emigrants, and these would have implications for what they would do
in the New World. Most of the hidalgos, with the exception of the
priests, professionals, and semiprofessionals among them, had no
specific occupation as such, although they probably had received
some education and training in the use of arms. So many of them
emigrated not with the intention of setting themselves up in a trade
or going to work for an already-established relative, but with the
expectation that their status and connections would ensure them a
living and a place in society. Naturally, being among the more
affluent emigrants, many hidalgos could take with them a stake in
merchandise or capital that would help them make their start.
Certainly a number of them proved to be resourceful and flexible as
they sought opportunities and adapted to the new context. Yet one
cannot discard altogether the other image of the hidalgo seeking
mercedes (rewards) and sinecures, frustrated that neither name nor
connections brought the anticipated rewards. This element existed
as well, especially after the first couple of generations in the Indies,
when the military conquest per se had been accomplished and
factional turmoil curtailed. The hidalgos who came later and missed
the fighting and distribution of rewards often were unable to find a
comfortable niche and had difficulty fitting into society.[5]

Alvaro de Paredes, the man who wrote the revealing series of
letters to his brother in Cáceres from Mexico in the late sixteenth
and early seventeenth century, is a fine example of this latter kind
of hidalgo. Paredes had problems in Mexico and, for whatever
reason, time and again failed to take advantage of what opportunities came his way. For years his letters reflected a constant concern
with connections and influence. He had some connection with the
Inquisitor Bonilla, who in 1590 left Mexico for Peru. Paredes asked

to accompany him, but Bonilla refused on the grounds he would not be able to do anything for him there. Later the same year, after his marriage, Alvaro urged his brother Licenciado Gutiérrez Espadero to get in touch with Juan Beltrán de Guevara on the Council of the Indies to "remind him of past friendship, so that he might help me in this kingdom with a letter of his and others of his friends on the council." In 1606 he wrote that "I am such that I need favor by any means." Despite all his difficulties in making his way, it was not until 1608 that he asked his brother to send him the bachelor's degree he had earned in law, so that he could be appointed to a position that required a lawyer (letrado). Evidently he had not expected to work in the profession for which he was trained.[6]

Artisans and semiprofessionals formed another important element in the emigrant group. Among the thirty-nine men from Trujillo who identified themselves as artisans, there were nine blacksmiths (including three locksmiths), eight tailors, seven stone-cutters (including the architect Francisco Becerra), five shoemakers, and four carpenters. In addition Trujillo sent three notaries, two surgeons, a barber, and a pharmacist. The data for the representation of trades from Cáceres are scant; the cacereño emigrants included two shoemakers and a blacksmith, as well as two notaries, a barber, and a pharmacist. Cáceres did send four labradores, however, whereas none of the trujillanos identified himself as a farmer (two labradores left Santa Cruz for Peru).

The larger number of artisans from Trujillo compared to Cáceres probably reflects the differences in the overall size and nature of the emigrant groups from the two cities. Artisans often were family men who had clear notions of what they planned to do once they reached their destinations, and many more families left Trujillo than Cáceres. Andrés Hernández, the carpenter who went to New Spain in 1580 with his wife and children under the sponsorship of the encomendero Gonzalo de las Casas, obtained permission to take a twenty-year-old apprentice and his nephew Alonso Sánchez, also a carpenter.[7] Melchor González, a locksmith who emigrated in 1555, declared he planned to settle in Peru and practice his trade there; he asked to take an apprentice with him.[8] These men would arrive in the New World well-prepared to establish their trades. The tailor Alonso Ramiro left Trujillo for New Spain in 1574 with his wife and three sons and an apprentice. Ramiro formed a partnership in Puebla de los Angeles with his cousin Alonso Morales, another tailor who was from Cabañas de la Peña. In 1576 Morales wrote to Juan Ramiro, Alonso Ramiro's brother, telling him about the store they had together and urging him to come and bring other relatives of theirs; "the work pays very well, " he wrote, "and food is cheap."[9] While doubtless a number of artisans and semiprofessionals did not work exclusively in their trades and some even discarded them altogether in face of unanticipated circumstances or better opportunities, most likely the intention of individuals who identified themselves by their trade or profession was to establish themselves in the occupation for which they were trained.

Probably the same was true for the secular clergy who emigrated; in the New World, as in Extremadura, they would serve as priests or work in other capacities. Twenty priests left Trujillo and five Cáceres, the majority for Peru. Opportunities there must have looked most promising, especially since the principal figure in the ecclesiastical establishment of Lima for decades was the Dominican Fray Jerónimo de Loaysa. A native of Trujillo, Loaysa was appointed bishop of Lima in 1541 and made archbishop several years later, serving in that capacity until his death in 1575. Fifteen of the priests from Trujillo went to Peru, almost all of them in the 1560s and 1570s, and three of the five cacereños went there as well.

Some of the priests achieved considerable prominence. Hernando Alonso Villarejo went to Cartagena in 1539 (at which time Fray Jerónimo de Loaysa was bishop of Cartagena) as the appointed archdeacon of the church there.[10] The more common pattern, however, was not appointment in Spain but gradual advancement after a priest established himself in the Indies. Juan de Llerena of Cáceres first went to Peru in the entourage of the Inquisitor Licenciado Fray Antonio Gutiérrez de Ulloa (from Cáceres) in 1570. Llerena returned to Spain in 1575 on business for the inquisitor, and when he went back to Peru in 1577 he said he had been given the "benefice of the port of Payta and pueblo of Escolar, in the diocese of Quito."[11] Bachiller Gonzalo de Torres of Trujillo was vicar of Arequipa until his patron, appointed bishop of Popayán, brought him to be vicar of Popayán. Later the bishop made Torres archdeacon and *chantre* (cantor).[12] While few priests achieved such distinction, most of them probably did well enough. Francisco Regodón, who went to Peru in the early 1550s, sent for his nephew in Trujillo, Alonso Regodón Calderón, in the 1570s and was said to be "very rich."[13] Priests frequently purchased censos in Spain in absentia, an indication that they had surplus capital to invest.[14]

Most officials left Spain with a definite appointment in hand, although emigrants who were in the New World might obtain positions that typically went to people already on the local scene. Treasury officials often emerged from the local milieu; Francisco González de Castro was treasurer of Santa Marta in the 1560s, Juan Rodríguez de Ocampo was treasurer of Quito in the 1570s and 1580s, and Pedro de Valencia treasurer of Arequipa in 1570.[15] Higher-ranking officials received their appointments in Spain. Cáceres and Trujillo both produced a number of governors and audiencia judges and presidents, some of whom had long and uninterrupted careers in the Indies and accumulated considerable experience there. Dr. Francisco de Sande from Cáceres served successively as prosecutor, criminal magistrate, and judge of the audiencia of Mexico between 1567 and 1574. He was governor and captain-general of the Philippines from 1575 to 1580, at which time he returned to Mexico to serve again on the audiencia. He later served as president of Guatemala (1593–1596) and Santa Fe de Bogotá (1596 until his death in 1602).[16] Another cacereño, Licenciado Diego García de Valverde, in 1556 went to New Granada as *fiscal* (prosecutor) of the audiencia of Bogota. In 1564 he was appointed oidor of the audiencia of Lima, then served as president in Quito in 1573–1574 and the following year became president of Guatemala; he died in 1587 before assuming the presidency of Guadalajara to which he had been appointed.[17]

Such lengthy careers must have resulted in (and reflected) substantial expertise and competence in the governance of the Indies, regardless of whether the policies and actions undertaken were popular or just. Licenciado García de Valverde was a determined reformer who arrived in Guatemala at the tail end of a major epidemic to find the population there much diminished. He tried to reform the encomiendas through improved recordkeeping that would allow a realistic adjustment of tribute quotas. This and other measures enraged the local encomenderos, who attempted to undermine the president's reputation and position.[18] Dr. Sande, in contrast, seems to have run afoul of his constituents not because of an interest in reform but more likely as a result of his ambitions. He accumulated substantial wealth during his career and doubtless was always alert to the opportunities afforded by his position. In 1578 in the Philippines, for example, he sent his captain, Esteban Rodrí-guez de Figueroa (also from Cáceres) to the island of "Xolo" to pacify the people and develop agriculture and the pearl industry. He also instructed Rodríguez to have the people tame two ele-phants for him, for which he would pay. Rodríguez conquered the "king" of Xolo and made him a vassal.[19]

In contrast to artisans and professionals, who usually went to the Indies intending to pursue their occupations or careers at least for a number of years (if not necessarily permanently), merchants often went there only temporarily, or moved back and forth. Thirteen men from Trujillo, one from Robledillo (in Trujillo's district), and three from Cáceres left for the Indies calling themselves merchants or merchants' factors, most of them in the 1560s and 1570s. Proba-bly many of them worked together. Gonzalo de Carmona, Juan de Ribera (brother of Bachiller Gonzalo de Torres, who became arch-deacon and cantor of Popayán), and the noble Andrés Calderón Puertocarrero, all left Trujillo for Tierra Firme and Peru in 1562. Juan Cotrina and Rafael Solana both left Cáceres in 1564. Andrés Calderón and Juan de Ribera were back in Trujillo within two or three years.

These self-identified merchants, who often remained more closely tied to Spain than the New World, actually formed only part of the much larger and flexible group of merchants and entrepreneurs which developed in response to the many opportunities offered by the Indies enterprise. Even a random look at the activities of emi-grants in the Indies suggests that almost everyone at one time or another engaged in some kind of commercial activity. Alonso Alva-rez de Altamirano went to Peru as a child with his father Licenciado Alvarez, the surgeon. When he returned to Spain in 1581 at the age of thirty on business, he called himself a "known merchant" ("mer-cader conocido").[20] Alvaro de Cáceres, long-time resident and lead-ing citizen of Puebla de los Angeles, became involved in the cacao trade between Mexico and Guatemala and Soconusco.[21] Since oppor-tunities abounded, many individuals, especially in the early years, were buying and selling as a sideline if not a principal occupation; Diego de Carvajal, a retainer of Juan Pizarro who returned to Trujillo to marry Juan's half-sister Isabel de Soto, in testimony regarding transactions of 1536 with Juan de Herrera in Peru, said that "at the time this witness invested in the City of the Kings [Lima] certain money and certain merchandise and he doubled them in the city of Cuzco."[22] Yet others invested in commerce while avoiding direct participation; Juan de Hinojosa of Cáceres, an encomendero of Arequipa, invested 20,000 ducados with the merchant Gaspar de Solís.[23] Alonso Carrasco of Zorita, another encomendero, had a mercantile company with his mayordomo Alonso de Fuentes and employed his own factors.[24]

Diversity and flexibility characterized the activities of extremeños, as of all emigrants in the Indies. An encomendero could be an entrepreneur, a miner, or a stockraiser. Lucas Martínez Vegaso, a veteran of Cajamarca and wealthy encomendero of Arequipa, from the outset of his career in Peru was involved in commercial activities. He owned a ship and had silver mines at Tarapaca, where he held his encomienda.[25] Another emigrant from Trujillo, Diego Pizarro de Olmos, who arrived in Peru around 1540 with his relative Alonso Pizarro de la Rua, who also received an encomienda, had an encomienda in the valley of Supe on the coast. He received a land grant of 210 acres in the valley of Charcay, near Lima, and in his will of 1562 left 910 head of cattle, 680 pigs, 178 goats, and 37 horses in the valley of Supe.[26] Non-encomenderos also diversified their economic activities. Diego de Nodera, a master stonecutter from Trujillo who lived for years and practiced his trade in Mexico, had a commercial partnership with a merchant from Seville and visited Spain at least once on business.[27] Francisco de Ojalvo of Cáceres had a mercantile company as well as a shoemaker's shop in Trujillo (Peru).[28]

Because many Spaniards in the New World pursued an array of economic undertakings, there is no very precise way of categorizing people according to their economic involvements, occupations, or status, nor was possession of an encomienda necessarily a crucial determinant of one's status or activities. Holding an encomienda did not guarantee economic success, although certainly a populous and well-located encomienda was a great asset to someone with agricultural, stockraising, or mining interests. But an encomienda was not essential to such activities. Juan de Cáceres Delgado, a cacereño involved in stockraising and the transport trade in and around Mexico City in the 1520s and 1530s, achieved wealth and prominence despite the fact that he never received an encomienda. In the 1520s he was "father and guardian of orphans" for New Spain, and his wife was called "doña."[29] Juan Pantoja de Ribera of Cáceres, who lived in San Jorge in Honduras in the 1540s, at the time of his marriage there owned thirteen black slaves "of the best miners . . . in Honduras" and a stand of cacao trees that annually yielded fourteen or fifteen *cargas* of cacao; together with his houses and other properties, his net worth was estimated at over 12,000 pesos.[30] Diego Martín de Trujillo of Garciaz, who went with his wife to Mexico in the early 1550s, held agricultural land and pastures on which he grazed sheep outside Mexico City. In a letter of 1562 he claimed that he had an annual income of 2,000 pesos. A vecino of Garciaz who had seen Diego Martín in Mexico said that he and his family were "rich and prosperous."[31] Andrés Pérez of Cáceres, a vecino of Puebla de los Angeles in the 1540s and 1550s, had owned mines and slaves in Zumpango in the 1530s.[32]

None of these men held an encomienda, and they all achieved a decent standard of living in the New World. But their economic circumstances on the whole were still fairly modest. In Spain in the 1560s the relatives of cacereño Juan Pantoja de Ribera, who died in Honduras, attempted to reclaim from Juan Pantoja's widow the cumulative value of his estate and assets over the twenty-four years since his death. By the claimants' own calculations the income from mines and cacao would not have much exceeded 600 pesos annually, hardly a fortune.[33] Commercial activity, in contrast to agriculture or small-scale mining, more likely could generate real wealth. Alvaro de Cáceres's activities in the cacao trade with Guatemala financed the upkeep of a large, well-furnished house in Puebla in which he had built a fountain that he let his neighbors use. He served as the steward of a local confraternity and was known for his charities to widows and orphans. His entrepreneurial success can be gauged by the fact that by the mid-1570s he apparently had retired from direct participation in commerce and acquired an estate in the countryside. In 1574 Cáceres received a sentence of one year's exile from New Spain for attempting to secure the bishopric of Tlaxcala for his own candidate. The sum of 7500 ducados that he proposed to use for this purpose reflects his substantial financial wherewithal.[34]

Encomenderos

Despite the relative success, even in the early years, of some non-encomenderos, the encomienda nonetheless was the dominant economic and political institution of early colonial society, mobilizing labor for Spanish enterprises as well as providing a direct source of income for those who received grants. Furthermore, encomenderos, since they often were among the wealthiest and best-established vecinos of a city, frequently served on town councils or in other official capacities and thus were in a good position to secure the land grants they wanted. Frey Nicolás de Ovando, during his term as governor of Hispaniola, was an encomendero and the largest landholder on the island (after King Ferdinand). He had extensive agricultural lands and holdings in livestock (mainly pigs) and was involved in mining and commercial imports. In fact Ovando implemented the royal cédula of 1503 authorizing the establishment of encomiendas (which actually had been in existence for some years). Probably most of the wealth that Ovando derived from his encomienda and other very profitable enterprises went to the Order of Alcántara or indirectly to the king (as grand master of the order) rather than to Ovando himself.[35]

Some encomiendas yielded disappointingly little in the way of tribute or labor or were rendered virtually worthless by epidemics that decimated indigenous populations. Others were not located sufficiently near to productive mining or agricultural areas to be of much use, or the encomendero lacked the necessary access to capital or political favor to use the encomienda to best advantage. In the 1540s cacereño Alonso Hidalgo, vecino of Ciudad Real de Chiapas, complained of his poverty, saying he had received only a small encomienda from Pedro de Alvarado worth about 70 pesos.[36] Some conquistadores and early settlers, victims of factionalism and favoritism, lost part or all of their encomiendas. Another cacereño, Diego Holguín, a vecino of Puebla de los Angeles in the 1530s and 1540s, lost part of his encomienda to Cortés's Marquesado. Nuño de Guzmán, first president of New Spain's audiencia, reassigned the remainder, leaving Holguín, a married man with two sons and two daughters, destitute.[37]

Politics, factionalism, and civil war frequently resulted in the loss or reassignment of encomiendas in Peru as well. Pedro Alonso Carrasco, a native of Zorita and conqueror and early settler of Cuzco, lost part of his encomienda of Carichane, which he had received from Juan Pizarro. Witnesses in the late 1550s said that Francisco Pizarro took Carrasco's grant because he was angry at him ("por estar mal con el") and because he thought Carrasco had too many Indians.[38] A number of encomiendas changed hands during or after Gonzalo Pizarro's rebellion. Lucas Martínez, who in 1547 became Gonzalo Pizarro's lieutenant governor for the region of Arequipa, lost his encomienda when the rebellion ended. Eventually he regained it, in 1557, allegedly bribing the new Viceroy, Cañete, and one of the judges of the audiencia to achieve that effect.[39] Although Martínez, like many of Pizarro's supporters, in the end switched his support to the side of the royal representative, President Licenciado Pedro de la Gasca, he did not fare as well as other supporters of Pizarro who did the same. Men like Lorenzo de Aldana and Gómez de Solís, nobles from Cáceres who played an active and important role in the rebellion, actually came out ahead, ending up with some of the best encomiendas in Peru.[40]

An encomienda could yield a substantial income and serve as the basis for a range of economic activities. But because encomiendas were grants made and held at the discretion of officials (or whoever exercized effective authority), they were a much more uncertain basis for the accumulation of wealth and perpetuation of family status than the rents and properties held in Extremadura—hence the need to diversify and develop the private aspects of estates and enterprises. Early grants went to a variety of individuals, from artisans and miners to hidalgos and officials, but people with wealth, prestige, and good connections were most successful in securing and retaining good encomiendas. On the whole hidalgos probably did best in using and keeping their grants, but certainly they were not immune to the capriciousness of events or officials. Lorenzo de Ulloa, one of the few cacereños in Peru who managed to survive Gonzalo Pizarro's rebellion while avoiding real commitment to the rebel side, lost one-third of his encomienda (which had been worth 4000 pesos) in the 1550s when the viceroy transferred 1400 pesos to seven vecinos of the town of Jaen. He never was reinstated in this grant, but later he succeeded to the repartimiento left vacant at the death of a fellow cacereño, Lorenzo de Aldana.[41]

The nature of the grants created other problems for their holders. An encomienda could not be held in absentia, although the encomendero could obtain permission for a short-term absence. Since encomenderos could not arrange to collect the income from their grants in absentia and could not legally sell their grants outright, the direct profits to be made from an encomienda only benefited the grantee who stayed in the Indies. There were, of course, some exceptions in both regards. Hernando Pizarro and his wife doña Francisca (the mestiza daughter of Francisco Pizarro) enjoyed the income from their encomiendas and mines in Peru to the end of their lives in Spain; but then the careers and circumstances of the Pizarro family in Peru in certain ways were quite atypical, just as in other ways they exemplified—if on a grander scale than most—the activities and occupations of many of their fellow countrymen.[42]

The question of succession to the grants also caused problems. Normally a son succeeded to his father's encomienda, at least in the first generation. Thus Gonzalo de las Casas succeeded to the encomienda first granted to his father Francisco de las Casas; Maestre Manuel Tomás, a surgeon from Trujillo who accompanied Francisco de las Casas to Mexico, in 1547 transferred his encomienda of Tututepec to his son Diego Rodríguez de Orozco, who arrived in Mexico in 1536; and Juan de Hinojosa, another trujillano who shared an encomienda about 150 miles northeast of Mexico City and died in 1533, was succeeded by his son Francisco, who arrived from Spain in 1537.[43] In each of these cases in the early years, the encomenderos were men who had started families in Spain and so had the appropriate heirs to succeed them. But the excitement, newness, and conflicts of the early years, in Peru especially, meant both high mortality rates and delays in establishing families in the New World. Lorenzo de Aldana had no legitimate heirs and apparently never married, so his encomienda went to Lorenzo de Ulloa, a fellow cacereño. Where there were no heirs, it was common for a grant to be assigned to someone from the same home town or region in Spain. Pedro de Valencia of Trujillo, the treasurer of Arequipa, in 1570 succeeded to the encomienda left vacant at the death of another trujillano, Captain Francisco de Chaves.[44]

An encomendero's widow usually could succeed to a grant, but a woman was seldom permitted to remain single and retain an encomienda. As a result men often became encomenderos through marriage to widows who held grants.[45] This practice could create conflicts in the next generation, however, if there were children by more than one husband. And the custom of allowing widows to succeed but hastening them into marriages doubtless at times had less than desirable results for the women involved. Alonso Carrasco of Zorita succeeded to his uncle Francisco Lobo's encomienda in the valley of Jayanca and married Lobo's widow, doña Isabel Palomino. Lobo had made Carrasco his heir in his will of 1551, and witnesses stated that Lobo had treated Carrasco like a son, giving him the run of his estate:

Alonso Carrasco commanded all the household . . . and his Indians, and everyone obeyed him, and he spent and distributed the goods and tributes of Francisco Lobo, and in everything he acted as if it were his, the same as Francisco Lobo himself could do.

Lobo's widow's feelings for Carrasco might not have been so fond; by the mid-1570s Carrasco was dead, allegedly at the hand of his wife, who poisoned his soup.[46]

Problems over succession and assignment of grants generated endless litigation that could involve officials who acted not only in their official capacity but in defense of their private interests as well; Pedro Alonso Carrasco tried to reclaim part of his grant from the son of the governor Licenciado Vaca de Castro.[47] Again, because of a high rate of mortality and considerable mobility, a series of individuals might succeed to a grant in a rather short period of time, fomenting legal chaos, especially since individuals who probably did not have the authority to assign grants often did so in the early years.

The acrimonious suit between the aforementioned Alonso Carrasco of Zorita and Alvaro Pizarro de la Rua of Trujillo arose from precisely those kinds of circumstances and was unusual only in that the customary solidarity of two men from the same "tierra"—they had many friends and even relatives in common—broke down. Carrasco's uncle Francisco Lobo received half the repartimiento of Jayanca, to which Carrasco succeeded. The other half passed through the hands of a couple of men and to the daughter of the second, who apparently died young. Since the holders of that half had never taken over administration very effectively, Lobo and Carrasco allegedly had expanded their part at the expense of the other. So when Alonso

Pizarro de la Rua was assigned half of Jayanca in 1566, probably as a reward for helping to put down the rebellion of Francisco Hernández Girón, he discovered that his share was of little value. Attempts to negotiate with Carrasco failed, and Alonso Pizarro's representatives were unable to contact Carrasco's wife, doña Isabel Palomino, who they claimed Carrasco had "very shut up and hidden," unable to leave the house; nor could a notary enter. Two long-time residents and early conquerors—Diego de Trujillo and Pedro Alonso Carrasco (the former from Trujillo, the latter from Zorita)—testified in 1570 in Alonso Carrasco's probanza; and several other trujillanos—Diego Pizarro de Olmos, Captain Francisco de Olmos, and the surgeon Licenciado Juan Alvarez—gave testimony for Alonso Pizarro de la Rua. Carrasco's mayordomo and business partner, Alonso de Fuentes, claimed he was a friend of both parties, and Juan de Valverde Pizarro, a second cousin of Alonso Pizarro de la Rua, was the man who testified regarding the key position Alonso Carrasco played in Francisco Lobo's establishment.[48]

Lucas Martínez Vegaso

The activities and often complex business affairs of Lucas Martínez of Trujillo provide a good illustration of how an early encomendero-entrepreneur operated. Martínez's long-time association with partner and fellow Cajamarca veteran Alonso Ruiz, who returned to Trujillo to marry Martínez's sister Isabel, and his connections with other people from Trujillo illustrate how the maintenance of ties to home and family put a particular stamp on the organization and operation of an early Spanish American establishment.

Martínez figured among the group of young recruits from Trujillo who accompanied Francisco Pizarro back to Peru in 1529. He was about twenty-one years old when he received his share of the spoils of Cajamarca, and his companion and business partner Alonso Ruiz was perhaps a year or two younger. Ruiz was not a native of Trujillo; he may have grown up there, but he also could have been recruited by Pizarro elsewhere. Whatever his origins, he and Martínez formed an enduring partnership almost from the inception of their enterprise in Peru, selling horses and other provisions, lending money, and for ten years—until Ruiz's departure for Spain in 1540—holding and managing their property in common. They did, however, receive separate encomiendas in Arequipa.[49] Despite their closeness and the similarity in age, Martínez was the dominant partner. He was informed and literate (Ruiz essentially was illiterate), and regardless of whether Martínez actually started out as a merchant, he had a talent for and knowledge of business affairs. He was a loyal Pizarrist and achieved some prominence in early Peru despite an undistinguished military record. A member of the Cuzco city council in the 1530s, he sat on the Arequipa council from the first year of its founding in 1539–1540; Ruiz in contrast scarcely appeared in a public capacity in Peru. Ruiz's encomienda was smaller than Martínez's encomienda of Tarapaca and Arica, one of the largest and most lucrative in the jurisdiction of Arequipa.

When Ruiz left for Spain in 1540 to marry Martínez's sister Isabel in Trujillo, the men divided up their property but did not terminate their partnership. Each of them put aside 2000 pesos for Isabel's dowry, and in addition Ruiz took to Spain over 20,000 pesos that belonged to both; the men gave each other their powers of attorney to administer properties and conduct transactions. Ruiz probably did not intend to return permanently to Spain, and three times he had his license to stay there extended.[50] But in the 1550s he was on the Trujillo city council, and in 1558 he purchased señorío of the village of Madroñera, where Martínez may have had family connections. Over the years the two men in their parallel and connected lives rose considerably beyond their rather humble origins, and both added surnames to bolster their new status. The encomendero of Arequipa became Lucas Martínez Vegaso, and the lord of Madroñera Alonso Ruiz de Albornoz.

Lucas Martínez created an integrated and efficient operation in Peru, based on the exploitation of his silver mines at Tarapaca, his encomienda, and agricultural holdings. His tributes and farms yielded a standard range of products—maize, wheat, alpacas and llamas (for wool, meat, and transport), sheep and pigs, salted fish, poultry—which he used to supply his employees, slaves, and retainers or sold in Potosí or elsewhere. Of over 1200 fanegas of maize collected in 1565, for example, more than half the total was sold or exchanged for livestock, while 43 percent went to feed encomienda and mine workers. Martínez's ship was crucial to the operation, and after he recovered his encomienda in 1557, he had new boats built that linked Tarapaca to Arica, Callao, and other ports.[51]

Martínez's will of 1566 declared that he held twenty black slaves, half of them working in the mines and half in his households in Arica and Lima, where he had gone to live in 1561. In addition to encomienda Indians, he had yanaconas (Indian dependents) working on his lands in Guaylacana, Tarapaca, and elsewhere.[52] One of the most interesting aspects of Martínez's staffing arrangements for his encomienda and mining operations was his employment of a number of members of the Valencia family, natives of Trujillo and Madroñera who possibly were related to Lucas Martínez on his mother's side (his mother was Francisca de Valencia). Soon after his return to Trujillo, Alonso Ruiz sent two first cousins, Martín de Valencia and Pedro Alonso de Valencia, to Peru to work for Martínez; Martín worked in Arica and Pedro Alonso in Tarapaca. About ten years later Martín de Valencia's son Gonzalo also departed Trujillo to work for Lucas Martínez in Peru. One of Gonzalo's brothers also apparently went to work for Martínez in the mines.

The men of the Valencia family did fairly well working for Martínez, although they remained primarily his dependents and employees. In the mid-1540s Pedro Alonso was the encomendero's chief mayordomo, earning an annual salary of 600 pesos. Later Gonzalo de Valencia's salary would be higher, since he received 650 pesos for just seven months' work. Gonzalo's father Martín owned a farm where he had an Indian woman and a black slave working for him. But apparently none of them left Martínez's establishment. Gonzalo de Valencia and Pedro Alonso de Valencia's widow each received a bequest of 1000 pesos in Lucas's will of 1566. Martínez made Gonzalo the custodian of his property and directed him to take his things back to Spain.[53]

Lucas Martínez's career in Peru provides a revealing picture of a man in transition between two worlds. He spent over thirty-five years—the greater part of his life—in Peru and took the fullest possible advantage of available opportunities to build up a flourishing and profitable enterprise. He apparently never visited home again and certainly did not plan to go back permanently, although he arranged for his friend and partner Alonso Ruiz to do so. Yet in a sense he never fully established himself in Peru, marrying a young woman only days before his death in April 1567 so that she could inherit the encomienda. Never having established a legitimate family, Martínez left no direct legal heirs. In the early years he did have an Indian noble woman, doña Isabel Yupanqui, as his mistress, and he had children by a morisca woman named Beatriz (formerly a slave). One of these children might have been his son Francisco Martínez Vegaso, who held an encomienda in Chile in 1546.[54] Martínez made his sisters Isabel and Lucía Martínez his universal heirs, and the executors of his will included Alonso Ruiz and Isabel Martínez in Spain and Martín de Meneses (of Trujillo) and Diego Velázquez (a native of Jaraicejo and long-time retainer of Hernando Pizarro) in Peru.

Despite his success and extensive involvement in Peruvian affairs and society, Lucas Martínez, then, remained to the end of his life strongly oriented toward Trujillo and his family there, maintaining close relations with Alonso Ruiz, who acted as a sort of surrogate for Martínez in his own home town, and continuing to rely on his fellow trujillanos (and possible relatives) the Valencias to staff and manage his business enterprise. A further irony of Martínez's rather paradoxical—if not irreconcilable—allegiances lies in the fact that at least one of his brothers, Alonso García Vegaso, was in Peru. He left this brother and his illegitimate son Lucas Martínez Vegaso only modest bequests in his will and does not seem to have associated closely with them.[55] Clearly Lucas much preferred Alonso Ruiz, and he chose to forge with him bonds of kinship and common origin—Alonso became his partner, then his brother-in-law and a trujillano—rather than rely on the ones already at hand.

Family, Kinship, and Recruitment

The importance of having someone to trust with one's economic affairs and properties accounted in part for the close connections extremeños maintained with one another in the Indies and their frequent efforts to recruit young relatives from home. The priest Francisco Regodón, who sent for his nephew Alonso Regodón Calderón in Trujillo, wrote to his brother-in-law Vasco Calderón in 1578 that he had lost 4000 pesos as a result of having trusted distant relatives.[56] Alvaro de Paredes wrote to his brother in February 1591 that a man to whom he had entrusted "a little capital" absconded with the money.[57] Others had similar experiences. Francisco González de Castro, the treasurer of Santa Marta, wrote to his brothers that he would be happy if one of them sent a son; but he qualified this, saying that "if he turns out to be as irresponsible and as much my enemy as was the son of Francisco García who came here, I'd prefer he doesn't come, because I don't see him nor do I know where he is."[58] Along with affection and family loyalty, letters from emigrants in the Indies often expressed a very real anxiety that the economic gains of years or even decades would be lost for lack of an heir or trusted relative to take charge of affairs. Francisco Ojalvo, the shoemaker whose business flourished in Trujillo (Peru), wrote to his nephew Gonzalo Ojalvo in Cáceres in the 1570s:

> The greatest pain and grief . . . I have is not to have you at present in this country to give you the little I have. . . . Because if I died, the greatest pain I would carry would be if you were not here to collect what I leave, because this country is such that almost everything is lost when a man shuts his eye.[59]

Inés Alonso Cervera wrote to her son in Trujillo in the late 1570s about "the need I have for you because, as I say, I have no help nor anyone to look after my property."[60]

On the whole, however, despite the dangers of travel and fac-tional turmoil, the frustration experienced by men like Alvaro de Paredes in Mexico or Diego de Ovando de Cáceres in Peru—who, despite his connections and loyal services to the crown, never re-ceived an encomienda or any kind of compensation[61]—and the economic risks and uncertainty that could spell disappointment or disaster, the evidence suggests that most emigrants to the Indies felt that they had substantially improved their condition and possi-bilities by making the move to the New World. Letters from emi-grants to family members did not paint exaggerated pictures of wealth, but instead emphasized the potential for a good life if one were willing to work. Lorenzo Gutiérrez, who in 1572 wrote from the valley of Ica in Peru urging his son Mateo in Cáceres to join the family, indicated that they certainly were comfortable if not rich. Two of his daughters had married there and a third was about to do so, all of them to "well-to-do and rich men."[62] Antonio and Andrés Pérez of Cáceres, vecinos of Puebla de los Angeles in the 1540s and 1550s, wrote to their brother Francisco Gutiérrez inviting him to join them; they also talked about their prosperity and the good life they had made for themselves. The two brothers had married two sisters, the daughters of "honorable parents," and lived in adjacent houses in Puebla.[63] When Inés Alonso Cervera wrote to her son García de Escobar in 1577, she had been recently widowed; "since our Lord has been served to take my husband," she wrote, "he has compensated me in possessions, of which I have many."[64]

The strength of family ties and the marked tendency to regard the pursuit of opportunities offered by the Indies as a collective, family undertaking, rather than an individual one, accounts for numerous examples already cited of family members emigrating together or joining each other in the New World. The evidence for this pattern is so abundant that one suspects that almost any emigrant identified from the passenger lists or other records probably had at least one other relative—parent, uncle, sibling, or cousin— in the Indies. The Guerra family of Cáceres provides a good case in point. Alonso Guerra was in Peru quite early. He received an encomienda from Francisco Pizarro and by 1537 was a vecino and councilman of San Miguel de Piura; in that year he appeared with fellow cacereño Francisco de Godoy to receive Godoy's power of attorney. Eventually no fewer than six members of Guerra's immediate family—five sons and a brother—would join him in Peru.[65]

Diego Guerra, who claimed to be an hidalgo and Alonso Guerra's legitimate son, prepared an información in 1562 detailing what he and his brothers had done in the New World. Diego had gone to the Indies looking for his father, arriving first in Puerto Rico and moving on to Hispaniola, where he helped put down an attempted slave revolt in Santo Domingo. After spending a couple of years there, he left for Tierra Firme and then Peru, having heard his father was there. Diego went to San Miguel but did not find his father until he went on an expedition to quell a local revolt; Alonso Guerra met the expedition with supplies. Diego stayed on in Peru, marrying around 1550 and inheriting his father's encomienda, which was located 140 leagues from San Miguel.

In 1562 Diego complained that the repartimiento's annual income of 1500 pesos was insufficient to support himself and his brother Juan Guerra "to whom he is obligated." Juan Guerra had been in Peru since some time in the 1540s. Two other sons of Alonso Guerra— Fray Alonso Guerra and Fray Ambrosio Guerra—both Dominicans—also were in Peru. Yet another son, Pedro Guerra, went on from Peru to Chile, where he died with Pedro de Valdivia. Diego Guerra also testified that his father's brother Diego Guerra de la

Vega had gone to the Indies as a secret envoy of the crown and later produced chronicles of the discovery and conquest of New Spain and other events. This uncle became a priest. Eventually he too went to Peru, where he died in the city of San Miguel.[66]

We have, then, six men in one family drawn to Peru, singly or in pairs—Diego Guerra and his uncle Diego Guerra de la Vega each got there on his own, the two Dominican brothers probably went there together—by the presence of Alonso Guerra. Alonso Guerra was in Peru from the 1530s, and his connection with Francisco de Godoy suggests that from the beginning he formed part of the closeknit cacereño group so active in the early years. In this case, as in others such as that of the early settler and encomendero of Trujillo, Lorenzo de Ulloa, who attracted three of his brothers and a sister to Peru,[67] the early and successful establishment of one family member in the Indies offered others not just a precedent to follow but seemingly a solid base from which to develop their own careers in the New World.

These hopes often met with disappointment. Diego Guerra found his father's encomienda barely sufficed to support him, his family, and his brother Juan and enable him to send money back to his mother in Spain, and not one of Lorenzo de Ulloa's brothers who came from Cáceres established himself successfully in Peru. Nonetheless such men, especially the hidalgos who (with the exception of the ecclesiastics) mostly lacked any particular vocation, operated according to standard notions of how to make one's way in the world. When a family member moved to the Indies, the Indies became part of the enlarged arena in which family and kinship networks could function to provide opportunities and a livelihood for other relatives.

The continuous recruitment of younger relatives by people established in the New World and the desires of parents for the children they had left behind to join them reflect one of the paradoxes of life for Spaniards in the Indies. While many emigrants' economic circumstances improved strikingly as a result of the move, for whatever reason—late marriages, mortality rates—they frequently failed to produce heirs. Thus while they often found the economic security that had eluded them back home in Spain, they were unable to pass the benefits on to their children. Francisco Ojalvo, who sent for his nephew in Cáceres, was married but childless. Antonio Pérez, vecino of Puebla, had no children, although his brother Andrés had several, legitimate and illegitimate. The encomendero Juan Ramiro had married doña María Martel in Lima but died without heirs, as did Juan Pantoja in Honduras and many, many others. Diego de Trujillo, the veteran of Cajamarca and encomendero of Cuzco who sent for his nephews in the 1570s, married four times but had no surviving heirs. Doubtless children born in the Indies were much more susceptible to the epidemic diseases that were ravaging Indian populations than were their parents. Alvaro de Paredes in 1602 had six small children. Two years later he had lost two; "there have been a thousand illnesses and three deaths" (the third was his mulatto servant).[68]

While marriages could bring personal fulfillment and happiness, they often hinged on pragmatic considerations. Thus Alonso Carrasco married his uncle's widow, who had inherited the encomienda. The consequences for Carrasco of that practical arrangement were quite literally fatal. A trujillano named Hernando Caballero entered into another type of situation when he wrote to the widow of his compatriot Pedro Martín about Martín's untimely death (following a failed business venture, Martín died trying to escape from a royal constable sent to arrest him for his debts; he threw himself into a river near Cuzco and drowned). Caballero was supposed to take charge of collecting what remained of Martín's estate—he had owned a mine at Potosí—for Martín's widow in Trujillo. He ended up marrying one of Pedro Martín's illegitimate daughters, who apparently had inherited the property.[69]

Common origins or relationship could influence choice of marriage partners, hence the strikingly anomalous marriage of the noble trujillano don Pedro Puertocarrero to the wealthy commoner María de Escobar, widow of Francisco de Chaves of Trujillo.[70] Gonzalo Pizarro intended to marry off his mistress María de Ulloa in Lima to a compatriot. He wrote to her in April 1547 that "an hidalgo of my country, who has served much in this land, named Pizarro de la Rua, I have married to you, because he is a good soldier and has my name; and I think you will be very happy with him."[71]

The same factors that resulted in a frequent lack of heirs—delayed marriages or no marriage at all, mortality among children—could enhance the importance of the mestizo children that Spaniards had with Indian women. While most mestizo children were illegitimate, their fathers often recognized and raised them. Francisco, Gonzalo, and Juan Pizarro all failed to marry in Peru and all fathered mestizo children, some of whom were sent to Spain;[72] it was not uncommon for mestizo children to end up there. Cristóbal de Ovando Paredes took his mestiza daughter doña Beatriz back to Cáceres in the 1580s and placed her in the convent of Santa María de Jesús.[73] Diego de Sanabria, an early vecino of Mexico City, in his will of 1528 left fifty pesos to his mestiza daughter Isabel and gave two of his fellow cacereños responsibility for his daughter, instructing them to take her to Castile so that his mother or brother (a priest) could care for her.[74]

More typically, however, mestizo children remained in the New World where their possibilities probably were much better. A son of Frey Nicolás de Ovando, Diego de Ovando, who became one of Gonzalo Pizarro's captains, was called a "mestizo natural de Extremadura."[75] Bartolomé Chico de Halia of Zorita, who died in Charcas in the 1560s, left his mestizo son 800 pesos and instructed that he not be sent to Spain.[76] Lorenzo de Aldana married his mestiza daughter to another encomendero, and don Pedro Puertocarrero, whose marriage to María de Escobar was childless, shortly before his death allegedly fathered a boy by an Indian woman, Ana Vispa, who had been his wife's servant. Although because of don Pedro's advanced age and illnesses some people doubted that the child could have been his, don Pedro recognized the boy, gave him his name, and made him his heir, and he sought to legitimate his son by marrying the boy's Indian mother just before his death (María de Escobar died before the child was born). In the 1590s Bachiller don Cristóbal de Albornoz, a dignitary of the cathedral of Cuzco, said that don Pedro had been very happy when his son was born and showed him to everyone who came to his house, "saying look how he resembles me in this and that."[77]

Local and Regional Ties

Emigrants' economic activities, legal involvements, marriages, and families all underscore the extent to which the extremeños maintained their connections with one another. These associations were so pervasive that they must be considered a crucial aspect of their lives in the Indies with many implications and repercussions. Emigrants frequently gave their power of attorney to relatives and other acquaintances from their home towns or regions. Extremeños served as witnesses for the transactions, wills, and other documents executed by their kinsmen and home town acquaintances, testified on their behalf in suits, took custody of orphaned children, and bought and sold property held in Spain or the Indies to each other. The encomendero Maestre Tomás in Mexico in 1527, for example, bought houses in Trujillo for 100 pesos from another trujillano in Mexico, Hernando Pizarro, who was acting as guardian of Francisco de Gaete.[78] Such patterns of association characterized not only the early years but persisted throughout the sixteenth century. Juan Rodríguez de Ocampo, the trujillano who was treasurer of Quito, bought some juros on the sales tax of Trujillo from Licenciado García de Valverde, doubtless while Valverde was oidor in Quito in the mid-1570s.[79] Francisco Calderón de Tapia of Trujillo, who went to Peru in 1573 in his mid-twenties, in 1580 became the guardian of don Pedro Puertocarrero, the mestizo son and heir of his noble father of the same name.[80] Continued reference to and association with relatives and other people from the same home town or region conditioned or affected the decisions and activities of extremeños in the Indies for years.

Letters home in particular shed light on these continuing connections. Andrés Pérez, after living in New Spain for some twenty years, mentioned two other cacereños, Cosme de Ovando and Alvaro de Cáceres, when he wrote to his brother in Spain in 1559.[81] Diego Martín de Trujillo of Garciaz in 1562 wrote to the priest Alonso de Aguilar (apparently his wife's uncle and the guardian of the daughter they had left behind) about several people who must have been from their town or nearby and known to Aguilar: "My sister and Juan López and Miguel Sánchez, my brother-in-law, and Hernan Martín are all alive and well. We know nothing of Andrés Martín for three years because [he went] to Peru with merchandise and we await him here."[82] Fray Gaspar de Carvajal wrote to his brother Diego de Carvajal in Trujillo that their compatriots Martín de Chaves and Alonso García Calderón had drowned together in Peru in 1549.[83] In two letters in 1606 Alvaro de Paredes mentioned the arrival in Vera Cruz of cacereño Alonso Gil, son of the man who owned the oven next to their father's house in Cáceres. Paredes passed along the rumor that Gil and his wife had disappeared from

Vera Cruz because they had emigrated without the proper legal authorization.[84]

Testimony of people who returned to Spain also reflects the network of contact and communication that extremeños maintained in the Indies. Alvaro Rodríguez Chacón, who returned to Trujillo from Mexico in the 1570s to get his children, testified that Francisco Gómez of Trujillo had a tailor's shop with a good business in Mexico City.[85] Seven returnees to Trujillo testified that they had been with Juan Ramiro in Lima before his death.[86] Juan de Ribera, who went to Tierra Firme and Peru in 1562 as a merchant and returned three or four years later, testified at different times in Trujillo regarding people he had seen in the Indies. In Lima he had met Felipe Rodríguez, a silversmith, and Pedro Gómez, whom he said he knew both in Trujillo and Lima; both of them had left young sons in Trujillo. In Santa Marta Ribera stayed in the house of the treasurer Francisco González de Castro.[87]

Emigrants frequently borrowed money from one another. Lorenzo de Aldana's will of 1562 mentioned a debt of 1100 pesos he owed to Leonor Méndez, the wife of cacereño Juan de Hinojosa.[88] The associations of people in the Indies also could generate complicated transactions that involved people at home in Spain as well. Jerónimo Holguín borrowed money from fellow cacereño Benito de la Peña in the 1550s and arranged for the sum to be repaid in Cáceres by making an agreement with a notary, Pedro Pérez, by which 2045 maravedís of rents that belonged to Holguín were transferred to Peña's brother in Cáceres.[89]

The mobility of many Spaniards in the Indies enhanced both the possibility and the importance of maintaining this network of acquaintance and association. Furthermore it must be remembered that the total numbers of Spaniards, even in the largest centers of settlement, were relatively small, which also helps account for their success in preserving and utilizing these connections. Mexico City in the midsixteenth century, for example, had perhaps 75,000 Indian residents but only about 8 to 10,000 Europeans and another 8,000 Blacks.[90] Thus the European element or community there constituted the equivalent of a contemporary small Castilian city. Since Spaniards in their everyday lives in the Indies generally took Indians into account only indirectly for the most part, for many intents and purposes they could maintain social relations with one another and pursue their economic activities within a frame of reference not entirely unlike that of their home towns and villages in Castile in scale. Naturally the greater diffusion of people over large areas made for some real and important differences in the New World setting; but mobility and the effectiveness of communications among people who were separated geographically to some degree compensated for the scattering of people and worked to bind them together.

The accounts and chronicles of the conquest and civil wars of Peru provide endless examples of the close association of extremeños. After Cajamarca, in which seventeen men from Trujillo and towns nearby and two from Cáceres participated,[91] perhaps the most spectacular episode in Peruvian history that involved virtually everyone from the region in one way or another was Gonzalo Pizarro's rebellion of the 1540s against the New Laws that restricted the encomienda.[92] Many extremeños—above all, the trujillanos— were loyal and enthusiastic supporters of Gonzalo Pizarro from the outset. Although the shrewdest ultimately defected, while the rebellion lasted their support was crucial. Extremeños were not drawn into Gonzalo Pizarro's entourage simply because of common origin, but rather because common origin, as seen, meant common ties of relationship and acquaintance. Pizarro's rebellion, in other words, did not in itself so much call forth local or regional solidarity as draw on it, and of course in turn reinforced already-existing networks and ties by involving people in acts of rebellion and treason. Gómez de Solís (of Cáceres), for example, wrote to Pizarro from Tumbez in December 1546:

I am bringing with me Benito de la Peña, who is the person I talked to you about the night before I left, because he's from my country [tierra] and I love him very much, and I have great trust in him because I know him, and also because he is very dedicated to you.[93]

The trujillano Fray Gaspar de Carvajal wrote from Jauja in May 1547:

I am going with all haste to see you. I bring a companion, father Fray Alonso Trueno of our country [tierra], who wishes to serve you. Although it's not legal for him to take up arms, I know he will use those of Jesus Christ and pray to God on your behalf, as do I.[94]

Naturally, given Gonzalo's strength and momentum during much of the rebellion, expressions of friendship and support might have been the only guarantee of safety. Fray Jerónimo de Loaysa, bishop of Lima, wrote to Gonzalo Pizarro at the end of 1546 "you understand that I an truly your servant and friend, although according to what I understood . . . and later was told . . . there has been no lack of suspicions to the contrary."[95] Given the close ties that extremeños maintained with one another, their mobility in Peru, and the constant communication that resulted, it was all but impossible not to take sides—and taking the wrong one likely had serious or even fatal consequences, as in the case of cacereño Hernando de Aldana. A veteran of Cajamarca and encomendero of Cuzco, Aldana was executed by one of Pizarro's lieutenants in 1546.[96]

Two young trujillanos, Alonso de Bibanco and Pedro Jara, who returned to Spain with Licenciado Gasca in 1549, were subsequently accused in the death of Nicolás de Heredia, executed by Pizarro's field marshal Francisco de Carvajal. Witnesses claimed that Bibanco and Jara had served only brief stints in Pizarro's camp, under coercion. Martín Casco, another returnee to Trujillo, said that Pedro Jara had been with Carvajal maybe two or three weeks. "He went with his merchandise and against his will because the said Pedro Jara told it to this witness later with tears in his eyes." Pedro de Cuevas, who had arrived in Peru with Pedro Jara in the 1530s, at one point managed to warn Jara that Carvajal intended to intercept him on his way back to Cuzco, and he arranged for Jara to hide for a few days. After Pizarro and Carvajal left Cuzco, Pedro Jara came to Cuevas's house, and they stayed in Cuzco until Gasca arrived. Pizarro had posted guards along the river between Cuzco and the royal camp so that no one would desert to the other side. Cuevas said that the guards captured and killed eight or nine men who tried to flee, including a man from Trujillo named Sotelo, after which everyone else stayed put to wait out the denouement of the revolt. [97]

The bonds of kinship and loyalty continued to play a key role to the very end as events unfolded. Gonzalo Pizarro had real difficulty accepting the possibility that such close friends and allies as Gómez de Solís or Pedro Alonso de Hinojosa might actually have betrayed him. When he wrote to cacereño Francisco Hernández Girón from Lima in April 1547, he was convinced that the delegation he had

sent to meet the crown's representative, Gasca, in Panama must
have come to a bad end. He wrote "it's fair that everyone should
know . . . what I will do in revenge of your friends Lorenzo de
Aldana and Gómez de Solís, because if anything has happened, it's
certain that they will receive the greatest part of the bad treatment,
as a result of being such friends of mine."[98] And Gasca's representative to Gonzalo Pizarro, Pedro Hernández Paniagua de Loaysa,
constantly stressed his extremeño ties and origins. He was a cousin
of the bishop, don Jerónimo de Loaysa, and Gómez de Solís was his
wife's cousin. According to the account of August 1547 that he
wrote to Gasca, he judged that these kinship ties had been crucial
in securing his safe conduct to Pizarro's camp. In conversation with
Gonzalo Pizarro he called the bishop his "nephew," said he had
brought with him one of his (the bishop's) brothers, and referred to
Aldana as a relative. No doubt tongue in cheek, he appealed to
Gonzalo on the basis of their common ties and origins:

I thought that [having] arrived to you, all my labors were done, in that you
would grant me a thousand favors and rewards for being from Extremadura, and a *deudo* and servant of your deudos, and of one friendship and
party [bando], and for the letter of Sr. Alvaro de Hinojosa [Pizarro's
brother-in-law].

He also pointed out that he had expected to benefit from the favors
that his "lord and cousin" the cardinal had always done for Gonzalo's brothers.[99]

The consequences for many of the extremeños who participated
in the rebellion were bad or fatal, although quite a few not only
escaped punishment but landed solidly on their feet. Some, like
Pedro de Bibanco and Blas de Soto, died before the end of the
conflict. Soto was Gonzalo Pizarro's maternal half-brother and died
just before his wife gave birth to a son.[100] Their deaths notwithstanding, these men were tried and convicted along with a number
of other men—Rodrigo Pizarro, Bartolomé de Aguilar, Gonzalo
Hernández, Cristóbal Pizarro, all of Trujillo, and Diego de Ovando
(son of Frey Nicolás de Ovando)—and their goods confiscated.
These confiscations often directly affected people in Spain, since
properties there were forfeit as well. Blas de Soto's sister Isabel de
Soto, who had been raised by Gonzalo Pizarro's sister Inés Rodríguez de Aguilar and had married the Pizarro retainer and returnee

Diego de Carvajal, had to give up the 1000 ducados that her brother had donated for her dowry.[101] The participants in the rebellion who survived to face trial usually were sentenced to exile from the Indies and condemned to the galleys. One man from Trujillo, Francisco Velázquez, went to trial and was sentenced, spent two or three months in jail, and then went free, according to returnees Alonso Cervantes and Pedro Jara who testified in Trujillo in 1550. Apparently he was recruited by Captain Juan Alonso Palomino to help apprehend other followers of Gonzalo Pizarro who were still at large and received a full pardon for his services.[102]

Certainly leniency and reconciliation played an important part in the process by which Gasca won over many of Pizarro's followers and secured their future loyalty. Alonso de Bibanco and Pedro Jara, who returned to Spain with Gasca when they were still young men of thirty or less, formed close ties to Gasca. Returnee Alonso de Cervantes testified in Trujillo that Gasca was fond of Bibanco and "showed him much love." Juan de Monroy, who returned to Spain on the same ship as Gasca, said that since Pedro Jara traveled on a different boat, Gasca sent "to find out how he was and if he needed something to eat" and then sent Jara a quintal of biscuits, saying that "if there were anything else he needed he should say, that he would provide it, and he showed him much love." Pedro de Cuevas testified that after they returned to Spain, he and Pedro Jara went to visit Licenciado Gasca at the home of the archbishop in Cantillana, where Gasca received them and then sent Jara on his way to Trujillo, commending him to Francisco de Loaysa, brother of the archbishop of Lima.[103]

The participation of people from Trujillo and Cáceres in Gonzalo Pizarro's rebellion, along with other less spectacular examples of close association in the Indies, raises the question of what the real scope and extent of associational networks were. Were the networks regional or subregional, or did real cohesion and solidarity actually extend little beyond one's home town? The question is complex. Certainly the appearance—in fact the prominence—of cacereños in Pizarrist camps from the earliest years in Peru attests to significant regional or subregional ties; yet the relations between cacereños and trujillanos on the whole do not reflect the almost invariable solidarity and loyalty that characterized the relations of trujillanos with one another. Essentially the cacereño supporters of

Gonzalo Pizarro were the same individuals who had actively and consistently associated with the Pizarros from the very beginning. But men such as Hernando de Aldana and Lorenzo de Ulloa distanced themselves from the Pizarros fairly early and did not flock to Gonzalo Pizarro's camp, nor did many later-arriving cacereños. In contrast, the trujillanos in Peru supported Gonzalo to a man. Similarly, while people from Trujillo and its town Zorita knew one another, and their ties of kinship, acquaintance, and common origin fostered frequent association, here again solidarity was less consistent, as seen in the dispute between Alonso Carrasco of Zorita and Alonso Pizarro de la Rua of Trujillo.

Other aspects of association reveal similar patterns. Officials assigned encomiendas for which there was no immediate heir not to a person from the same region but rather to someone from the same home town, if possible. Only in their marriage choices for themselves or their children did emigrants abandon their preference for partners from their home towns, and surely this was so because they had no real choice, given the limited possibilities in the New World. If they could make such alliances, they did. It would appear, then, that the more regional (rather than local) nature of marriage choices reflected not the most characteristic or preferred pattern of association by place of origin but rather a much more diluted form forged by the circumstances and context of the New World.

In the end the conservatism manifested in preferences for association failed to become the dominant feature of social organization in the Indies largely because there simply were not enough trujillanos or cacereños available to do everything that needed to be done. Had there been, the factionalism that was so prevalent and disruptive in early Peru doubtless would have been even more pronounced and enduring. Yet if home town identification, clustering, and cohesion were so important and tenacious, why then did people from Seville, for example, not take over and run everything in the Indies? The answer to that question touches on a complicated set of factors involving timing, leadership, occupations, and destinations. But the answer also would underscore the same point made earlier about local society in Spain: Spanish cities and towns were quite separate, with their own distinctive patterns of development and organization. Given its remarkable expansion and dynamism in the sixteenth century, Seville certainly was a far more varied and complex, and therefore far less cohesive, place than the small, conservative cities of Alta Extremadura.

Ties to Home

The ties that extremeños maintained with home manifested themselves as clearly and frequently as those that bound them to one another in the New World. As did association with other extremeños in the Indies, ties to home conditioned the decisions made by emigrants and the people they left behind and reflected their concerns and objectives. Emigrants wrote letters, sent home for relatives, visited (or returned permanently), sent back money to support family members and further family strategies and objectives, and invested in rents and properties, chaplaincies, and charitable works. These activities resulted from some rather distinct concerns. Continued investment in properties in Spain could indicate that an emigrant had plans (or at least intentions) to return there to live, while endowing charitable works in one's will obviously reflected another kind of aspiration. But in a larger sense all these concerns were related, because they were rooted in emigrants' perception of what their place of origin represented. The home town and all it encompassed—family, friendship, reputation—continued to serve as a major point of reference even after years of absence. Ultimately emigrants made their choice either for Old World or New, but this decision, whether conscious or not, could evolve slowly. It is in the context of this sometimes protracted process of transferring allegiance and interest from one side of the Atlantic to the other that one must consider the emphasis emigrants placed on obligations to and ties of affection with relatives at home, their cohesiveness in the Indies, their desire to reunite with family members, their investments in property to assure themselves or their heirs a secure place in their home town, and their concern for status and prestige in a distant "tierra" they might never see again.

Furthermore, people at home often continued to view absent family members as a vital part of the family unit, to be consulted or considered when important decisions were made. In 1560 Lorenzo de Aldana's mother in Cáceres, doña María de Ulloa, said that in donating a part of her estate to her eldest son, Alvaro, and making her will, "her intent and will has never been nor was nor is to deny her son Lorenzo de Aldana, presently in the Indies, nor her grandson," of what was rightfully theirs.[104] When Isabel González, the mother of emigrant sons Antonio and Juan Cotrina, made her will in 1579, she instructed that none of her properties should be sold nor was her daughter Juana to leave the house until Antonio Cotrina arrived (he probably was in Seville at the time). If Antonio died, then the executors should wait at least until her son Juan, still in the Indies, had been informed by letter.[105]

People in Spain sometimes continued to involve themselves in the affairs of people in the Indies even after the death of the immediate family member. Lorenzo de Ulloa Solís in Cáceres spent years trying to settle the affairs of his brothers Gómez de Solís and Juan de Hinojosa, who died in Peru. The business dealings of the latter were complex, and even matters that really concerned his sister-in-law Leonor Méndez rather than his brother occupied Lorenzo de Ulloa's attention. Leonor Méndez had been married first to Miguel Cornejo, and a suit that she brought against someone in Córdoba probably involved money owed to her first husband. Lorenzo de Ulloa Solís handled the matter nonetheless. When Leonor Méndez won her claim in 1579, the money went to the sons of her first marriage.[106]

People at home in Cáceres and Trujillo assigned their power of attorney to friends and relatives in the Indies to collect the legacies of deceased relatives, or undertook the journey themselves for that purpose, or sent a young relative or representative in their place. They also responded with some frequency to the invitations of relatives in the Indies to join them there. Thus people on both sides of the Atlantic had strong motivations—economic, legal, and emotional—to maintain their connections with one another.

The flow of money from emigrants to relatives or acquaintances in Spain was constant if erratic. Almost all the private letters that survive either referred to money that had been or would be sent or offered apologies if none was forthcoming immediately.[107] In her letter from Lima of March 1578 to her son in Trujillo, for example, Inés Alonso Cervera said she had sent 700 reales with the last fleet—500 for one of her daughters and 200 for her son—and that she was now sending another 40 ducados.[108] The amounts and form that such remittances took varied considerably, as did the purposes for which they intended. If the money was meant to cover the passage and travel expenses of a family member or members, most likely the amount sent would exceed those costs by very little. But the provision of dowries, acquisition of offices, or support of family members could generate much larger remittances. Francisco Picón sent 500 ducados from Peru to Bachiller Antonio Picón in Cáceres to buy rents for the dowries of his sisters "las Piconas" in the late 1570s. Around the same time Dr. Francisco de Sande sent approximately 1100 ducados to his mother to cover the costs of business that his brother don Juan de Sande was conducting at the court and to purchase a seat on Cáceres's city council for don Juan.[109] Martín López, a vecino of Arequipa, sent his wife and children in Trujillo more than 2500 ducados in 1549.[110]

People at home in Spain could receive varying quantities by various means over an extended period. Juan Rodríguez de Cepeda, a cacereño who acquired a position as notary in Huamanga, sent 3000 pesos to his father in the early 1570s and 128,118 maravedís to his brother Alonso Domínguez in 1580. Domínguez's sister and niece received the money via the regidor don Juan de Sande (brother of Dr. Francisco de Sande) and another vecino of Cáceres; they in turn had gotten it from the priest of the church of San Pedro in Seville. Alonso Domínguez himself had been in Peru and had sent 600 ducados for his sister's dowry in the 1560s. Domínguez sent the money to Francisco de Ovando, mayorazgo, and his sister collected the 600 ducados from a priest who worked as Ovando's agent.[111]

Such cases reveal the complexity that recovering money coming from the Indies often entailed. In 1571 a vecina of Cáceres, Francisca Jiménez Durán, stated that she had received 480 reales that her son Lorenzo de Montanos had sent from Honduras via a merchant from Seville. At the same time Montanos sent another 565 reales to two brothers and a sister, possibly his cousins. They had to spend 30 reales of this for "certain inquiries and suits" to get the money from the Casa de Contratación, and the merchant who had brought the money from Honduras sent the remainder on with a muleteer from Cáceres.[112] Thus the number of middlemen involved in the transfer of money could proliferate. Madalena Pérez, whose husband was in the Indies, received several sums of money for her daughter Costanza Pérez. A sum of 24,000 maravedís came from Madalena's brother in the Indies, Rodrigo de Soria, via a

vecino of La Serradilla (a town in Extremadura), as well as a separate amount of 30,800 maravedís. Madalena Pérez also acknowledged receipt of another 20,000 maravedís from her daughter's
aunt who was a vecina of Trujillo. In 1577 Costanza Pérez and her
sister Catalina received another 200 ducados from their uncle Rodrigo de Soria, via a cacereño merchant who in turn had received
the money from a vecino of Alcaraz. Rodrigo de Soria also sent his
nieces documents so that they could collect another 130 ducados
from a banker in Madrid.[113]

The frequency and size of these remittances and of other kinds of
financial arrangements made indicate that many emigrants took
their continuing ties and obligations to the families they left behind
quite seriously. Alonso Delvás wrote to his brother Francisco Delvás, a silversmith, from Victoria (New Granada) in January 1568,
saying he had sent 50 pesos and that Francisco "should do what is
obligated for the lady our mother and our sister until I provide
more.[114] Diego de Trujillo wrote to his sister from Cuzco in 1565,
saying he had sent her 224 ducados and another 50 ducados to his
wife's sister in Fuente de Cantos. He also was sending another 100
ducados for Christmas: "be certain," he wrote, "that every Christmas while I live I'll send money."[115]

Emigrants also remembered people back home in their wills. In
the same letter of 1568 Diego de Trujillo told his sister that he had
more than 1500 ducados for her and her son and that in his will he
was leaving another 3000 ducados for his brothers and their sons.
Juan Rubio, a native of Santa Cruz de la Sierra who died in
Popayán, left half his estate to his nephew Hernán Pérez Rubio and
one-fourth each to his brother Juan Sánchez Rubio and a niece
Leonor Alonso, his sister's daughter. In 1583 this niece's husband,
Juan Sánchez of Santa Cruz, asked permission to go to Popayán for
four years to collect the legacy, taking with him a son who could
help him with the estate because he knew how to read and write,
which Sánchez could not.[116] Collecting legacies often occasioned
applications for short-term sojourns in the Indies. Juan Ramiro's
mother sent another of her sons, García Ramiro, to Lima in 1555 to
collect the "many goods and estate, gold and silver and other
things" Juan Ramiro had left. García Ramiro posted a bond of
100,000 maravedís, pledging to return in three years.[117]

Probably more commonly people assigned their powers of attorney to acquaintances already in or en route to the Indies to collect on the estates of relatives. On his second trip to Peru in 1569 Licenciado Altamirano of Trujillo took with him a power of attorney of the heirs of Bartolomé Chico de Halia of Zorita, who had died in Peru leaving them about 3600 pesos. Apparently the family was having difficulty extricating this legacy from the executor, Pedro Alonso Carrasco, and eventually Bartolomé Chico de Halia's son Pedro went himself.[118] In 1551 a man and woman who claimed to be the siblings of Alonso de Toro, a veteran of Cajamarca, encomendero and lieutenant of Gonzalo Pizarro who was killed by his father-in-law in 1546, made an arrangement with Juan Velázquez to collect Alonso de Toro's legacy. Velázquez, who was the brother of Licenciado Altamirano, was to keep one-third of whatever he recovered.[119] While this probably fraudulent effort doubtless yielded nothing, since the crown in any case confiscated Toro's property at the end of Gonzalo Pizarro's rebellion, identical or similar names and circumstances at times might have created genuine confusion. In 1579 three sisters, their husbands, and the husband of a fourth sister who had died (in the name of their five children) gave their power of attorney to returnee Antonio Cotrina to collect 726 silver pesos from the Casa de Contratación. They said that the money came from their brother Vasco Gallego, who had died in San Miguel de Piura in Peru, and presented evidence demonstrating that he was in fact the Vasco Gallego of Cáceres and not another man from Plasencia.[120]

Conclusion

Remittances of money, the purposes for which such money was intended and used, and the emphasis in emigrants' letters on business and practical affairs and economic opportunities underscore and reflect the principal expectations and aims of the people who went to the New World. Adventure and excitement (along with the quest for gain and opportunity) unquestionably motivated many people to go to the Indies in the early years. But Spanish American society consolidated rapidly, and emigrants chose destinations where they had relatives or acquaintances; increasingly, therefore, people were going to America not to meet the challenges of adventure and risk but rather those of making a livelihood and rising in the world, whether they stayed in the Indies or returned to Spain. Although extremeños sought to preserve or recreate a context defined by relations of family, kinship, and common origin whenever possible, the circumstances of their lives in the New World often limited their ability to do so and introduced new elements into the traditional social equation based on family and home. In their objectives and activities extremeños over time proved to be no different from all the other emigrants who left Spain—nor, for that matter, did they differ markedly in these regards from all the other hundreds of thousands of emigrants who left the Old World for the New from that time until the present day.

VII

Return Migration

The available data indicate that sixty-two trujillanos and twenty-six cacereños returned to Spain permanently, while temporary return-ees (visitors) numbered twenty-six and twelve for Trujillo and Cáceres respectively. Even assuming that these figures (like the figures for emigrants in general) are low, the actual movement of people was greater than the numbers suggest, since some individu-als visited home at least once before returning for good (for exam-ple, Juan Cano, the encomendero of Mexico who eventually settled in Seville, visited Cáceres in the 1540s), whereas others traveled to Spain more than once but chose to live in the Indies (or the re-verse, as was true for some merchants and entrepreneurs). Other patterns emerged as well. Diego de Trujillo returned to Trujillo shortly after Cajamarca and the division of Atahuallpa's treasure, but left again after ten years; Martín Alonso, another wealthy, non-hidalgo veteran of Cajamarca, returned to Peru after nearly twenty years in Trujillo. Licenciado Diego González Altamirano served two separate terms on the audiencia of Lima (1551–1558, 1569–1578) and died in Trujillo soon after his second return from Peru. People returned voluntarily and involuntarily for a number of rea-sons; the return home need not have fulfilled their expectations any more than did the move to the New World. Among the returnees there were spectacular successes, obscure failures, and a varied spectrum in between.

The volume of the return movement and the often notable im-pact of returnees and their activities on local society suggest that return migration was more than a simple by-product of the movement to the Indies; rather it was, in many senses, crucial and central to the whole phenomenon. Returnees linked the home society in a concrete and visible way with the Indies. The activities of returnees and visitors, their maintenance of connections with one another and with individuals and events in America, and their direct and indirect promotion of emigration of family members and fellow townspeople gave them an importance in the movement to the New World out of proportion to their relatively small numbers. Return migration from the Indies has been estimated to have been on the order of 10 percent, with possibly another 10 percent of emigrants returning temporarily—to visit, bring back family or other relatives, negotiate business, or some combination of these things.[1] The figures available for Cáceres and Trujillo fall well below this estimate, with the total known volume of temporary and permanent migration closer to 10 than 20 percent. But the only available general estimates of return migration are based on scanty and fragmentary evidence, so it is impossible to know if the Cáceres and Trujillo figures are particularly low. It is clear, however, that in both cities—most notably in Trujillo—returnees were much in evidence, associated with one another, and stimulated subsequent emigration.

Given the relative smallness of the known returnee group and the disparate experiences of emigrants, no single returnee really typified the group as a whole, although certain individuals might have epitomized the image of the wealthy and successful *perulero*.[2] The decision to return to Spain, like the decision to leave, hinged on a number of factors both situational and individual. Family background and social and economic status, position within the family, timing of arrival in the Indies and connections and opportunities found there, and, of course, individual capabilities and even personalities all figured. It is often assumed that the most successful individuals—such as the men who participated in the division of treasure of Cajamarca—returned home, but they simply might have been the most visible members of the returnee group. The most successful returnees made good marriages with women from noble families, bought, built, or renovated urban residences, invested in rents, properties, charities, and chaplaincies, and acquired seats on the city council. All these activities brought them into the public limelight and left ample record in the documents. Failures, or people whose success was more modest, do not emerge so clearly, since their activities often left little trace. People who returned to visit, or who (like Diego de Trujillo and Martín Alonso) returned with the apparent intention of establishing themselves permanently at home but then left again, represented yet other variants in the possible response to the options offered by New World or Old.

Despite the variation in the experience and decisions of return-ees, however, return migration was significant not only because of its perceptible impact on the home society and on subsequent emi-gration, but also because in a sense it represented a phenomenon new to local society. Returning from the New World in some re-spects differed from other kinds of physical mobility that had taken people away from local society. People who moved relatively short distances—within the region, or to Seville—frequently returned, but individuals who left home for destinations farther afield—the royal court, Rome, Vienna—generally did not return permanently, even though they might retain their ties with home. The people whose careers most closely paralleled those of the returnees from the Indies were military officers who served in Granada, Italy, or Flanders and then came back to their native city. Yet here again there was a difference, since military officers often left home with a commission and a specific charge, and emigrants usually departed with fairly vague notions as to what they would do in the Indies and whether or not they would be able to return home. Those who returned, and especially those who returned wealthy, did so largely as a result of personal initiative and enterprise and their ability to manipulate circumstances in the New World, not because they had received a commission or a bureaucratic appointment with a guaran-teed salary and the perquisites of office.

Thus the returnee group, small as it was, represented the possibil-ity that an individual could go off to a relatively unknown situation, with few guarantees of success and no previously established time limitation, and still come home to achieve acceptance and high social standing. If by the second and third generations of emigrants to the New World there surely were many individuals who left with no serious intentions of returning—or at least not permanently—nonetheless others must have hoped for or anticipated a finite so-journ away from home. For those emigrants, the successful return-ees must have exemplified fulfillment of their dreams.

Patterns of Return Migration

Despite the smallness of the returnee group, certain patterns emerge, although on the whole the conclusions they point to are fairly tentative. The little work that has been done on early return migration has suggested that individuals of better social standing would be more likely to return to Spain permanently, since they could expect a good reception there;[3] so it is worth considering the social composition of the returnee group. Nearly two-thirds of the permanent returnees to Cáceres were hidalgos, but perhaps no more than a third of the trujillanos who went home were hidalgos, and those not necessarily of very high standing. Like the discrepancy in the overall social composition of the emigrant groups from the two cities, these rather distinctive patterns require some explanation. Most important, the Cáceres emigrant group included a higher proportion of hidalgos than did the Trujillo group, so logically they would figure proportionately more frequently among the returnees as well.

Once again the size of the movements in both directions might have had some rather complex ramifications. It was suggested in chapter 5 that the larger size of the Trujillo emigrant group probably accounted for its more varied occupational and demographic composition. Given the crucial importance in the Indies of networks and associations tied to point of origin in Spain, presumably the possibilities for people from Trujillo who contemplated emigration—especially to Peru—were much better than for cacereños; the trujillanos' potential for finding patrons and opportunities was greater. As a result, possibly more people from Trujillo decided (or were able) to emigrate for a particular purpose (such as work for a relative or someone else from their home town) and for a finite period, with fairly modest objectives in mind. The nobles and hidalgos of Cáceres, who formed a large part of the emigrant group from that city, probably felt that they could return only if their gains in wealth were such that they could set themselves up in impressive style. Two of the early returnees to Cáceres—Francisco de Godoy and Sancho de Figueroa—did precisely that (although Godoy was away sixteen years and Figueroa twenty-three). But as time went on, this became more difficult; Cosme and Cristóbal de Ovando Paredes were in Peru for eighteen and twenty-three years respectively, returning only when it seemed likely that each in turn would inherit the family entail that originally had passed to their older brother, who died without heirs.[4] Antonio de Ulloa, another cacereño noble, also decided to leave Peru only when news came of the death of his older brother, heir to the family estate; but he died before reaching Spain.[5] In contrast, in Trujillo many commoners or even relatively humble hidalgos evidently did not feel that they had to return with great riches. Taking advantage of the differential value of silver in Spain compared to the Indies, a number of men returned to Trujillo fairly young probably with limited gains, sufficient to purchase some property or invest in censos and establish themselves comfortably but modestly.

The questions of how much wealth one needed to return and how long it took to accumulate it relate to two other aspects of return migration—the length of time people stayed away, and their age when they came back. If we accept that higher-ranking hidalgos and nobles needed substantial wealth before they would consider returning home permanently, and bear in mind that people who missed out on the first spectacular division of treasure in Peru usually had to work a number of years to amass such wealth, then it is not surprising that many cacereños stayed away a long time. Of the sixteen returnees to Cáceres for whom the period of absence can be established with reasonable certainty, nine stayed away at least sixteen years and another three were absent eleven years or more; 75 percent, then, lived in the New World for more than ten years. In contrast the periods of absence that can be ascertained for forty-five returnees to Trujillo show a more even distribution. Half of them (twenty-three) stayed away ten years or less (this category includes six early-returning veterans of Cajamarca), another twelve were absent for eleven to fifteen years, and ten for sixteen or more. This more varied pattern of length of sojourn in the Indies for returning trujillanos is in line with the possibility that more of these returnees had gone to the New World with finite objectives and expectations.

Ages at return further substantiate this idea. Almost a third (nineteen) of the sixty-two permanent returnees were thirty-five years of age or younger when they went back to Trujillo. Many of them, then, were in early middle age or younger, still young enough to marry and establish households, presumably with improved means to do so as a result of their years in the New World. A number of men who returned to Spain with Gasca at the end of Gonzalo Pizarro's rebellion fell within this age group despite having spent some fifteen years in the Indies. Pedro Jara was twenty-eight, Alonso Bibanco thirty, and Diego Jiménez thirty-five. Alonso García de Cervantes, who also returned with Gasca, was thirty and had been away about ten years; Martín Casco, who returned a couple of years later, in 1551, at the age of thirty-five, had spent fifteen years in the Indies, working at least part of that time as an agent for an encomendero of Arequipa.[6] There are a number of other similar cases among the Trujillo group, such as the locksmith Santos García. García emigrated to Peru in 1555 with his half-brother and returned to Trujillo before 1574, probably in his midthirties.[7] These men's careers suggest a pattern that resembles the long-term but temporary labor migration of modern times, in which single young men work for some years outside their own country, ultimately returning to marry and settle at home. Certainly this was not the predominant pattern of movement among extremeño migrants, but apparently it existed in this period. The data for age at return among the Cáceres group are very sparse, making it impossible to judge whether such a process affected young men there as well.

While certain overall patterns can be identified, the actual length of sojourn in the New World of any individual doubtless depended on and reflected a combination of personal circumstances and aspirations and external events rather than the less tangible question of social acceptability. Obviously some people returned having fulfilled short-term objectives. Juan de Ribera, an hidalgo who left for Tierra Firme and Peru as a merchant in 1562 at the age of thirty-two, returned three years later. Andrés Calderón Puertocarrero, the noble who also declared himself a merchant and probably accompanied Ribera, came back even sooner, fleeing authorities who sought him on murder charges in Peru.[8] The two sons of Diego de Vargas Carvajal who accompanied him to Peru in 1560 returned to Trujillo in 1563, right after their father's death and the expulsion of the remaining Comisarios de Perpetuidad, although one of them—don Diego—might have gone to Peru again in the late 1560s.[9]

As part of the terms on which they received licenses to go to the Indies, some prospective emigrants posted bonds as assurance that they would stay there only a specified period of time. García Ramiro,

a twenty-five-year-old bachelor from Trujillo, in 1555 posted a bond
of 100,000 maravedís in Seville as a guarantee that he would return
in three years from Lima, where his brother Juan Ramiro, an
encomendero, had died without heirs.[10] Juan Sánchez, a vecino of
Santa Cruz de la Sierra, in 1583 petitioned for a license to go to
Popayán under bond for four years to collect his wife's legacy from
her uncle, Juan Rubio; he proposed to take his son with him.[11]
Whether these men returned, or returned when they proposed, is
not known; but the posting of bonds at least implies the intention of
making the stay finite.

In contrast other returnees stayed away many years. Captain
Martín de Meneses was in Peru over forty years (he went to Santa
Marta in 1536 and returned to Spain in 1578) and very likely did
not plan to return permanently to Spain. An encomendero of
Cuzco, he obtained permission to leave and retain the income of
his encomienda in his absence. In 1583 he was at court, seeking to
extend his stay in Spain. Apparently he went there to protest the
viceroy's reduction of his encomienda and to request a habit in one
of the military orders for one of his sons. After arriving Meneses's
wife died, two of his sons became seriously ill, and Meneses himself was frail and under stress. He died in Spain before the question
of extending his stay was resolved.[12]

Others did return permanently notwithstanding long absences.
Francisco de Avila, one of three hidalgo brothers from Cáceres who
went to the Indies, was away over thirty years; his activities in the
1570s after his return clearly demonstrated that he meant to reestablish himself in Cáceres. His brother Sancho de Figueroa also
had returned to Cáceres, in 1548 after an absence of over twenty
years; but Figueroa died shortly after his return and marriage. Juan
Cano, the cacereño who married doña Isabel Moctezuma in Mexico
and became the encomendero of Tacuba, was absent some forty
years before returning to Spain in the early 1560s. Cano, however,
did not settle down in Cáceres but rather in Seville. His third son,
don Juan Cano Moctezuma (born in Mexico), did go to Cáceres,
where he married in 1559 and built the "Palacio de Moctezuma"
near the plaza of Santa María.[13]

Most known returnees settled down in their home towns, but a
few, like Juan Cano, chose Seville or the court. Some returnees
might have preferred the more open and cosmopolitan atmosphere

of Seville compared to their small home cities or felt that the incongruity between their newly gained wealth and relatively modest social status barred easy acceptance at home. But probably most returnees who opted for Seville were entrepreneurs and merchants. Francisco Sánchez de Melo, a native of Trujillo, already had become a vecino of Seville by the time he traveled to Peru in the 1550s. Two young relatives of his, the brothers Pedro and Baltasar de Melo, went to Peru as his factors in the late 1550s. Pedro de Melo returned in 1575 and also became a vecino of Seville.[14] Antonio de Cotrina, a marginal hidalgo of Cáceres, traveled to the Indies at least twice before settling in Seville. There in the 1570s he undoubtedly was an entrepreneur of sorts and frequently acted as a middleman on behalf of fellow cacereños in their dealings with the Casa de Contratación.

Returnees, like emigrants, often made the journey home with their families, relatives, and acquaintances. Martín de Meneses returned in 1578 with his wife, three sons, a daughter, and niece, as well as three women of uncertain relationship, and a criada. Also in his party were Rodrigo Alonso, an ironsmith from Trujillo, and his wife Isabel Alvarez. He had gone to Peru in 1569 with his wife and one son.[15] Juan de Castro traveled in the 1573 fleet from Tierra Firme with his wife, two daughters, and a son, plus a mestiza and a black woman.[16]

At least seven or eight men from Trujillo accompanied Gasca to Spain in 1549. Apart from the men who had been at Cajamarca, this was the single largest group of returnees who were not related to one another; but doubtless these men's decision to return was based on very different considerations from those of the Cajamarca veterans. Most of the Gasca group, as mentioned, were fairly young, but all had been in the Indies ten years or more. Why did they leave? Though none of these men were prosecuted for participation in the Gonzalo Pizarro rebellion, the end of the rebellion and the reimposition of royal authority might have left them stranded in a sense. Unlike the great captains (most of whom were cacereños, in any case) who ensured their future in Peru by switching to Gasca's side at the right moment, these trujillanos who left Peru in 1549 had received no rewards, even though probably none was a willing participant in the rebellion. The rebellion and its denouement probably disrupted—at least temporarily—networks of association and patronage and discredited the trujillanos, so these men opted to return home. Significantly almost none of them achieved substantial wealth or position, with the possible exception of Diego Jiménez, whose daughter married into a noble family of good standing.[17]

Reasons for Returning

The resounding success of a number of returnees in itself suffices to explain their motivation for going home. Once back in Spain their activities suggest that these men had well-defined objectives and clear ideas for how they would go about reestablishing themselves in their home towns. Some returnees started to lay their plans well in advance of their return. In 1578, while still in Peru, Cristóbal de Ovando Paredes had his brother Cosme buy a house for him in the parish of San Mateo for 900 ducados; after returning in 1583 Cristóbal spent another 2400 ducados to renovate the house.[18] Juan Cano had been investing in rents and property in Cáceres in absentia for years through his brother, Pedro Cano. His son don Juan Cano Moctezuma (mentioned earlier), who settled in Cáceres, probably inherited most of these holdings.[19] Perhaps the best way to see how successful returnees functioned is to examine in detail the activities of one person.

Francisco de Godoy

Possibly better than any other individual, Francisco de Godoy personified the ideal of the successful emigrant and returnee. Member of a fairly high-ranking hidalgo family of Cáceres related to the Aldanas, Godoy was heir to the bulk (the tercio y quinto) of his father's estate but chose nonetheless to go to the Indies. Born in 1515, he went to Nicaragua in the 1520s and from there to Peru in 1533. In Peru he became a captain and participated in the conquest and civil wars, associating closely with his equally illustrious first cousins, Lorenzo de Aldana and Perálvarez Holguín. He was often in the company of other cacereños in Peru as well. The inventory of his estate and other papers prepared after his death in Cáceres in the 1560s showed the transfer in 1537 of a house that had belonged to Antonio de Ulloa to Godoy and his cousin Alvaro de Aldana. The same inventory included a loan of 220 pesos that Godoy made to fellow cacereño Sancho de Perero (also a returnee) in Lima in 1541.[20]

Although he was not at Cajamarca, Godoy's activities and connections brought him a number of military and official positions in Peru. He received an encomienda in Lima, where he amassed considerable wealth. When he decided to leave Peru, he actually managed to sell off his encomienda in 1542 for some 9000 pesos, although such a practice was strictly illegal.[21] Also in preparation for departure he registered some pieces of silver to be sent from Panama in 1540 and executed a will in Lima in February 1542. In this will he established a capellanía under the patronage of his nephew Lorenzo de Godoy. In August 1541 he had made a donation to the monastery of Santo Domingo in Lima.[22]

Back in Cáceres by the mid-1540s, Francisco de Godoy initiated a remarkable period of activity in which he invested in land, rents, and chapels and, during the remaining twenty years of his life, attained all the trappings of an important noble. He married a woman from a leading noble family, doña Leonor de Ulloa, the daughter of the regidor Lorenzo de Ulloa Porcallo and doña Juana de Ovando, daughter of Francisco de Ovando, el rico. He founded an entail for his son Rodrigo de Godoy; built a splendid house in the parish of Santiago, outside the walls of the old city; spent several thousand ducados on lands and rents; and acquired a seat on the city council in 1555.[23] He also maintained contact with people and events in Peru. Along with accounts and unspecified letters having to do with the Indies, the 1564 inventory of his estate included a bundle of letters from a Pablo Pérez regarding "cosas de Indias" and a large number of other letters and documents (including wills, accounts, and probanzas) pertaining to people he had known in Peru.

Among these documents were letters and accounts of Juan Morgovejo de Quiñones, member of an important noble family of Mayorga in Old Castile with whom Godoy had close connections. They may have met in Nicaragua, although Morgovejo was present at Cajamarca and Godoy was not. Morgovejo's promising career was cut short in 1536 when he died during the attempt to lift the siege of Cuzco.[24] Godoy took charge of Morgovejo's son Francisco from the time of his death and brought him back to Spain. The boy remained in Cáceres, directly or indirectly under Godoy's care,

until he died in 1550. He probably was illegitimate, and Morgovejo's family made no effort to take charge of him while he was still
alive. Godoy, on the other hand, went to some effort for his ward,
investing money he had inherited from his father in juros and
censos and seeing to Francisco's education. In 1546 he sent him to
live with a priest in Cáceres named Suero Díaz Barroso.[25]

Godoy began work on his house after his return. He had inherited the property near the church of Santiago and an additional lot
across the street from his father, and most likely a house already
stood at the site; but Godoy rebuilt it entirely, employing the
master stonecutter Pero Gómez, and expanded the site by acquir-
ing a house owned by the cofradía of Santa María la Vieja. The
cofradía used the house on the "calle de Godoy" for their meetings
and allowed two poor women to live there. Godoy offered the
cofradía "another new and good house" in exchange for the one he
wanted and donated 1000 maravedís of rents.[26]

In 1560 Godoy purchased the upper and lower sacristy of the
church of Santa María for 600 ducados,[27] but most of his acquisitions were in rents and properties. He had already purchased rents
in three different dehesas before he returned, and in the 1540s and
1550s accumulated many more. He frequently bought rents from
several individuals holding title to portions of the same dehesa,
thus achieving controlling interest or even exclusive ownership of
certain pastures. In 1546, for example, he bought rents in one
dehesa from four different people—a vecino of Medellín and three
cacereños, one of whom was his father-in-law and another his
nephew by marriage Benito Moraga. In the same year he purchased a pasture called the "Suerte del Patrón" by buying a quarter
from Benito Moraga and three-quarters from another cacereño noble. In the 1540s and 1550s he acquired additional rights to rents in
the Atalaya, parts of which he and his brother Martín de Godoy
(who had managed his affairs in his absence) already owned. On his
acquisitions in pastures alone during the 1540s and 1550s Godoy
probably spent over a million and a half maravedís, or 4000 ducados; and these purchases by no means represented the entirety of
his holdings. The donation of the tercio y quinto that he made in
1558 to his son Rodrigo de Godoy which—together with Francisco's inheritance from his own father—became the basis of the entail, included substantial winter rents in six other dehesas. Godoy

also acquired other kinds of property and censos. He bought a
vineyard in 1547, a dovecote and an *alcacer* (barley field) in 1562,
and owned a mill. In the 1540s he bought a number of censos,
including one for 10,000 maravedís from the council of Cañaveral, a
village belonging to Garrovillas, as well as a number of smaller
censos from vecinos of Garrovillas. Not surprisingly Godoy was a
stockraiser who was selling wool in the 1550s.[28]

In his will of 1564 Francisco de Godoy reiterated the terms of
the entail he had established in 1558 and reserved for himself the
right to dispose of half the rents of pasturage for four years in his
final testament. By the time of his death, Godoy had three sons and
three daughters (the oldest son, Rodrigo, was about twenty); the
five younger children were to receive 1000 ducados each on reaching the age of twenty. Godoy also had an illegitimate daughter
named doña Mencía de Aldana, a nun in the convent of San Pablo.
Godoy's father-in-law became the guardian of his children.[29]

In his will Godoy established a capellanía in the church of Santa
María for weekly masses to be recited in his chapel of San Juan
Evangelista for his parents, his wife, and himself. He named his
son Lorenzo de Ulloa, who was studying for the priesthood but not
yet ordained, the chaplain; the successor to the entail could name
the next chaplain, preferably a priest of Godoy's lineage or otherwise the nearest available relative. In 1579 Francisco de Paredes,
the son of Lorenzo de Aldana, was chaplain.[30] Godoy also mentioned in his will the donation he had made in 1541 of a house and
store in Lima to the monastery of Santo Domingo and the capellanía he had endowed with houses in Lima in 1542.

Francisco de Godoy's story was one of consistent success. He
survived the political and physical dangers of the civil wars in Peru
and the arduous journey to the New World and back and returned
with a fortune that probably much exceeded his paternal inheritance. That inheritance might have allowed him to live well but not
splendidly; his ventures in the Indies, however, brought him rewards that would have been beyond his reach and enabled him to
establish his family among the top-ranking nobility of the city. His
heir, Rodrigo de Godoy, and daughter, doña María de Godoy,
married siblings who were their mother's first cousins and members of the important Ovando family.[31]

The specific factors that combined to assure Francisco de Godoy's success—his early presence and good connections in Peru, the sale of his encomienda, his family's position in Cáceres—might have been unique, but his choices and ambitions were not. This is clear from the activities and accomplishments of other returnees. By the mid-1550s, five returnees from Peru, all of them veterans of Cajamarca, were on Trujillo's city countil; in addition, Hernando Pizarro controlled two city council seats. One of the returnee regidors, Alonso Ruiz, was not even a native of Trujillo, but as seen he had formed a close partnership and friendship with the encomendero Lucas Martínez in Peru. Alonso Ruiz left Peru in 1540 for Trujillo, married Martínez's sister Isabel, became a vecino and councilman, and in 1558 acquired title to the village of Madroñera near the city. By the mid-1540s he had a house and lands and was grazing cattle in and around Madroñera, but he maintained his principal residence in the city in the parish of San Martín.[32]

Juan Pizarro de Orellana, socially the highest-ranking of the Cajamarca veterans, obtained the title of "señor de Magasquilla" (a dehesa, not a village), built a magnificent house just off Trujillo's plaza, and married his son and principal heir, Hernando de Orellana, to doña Francisca Pizarro, the illegitimate daughter of Hernando Pizarro and doña Isabel Mercado. Pedro Barrantes, also from a high-ranking family, became the lord of La Cumbre. His son, Juan Barrantes, married doña Catalina de Orellana, daughter of Juan Pizarro de Orellana. Even returnees of humbler origins could come close to achieving the noble lifestyle. Pizarro retainer Martín Alonso, by the time of his second departure for Peru in 1552, owned a house on Trujillo's plaza worth 1000 ducados and a vineyard in the Sierra de Herguijuela and a garden near the city worth about 1500 ducados; he also held 200,000 maravedís of juros in Seville and Trujillo and 40,000 maravedís of rents of pasturage. In 1534 Alonso had purchased a censo of 100,000 maravedís from the Duke of Béjar through Juan Cortés, another Pizarro retainer and Cajamarca veteran.[33]

Once again, however, it must be emphasized that the Cajamarca men were unusual, not in their ambitions and objectives, but rather in the means they possessed for achieving them. Even years of work or service in the Indies did not guarantee real wealth. Licenciado Diego González Altamirano renovated his father's house on Trujillo's plaza and founded an entail for his eldest son. But despite his two terms of service on the audiencia of Lima, he had no great fortune; his wife had to add her dowry to her husband's entail in order to make it solvent.[34] Another Trujillo returnee, Diego de Carvajal, who had accompanied Hernando Pizarro back to Peru, participated in the siege of Cuzco and received shares of gold and silver. His Pizarro connections notwithstanding—he married Juan Pizarro's half-sister Isabel de Soto—after his return to Trujillo in 1541 his status was modest, so much so that in the 1550s he and his brother Gonzalo brought a suit in Granada against the city for including them in the padrón of taxpayers. While Carvajal clearly had some means—he bought a censo on a mill in 1551 from two merchants for 500 ducados—he did not occupy a very prestigious position in local society.[35] Other returnees were humbler yet; a Juan Jiménez, perulero, was listed in the 1561 census of Santa Cruz de la Sierra as a "labrador mediano."[36]

While most returnees probably tailored their ambitions to their social station and financial wherewithal, some people must have returned because they failed to find a place or do well in the New World. Someone who was unable to take advantage of opportunities in the Indies probably would not find his circumstances much altered on his return home. One less than outstandingly successful returnee was Hernando de Sande, member of an ambitious family recently established in Cáceres that claimed hidalgo status and relationship to the illustrious and powerful Sande clan of Cáceres and Plasencia. Hernando's older brother, Dr. Francisco de Sande, had a long and successful career in the Indies in the last third of the sixteenth century, serving twice on the audiencia of Mexico, as governor of the Philippines, and as president of Guatemala and Santa Fe de Bogota. Several of his other brothers also had successful careers in Spain or the Indies. One served in Flanders and ended up on the Cáceres city council, another as an army officer in the Philippines, and a third was a Franciscan who became head of the monastery of San Francisco de Bogotá at the end of the sixteenth century. All his brothers used the honorific "don," but Hernando did not, although he was their full legitimate brother. He traveled to the Indies in the 1560s and spent some time with Dr. Sande in Mexico, but apparently never found a niche there. After a few years he returned home, where he handled some affairs for his brother Dr. Sande, and died in Cáceres in 1577.[37] One suspects that his failure was largely personal, because Dr. Sande worked hard to bolster the careers and prestige of his other brothers.

Some men were literally forced out of the Indies or, like Andrés Calderón Puertocarrero, fled from authorities there. Diego García de Paredes, member of a leading noble family of Cáceres who had a ten-year military career in Europe before going to Peru in 1546 to join Gasca, ran afoul of Gasca or his officers and was sent back to Spain within a few years. Charges that he had participated in the Gonzalo Pizarro rebellion were never proven and in the 1550s Paredes was released from prison; but his career was ruined, and he lived the remainder of his life in obscurity.[38] Hernando Pizarro himself, of course, spent years in prison after returning to Spain because of his involvement in the execution of Diego de Almagro. His confinement in the castle of Medina del Campo, however, in no way inhibited him from actively overseeing his family's affairs and furthering the family interests at every turn. Other returnees may have gotten into trouble once they were back. Pedro Jara and Alonso de Bibanco, two of the Trujillo men who accompanied Gasca back to Spain, had to defend themselves against charges of complicity in the execution of Captain Nicolás de Heredia, a victim in Peru in the 1540s of Gonzalo Pizarro's field marshal Francisco de Carvajal.[39] A Francisco de Rodas left Popayán in the mid-1540s and died within a few days of reaching Trujillo. He left an emerald belonging to the governor of Popayán, don Sebastián de Benalcázar, in the house of a priest, also Francisco de Rodas (no doubt a relative). Rodas apparently had smuggled the emerald into Spain,[40] but with his death escaped prosecution by authorities.

These cases, like the careers of the most successful returnees, underline the interconnectedness of people and events on both sides of the Atlantic. The effective authority of royal officials often was limited by their available resources and the resistance of local people to outside interference (royal officials never were able to arrest Andrés Calderón Puertocarrero, despite a couple of determined attempts). Nonetheless the prosecution of individuals who had returned to Spain for activities that took place thousands of miles away in Peru or elsewhere reflects not only a high degree of awareness of the actions and whereabouts of people who were moving around, but also the extent to which the entire Hispanic world formed a single arena. Distance notwithstanding, Trujillo was as closely tied to Peru as it was to Seville or the court. Emigrants and returnees, whether they succeeded or failed, moved through channels of communication, advancement, or misadventure that were known and predictable to authorities and private individuals alike.

Visitors

Individuals of all types and for a variety of reasons went back to Spain temporarily. Doubtless a distinction should be made between people who went to Spain to visit—for a finite period, with definite intentions—and people who returned intending to stay or undecided as to their future plans who subsequently left again. The latter group, which would include Cajamarca veterans Martín Alonso and Diego de Trujillo, were not visitors strictly speaking but rather second-time emigrants. Francisco de Orellana, for example, after participating in Gonzalo Pizarro's expedition to the Amazon region, returned to Spain only long enough (1543–1544) to obtain the capitulaciones for the further exploration of the Amazon and to organize the expedition. In contrast his fellow trujillano Diego García de Paredes, who accompanied him to the Amazon, had returned to Spain in 1534 with Hernando Pizarro and spent the next ten years fighting in Europe. He did not necessarily intend to return to the Indies when he left there in 1534; his second return, in 1562, followed within the year by his departure as the appointed governor of Popayán, much more likely was a visit. Another trujillano, Rodrigo Bravo, had a similar career. Having already fought in Italy, Bravo went to the Indies in 1555 and served the crown in Chile and Peru; returning to Spain in the 1560s, he fought in the Alpujarras rebellion of 1568–1570. In 1571 he petitioned to go back to Peru, taking with him a relative and two criados.[41] Bravo, and others like him, may have found it difficult to fit in and settle down on either side of the Atlantic.

Some people got into trouble in the Indies and found themselves making a temporary return to Spain. Alvaro de Cáceres, exiled from the Indies for one year, returned to New Spain in 1575, taking two of his nieces with him.[42] A Diego de Ovando de Cáceres was sent back to Spain in the 1550s by the viceroy of Peru, the Marqués de Cañete. Ovando, whose older brother Lorenzo de Ulloa was an important settler and encomendero of Trujillo in Peru, had arrived in Peru with Licenciado Pedro de la Gasca in 1547. But despite a solid record of service, Diego de Ovando failed to establish himself very well in Peru. Furthermore he had taken on responsibility for his sister, whose husband had died in one of the civil wars; she received only a small pension to support herself and her children. Ovando complained of their situation and clashed with the viceroy, who sent him to Spain. Although he went back to Peru in 1558, Ovando once again was shunted off, this time to Chile. He died shortly thereafter.[43]

Another cacereño, Juan de Hinojosa, also got into trouble and paid an unanticipated visit home. Hinojosa was a younger son in a prominent noble family of Cáceres who became a wealthy and successful entrepreneur and encomendero of Arequipa. In the 1560s he wrote a provocative and defamatory letter to the corregidor of that city, who sent out ten or twelve horsemen to a farm of Hinojosa's to arrest him. He eluded his pursuers and fled to Lima, where his lawyer impressed upon him the seriousness of the charges against him. Hinojosa decided it was an opportune moment to pay a visit home and left for Spain without returning to Arequipa, where the corregidor had his properties confiscated. He later returned to Peru.[44]

Restless and troublemaking types aside, the majority of temporary returnees were people who were unable or unwilling to return permanently and decided to visit Spain to see family and friends, bring back their families or relatives to the Indies, or take care of legal and other business. Hernando de Aldana and Gonzalo de los Nidos, two cacereños who were in Peru quite early, both obtained permission to go to Spain in the mid-1530s and retain their encomiendas. Both went back to Peru with siblings—Aldana with his brother, and Nidos with two of his sisters and possibly a brother as well.[45] Francisco Calderón de Tapia of Trujillo in 1581 returned from Peru after about eight years there to act as the representative and guardian of the mestizo son of the encomendero don Pedro Puertocarrero. He planned to take back not only his own children but also the wife and children of Juan Carrasco, a native of Zorita living in Lima, who had given him his power of attorney for that purpose.[46] Doubtless the visit with the most far-reaching consequences was that of Francisco Pizarro, who returned to Spain in 1529 to obtain the capitulaciones for the conquest of Peru and recruit men to join his expedition. Yet the fame and many repercussions of this visit aside, Pizarro did much the same things as other visitors. He transacted business at court; visited his home town and recruited people from Trujillo and the region; and took back family members—four of his half-brothers—with him to Peru.

The motivations of visitors for the most part are clear from their activities and circumstances. At least seven encomenderos from Trujillo and Cáceres visited Spain. Permanent return would have meant forfeiting the income of their encomiendas, so these men opted for America. Antón de Andrada, who first left Spain at the age of twenty as part of Lucas de Ayllón's expedition to Florida, returned to take up residence in Seville, where he married. In 1576 he took his family to New Spain. Andrada was a younger son of a leading noble family in Cáceres,[47] and one might guess that his first sojourn in the Indies did not enrich him sufficiently to return to Cáceres and set himself up in the style to be expected, given his family's position in society. Like many others, he foresaw better opportunities in the New World.

Impact of Returnees

A very perceptible effect of returnees, both permanent and temporary, was that they directly stimulated further emigration, not only of their fellow townspeople but often of their own family members and other relatives. The visit from Mexico of Alvaro Rodríguez Chacón to Trujillo in the 1570s, discussed in chapter 5, serves as an excellent illustration of the impact a visitor could have on subsequent emigration. He went back to Mexico with an entourage that included his three unmarried sons, his married daughter with her husband and four children, and his daughter's brother-in-law, wife, and children, as well as several criados.[48] Alvaro Rodríguez Chacón's visit, then, resulted in the emigration of perhaps fifteen or more people. A number of similar examples of people who returned from the Indies and went back accompanied by relatives or servants already have been mentioned. Diego de Trujillo, the Cajamarca veteran who lived in Trujillo for ten years before deciding to return to Peru, was followed a few years later by his wife, Costanza Rodríguez, their two sons, and her two brothers. She also took servants and slaves.[49]

Permanent returnees also stimulated emigration. Juan de Ribera, who made a short trip to the Indies in the mid-1560s as a merchant, sent his sixteen-year-old son Cristóbal de Ribera to join his uncle (Juan de Ribera's brother) in Popayán in 1578, the year that Cristóbal's mother died. Cristóbal's uncle, Bachiller Gonzalo de Torres, by then a high-ranking church official in Popayán, had written many times asking that Juan de Ribera send his son. Cristóbal could "read and write and count," and possibly he, like his uncle, embarked on an ecclesiastical career.[50] Two sons of wealthy Cajamarca veteran Pedro Barrantes—the older a priest in his thirties, the younger an adolescent—went to Peru in 1579, decades after their father's brief sojourn there. Another man from Trujillo accompanied them as their criado.[51] Families associated with bureaucratic service might maintain the tradition over generations. Don Blas de Torres Altamirano, one of the sons of returnee Licenciado Diego González Altamirano, in the seventeenth century served as *fiscal* in Lima and Quito and as both criminal magistrate and judge of the audiencia of Lima, as his father had done.[52]

Returnees played an important role in creating and perpetuating cycles of emigration in which family members of successive generations followed one another to the same destination and established themselves in the New World. Juan de Castro of Trujillo, who went to New Granada in 1569 to join his uncle Francisco González de Castro, treasurer and long-time resident of Santa Marta, doubtless departed with another uncle, Pedro de Castro, who returned to New Granada that year with his family.[53] Juan de Castro's decision to emigrate probably hinged as much on the visit and actual presence in Trujillo of his uncle Pedro de Castro as on the letters that his uncle Francisco wrote from Santa Marta.

Returnees and visitors also contributed to the formation and maintenance of networks of friendship and association tied to place of origin that characterized and shaped so many of the activities of people involved in the New World enterprise. The cacereño Benito de la Peña, who had participated in the Gonzalo Pizarro rebellion in Peru in the 1540s (but, like most of the prominent cacereños involved, suffered no dire consequences as a result) was in Cáceres in 1547. By 1549 he was back in Peru. That year he sent his power of attorney to two of his brothers in Cáceres authorizing them to collect a sum of 90,000 maravedís that Peña had lent to another cacereño, Pedro de Vita, in Peru from Vita's estate in Cáceres. Since Vita was arranging for the administration of his property in Cáceres in late 1546, and was with Peña in Potosí in 1549, it seems likely that the two men—visitor and first-time emigrant—traveled together to Peru and continued their association once there.[54]

Even where it cannot be shown that returnees directly fostered further emigration, their very presence in their home towns as examples and sources of advice and expertise must have encouraged people to consider going to the Indies. Three returnees testified on behalf of Francisco Cervantes, who petitioned for a license to go to Peru in 1571 to join his uncle Diego de Trujillo. Three other returnees in Trujillo testified for Sancho de Cabañas, who wanted to join his sister in Lima in 1575.[55] There are many such examples, and certainly it was no coincidence that intended emigrants chose returnees as their witnesses. Individuals who had been in the Indies not only could assist them in completing the necessary legal and other preparations for departure but they had contacts in and knowledge of Seville and the Indies that could make a crucial difference in the emigrant's experience, both during the journey and after arriving in the New World.

Returnees forged friendships and associations in the New World that they maintained after their return home, thereby creating networks of association that could encompass people in the Indies, Seville, the court, or other parts of Castile. The example of Francisco de Godoy, discussed earlier, indicates the existence of such a network extending well beyond his home city of Cáceres to include people still in Peru and the family of his ward in Mayorga. People in the New World frequently looked to friends and relatives who had returned home to take care of legal or economic transactions, and they sent money back to Spain for their families or to invest via returnees. For their part the returnees called upon people still in the Indies to administer their properties, take charge of mestizo children they had left behind, and settle various debts. Sancho de Perero, who had been an encomendero in Peru and was back in Cáceres by his midthirties, in 1559 arranged for fellow cacereño Gómez de Solís in Peru to give the Indians of his encomienda 2000 ducados to relieve them of their tribute obligations. Francisco de Ulloa Solís, Gómez de Solís's brother, was a party to the arrangement made in Cáceres. Such restitutions, often made rather late in life or at a time when the original wealth and population of an encomienda had diminished considerably, were not at all uncommon.[56]

Business dealings, friendships, and family relationships linked not only emigrants and returnees but also people who never left Spain but were themselves associated—through family, business, or acquaintance—with those who did. An episode involving a returnee to Cáceres, a barber named Francisco Durán, illustrates the expanded circles of contact and acquaintance within which emigrants and returnees moved. In 1561 Durán stated that he owed 45,000 maravedís to Juan de la Cueva, native of the "city of Baeza and Ubeda [sic]." Cueva had given him the money in Lima to take back to his father in Spain, but instead Durán spent it all during the journey. Cueva asked that Durán repay the money to Francisco de Ulloa Solís, who then would send it to doña Ana de Navarreta, abbess of the cloister of San Millán de Ubeda, perhaps a relative of Cueva's or someone to whom he owed money.[57] Francisco de Ulloa Solís had two brothers in the Indies—the aforementioned captain and encomendero Gómez de Solís, and the encomendero-entrepreneur Juan de Hinojosa—but never went there himself.

By no means of least importance in terms of understanding the changed (and expanded) context in which returnees functioned as a result of their New World experience, they often formed close ties with one another that they maintained and elaborated after reestablishing themselves at home. As already observed, Trujillo society from at least the middle of the sixteenth century showed a perceptible impact of the clustering and association of returnees in the composition of the city council and the marriage choices of returnees and their children. The returnees remained aware of one another's whereabouts and activities. In 1552 when Alonso de Bibanco and Pedro Jara defended themselves against charges brought in connection with Captain Nicolás de Heredia's death in Peru, they elicited testimony from six other returnees who were vecinos of Trujillo and a returnee from Deleitosa, a town near Trujillo and closely connected with it (although in the jurisdiction of Jaraicejo). Bibanco also traveled to Cáceres to get testimony from the returnee Sancho de Perero. Other witnesses were returnees who were natives of Zafra, Garrovillas, Valverde (jurisdiction of Badajoz), and Cazalla de la Sierra (near Seville).

The men who testified in this criminal proceeding—both the accused and their witnesses—had many years of association and acquaintance behind them. Pedro de Cuevas, a witness, went to Peru in 1534, at the same time as the accused Pedro Jara, although the two did not travel on the same boat. Both participated in the fighting at Cuzco and supported Licenciado Vaca de Castro against Almagro, and Cuevas and Jara both inadvertently became embroiled in Gonzalo Pizarro's rebellion. At one point during those unsettled times, Cuevas found out that Pizarro's henchman Francisco de Carvajal planned to seize Jara on his way back from Potosí to Cuzco in order to confiscate his goods or money (Jara was a merchant). Cuevas managed to warn Jara to leave the main road and arranged for him to hide for a few days in a cave, where he sent him food; thus Jara eluded capture. The two men returned to Spain together in Gasca's entourage.[58] Despite perhaps ten years' difference in age, their shared experiences and close association suggest an almost brotherly relationship.

At the same time, long acquaintance and experiences shared in common by no means guaranteed friendship and solidarity. In Trujillo the best illustration of this was the long-term and bitter enmity between returnees Juan Cortés and Juan de Herrera, the origins—if not the consequences—of which remain obscure. Both Cortés and Herrera were at Cajamarca, both returned to Spain early (Cortés in 1533, Herrera in 1535), acquired seats on the city council, and married. Both were associated with the Pizarros, although Cortés was some twenty years older and his relationship with the Pizarros (especially Hernando) was of much longer standing and more important than Herrera's. Herrera was in his late teens when he left Trujillo for Peru, and at Cajamarca Cortés received much larger shares of gold and silver, a reflection of his role and his close connections with the Pizarros. The break between the two men occurred because Cortés challenged Herrera's handling of part of the sum of 25,000 pesos that Juan Pizarro had entrusted Herrera to bring back to Spain. The amount of money in dispute was in relative terms so trivial, and Cortés's behavior so vindictive, that the episode surely reflected some already-existing antagonism.

The story went as follows. While Herrera was in Lima and about to leave for Spain with Juan Pizarro's money, Diego de Carvajal arrived with instructions to buy a horse for Juan Pizarro. Since

Carvajal had no money for the purchase, Herrera paid 1300 pesos for the horse out of the money he was taking to Spain. Despite ample testimony and proof that the transaction had taken place as Herrera described, Cortés won the suit and recovered the sum. Herrera forfeited his house in Trujillo and 21,000 maravedís in juros and also spent some time in jail. Furthermore the boat in which Herrera returned to Spain had been forced ashore in southern Portugal and the money he was carrying confiscated, so that he had to go to considerable effort and some expense to retrieve it and fulfill his charge.[59] If there had been bad feeling between the two men before the dispute, the suit and Cortés's unbending attitude (very likely a reflection of Hernando Pizarro's) fanned the flames of hostility into a burning hatred and "enemistad."

The roots of the conflict seem to have lain principally in Cortés's personality. Significantly, other long-time associates of the Pizarros and Cortés, such as Diego de Carvajal, did not rally to Cortés's side; in fact Carvajal's evidence by all rights should have exonerated Herrera. Returnee Martín Alonso, perhaps the most sympathetic member of the Pizarro circle, once stated that he had tried to reconcile the antagonists but failed. Cortés's propensity for overt conflict and his unwavering devotion to the Pizarros emerged again in a near-violent confrontation with an important Trujillo noble, Juan de Escobar (the brother of the royal confessor, Fray Diego de Chaves). Cortés apparently proclaimed publicly and repeatedly that Pedro Alonso Hinojosa, a captain in Peru and Escobar's brother-in-law, had not acted as a "caballero" and had betrayed Gonzalo Pizarro by turning to Gasca's side. Escobar wrote a letter to Cortés defending Hinojosa's actions in Peru, and Cortés responded by demanding a meeting. The two men nearly came to blows in the church of Santa María and were about to adjourn to fight it out in the countryside, when a friend of Cortés persuaded him to desist by pointing out that the matter did, after all, involve the delicate question of allegiance to the crown as well as loyalty to Gonzalo Pizarro. The disagreement among the men and rancor over events in Peru touched the women close to them as well. Cortés's wife, doña María de Ribera, and Juan de Escobar's mother got into the same argument over Pedro Alonso Hinojosa while visiting in the house of noblewoman doña Juana de Acuna. Their hostess and Juan de Herrera's wife, doña Ana de Hinojosa, managed to make peace between them.[60]

Apart from their contribution to generating emigration from their home towns and their role in maintaining connections between New World and Old, the greatest impact of the returnees on local society lay in the wealth they brought home. As seen, they used their capital to build and renovate houses; acquire urban and rural properties, rents, censos, and juros; purchase seats on the city council and jurisdiction or señorío over small towns and villages; provide dowries for daughters or sisters to marry well or enter convents; establish or enlarge entails for sons; refurbish and construct chapels; and found capellanías and charitable works. Some people came home with substantial capital resources at their disposal, which was not very common in provincial towns where wealth was mainly agrarian rather than mercantile. The inventory of returnee Cristóbal de Ovando Paredes's assets prepared in 1588 showed that in addition to 4000 ducados he had lent to people in the Indies, relatives and acquaintances in Cáceres owed him more than 5000 ducados altogether; one of his cousins, Hernando de Ovando de la Cerda, had borrowed 1000 ducados. These debts were not owed on censos or other transactions, but rather represented loans Ovando Paredes had made.[61] In 1578 returnee Licenciado Diego González Altamirano lent 3500 ducados to four regidores of Trujillo.[62]

The uses to which returnees put their capital were conservative, at least in kind. Certainly they did nothing especially innovative with the wealth they had at their disposal, but rather followed a predictable course in their economic, social, and political investments that was largely shaped (depending on their status and means) by the ideals and aspirations of the upper or middle classes. But despite this basic conservatism in kind, there was a real difference in degree. The amount of wealth brought back and the very size of the return phenomenon led to some striking developments in local society. In Trujillo the altered composition of the city council, acquisition of towns and titles by returnees or their descendants in the sixteenth and seventeenth centuries, and the sometimes dazzlingly high dowries (at least by local standards) returnee families provided daughters in order to form illustrious marriage alliances combined to produce a returnee elite that directly challenged the wealth and position of the nobility hitherto so dominant in local society. Of course one might argue that the change was far from revolutionary and that, for the most part, only the returnees of fairly solid social origins (that is, hidalgos) attained these heights of prestige and position; commoners Diego de Trujillo and Martín Alonso could not make the leap into the upper ranks. Nonetheless if the achievements of the wealthy returnees fell considerably short of transforming social structure as such, they undeniably caused a shakeup and realignment in the upper ranks of local society, especially in Trujillo. This new configuration underscores again the flexibility and adaptability of social structures that tend to convey, at least outwardly, an impression of great conservatism and stability. The wealth the returnees brought home wrought concrete and perceptible changes in local society, from the appearance of huge and splendid new houses to the formation of a new aristocracy that intermarried and acquired new titles and possessions. These innovations suggest that the fairly closed and stable nature of the old upper class was a result at least in part of the relatively limited resources of local society. By expanding the resources and opportunities available to people in these towns in Extremadura, the Indies enterprise made change possible in local society.

Family Ties

Emigration to the Indies often meant the temporary or long-term separation of families; as seen, men might leave their families behind, or parents would take older children with them but leave the younger ones at home. While return migration could mean reuniting with spouses or children, it too could work to perpetuate or complicate the geographical dispersion of families. In 1581, at the time of the final division of the estate of Captain Gonzalo de Olmos, a returnee from Peru who died in 1574, three of his sons were in Peru, while two other sons and four daughters (one was a nun in the convent of San Pedro) were living in Trujillo. Olmos may have returned early to Spain, in the 1530s, so possibly his sons were born in Trujillo and later emigrated to Peru on their own.[63] A daughter of Licenciado Diego González Altamirano stayed behind in Peru and entered a convent in Lima and, as mentioned, one of her brothers later returned there to serve on the audiencia.

Children who were born in the Indies or had been there from an early age, however, might come to Spain, sometimes with parents

or guardians, other times on their own. A man named Domingo de
Arquinigo, who in 1578 testified that he had known some trujillanos in Peru, said he had lived there since he was a child and had
come to Spain only recently. He was thirty-two years old.[64] Families with strong ties and stakes on both sides of the Atlantic could
generate a good deal of movement back and forth and end up fairly
well scattered. The Loaysa family of Trujillo was a case in point.
Two brothers, Alonso and Francisco de Loaysa (nephews of the
archbishop of Lima, Fray Jerónimo de Loaysa), went to Peru in the
mid-1530s, probably with Hernando Pizarro. Alonso de Loaysa
married doña María de Ayala, and possibly some of their children
were born in Peru before they went to Trujillo, where Loaysa died
in 1574. One of their sons, don Gaspar de Ayala, went to Peru in
the late 1580s, returning to Trujillo in 1596. At least one other son,
Captain Francisco de Loaysa, and possibly a daughter, made Peru
their permanent place of residence.[65]

The careers and choices of the cacereño Juan Cano and his descendants reflect the complexities that could arise in families that
maintained a foothold in both Old World and New. An associate of
Hernando Cortés, Juan Cano received an encomienda after the
conquest of Mexico but lost most of it. He became an important
encomendero only by virtue of his marriage to doña Isabel, daughter of the Mexican emperor Moctezuma. Doña Isabel received the
large encomienda of Tacuba from Cortés before she married Cano,
with whom she had three sons (Pedro, Gonzalo, and Juan) and two
daughters, who entered a convent in Mexico City. Doña Isabel's
son by a previous marriage, Juan de Andrade de Moctezuma, after
his mother's death in 1551 disputed Cano's claim to the encomienda, and eventually it was divided; in the 1560s the encomenderos were Juan de Andrade, Juan Cano, and the latter's sons
Gonzalo and Pedro Cano. But the encomienda represented only
part of the basis of the Cano Moctezuma family's fortunes. In the
1530s and 1540s Cano initiated petitions for *mercedes* (grants or
awards) from the crown, alleging that his wife had received only a
portion of the patrimony due to her from her father, Moctezuma.
Cano's son Gonzalo pursued these claims with some success, and
the family also accumulated large landholdings in New Spain.
Gonzalo Cano also received several pueblos outside the Tacuba

encomienda and the Valley of Mexico through the terms of his mother's will.[66] At the same time, before he returned to Seville in the 1560s, Juan Cano was buying lands and rents in and around Cáceres.

Juan Cano's third son, don Juan Cano Moctezuma, left Mexico to settle in Cáceres, where he married doña Elvira de Paredes Toledo and probably inherited most of his father's estate in Spain. He received a royal annuity of 1800 ducados and in the 1570s apparently still had some income from the encomienda or other family properties in Mexico. Contacts between family members in Cáceres and Mexico continued even beyond the generation of Juan Cano and his sons. In 1602 another don Juan Cano Moctezuma (grandson of Juan Cano and the son of Gonzalo Cano, who remained in New Spain) was in Cáceres litigating with his cousins, the sons of his uncle don Juan Cano Moctezuma. The dispute concerned Juan Cano's entail and legacy, which included 300,000 maravedís of juros that Juan Cano had held in the rents of the *almojarifazgo* (customs duties) of Seville.[67]

Did these lingering connections between people in Spain and the Indies, sometimes enduring over two generations, mean that some extremeño families were able to maintain themselves as true transatlantic units, comparable to some of the great mercantile families of Spain? Probably only to a very limited extent. Mercantile fortunes were fairly manipulable, but the properties held by extremeños both in Spain and America often were not. Transferring the income from properties and holdings in the Indies back to Spain could cause problems, and maintaining holdings in absentia—especially encomiendas—was difficult or impossible. As a result the familial center of gravity usually could not be shared between family members in Spain and the Indies for long and ultimately came to rest on one side of the Atlantic or the other. If some extremeños returned home to live, others became important figures in colonial society and founded new family dynasties quite independent of family and relatives in Spain. The Cano Moctezumas achieved sufficient wealth and prominence to establish themselves firmly on both sides of the Atlantic. But while Juan Cano's sons and grandsons in Mexico and Cáceres maintained some contacts (if nothing else because of properties held in absen-

tia and occasionally in dispute), the Mexican and extremeño relatives soon came to constitute distinct and independent branches
of the family and no longer comprised a single unit.

Conclusion

The background, careers and accomplishments of returnees and
visitors were sufficiently diverse that it would be fair to regard
them essentially as a subset of the overall emigrant group, distinguished from the rest mainly by reason of their return. On the
whole returnees were exceptional within the larger group of emigrants because they possessed the means and motivation to return
to Spain; individual objectives and personal assessments of what
constituted sufficient means could vary considerably. Yet by returning these particular emigrants played a special role, both in stimu-
lating further emigration and altering the fabric and facade of their
home societies. The significance of the Indies for local society certainly was not limited to the activities and presence of the returnees; but without the returnees and their accomplishments, the
impact of the Indies surely would have been much less tangible and
immediate, and therefore far less central.

Conclusion

The study of emigration from the Cáceres-Trujillo region and the participation of people from that area in the Indies enterprise points to two conclusions that show the interconnectedness of Spain and Spanish America in the sixteenth century. First, involvement in America had a direct, tangible, ongoing impact on local society in Spain. Second, the strength of the ties of family, kinship, and common origin rooted in the home town and region in Spain could have long-term repercussions for the activities and objectives of emigrants in the New World. From the point of view of many people in Cáceres and Trujillo, the Indies were not an isolated and remote enclave of the royal domain but instead an important extension of the arena in which they could function to pursue opportunity and advancement for themselves and their families. For emigrants in the New World, attachments to home continued to play a vital part in shaping their choices and objectives.

The most common view of the relationship of Spain to Spanish America in the sixteenth century has been nearly unilateral, reflecting a model of change and impact in which the major currents of influence flowed in one direction—westward. Castile exported its institutions of government and church, forms of economic organization, and people to the New World. The new society of Spanish America developed within the institutional and socioeconomic framework imposed by Spaniards, and it preserved the language, religion, and many of the social patterns of the Spanish settlers. Although it is clear that Spain to a great extent did provide the basic outline and direction for the development of postconquest society in the Indies, we also have abundant evidence of the resilience and creative adaptation of indigenous cultures in face of the European conquest and colonization of the New World. Scholars are discovering more and more about how those cultures affected and persisted within Spanish American society.[1] The American context and cultures influenced and at times transformed Spanish expectations and forms of activity and organization. The new Spanish American societies were the product of the encounter, confrontation, and accommodation that took place between the people and cultures of Old World and New in the western hemisphere.

Spain and America also met in Europe, but the process and results of that encounter have not been examined in the same terms or with a specificity comparable to that which scholars have brought to bear on the question of contact between the two societies in the New World. Inquiry into the significance of America for sixteenth-century Spain and Europe has been confined largely to the realm of intellectual perception and response and the topics of economic and demographic impact.[2] But the ramifications and repercussions of the Indies enterprise for Spanish society were more complex and subtle than consideration of scholarly debates or inflationary trends in prices alone would suggest. The assumption that socioeconomic transformation was limited to the American side of the Atlantic reflects a static, generalized view of Spanish society that fails to account for the dynamic changes that already were underway from the late Middle Ages and that would accelerate and become more complicated with the opening of the New World. From the sixteenth century on the Atlantic did not separate Old World and New but rather bound them together; the currents of influence and impact flowed in both directions. If the forces for change did not affect the towns and villages of Castile as suddenly and drastically as those of, say, central Mexico, nonetheless they could touch the lives of people in Spain closely and sometimes dramatically. Perhaps even more important, to people in places like Cáceres and Trujillo the Indies quickly came to represent not an exotic and distant destination that attracted only the most adventurous but a sphere in which they, their relatives, and acquaintances were directly and indirectly involved. Consider the following statement made in testimony in Trujillo in 1549:

In this city it's the fashion and custom, since there are many people in Peru who are citizens of this city, that when a stranger or native comes from there, those who have relatives there—who are many—as well as others who don't, in order to know [about them] go to ask and find out from such persons the news of the Indies.[3]

Experience of and involvement in the Indies permeated local society in Cáceres and Trujillo.

The first four chapters of this book offered a detailed account and analysis of the structure, composition, and functioning of local society in Cáceres and Trujillo and the surrounding smaller towns and villages by examining the variety of social and occupational groups and corporate and family units that constituted that society. Describing and analyzing local society and the people who participated in it made it possible to view the careers of emigrants and returnees in the context that played a crucial role in shaping their decisions and future activities. Furthermore, considering the lives of emigrants from the point of view of how they functioned within their home society allowed us to see the extent to which their activities and motivations reflected and conformed to those of many of their kinspeople and neighbors.

Emigrants and returnees were, of course, exceptional in some ways. They undertook ambitious and drastic changes in their lives that went well beyond the more limited moves in search of opportunities made by others who stayed much closer to home, and they often took considerable risks to do so. One cannot discard altogether the notion that an emigrant group tends to draw on the more dynamic and determined elements in a society. Yet we have seen that major, risky moves and career choices, comparable to departure for the Indies, were not unprecedented in this society. Military service probably offers the closest parallel to emigration, since it could entail extended absences from home and an array of dangers (and possible rewards); but even entry into a religious order, for men at any rate, could mean definitive separation from home and family. Certainly emigrants must have been tough and determined people for the most part. But no individual's life or decisions can stand for the experience of an entire group; and a person who decided to go to the Indies no more typified society or some facet of it than did someone who stayed at home. Still, neither the aspirations nor the achievements of emigrants were so distinctive that they separated them clearly from their compatriots in most regards; the only consistently distinguishing factor that characterized them was their choice to go to the New World.

Local society merited a great deal of detailed attention in the book because it was the primary milieu in which the majority of people functioned and the main focus for their loyalty and interest. The word "pueblo" embodies most accurately the significance of the relationship of people to place because it stands for both. Citizens of Trujillo referred to their city as a "pueblo," as did residents of much smaller towns; "pueblo" did not connote the size of a place but rather its perceived unity and integrity.[4] As has been observed in modern times as well, in the sixteenth century the city, town, or village—the pueblo—was the principal arena in which family, social, and economic relations developed and functioned, and therefore it was the main context for achieving and preserving reputation and position. If the nobility based their idea of status and privilege on tradition and lineage, these notions were also closely associated with historical ties to a particular place. As the latter chapters of the book have shown, emigrants carried with them and were strongly affected and even in some ways sustained by their ties to their home towns. Their nostalgia was not for Spain but for their real "patria," which was their tierra and home town. Emigrants who could return usually went back to their home towns. If they endowed a chapel or established a charitable work (regardless of whether they stayed in the Indies), that too would be in their home town. Reputation and status had meaning only where one knew people and was known, in the place where one's family had its roots and would continue to live.

Discussion of the many social and occupational groups also has shown the considerable degree of cultural and social homogeneity that characterized the various ranks and groupings of society. Family structure and strategies were similar at all levels of society. The distinctive practices that were evolving among the nobility, such as the creation of entails and unequal division among heirs, should be seen more as variants of the general pattern than as deviations; these practices could in fact be found among commoners as well, if to a much more limited degree. The nobles were set apart from the rest of society by their privileges and perceived status; but virtually no aspect of their lifestyle—including their wealth—was unique to them, as the arrival of wealthy returnees from Peru so dramatically underscored. Furthermore nobles were closely tied to commoners through business and legal affairs and patron–client, employer–employee, and even kinship relations (consider the illegitimate children who were the products of liaisons between noble men and common women), as well as the face-to-face, ongoing contacts that people who lived in small cities and towns maintained.

The cultural and behavioral homogeneity of Spaniards so notable in the New World setting had its roots in local society in Spain. Spanish emigrants were accustomed to orienting themselves to small units—the parish, village, or town—and at home they were organized into and participated in a range of associations that encouraged vertical integration as well as corporate solidarity. Perhaps one of the most impressive aspects of postconquest Spanish American society was how smoothly and efficiently it seemed to function from a very early time. While there were a number of elements in the New World context that contributed to the rapid settling and consolidation of Spanish American society (especially in the two great foci of Spanish activity, Peru and Mexico), the strength and efficacy of Spanish modes of organization imported to the Indies also played an important part. Emigrants were used to functioning in an organizational framework based on family and kinship, common point of origin, patron–client relations, and deference to social superiors. They could transfer these organizing principles to the New World and thus continue to operate much as they always had, even though the setting was quite different from that of home.

Once there were enough people available in Mexico or Peru or elsewhere to do so, emigrants could recreate in some part their customary socioeconomic relations. In the earliest years of conquest and settlement the Spanish presence was still skeletal and experimental; increased emigration after the conquests of the mainland areas in the 1520s and 1530s meant there would be greater concentrations of people from one place together in the New World. This clustering of people fostered the formation of networks of association and cycles of emigration and encouraged a perceptible rise in the emigration of women and families. The emigration movement from the Trujillo-Cáceres region provides a somewhat unusual but nonetheless apt illustration of this process, because of the strong impetus

provided by the activities and success of Francisco Pizarro in Peru.
Pizarro's extremeño contingent, if rather short on business and legal
skills and expertise, nevertheless formed the nucleus for a viable and
visible network based on kinship and common origin. The network
tied people from Trujillo and Cáceres in Peru to one another and to
people back home and allowed them to exploit opportunities in Peru
systematically and successfully.

The connections between the cities of northeastern Extremadura
and the Indies also would suggest that places the size of Cáceres and
Trujillo were almost ideal for taking advantage of opportunities in
the Indies in the collective sense. The cities were small and coherent, characterized by direct, personal relations and long-term, stable associations within and between a number of groups. The early
participation of cacereños and trujillanos in the conquest and settlement of Mexico and Peru set the stage for the rapid development of
mechanisms that would help to assure future emigrants a basis for
getting their start in society. Certainly emigration from the Cáceres-
Trujillo region was not a mass phenomenon organized deliberately
or publicly; nonetheless there is abundant evidence that it was in
many senses a collective undertaking that hinged on the existence of
networks of kinship and association and ongoing contacts that linked
people in the Indies, Seville, and Extremadura. The close relations
that existed between people who lived in the relatively small cities
and towns of that part of Extremadura enabled them to develop and
maintain networks that facilitated the move to the New World and
exploitation of its possibilities.

The Indies meant above all an expansion of the resources and
career alternatives available to people in Spain. Given emigrants'
orientation toward and continuing attachments to home, this expansion of opportunities would have direct consequences not only for
the individuals who took advantage of them but for their home
towns as well. At home the participation of people in the Indies
enterprise meant unanticipated increments of wealth that financed
the construction of houses and chapels, the purchase of lands and
rents, and the rise of families outside the traditional nobility to new
positions of power and influence. The New World offered potential
emigrants the chance to break away from the social restrictions and
economic limitations that governed their lives in Spain. Although
personal and political connections and social status certainly contin-

ued to be of great importance in the Indies, it is clear that the New World could reward talent and ambition far more frequently than the Old one. Artisans became encomenderos, and wealthy commoners married nobles. Francisco Pizarro, the illegitimate son of a middling hidalgo, became a marqués and the first governor of Peru; and his career set in motion events that would take the remnants of his family to the pinnacle of wealth and power in his home town of Trujillo and provide the basis for many of his fellow townspeople to establish themselves successfully in Peru.

The Indies allowed emigrants to discard old conventions and find new ways of making a livelihood and a place in society. The career of Juan de Hinojosa, a younger son from a prominent noble family of Cáceres who, because of the family entail, could only anticipate a limited inheritance, illustrates how this could happen. Hinojosa followed his older brother Gómez de Solís, a successful captain and encomendero, to Peru. There he became an encomendero and wealthy entrepreneur and married a woman named Leonor Méndez. Leonor was a commoner, the widow of a man from Salamanca, possibly an artisan, who had been present at Cajamarca.[5] Leonor Méndez was not Hinojosa's social equal, and such a marriage would have been utterly impossible in the more constrained and status-conscious society of Cáceres. Had Hinojosa remained in Spain, most likely he never would have married at all or attained any degree of economic independence. In Peru his marriage made a great deal of sense and probably provided the initial basis for his economic success there.

The careers of individuals like Francisco Pizarro, Juan de Hinojosa, and many others reflect a notable ability to adapt readily and willingly to the new circumstances and possibilities of the Indies. Yet we should not imagine that the opportunities created by the settlement and exploitation of the Indies introduced flexibility and pragmatism into Spanish society. Fluidity and adaptability already existed, but they were hampered by the reality of limited economic resources in many places and a restrictive and tenacious social system based on privilege and wealth. We have seen that upward socioeconomic mobility was by no means impossible even in small cities like Cáceres and Trujillo; but the pastoral-agrarian economic base of the region could provide only so much wealth, and the local nobility had a strong hold over what resources there were. The relatively

open and varied circumstances of the New World created an ambi-
ence in which the flexibility and pragmatism of Spanish socioeconomic patterns and relations could flourish, at least for a time.

We must, of course, qualify what opportunity in the New World
meant. Apart from the first conquerors and earliest arrivals, few
individuals who went to the Indies were able to ascend the social
scale to any significant degree; Juan de Hinojosa's wife, Leonor
Méndez, did not become a "doña" because she married a cachereño
noble, and Francisco Pizarro's essentially plebeian background was
so at odds with his power and ennobled status that finding a suitable marriage partner was impossible. But the majority of emigrants neither sought nor anticipated social elevation; they wanted
to improve their economic circumstances, which at home were
often tenuous at best. The Indies not only offered the prospect of a
better way of life but the added attraction of living in a milieu
where wealth and economic success need not necessarily be accompanied by privileged social status.

The example of Alvaro Rodríguez Chacón, who returned to
Trujillo in the mid-1570s to take his children back to Mexico, shows
how the move to the New World could work to modify certain
values. By his own statement Alvaro had become a well-established
merchant in Mexico, where he was financially successful and prosperous. He was from a family of probably marginal hidalgos. Witnesses testified to the family's hidalgo status; but most of these
witnesses were tailors, and the wife of one was the cousin of Alvaro
Rodríguez's daughter. Significantly, Alvaro himself said nothing
about his social rank; what counted was the financial wherewithal
that enabled him to take his children away from Trujillo to a place
where their improved economic situation would outweigh considerations of social status.

Naturally the reverse process occurred as well, since the altered
social landscape of the New World did not benefit everyone. The
kinds of opportunities available after the early years were not always very attractive for hidalgos who went to the Indies assuming
that their social status would guarantee them a comfortable place
that not only preserved or enhanced their social rank but compensated them amply as well. For individuals with those kinds of expectations, the opportunities of the New World must have seemed
limited and disappointing. But the majority of emigrants were not

hidalgos but rather working men and women. In the Indies many of them found circumstances in which their hard work paid off and enabled them to provide for their families, send home for relatives, or even return to Spain with sufficient gains to reestablish themselves there. For these people the promise of the Indies was not at all a false one.

Along with the more dramatic and visible effects on local society of involvement in the Indies came subtler changes in the lives of individuals. The existence of the Indies and their links to that distant place altered people's perceptions of the world and their relationship to it. We have seen that by midcentury residents of Trujillo were acutely aware of their many fellow townspeople who were living in or had returned from Peru. Individuals who never left Spain developed a kind of expertise on the Indies. A shoemaker named Juan López, the brother-in-law of Diego de Trujillo, the veteran of Cajamarca and encomendero of Cuzco, constantly served as a witness for the testimonies of people petitioning to go to America; although his experience of the Indies was strictly secondhand, López probably was considered to be one of the local experts. We have seen that people in Spain could almost come to blows over opinions about events far away in Peru. And involvement in the New World created new legal and logistical complexities. Disputes over legacies, for example, were hardly uncommon in any case; but if a relative died in Peru or Mexico, settling the estate could become very complicated. It could mean that someone who otherwise might never have contemplated a trip across the Atlantic would decide to go. Similarly the continuing involvement of emigrants in the New World with people and affairs at home could bring them back to Spain to visit or stay. Cáceres and Trujillo were connected to the Indies through kinship and acquaintance. These networks and relationships, which were basic to socioeconomic organization at home, retained their strength and significance even when the geographical context expanded so notably.

Detailed examination of emigration from and return migration to the cities of Alta Extremadura suggests some conclusions regarding the relationship of sixteenth-century Spanish emigration to the larger movement of people from Europe to the western hemisphere in modern times. Although a comparison of the various early modern European migration movements is too large and complicated a topic to treat here, it should be stated that the patterns and forms of emigration identified for sixteenth-century Castile did not differ significantly from those that have been observed for other colonizing societies of Europe. As was true for English or French emigration in the seventeenth or eighteenth centuries, the movement of people between Extremadura and America encompassed the migration of families and of young single people (who often went as servants), return migration, re-emigration, moving back and forth, and even something resembling labor migration. Again, like the other early modern European emigration movements that got their start a century or so later, Castilian emigration involved varying forms of recruitment and state and legal mechanisms that at times acted to restrict, at other times to encourage, migration. None of the movements was monolithic but rather each incorporated a number of patterns and variants; emigration from all the colonizing countries was affected by complex sets of circumstances and actors in both the home societies and the intended destinations.

This study of Cáceres and Trujillo makes it possible to consider Spanish emigration in much the same light as the heretofore much better studied movement from Britain.[6] Furthermore the detailed consideration of local society in Extremadura reveals that, despite its rather distinctive history, Castile was neither unique nor peculiar; in its socioeconomic structures and organization Castile much resembled other societies of early modern Europe. Castile in certain respects might have been better prepared than other states for the task of expansion to the New World because of its traditions of conquest and incorporation of peoples and territories and the institutions it had developed partly in response to the exigencies of that process. But such initial differences and advantages as Castile possessed diminished in importance over time as other countries also successfully worked out their own colonizing systems. In the end the whole European colonizing effort in the Americas appears to have been a coherent phenomenon more characterized by similarities and continuities than sharp contrasts, and patterns of emigration prove to be no exception. Modern European migration to the western hemisphere arguably began in the late fifteenth and sixteenth centuries with the movement from the Iberian peninsula and essentially developed over the centuries along the lines set out by emigrants from towns like Cáceres and Trujillo.

Notes

Introduction

1. The first two volumes of Peter Boyd-Bowman's *Indice geobiográfico de cuarenta mil pobladores españoles de América en el siglo XVI* (Bogota, 1964; Mexico, 1968) list emigrants for the period 1493–1539, and three other volumes covering the rest of the sixteenth century have yet to be published. Boyd-Bowman's articles analyzing his data have appeared in a number of journals, and several were reprinted in *Patterns of Spanish Emigration to the New World (1493–1580)* (Buffalo, N.Y., 1973); these are supplemented by his "Patterns of Spanish Emigration to the Indies until 1600," *Hispanic American Historical Review* 56 (1976): 580–604.

2. J. H. Elliott, *The Old World and the New, 1492–1650* (New York, 1970) discusses a number of themes related to the impact of America on Spain. Fredi Chiappelli, ed., *First Images of America: The Impact of the New World on the Old*. 2 vols. (Berkeley and Los Angeles, 1976) contains excellent articles on aspects of migration and return migration in the Spanish world by Peter Boyd-Bowman, Woodrow Borah, James Lockhart, and Magnus Mörner, who also compiled a bibliography of relevant works (see 2: 707–804). Jose Luis Martínez, *Pasajeros de Indias: Viajes transatlánticos en el siglo XVI* (Madrid, 1983) also summarizes a great deal of material from printed and published sources.

3. See Mario Góngora, *Los grupos de conquistadores en Tierra Firme (1509–1530)* (Santiago, 1962); James Lockhart, *The Men of Cajamarca* (Austin, 1972); Enrique Otte, "Cartas privadas de Puebla del siglo XVI," *Jahrbuch für Geschichte von Staat, Wirtschaft und Gesellschaft Lateinamerikas* 3 (1966): 10–87; James Lockhart and Enrique Otte, *Letters and People of the Spanish Indies* (New York, 1976).

4. The first volume of *Primeras jornadas de Andalucía y América* (La

Rábida, 1981) includes several studies that focus on emigration from a specific locality; see, for example, Lourdes Díez Trechuelo Spinola, "Emigración cordobesa a las Indias, siglo XVI," 405–426. However, although they are concerned with emigration from particular localities, the studies rely mainly on records in the Archive of the Indies rather than on local documentation.

5. Two studies that examine local society in Extremadura in the late fifteenth and sixteenth century at least raise the question of the relationship between local society and emigration; they are Mario Góngora, "Régimen señorial y rural en la Extremadura de la Orden de Santiago en el momento de la emigración a Indias," *Jahrbuch für Geschichte von Staat, Wirtschaft und Gesellschaft Lateinamerikas* 2 (1965): 1–19, and David E. Vassberg, "La coyuntura socioeconómica de la ciudad de Trujillo durante la época de la conquista de América," Publicaciones de la Diputación Provincial de Badajoz (Badajoz, 1979). Neither article, however, makes any direct connections between the localities studied and emigration to America.

6. Ida Altman, "Emigrants, Returnees and Society in Sixteenth-Century Cáceres" (Ph.D. diss., Johns Hopkins University, 1981).

7. I have identified 410 known emigrants from Cáceres in the sixteenth century and 921 from Trujillo in the same period (these figures do not include the villages and towns of their jurisdictions).

8. George M. Foster, *Culture and Conquest: America's Spanish Heritage* (Chicago, 1960). See also my article "Emigrants and Society: An Approach to the Background of Colonial Spanish America," *Comparative Studies in Society and History* 30, 1 (January 1988): 170–190, which addresses this question.

9. Marie-Claude Gerbet's *La noblesse dans le royaume de Castille: Etudes sur ses structures sociales en Estrémadure (1454–1516)* (Paris, 1979) is a major work for the period. For the Jewish community in Trujillo, see Haim Beinart, *Trujillo: A Jewish Community in Extremadura on the Eve of the Expulsion from Spain* (Jerusalem, 1980). Two articles in *La ciudad hispánica durante los siglos XIII al XVI* (Madrid, 1985)— Carmen Fernández-Daza Alvear, "Linajes trujillanos y cargos concejiles en el siglo XV," 1: 419–432 and María Angeles Sánchez Rubio, "Estructura socio-económica de la ciudad de Trujillo a través de sus Ordenanzas Municipales (siglo XV)," 1: 433–442.—do not greatly extend our picture of the period.

10. A multivolume *Historia de Extremadura* (Badajoz, 1985), authored mainly by faculty members of the University of Extremadura, summarizes much of the most recent research on the region as a whole. Another multivolume history is being compiled as well. Monographs such as Angel

Rodríguez Sánchez's *Cáceres: población y comportamientos demográficos en el siglo XVI* (Cáceres, 1977) and Gerbet's *La noblesse* represent important contributions not only to the study of Extremadura but also to the historiography of Castile in general. And the study of Extremadura has long benefited from the *Revista de Estudios Extremeños*, which has been published (in one form or another) since the late nineteenth century and reflects much of the scholarship on the region.

11. Clodoaldo Naranjo Alonso, *Trujillo y su tierra: Historia, monumentos e hijos ilustres*, 2 vols. (Trujillo, 1924); and Juan Tena Fernández, *Trujillo histórico y monumental* (Alicante, 1967).

12. For those interested in further study of the Pizarros, the biographies of the brothers included in Lockhart, *Men of Cajamarca*, are an excellent starting point. Lockhart's biographies of the Pizarros and other men from Extremadura portray tellingly the outlook, objectives, capacities, and limitations of the men of that region. They are thorough, balanced, and perceptive and provide extensive bibliography and references to archival sources. An important recent addition to the literature on the Pizarros is Rafael Varón Gabai and Auke Pieter Jacobs, "Peruvian Wealth and Spanish Investment: The Pizarro Family during the Sixteenth Century," *Hispanic American Historical Review* 67, 4 (November 1987): 657–695.

13. This material is drawn largely from Lochart's biographies in *Men of Cajamarca*; for the principal events in the conquest of Peru, see pp. 3–16. Also essential for understanding early Peru is James Lockhart's *Spanish Peru, 1532–1560* (Madison, Wis., 1968).

I. Local Society in Northern Extremudura

1. Eugenio García Zarza, *Evolución, estructura y otros aspectos de la población cacereña* (Badajoz, 1977), 50 writes "la extensa comarca cacereño-trujillana es la que mejor encarna el severo y grandioso paisaje extremeño."

2. García Zarza, *Población cacereña*, 41. See also Gonzalo Martínez, S.I., *Las comunidades de villa y tierra de la Extremeña Castellana* (Madrid, 1983), 658.

3. Antonio C. Floriano, *Estudios de historia de Cáceres*, 1 (Oviedo, 1957): 53, 58.

4. Floriano, *Estudios*, 1:72; Tena Fernández, *Trujillo histórico*, 447; a Roman burial site was found behind the castle.

5. Floriano, *Estudios*, 1: 44, 68, 77, 98–99.

6. Ibid., pp. 165, 167; García Zarza, *Población cacereña*, 39–40; Tena Fernández, *Trujillo histórico*, 15. Martínez, *Las comunidades*, 661 says that the orders of Santiago and Calatrava and the militia of Plasencia

played an important role in the reconquest of Trujillo under Fernando III el Santo. The key town of Santa Cruz was reconquered in 1234.

7. In principle Cáceres was within the lands of León and Trujillo belonged to Castile, and therefore each should have been settled accordingly; see García Zarza, *Población cacereña*, 41. In reality, however, given the difficulties of reoccupying such a large region, probably virtually anyone willing to come could settle wherever.

8. Ibid., 40–42.

9. Floriano, *Estudios*, 2: 53; he writes that Jews were coming to settle in Cáceres from the late thirteenth century. For the Jewish community in Trujillo, see Haim Beinart, *Trujillo: A Jewish Community in Extremadura on the Eve of the Expulsion from Spain* (Jerusalem, 1980).

10. Miguel Muñoz de San Pedro, *Extremadura: La tierra en la que nacían los dioses* (Cáceres, 1981), 33–34.

11. Floriano, *Estudios*, 1: 126, 149, 171.

12. See Miguel Muñoz de San Pedro, *La Extremadura del siglo XV en tres de sus paladines* (Madrid, 1964) for the careers of Gutierre de Sotomayor, Francisco de Hinojosa, Captain Diego de Ovando de Cáceres, and other men from Cáceres and Trujillo.

13. Simón Benito Boxoyo, *Historia de Cáceres y su patrona* (Cáceres, 1952), 124–125. For a critical discussion of the earliest manuscripts and interpretation of the legend, see Jacques Lafaye, *Quetzalcoatl y Guadalupe: La formación de la conciencia de México* (Mexico, 1977), 304–407.

14. Lafaye, *Quetzalcoatl y Guadalupe*, 309–310 points out the connections between the important Jeronymite monasteries and the Spanish crown. Monks from San Bartolomé de Lupiana founded the Jeronymite monastery at Guadalupe, and subsequently members of the Guadalupe monastery went to Yuste (founded 1408) and the Escorial (sixteenth century); the prior of Guadalupe himself went to the Escorial. The monastery also had connections with the Indies from the start. The royal capitulaciones granted Columbus were signed there, and on his return the first Indians brought to Spain were baptized there (see p. 311).

15. See Muñoz de San Pedro, *La Extremadura del siglo XV*, 258, 269, 298. Captain Diego did not actually ally himself with the Catholic monarchs until Isabella's brother Henry died in 1474, and he only handed over the fortress of Benquerencia in 1480. Two years later he received 250,000 maravedís in juros from the crown, subsequently the basis of the family entail. His son Nicolás de Ovando succeeded him as Comendador de Lares of the Order of Alcántara (Captain Diego de Ovando had accepted the encomienda of Lares in exchange for giving up the fortress). In 1502 King Ferdinand appointed Frey Nicolás de Ovando governor of the island of Hispaniola. Sancho de Paredes's descendants also upheld the tradition of

service to the crown. One of his grandsons, don Alvaro de Sande, became a high-ranking military officer and eventually the marqués de Piobera. In 1535 the Emperor Charles V's brother Ferdinand wrote to Sancho de Paredes in Cáceres in response to the letter that Sancho had sent with his grandson don Alvaro when he went to the Habsburg court. The German Habsburgs later played a key part in arranging Sande's ransom from the Turks in the 1560s; see Boxoyo, *Historia de Cáceres*, 47–48 and Huberto Foglietta, *Vida de don Alvaro de Sande*, with notes by Miguel Angel Orti Belmonte (Madrid, 1962), 88 (notes on book 1). The Chaves family also maintained the royal connection. A great-great-grandson of Luis de Chaves, el viejo, Juan de Chaves, accompanied the queens of Portugal and Hungary (sisters of Charles V) when they traveled through Extremadura in 1558; see Miguel Muñoz de San Pedro, ed., *Crónicas trujillanas del siglo XVI* (Hinojosa manuscript) (Cáceres, 1952), xxx, 138.

16. Tena Fernández, *Trujillo histórico*, 17 writes that one or the other or both visited Trujillo seven times between June 1477 and August 1479; Isabella spent a total of nine months in the city. Ferdinand in fact died in the village of Madrigalejo (in Trujillo's district) in January 1516, in a house owned by the monastery of Guadalupe.

17. Archivo Municipal de Trujillo García de Sanabria A-1-1. (Hereafter cited as AMT.)

18. AMT Francisco Enríquez A-1-5-1.

19. Changes in the status of a town or village did modify the use of the term. People often continued to refer to towns like Berzocana and Cañamero that became independent in the sixteenth century as being in Trujillo's tierra (in fact, even after they became independent Trujillo continued to exercise certain kinds of jurisdictional functions, such as summoning people for military levies). Furthermore, certain places like Orellana la Vieja that were under señorial jurisdiction had longstanding and close ties with Trujillo because they belonged to noble families of the city and for most intents they were considered to be part of the city's tierra.

20. Juan Pérez de Tudela, ed., *Documentos relativos a don Pedro de la Gasca y a Gonzalo Pizarro*, 1 (Madrid, 1964): 80.

21. AMT 1584: IX–8.

22. David E. Vassberg, *Land and Society in Golden Age Castile* (Cambridge, 1984), 62. The agreement included the right to graze pigs during the acorn season but excluded hunting, fishing, or cutting wood in the montes.

23. AMT Pedro de Carmona B-1-23.

24. Archivo General de Indias (Hereafter cited as AGI.) Indif. General 2083.

25. In the sixteenth century there actually were two types of censos;

Vassberg, *Land and Society*, 205 defines a censo as a "contract involving an annual payment." The "censo al quitar" was essentially a mortgage on property in which the principal was redeemable. The other type, the "censo enfitéutico" was really a quitrent or agricultural lease that usually was long term, staying in families over generations. For discussion of these two types of censos, see Vassberg, *Land and Society*, 94–95 and 205–207.

26. Julius Klein, *The Mesta: A Study in Spanish Economic History, 1273–1836* (Cambridge, Mass., 1920), 332–333. Klein did not list all the towns that protested, so it is not clear if Trujillo participated.

27. Henry IV in the fifteenth century also granted Trujillo a mercado franco, but the privilege lapsed under Ferdinand and Isabella.

28. AMT Pedro de Carmona B-1-23.

29. Calculations of the cities' populations in the sixteenth century vary a great deal, according to the source, and further variations result from the use of different multipliers (usually 4.5 or 5.0); see Vicente Pérez Moreda, "El crecimiento demográfico español en el siglo XVI," in *Jerónimo Zurita: Su época y su escuela* (Zaragoza, 1986), 62–64 for discussion of coefficients. He suggests that 4.0 may be preferable to 4.5. For population figures for Cáceres and Trujillo, see Jean-Paul LeFlem, "Cáceres, Plasencia y Trujillo en la segunda mitad del siglo XVI (1557–1596)" *Cuadernos de historia de España* 45–46 (1967): 248–299. Angel Rodríguez Sánchez, *Cáceres: población y comportamientos demográficos en el siglo XVI* (Cáceres, 1977), 53 says censuses for Cáceres listed 1401 vecinos in 1557, 1471 in 1561, 1463 in 1584, 1547 in 1586, and 1647 in 1595. For population figures, see also *Historia de Extremadura*, 9 vols. (Badajoz, 1983), 3: 486; and Annie Molinié-Bertrand, "Contributions a l'étude de la société rurale dans la province de Trujillo au XVIe siècle," *Mélanges offerts a Charles Vincent Aubrun*, 2 vols. (Paris, 1972), 2: 128. While the exact figures cannot be established, it is clear that at midcentury the cities had between 6000 and 9000 inhabitants and that Trujillo was somewhat larger than Cáceres.

30. In 1532 something less than half the district's taxpaying population were vecinos of Cáceres itself—854 out of 1896 taxpayers; see Jose Luis Pereira Iglesias, "Atraso económico, régimen señorial y economía deficitaria en Cáceres durante el siglo XVI" (Memorial de licenciatura, Universidad de Extremadura, 1977), 148.

31. See LeFlem, "Cáceres, Plasencia y Trujillo," 254–255. For the most recent work on population levels and growth in the period, see Annie Molinié-Bertrand, *Au siécle d'or: l'Espagne et ses hommes: La population du royaume de Castille au XVIe siècle* (Paris, 1985). Urban populations especially were growing rapidly in this period. She calculates, for example, that Burgos grew 192 percent, to 20,000 inhabitants, in the

period from 1528 to 1561 (p. 135). Rates of growth in Castile's towns and cities, however, were far from uniform.

32. The status "ciudad," which the crown conceded to Trujillo in the fifteenth century, was a legal distinction that seems to have been mainly honorific. Madrid, for example, remained a "villa" even after it became Spain's capital.

33. Archivo General de Simancas Expedientes Hacienda 189–56 (hereafter cited as AGS); Exped. Hac. 66; Exped. Hac. 906. Generally the number of vecinos indicates the number of households; see note 29 above on multipliers.

34. AGS Exped. Hac. 189-56, Exped. Hac. 66.

35. Clodoaldo Naranjo Alonso, *Solar de conquistadores: Trujillo, sus hijos y monumentos* (Serradilla, Cáceres, 1929), 280–281. Cañamero and Berzocana, each with over 400 vecinos, purchased their independence from the crown in 1538 for 6000 ducados each.

36. According to Naranjo Alonso, *Solar de conquistadores*, 289, in 1585 Trujillo still held Herguijuela, Zarza (later Conquista), Zorita, Logrosán, Navalvillar, Madrigalejo, Campo, Alcollarín, Santa Cruz, Abertura, Escurial, Búrdalo (later Villamesías), Santa Ana, Ibahernando, and Robledillo. In the early seventeenth century Trujillo was ordered to sell Zarza, Herguijuela, Santa Cruz, Escurial, Búrdalo, Ruanes and Santa Ana (see p. 304). Martínez, *Las comunidades*, 661–662 lists a total of thirty-six pueblos that were once part of Trujillo's término.

37. See Archivo Municipal de Cáceres Libros de Acuerdo del Consejo, March 1554 (hereafter cited as AMC); and AGS Exped. Hacienda 240. The council maintained that it was only seven or eight related vecinos ("de una parentela") of Casar who were campaigning for independence for their own particular interests. Gonzalo Ulloa de Carvajal bought Torreorgaz in 1559; see *Historia de Extremadura*, 3: 440.

38. Pascual Madoz, *Diccionario geográfico-estadístico-histórico de España y sus posesiones de Ultramar*, 3d. ed. (Madrid, 1848–1850), 6: 35–36; Pedro Ulloa Golfín, *Privilegios y documentos relativos a la ciudad de Cáceres*. Biblioteca Nacional, Madrid, Ms. 430 (18?) fols. 72–77.

39. See AGS Exped. Hac. 66; "primeramente decimos que este dicho lugar no tiene tierras ni los arrenda porque se las toma la villa de Cáceres como cabecera."

40. See Carmelo Solís Rodríguez, "El arquitecto Francisco Becerra: Su etapa extremeña," *Revista de Estudios Extremeños* 29 (1973):333.

41. AMC Libros de Acuerdo 1580; AMT Libros de Acuerdo 1580.

42. AGS Exped. Hac. 189-56. Nearly 60 percent of Herguijuela's vecinos had vineyards as well, for a total of about thirty hectares; see *Historia de Extremadura*, 3: 598.

43. Archivo de la Real Chancillería de Granada (hereafter cited as ARCG) 511-2284-8.

44. Madoz, *Diccionario*, 5: 86, 87.

45. Tena Fernández, *Trujillo histórico*, 123, 563–564; Solís Rodríguez, "Francisco Becerra," 330.

46. The usual term of office for the corregidor was one or two years in the sixteenth century, and the practice of changing corregidors frequently seems to have been strictly observed. Benjamin González Alonso, *El corregidor castellano (1348–1808)* (Madrid, 1970), 140, 160 says that corregidors were nobles and tenientes were always letrados. If the corregidor was not himself a letrado, the teniente routinely performed the judicial functions of the office. At least one corregidor, Pedro Riquelme de Villavicencio, served both in Trujillo (1566–?) and Cáceres (term ended in 1570). The origins and development of the institution in the Middle Ages have been studied by Agustín Bermúdez Aznar, *El corregidor en Castilla durante la Baja Edad Media (1348–1474)* (Murcia, 1974). Cáceres had a "juez del rey" by 1345 and was one of fifteen cities in Castile that had a corregidor under Henry III (see p. 54, map, p. 64) and apparently continuously throughout the fifteenth century. Trujillo had a corregidor by 1480, and only three other cities in Extremadura had corregidors in the sixteenth century (Plasencia, Badajoz, and Mérida until 1520, Jerez de los Caballeros after 1520); see *Historia de Extremadura*, 3: 423.

47. Antonio C. Floriano, *La villa de Cáceres y la Reina Católica: Ordenanzas que a Cáceres dio la Reina Doña Isabel Primera de Castilla* (Cáceres, 1917), 36; Naranjo Alonso, *Solar de conquistadores*, 118. I have not seen a copy of Trujillo's fifteenth-century ordinances, but it is clear from the city council records that the señores de vasallos were not barred from serving on its council as was true in Cáceres.

48. See Carmen Fernández-Daza Alvear, "Linajes trujillanos y cargos concejiles en el siglo XV," in *La ciudad hispánica durante los siglos XIII al XVI* (Madrid, 1985), 419–432. She writes (p. 429) that Charles V curtailed the existing system of election to city council offices in 1544 because of the disturbances and factionalism that arose and made the thirteen regimientos proprietary offices. This change doubtless paved the way for the wealthy returnees from Peru to gain municipal office.

49. See AMC Libros de Acuerdo 1555 or AMT Actas 1558 for examples of disagreements between the corregidor and regidores of the cities.

50. See Tena Fernández, *Trujillo histórico*, 208, 216, 218, 323. In Trujillo a gunsmith was employed for six years at an annual salary of 6000 maravedís; a harnessmaker in 1585 for 4000 maravedís and eight fanegas of wheat; an esparto grass weaver for 2000 maravedís in 1563; see AMT 1-2-70-101, 1-3-78-1.

51. AMC Libros de Acuerdo 1574. The "mayordomo de propios y rentas" in Trujillo received 17,000 maravedís in 1564 and 24,000 maravedís in 1584; AMT 1-2-70-92.

52. AMC Libros de Acuerdo 1575; AMT 1-2-70-74; 1-3-78-1; 1-2-70-90; 1-2-70-64.

53. Tena Fernández, *Trujillo histórico*, 278.

54. AMC Libros de Acuerdo 1553, 1571, 1575, 1578, 1579.

55. AMT 1-3-78-1, 1-2-70-44, 1-2-70-34; AMC Libros de Acuerdo 1558.

56. AMC Libros de Acuerdo 1574.

57. AMT 1-2-70-92, 1-2-70-136; it also paid an "algebrista" 3000 maravedís in the 1570s and 1580s; see AMT 1-2-70-103 and others.

58. AMC Libros de Acuerdo 1579; Tena Fernández, *Trujillo histórico*, 21.

59. AMC Libros de Acuerdo 1575.

60. Trujillo's council gave the Hospital of Santa Lucía 50 ducados in 1564 and contributed 300 ducados to the construction of the Hospital of Espíritu Santo in 1591; see Tena Fernández, *Trujillo histórico*, 289, 112.

61. AGS Diversos de Castilla 28, no. 1.

62. AMT 1-2-70-90; AMC Libros de Acuerdo 1575.

63. In November 1576 Trujillo's council made a contract with Juan Granado, vecino of Baeza and "author of comedies," for 130 ducados; Granado's wife was one of the players. The council spent 60,000 maravedís for Corpus Christi in 1565 and in 1587 obtained royal authorization to spend 300 ducados a year for the next six years to celebrate the holiday; see AMT 1-20-70-58 and Libros de Acuerdo 1576; see also AMC Libros de Acuerdo 1577.

64. The arciprestazgo included a group of parishes and usually coincided with the district of a city ("comunidad de villa y tierra"). But the label was not just administrative, since the arciprestazgo functioned with some independence with respect to the authority of the bishop, and the archpriest worked with the bishop in the planning and convocation of synods and diocesan councils; see *Historia de Extremadura*, 3: 428.

65. AMT 1585:I-7; Archivo del Conde de Canilleros (hereafter cited as ACC), Casa de Hernando de Ovando (HO), leg. 4, no. 47; Archivo Histórico Provincial de Cáceres Diego Pacheco 4113 (Godoy's will) (hereafter cited as AHPC).

66. Tena Fernández, *Trujillo histórico*, 170–175.

67. See Tena Fernández, *Trujillo histórico*, 94–106 for the complicated debates and maneuvers that resulted in the establishment of this monastery.

68. In 1551 Pedro de Sosa, alcalde of the cofradía, rented out part of the dehesa of Cañadas de Orellana for three years at 14,200 maravedís a

year; see AMT García de Sanabria A-1-1. In 1578 Francisco de Herrera, as the cofradía's mayordomo, rented half the estate of Cabeza de la Sal to two vecinos of La Cumbre for 11,000 a year; see AMT Pedro de Carmona B-1-23. See also Tena Fernández, *Trujillo histórico*, 112.

69. Tena Fernández, *Trujillo histórico*, 149, 150, 118, 311.

70. Naranjo Alonso, *Solar de conquistadores*, 504. Don Juan Pizarro Carvajal, who died in 1580, was a graduate of Salamanca who had spent time in Rome.

71. AMT 1585: I-7.

72. Muñoz de San Pedro, *Crónicas trujillanas*, 80.

II. Nobles and Hidalgos

1. See Ruth Pike, *Aristocrats and Traders: Sevillian Society in the Sixteenth Century* (Ithaca, N.Y., 1972), 22–24 for intermarriage between the nobility and merchant and converso families and the ennoblement of merchants. In her conclusion (p. 213) she writes: "The Sevillian nobility was never a closed homogeneous class. . . . By the middle of . . . [the sixteenth] century the majority of the Sevillian nobility consisted of recently ennobled families of mixed social and racial origins whose commercial orientation and activities reflected their mercantile background."

2. Juan Pérez de Tudela Bueso, ed., *Documentos relativos a don Pedro de la Gasca y a Gonzalo Pizarro*, 2 vols. (Madrid, 1964), 2: 315; Gonzalo Pizarro's statement was quoted by Pedro Hernández Paniagua de Loaysa in his *relación* (account) written to Gasca, August 1547.

3. For Dr. Lorenzo Galíndez de Carvajal (dates 1472–1532), see Ernest Schäfer, *El consejo real y supremo de las Indias*, 2 vols. (Seville, 1935 and 1947), 1: 27; and Helen Nader, *The Mendoza Family in the Spanish Renaissance, 1350 to 1550* (New Brunswick, 1979), 129–130. For Diego de Vargas Carvajal, see Schäfer, *El consejo de Indias*, 2: 287–288; for his will, see Federico Acedo Trigo, "Linajes de Trujillo." (Ms. in AMT), Vargas, 48[a12–13].

4. See J. G. Peristiany, ed., *El concepto de honor en la sociedad mediterránea* (Barcelona, 1968), especially the article by Julio Caro Baroja, "Honor y vergüenza. Examen histórico de varios conflictos," 77–126. The English edition is entitled *Honour and Shame: The Values of Mediterranean Society* (London, 1966).

5. See Nader, *The Mendoza Family*; essentially the entire book deals with the impact of humanism and Renaissance ideas and styles on the Castilian nobility. Nader claims that the letrados were not humanists in their ideas and they were essentially "anti-Renaissance" (p. 133).

6. Miguel Muñoz de San Pedro traced the career of this Diego García de Paredes in his article "Aventuras y desventuras del tercer Diego García de Paredes," *Revista de Estudios Extremeños* 13 (1957): 5–93.

7. Archivo del Monasterio de Guadalupe (AMG) Fondo Barrantes, Ms. B/3. In 1590 Alvaro de Paredes wrote to his brother Licenciado Gutiérrez de Espadero that he had borrowed 1000 pesos from a friend leaving for Spain and said "me ofrecio el viaje a España, lo cual no acepté de vergüenza" (fol. 167).

8. See Muñoz de San Pedro, *Crónicas trujillanas*, Hinojosa, 122 for the reference to the Cid; see p. 177 for the description of how Hernando Alonso de Hinojosa avenged his cousin and many years later was himself killed in vengeance; see p. 157 for a description of Alonso García Calderón, an uncle of Andrés Calderón Puertocarrero, which included the following: "es muy varon y liberal, es amigo de su sangre, sin haber respecto al bando, lo cual hacen pocos en esta ciudad." The Hinojosa manuscript was written in 1548 by Diego de Hinojosa and amended and expanded by his nephew Alonso in 1563.

9. Gerbet, *La noblesse*, 105–127, 134–135 discusses the different types of nobles and hidalgos. See also Marie-Claude Gerbet and Janine Fayard, "Fermeture de la noblesse et pureté de sang dans les *concejos* de Castille au XVème siècle: à travers les procès d'*hidalguía*" in *La ciudad hispánica*, 1: 443–474 for access to noble status.

10. Diego de la Rocha's entail is in AHPC Pedro de Grajos 3923. For Juan de Chaves, see Muñoz de San Pedro, *Crónicas trujillanas*, 138. The wife of Luis de Chaves, el viejo, was doña María de Sotomayor, who was the sister of the first count of Belalcazar, don Alonso de Sotomayor; they were the illegitimate children of don Gutierre de Sotomayor, the famous master of Alcántara; see Muñoz de San Pedro, *Crónicas trujillanas*, 189. Some other cacereños involved with the duke of Béjar were Francisco de Villalobos, who in 1534 was trying to recover money owed to him for four years of service to the deceased duke; Francisco de Ribera, who sought compensation for services rendered and money lent to the same; and Comendador Hernando de Ovando (brother of Frey Nicolás de Ovando), who was trying to collect money owed to his dead son Gonzalo de Ulloa in the same year; see AHPC Hernando Conde 3712. In that year also Martín Alonso, nonnoble returnee to Trujillo from Cajamarca, purchased 100,000 maravedís de censos from the duke of Béjar. Diego Mejía de Grado, a vecino of Trujillo with the power of attorney (*poder*) of Señor don Francisco de Zúñiga Guzmán y Sotomayor, duke of Béjar, carried out the transaction with Juan Cortés, another returnee who had been at Cajamarca, acting in Martín Alonso's name; AMT García de Sanabria A-1-1. See Acedo, "Linajes," Mejía, 406, for the censo that don Diego Mejía de

Ovando sold on the "villa y dehesa" of Loriana to the wealthy returnee Señor Juan Pizarro de Orellana, vecino of Trujillo.

11. Muñoz de San Pedro, *Crónicas trujillanas,* xxx (introduction), Hinojosa, 138.

12. A number of these suits involved people who had been in the Indies or had family members there; their newly acquired wealth might have been a factor in the decision to go to court. Luis García Polido (who had been in the Indies; see AHPC Diego Pacheco 4113) and the brothers of Dr. Francisco de Sande of Cáceres (see note 15 below) had suits in Granada, as did Diego de Carvajal, returnee from Peru to Trujillo who married a half-sister of Gonzalo and Juan Pizarro (see AMT García de Sanabria A-1-2; he initiated the suit with his brother Gonzalo de Carvajal) and Florencio Carrasco, vecino of Zorita and brother of Pedro Alonso Carrasco, long-time resident of Cuzco; see ARCG 303-290-10.

13. Caro Baroja, "Honor y vergüenza," 100 points out that, with the growing importance of "limpieza de sangre" (purity of blood) in the sixteenth century, it no longer was only the male lineage that counted but one's antecedents on both sides and through both maternal and paternal lines.

14. Acedo, "Linajes," Escobar, 380–386 quotes extensively from the testimony on the Escobars of Trujillo and Robledillo. Francisco de Escobar was listed as "soltero, mercader" when he went to Cartagena in 1574; see AGI Indif. General 2087.

15. ARCG, Hidalguía 301-181-153 and 301-55-21. Miguel Angel Orti Belmonte in his notes for Huberto Foglietta, *Vida de don Alvaro de Sande* (Madrid, 1962), 85 says that the Sandes of Cáceres descended from Alvaro de Sande, "señor de la casa del valle de Sande" in Galicia, who came to Cáceres in the fifteenth century with King Juan II.

16. Further evidence of the unimpressive status of the family in Cáceres was that in the 1570s, when she was a widow, Francisca Picón's closest associate and agent was Bachiller Antonio Picón, a man of modest status who probably was a relative. Other than the testimony in the *pleito de hidalguía,* there is no evidence of the family of Pedro de Sande having any dealings or connections with the "important" Sandes of the city. Francisca Picón made her will in 1580 and named as her children and heirs Dr. Francisco de Sande, don Juan de Sande, don Bernardino de Sande, capitán de Su Majestad, don Antonio de Sande, doña Juana de Sande, and doña Teresa de Sande. Another son, Hernando, who died in the late 1570s, never used the don. In 1578 Antonio de Sande witnessed a document for his mother in which he did not use don (this document and his mother's will are in AHPC Alonso Pacheco 4104). For more information on this family, see Altman, "Emigrants and Society," 182–185.

17. See the 1579 wills of Baltasar de Valverde and Bachiller Francisco Romero in AHPC Alonso Pacheco 4104.

18. See, for example, Caro Baroja, "Honor y vergüenza," 96–98, 100, 104–105.

19. AGI Contratación 5234B. Hernando de Encinas was a vecino of Trujillo.

20. In 1571 Cotrina's mother, Isabel González, was called the widow of "Juan Cotrina, sastre"; see AHPC Martín de Cabrera 3636. Cotrina's wife was "doña María"; see his mother's will of 1579 in AHPC Alonso Pacheco 4103.

21. AGS Exped. Hacienda 66.

22. AGS Exped. Hacienda 189-56. For the dispute over the offices of Zorita, see AMT García de Sanabria A-1-1. In their petition to the crown the hidalgos of Zorita estimated that the village had 230 vecinos "entre viudos y casados y que de ellos era mas de ochenta hijosdalgo." The 1561 padrón included widows also among the vecinos, so the discrepancy in the figures is not all that great.

23. For Zarza, see Vassberg, *Land and Society*, 108. In the small pueblo of Ruanes, all but one of fifty-two vecinos were hidalgos, but they were all labradores; see p. 139.

24. AGS Exped. Hacienda 189-56, 1561 padrón of Ibahernando.

25. See Naranjo Alonso, *Trujillo*, 2: 45–54 for the sale of villages in the sixteenth century. In 1627 don Juan de Chaves y Mendoza bought Herguijuela (p. 35), don Juan de Chaves Sotomayor bought Aldea del Pastor (later Santa Ana) and Ruanes (p. 49), and Hernando Pizarro's grandson don Juan Hernando Pizarro bought Zarza (pp. 32–33), later known as La Conquista. See also Clodoaldo Naranjo Alonso, *Solar de conquistadores: Trujillo, sus hijos y monumentos*, 3d. ed. (Madrid, 1983), 234–236.

26. AGS Exped. Hacienda 66.

27. Naranjo Alonso, *Trujillo*, 2: 29, 46–48.

28. ACC-HO leg. 5, pt. 2, no. 20.

29. See Carlos Callejo, *Cáceres monumental* (Madrid, 1973), 98, 106, 111, 126, as well as references throughout Tena Fernández, *Trujillo histórico*, to new constructions and renovations; see, for example pp. 347–348 for the house of Juan Pizarro de Orellana and pp. 362–363 for the Ayuntamiento. See also Carmelo Solís Rodríguez, "La plaza mayor de Trujillo," in *Actas del VI Congreso de Estudios Extremeños*, (Cáceres, 1981): 277–299, especially 282, 285. The article offers an excellent description of the growth of the city around the plaza from the time of the reconquest.

30. AMT Pedro de Carmona B-1-27.

1. Miguel Muñoz de San Pedro, "Las últimas disposiciones del último

Pizarro de la Conquista," *Boletín de la Real Academia de Historia* 126 (1950): 398. She also owned jewelry with pearls, rubies, and diamonds.

32. AMC Libros de Acuerdo 1570.

33. Miguel Angel Orti Belmonte, *La vida en Cáceres en los siglos XIII y XVI al XVIII* (Cáceres, 1949), 26, 28–30; Ida Altman, "Spanish Hidalgos and America: The Ovandos of Cáceres," *The Americas* 43, 3 (1987): 325. Gerbet, *La noblesse,* 301 estimates that the net worth of Diego de Ovando's father (of the same name) was about 5 million maravedís at his death in 1505.

34. See Orti Belmonte, *La vida en Cáceres,* 37–40 for examples of inventories of noble households, and 96–97 for country life. In addition to riding, women might also take part in vigorous outdoor activities and games; Miguel Muñoz de San Pedro, *Diego García de Paredes. Hércules y Sansón de España* (Madrid, 1946), 88–89 says that the famous hero's older half-sister, María Jiménez de Paredes, often initiated games of physical skill in which Diego García came to excell.

35. In June 1558 nobleman Diego de Vargas Carvajal "went with his criados as he normally does . . . to his house and lands at Balhondo. . . . He went dealing with and looking over his estates and from there went to the city of Cáceres," where he saw his daughter and her mother-in-law (who had recently lost her husband) "and he was there in that city . . . visiting some caballeros." This information was included in testimony in a suit brought by Pedro Calderón de Vargas against his cousin doña Beatriz de Vargas, wife of Diego de Vargas Carvajal, over the Vargas family entail that she inherited; see ARCG 508-1987-8.

36. AGI Contratación 5234A (testimony of 1591).

37. AMT Pedro de Carmona A-1-9; Acedo, "Linajes," Escobar, 379–380. Gómez Nuño de Escobar lived "temporadas en Trujillo y otras en Robledillo, donde hizo una casa muy buena."

38. AGI Justicia 1061, no. 2, ramo 2 and Justicia 1062 no. 1, ramo 2.

39. Vassberg, *Land and Society,* 28.

40. Vassberg, *Land and Society,* 23–24. Owners of private dehesas might make similar arrangements for rental as well.

41. I reached this conclusion after reading dozens of land transactions in the sixteenth-century notarial records of Cáceres; see Altman, "Emigrants, Returnees and Society," 29–30.

42. AHPC Diego Pacheco 4101. Juan Pizarro rented a dehesa for six years from Juan de Ovando Perero, a regidor, for 384,000 maravedís and another for 354,000 maravedís from Dr. Bernaldino de Saavedra, Martín de Paredes, and his brother Francisco de Paredes.

43. Muñoz de San Pedro, *Crónicas trujillanas,* Hinojosa, 19–21. Pascual Gil de Cervantes was an ancestor of Pedro Barrantes (through his

mother, Francisca de Cervantes), returnee from Peru and señor of La Cumbre (see p. 99). Diego de Hinojosa, the chronicler, was married to Pedro Barrantes's sister Ana Barrantes. Antonio C. Floriano, "Cáceres ante la historia: el problema medieval de la propiedad de la tierra," *Revista de Estudios Extremeños* 5 (1949): 11 says that anyone in Cáceres who wanted to sell a part of an estate ("heredad") had to offer it first to relatives or to those who would have inherited the property. A suit in Cáceres in the 1550s involved the purchase of four houses on Pintores street by the pharmacist Cristóbal García. García bought the houses from Señor Gonzalo de Saavedra, and Saavedra's cousin Hernando de Ovando said he should have had the right of purchase as a near relative of doña Leonor de Orellana; see AHPC Pedro de Grajos 3924. A settlement was made in 1556.

44. This example is, of course, further evidence of the practice of keeping properties within families. Gonzalo de Saavedra and his cousin Francisco de Ovando were descendants of Francisco de Ovando, el viejo, brother of Captain Diego de Ovando de Cáceres; see Altman, "Spanish Hidalgos," 335–336 and table following 344. Saavedra was the nephew of Dr. Bernaldino de Saavedra mentioned above, note 42.

45. See Gerbet, *La noblesse*, 94.

46. See Muñoz de San Pedro, "Ultimas disposiciones," 345 and Varón Gabai and Jacobs, "Peruvian Wealth," 768–782, 685–691.

47. Acedo, "Linajes," Hinojosa, 363–364.

48. The listing of properties appears in the suit brought against doña Beatriz de Vargas by her cousin Pedro Calderón de Vargas; see ARCG 508-1987-8.

49. AGI Justicia 1144, no. 3.

50. AGI Justicia 1176, no. 2, ramo 1. The suit hinged on the question of whether Martín de Chaves, who went to Peru in 1534, actually had been the owner of the dehesa at the time of his departure (it subsequently was sold by his heir, a first cousin). Chaves died in Peru owing Gonzalo Pizarro 500 pesos, which royal officials were trying to collect as part of the confiscation of Pizarro's property after his trial and execution.

51. Muñoz de San Pedro, *Crónicas trujillanas*, 135.

52. The transaction of 1547 came to a total of 607,920 maravedís, see AHPC Pedro de Grajos 3923, and the transaction of 1552 came to 353,600 maravedís and 435,135 maravedís, see AHPC Diego Pacheco 4101, to be made good in Medina del Campo in July 1552 and 1553.

53. The yearlings were purchased from doña Teresa de Carvajal, and the same buyers purchased 496 sheep (187 shorn) from Alvaro de Ulloa, regidor of Cáceres; see AHPC Pedro de Grajos 3925.

54. AHPC Pedro de Grajos 3924. Wool was sold by weight and the

price determined according to quality, color, and whether the wool was washed or dirty.

55. AHPC Pedro González 3827. The carter, a vecino of Toro, received 46 reales (1564 maravedís) per cartload, or a total of 644 reales, half of which was paid in advance. He used oxen, not mules, to haul his carts.

56. AMC Libros de Acuerdo 1572.

57. The wool sold at 3125 maravedís per arroba and at the time of the 1588 inventory, some of it was already sold, for which Cristóbal de Ovando had received 9000 ducados. See ACC-HO, leg. 5, pt. 2, no. 20.

58. AMT Pedro de Carmona B-1-23. Don Diego de Vargas Carvajal was the son of Diego de Vargas Carvajal, whom he accompanied to Peru in 1560.

59. Klein, *The Mesta*, 332–333. Klein's is still the most comprehensive study both of the organization, privileges, and political power of the Mesta and of stockraising in the peninsula in general. Nevertheless the book is dated, and the subject demands thorough research and restudy. Vassberg, *Land and Society*, 81–82, for example, touches on aspects of the relations between the Mesta and local economy and society in Extremadura. His findings indicate clearly that the Mesta was not very powerful there in the sixteenth century and that Klein's study conveys only part of the picture.

60. See Vassberg, *Land and Society*, 82. In the 1560s Juan Pizarro twice sent representatives to appear before the council of the Mesta to protest the usurpation and illegal use of his pastures; AHPC Diego Pacheco 4102, 4113.

61. AMT García de Sanabria A-1-1.

62. For the use and regulation of the montes around Trujillo, see Vassberg, *Land and Society*, 36–37, 69, 73. For an excellent discussion of the rural economy of Trujillo, especially breeding pigs, see Vassberg, "La coyuntura socioeconómica."

63. AMC Libros de Acuerdo 1553; LeFlem, "Cáceres, Plasencia y Trujillo," 266.

64. Vassberg, *Land and Society*, 186.

65. Muñoz de San Pedro, *Crónicas trujillanas*, Hinojosa, 138.

66. See AHPC Pedro de Grajos 3924 for Sancho de Figueroa's will of 1549 and for Juan de Carvajal Villalobos; see Pedro de Grajos 3923 for don Juan de Ulloa Carvajal.

67. This was especially true in the case of criados who accompanied employers to the New World; see chap. 5.

68. For Nuño de Ortega, see AGI Justicia 1176, no. 2, ramo 1; AGI

Indif. General 2090 for González; Muñoz de San Pedro, "Ultimas disposiciones," 406, 546 for Hernando Pizarro.

69. AGI Contratación 5227.

70. AHPC Pedro González 3828. Francisco de Ovando Paredes was the oldest son and heir to the entail of his father, Cosme de Ovando, who had inherited one of three entails established by his father, Francisco de Ovando, el rico; see Altman, "Spanish Hidalgos," 338–339. Since he had no legitimate heirs, at Francisco de Ovando Paredes's death the entail passed first to his brother Cosme de Ovando Paredes and then to Cristóbal de Ovando Paredes, both of whom spent long periods in Peru before returning to Cáceres in the 1580s.

71. For comparison, see Pike, *Aristocrats and Traders*, 170–192 for slaves in Seville; 183–185 deal with the training and employment of slaves there.

72. AHPC Pedro de Grajos 3923, Diego Pacheco 4100.

73. Hernando Corajo freed his elderly slave Isabel in his will of 1513 and provided her with eight fanegas of wheat and 1000 maravedís a year and a new set of clothing every two years; see ACC Asuntos de Trujillo leg. 3, no. 2. He also freed his cousin Sancho de Paredes.

74. The incident was described in testimony in a suit of 1549 brought against Juan Cortés. He was accused of having aided a man named Pablo Vicencio (also known as Francisco Pérez), who had come from Peru and in Spain escaped from a royal prison; see AGI Justicia 1176, no. 2, ramo 8. The incident between Cortés's criados and Herrera figured in the testimony because it was suspected that Herrera helped fabricate charges against Cortés.

75. Gerbet, *La noblesse*, 316.

76. AMT leg. 1-1-30, Actas de 1576-83. For the guards of the montes, see Vassberg, *Land and Society*, 70–71.

77. AMC Libros de Acuerdo 1570. The alcalde, Benito Rodríguez Sanabria, had come before the city council to ask for a loan of 200 reales so that the hermandad could go to the mountains to apprehend the servant and his fellow delinquents. The council reluctantly granted the loan, noting that they were under no obligation to give the hermandad money to pursue thieves.

78. Muñoz de San Pedro, *Crónicas trujillanas*, 79, 137.

79. See Caro Baroja, "Honor y vergüenza," 84–85 for discussion of the concepts of "valer mas" and collective honor; "este honor colectivo se ajusta a un sistema de linajes patrilineales. . . . Las glorias de un individuo de linaje alcanzan a la totalidad de éste, las vergüenzas también. . . . Por eso cada linaje en conjunto pretende *valer mas* que otros" (p. 85).

80. Muñoz de San Pedro, *Crónicas trujillanas*, 135–136 (for Juan de Chaves), 157.

81. In his article on "Lope de Aguirre, 'traidor' " in *El señor inquisidor y otras vidas por oficio*, 2d ed. (Madrid, 1970) 65–122, Julio Caro Baroja relates the concept of "valer mas" to the conflicts and bandos of the late Middle Ages. He writes, "la consecuencia última de esta concepción bélica de la vida es el derecho del mas fuerte y la noción de una especie de dualismo, de división continua, entre dos contrarios en perpetua lucha" (p. 106). Julian Pitt-Rivers, in his chapter entitled "Honour and Social Status" in Peristiany, *Honour and Shame*, observes that "seen from the individual's point of view, to have recourse to justice is to abnegate one's claim to settle one's debts of honour for oneself" (p. 30) and "the aristocracy claims the right to honour=precedence by the tradition which makes them the leaders of society. . . . The sacred quality of high status is demonstrated in freedom from the sanctions which apply to ordinary mortals" (p. 31). "Enemistad" did have a specific legal meaning in many parts of Spain in the Middle Ages. Heath Dillard. *Daughters of the Reconquest: Women in Castilian Town Society, 1100–1300* (Cambridge, 1984), 31 writes that "at Sepúlveda . . . municipal law prescribed *enemistad* for serious crimes, meaning banishment under threat of legal execution by one's enemies."

82. AMT Pedro de Carmona A-1-9.

83. The protesting regidores were Bernaldino de Tapia, Alvaro de Hinojosa (brother-in-law of Gonzalo Pizarro), don Juan de Vargas Carvajal (son of Diego de Vargas Carvajal), Juan de Chaves (the chronicler), Martín de Chaves, and the returnees Pedro Barrantes, Alonso Ruiz, and Juan Pizarro de Orellana; see AMG leg. 134.

84. AMC Libros de Acuerdo 1571.

85. AMG leg. 134.

86. See Caro Baroja, "Lope de Aguirre," 96–97. He sees the "libertades de grupo" as "libertades de acción frente al poder" (p. 97).

87. AGI Justicia 1061, no. 2, ramo 2 (for quotation); Justicia 1062, no. 1, ramo 2; Justicia 1064, no. 3, ramo 1. The settlement appears in Acedo, "Linajes," Calderón, 333[a13]; he gave his poder to Alonso de Loaysa, don Pedro Puertocarrero (his uncle), don Diego de Carvajal, and Fray Jerónimo de Loaysa (archbishop of Lima). Andrés Calderón was related to a number of prominent families (see table 3). His maternal grandfather was Juan de Hinojosa, an encomendero in New Spain (among Hinojosa's children with his wife doña Beatriz de Tapia was doña Juana de Hinojosa, Andrés Calderón's mother; see Muñoz de San Pedro, *Crónicas trujillanas*, 175). Despite these family connections and the fact that he was heir to his father, Gabriel Calderón, either his inheritance was small or he

squandered a great deal of it. There is no doubt that he went to Peru as a merchant. He was listed as a merchant in the asientos of 1562; see *Catálogo*, 4, no. 2281. In October 1561 he appeared as the witness in a power of attorney of a merchant of Trujillo, Juan González de Victoria, to his son Diego González in Peru; see AMT Francisco Enríquez A-1-5-1. Two other men from Trujillo went to Peru as merchants at the same time, Gonzalo de Carmona and Juan de Ribera.

88. See ARCG 3ª-599-3.

89. Caro Baroja, "Honor y vergüenza," 92–93, note 37 quotes Francisco Núñez de Velasco, *Diálogos de contención entre la milicia y la ciencia* (Valladolid, 1614), fol. 417 as follows: "En algunas ciudades destos reinos de España aun no acaba de extinguir el fuego destos negros bandos, especialmente en Trujillo, Cáceres y Plasencia, adonde no solamente la gente principal es banderiza, pero aun la comun y plebeya esta dividida entre Carvajales y Ovandos."

90. Tena Fernández, *Trujillo histórico*, 392.

91. Muñoz de San Pedro, "Aventuras y desventuras," 14. García Holguín was the husband of doña Mencía de Ulloa, the eldest daughter of the camarero Sancho de Paredes Golfín and his wife, doña Isabel Coello.

92. Pérez de Tudela, *Documentos relativos a la Gasca*, 1: 356.

93. In 1570, for example, there were forty-five students from the diocese of Coria and sixty-six from Plasencia enrolled in the faculty of canon law in Salamanca, compared to only three students from each diocese enrolled in Valladolid in the same year. In 1550 three students from Coria and thirteen from Plasencia were enrolled at Alcalá de Henares. See Richard L. Kagan, *Students and Society in Early Modern Spain* (Baltimore, 1974), 240, 242–243, tables III, IV, and V.

94. AHPC Pedro González 3829.

95. ACC-HO leg. 1, no. 10. Ovando's will is in ACC-HO leg. 1, no. 16.

96. J. M. Lodo de Mayoralgo, *Viejos linajes de Cáceres* (Cáceres, 1971), 680. Schäfer, *El consejo de Indias*, 1: 130; 2: 303–307. Noel Geoffrey Parker, *Philip II* (Boston, 1978), 113–122.

97. Cacereño Licenciado Alonso Martínez Espadero was oidor of the audiencia of Valladolid before becoming a member of the Council of the Indies in 1572, where he served until his death in 1589; see Schäfer, *El consejo de Indias*, 1: 355; AHPC Alonso Pacheco 4104. Many of his relative in Cáceres were also letrados; see discussion of emigrant Alvaro de Paredes in chap. 4.

98. For don Gaspar Cervantes de Gaete, see Tena Fernández, *Trujillo histórico*, 58–60; and Costancio Gutiérrez, *Españoles en Trento* (Valladolid, 1951), 523–527. He was made cardinal in 1570. Before his appointment as archbishop of Messina, in 1561 as inquisitor of Aragon Cervantes

de Gaete gave his power of attorney to his nephews in Trujillo, Alonso Pizarro de Torres, Hernando Cervantes, and Francisco de Gaete, in preparation for his departure from Spain; AMT Pedro de Carmona A-1-9.

99. Tena Fernández, *Trujillo histórico*, 137. He was the brother of Martín de Meneses, captain and encomendero in Peru who returned to Spain late in life and died before he could go back.

100. In the late fifteenth century don Bernardino de Carvajal, nephew of don Juan de Carvajal, cardinal of Sant Angelo, was cardinal of Santa Cruz in Rome and also served in a number of bishoprics. Diego García de Paredes ("el Sansón") called him his cousin and met him when he went to serve in Italy. Don Francisco de Carvajal, arcediano of Plasencia who died in 1556, was his nephew. Don Francisco's brother don Bernardino de Carvajal and his first cousin Sancho de Sande were tesoreros of Plasencia. For the Carvajals, see Acedo, "Linajes," Carvajal, 62–63, and Antonio Rubio Rojas, *Las disposiciones de don Francisco de Carvajal, arcediano de Plasencia y Mecenas de Cáceres, su villa natal* (Cáceres, 1975), 64, 76.

101. From bequests and provisions in wills it is clear that hidalgos who entered religious orders often continued to depend on stipends from their families, whereas a secular priest with a benefice could be self-supporting. In 1577 Pedro Rol de la Cerda agreed to give his brother Cosme de Ovando, member of the Order of San Juan de los Caballeros, 100,000 maravedís a year; see AHPC Diego Pacheco 4113. The returnee Cristóbal de Ovando Paredes willed 24 ducados a year to his brother Fray Juan de Ovando, a Franciscan in Salamanca, and the same to another brother, Fray Gómez de la Rocha; see ACC-HO leg. 1, no. 21. In 1574 don Rodrigo de Godoy, regidor of Cáceres, arranged to send 500 escudos (escudo = 400 maravedís) to his brother don Lorenzo de Godoy, "caballero de la orden de San Juan," who was in Palermo, via some Genoese merchants; see AHPC Pedro Gonzalez 3829. Don Lorenzo and Don Rodrigo were the sons of wealthy returnee Francisco de Godoy.

102. Muñoz de San Pedro, *Crónicas trujillanas*, Chaves, 191–192; AMT Actas 1558–1560.

103. AGI Lima 199.

104. The biography by Muñoz de San Pedro, *Diego García de Paredes*, provides considerable detail on the campaigns and events in which he took part. " 'El Sansón Extremeño' (Diego García de Paredes)," *Revista de Extremadura* 10 (1908): 465–472 is a transcription of the *memoria* of his career that Diego García wrote for his son shortly before his death; Muñoz de San Pedro has concluded that the memoria is genuine. See also Miguel Muñoz de San Pedro and H. Nectario María, *El gobernador y maestre de campo Diego García de Paredes, fundador de Trujillo de Venezuela* (Madrid, 1957), 76, 125–127, 149, 277.

105. See Miguel Muñoz de San Pedro, "Don Alvaro de Sande. Cronista del desastre de los Gelves," *Revista de Estudios Extremeños* 10 (1954): 468–473 for details of his career and a transcription of the chronicle, and Orti Belmonte's notes to Foglietta, *Vida de don Alvaro de Sande*, especially 18–24, 88, 246. Orti Belmonte's edition of Foglietta's biography of Sande, which probably was commissioned by Sande's son don Rodrigo de Sande, contains an appendix of documents related to Sande's life and career—for example, his 1550 marriage to doña Ana de Guzmán, "dama de la reina de Bohemia," and the negotiations for his ransom. Maximilian's letter of 1562 to his brother, the "king of Bohemia," asking him to help Sande stated "yo tengo tanta obligación a su tio y sus parientes que han servido a mi padre" (p. 331).

106. See the testimony for don Juan de Sande's illegitimate son don Jerónimo de Sande in AGI Contratación 5234A and AHPC Pedro González 3827 for the loan of 200 ducados that don Juan de Sande took to go to Granada. The city council recorded his departure in December 1569; see AMC Libros de Acuerdo 1569. A brother of don Juan de Sande, don Alvaro de Sande, in 1558 was called captain—see AHPC Diego Pacheco 4101—and in 1563 coronel—see AHPC Pedro de Grajos 3925. He is said to have been in Gelves with his uncle and probably was the brother who died later in Italy. Another relative by marriage, Pedro Alvarez Holguín (brother of Pedro de Sande's wife, doña Aldonza de Torres) also fought at Gelves. He was thought to have been captured by the Turks but eventually was found in Sicily; see AHPC Pedro de Grajos 3926.

107. Don Juan de Sande was nominated as candidate for the captaincy of the 1580 levy of soldiers for the war in Portugal. Other nominees were Martín de Paredes, a "caballero principal" who had served in Italy and Spain, and another caballero named Diego García de Paredes, a widower, who had served in Italy. In the end don Juan Perero, whose military background was not detailed, led the troops; see AMC Libros de Acuerdo 1580.

108. AHPC Alonso Pacheco 4104.

109. ACC-HO leg. 1, no. 16 contains Dr. Nicolás de Ovando's will; he handled the negotiations at least in part in both cases. See AHPC 3926 for the efforts initiated by doña Aldonza de Torres, his sister (see above, note 106) to find Pedro Alvarez Holguín. Half the ransom money was lent by Francisco de Godoy (the returnee) and Comendador Aldana, both of whom were probably relatives.

110. AHPC Pedro de Grajos 3924.

111. See Acedo, "Linajes," Vargas, 48[a13] and ARCG 508-1987-8.

112. See Muñoz de San Pedro, "Ultimas disposiciones," 407; Acedo, "Linajes," Hinojosa, 366[a18].

113. AMC Libros de Acuerdo 1571.

114. ACC-HO leg. 1, no. 16. In 1571 Hernando Calderón de Chaves donated to the city of Trujillo two pieces of land and 600 maravedís of censo perpetuo on some houses, saying that when he was a regidor over thirty-two years before "no podía dejar de alagarme en algunas cosas y en otras ser corto por ser como era mozo en el dicho tiempo." See AMT 1571: VI-9.

115. AMC Libros de Acuerdo 1571.

III. Commoners, Clergy, and Professionals

1. Jose Antonio Maravall in *El mundo social de "La Celestina"* (Madrid, 1968), 21–22 pictures the nobility as shaping the important social structures and relations:

La clase de los señores, como clase dominante, es, sin duda, la responsable de la estructura y perfil de la sociedad. Mediante su dominio de los recursos de que la sociedad en cuestión dispone, aquella clase determina el puesto de cada grupo social en el conjunto, el sistema de sus funciones, el cuadro de sus deberes y derechos, es decir, la figura moral de cada uno de esos grupos. Como de la clase señorial depende la selección de los bienes y valores que en una sociedad se busca conseguir, es también esa clase superior la que determina los valores que a los demás corresponden y los que ella misma se atribuye y monopoliza. En definitiva, la clase dominante es la responsable de las relaciones ético-sociales entre los diferentes grupos.

2. See chap. 2. This situation might have been changing, of course. In Zorita, where the hidalgos petitioned the crown to be allowed to hold municipal offices, by 1561 the alcalde was Diego de Trejo, an hidalgo; see AGI Indif. General 2088, información of Jorge Holgado, vecino of Orellana.

3. On the lifestyle of the people of the villages, Michael R. Weisser, *The Peasants of the Montes* (Chicago, 1976), 53, comments:

Contrary to rejecting urban mores and styles, the peasantry adopted and adapted them to fit the realities of rural life. The social cohesion of the pueblo did not result from any denial of an alien culture, but was enhanced by the acceptance of the culture of the larger society by the entire rural community.

4. In 1554 a fifty-year-old shoemaker, Juan García, was called "rico" (see AGI Indif. Gen. 2078), and the brothers García Hernández and Gonzalo Cabezas, zapateros, in the same year were called "hombres ricos de caudal y bienes raíces" (see AGI Justicia 1074, no. 4). Alonso Blanco, who lost his property and became impoverished, in 1578 said he had been "hombre rico y principal" of Trujillo, AGI Indif. General 2059.

5. See chap. 5.

6. Teresa Muñoz, a widow from Cáceres, was living in Seville by

1535; by 1554 a dealer in oil named Francisco Hernández and his wife, both also from Cáceres, had become vecinos of Seville; and in the 1570s a cacereño priest named Juan Digán also was a vecino of the city. See AHPC Hernando Conde 3712; Pedro de Grajos 3924; Pedro González 3828 (1573); and Alonso Pacheco 4104.

7. AHPC Alonso Pacheco 4103; AGI Indif. General 2049.

8. Rodríguez Sanchez, *Cáceres*, 198–209; see also 180–183.

9. See AGS Exped. Hacienda 311, padrón of Madroñera.

10. AMT 1584: IX-8.

11. In 1570 Cáceres and Trujillo each had at least four inns ("mesones y posadas"), and in both cities at least one of the innkeepers was a woman; see ARCG 303-490-10, pleito de hidalguía of Alonso de Loaysa. There probably were at least twice that many inns, since in 1578 in Trujillo four different mesoneros and taverneros testified in two informaciones; see AGI Indif. General 2059, informaciones of Juan Rubio and Isabel García la Castra. Probably the larger towns in the cities' jurisdictions also had inns, since one of the smallest—Orellana la Nueva, with thirty-two vecinos—in 1575 was called "lugar donde no hay taverna ni carnicería"; AGS Exped. Hacienda 906.

12. AHPC Pedro de Grajos 3923, Pedro González 3827.

13. AHPC Diego Pacheco 4100.

14. Carmelo Solís Rodríguez, "El arquitecto Francisco Becerra" 287–383.

15. See Geoffrey Parker, *The Army of Flanders and the Spanish Road* (Cambridge, 1972), 35–43 for a description of how recruitment took place.

16. For example, Gonzalo Durán of Cáceres had died in Flanders by 1571. His brother Lorenzo de Montanos went to the Indies; see AHPC Alonso Pacheco 4102. In 1578 Juan Pérez, son of Juan Pérez tintorero, was a captive in Algiers; AHPC Pedro Gonzalez 3830.

17. AMT 1-1-30, Actas del Consejo 1580.

18. AHPC Pedro González 3827, 3831.

19. See Rodríguez Sánchez, *Cáceres*, 134, notes 15 and 16, and 88–89; AMC Libros de Acuerdo 1569, 1580; AMT Actas 1558, 1576–83.

20. AHPC Alonso Pacheco 4103; AMC Libros de Acuerdo 1575.

21. AMC Libros de Acuerdo 1580; AMT Actas 1580.

22. AMT 1-1-30.

23. AMC Libros de Acuerdo 1578.

24. AHPC Pedro de Grajos 3923.

25. AMT García de Sanabria A-1-1.

26. AHPC Pedro González 3827 (he was mayordomo in 1567), 3830. At some time before 1572 Lorenzo de Ulloa Solís took 1400 ducados in censos al quitar—400 from Diego García de Ulloa, 500 from Rodrigo

Silvestre (probably the merchant), and 500 from Cristóbal García. García had other financial dealings with Lorenzo and his brother Francisco de Ulloa Solís; see AHPC Alonso Pacheco 4102.

27. AGI Justicia 1074, no. 4; AGI Indif. General 2058 for información of Lorenzo del Puerto.

28. AHPC Hernando Conde 3712.

29. AHPC Pedro González 3830.

30. In 1550 Pedro del Toril, a shoemaker of Trujillo "over 57 years" of age, signed his name; AGI Justicia 1074, no. 4. In 1574 four witnesses for Alonso Ramiro, a tailor from Trujillo emigrating to New Spain, all could sign. They were a locksmith, a blacksmith, a tailor, and a merchant; AGI Indif. General 2055. There are, of course, many such examples of literate commoners.

31. AGI Indif. General 2051 (testimony of 1567).

32. Francisco Rodríguez was about thirty years old in 1575 when he petitioned to join his parents Rodrigo Alonso herrero (also called herrador) and Isabel Alvarez in Peru (Lima), taking with him his wife and two children. He subsequently returned to Trujillo, where in 1582 he was calling himself Francisco Rodríguez Godoy; see AGI Indif. General 2087 and 2093. His parents returned to Trujillo in 1578 in the entourage of the prominent Captain Martín de Meneses, long-time resident of Peru; see AGI Indif. General 2162A.

33. AMT 1570:III-4. There were at least two other men of the same name who were herradores in Trujillo: Hernán González, who emigrated in 1574, and Hernando González, who emigrated in 1575, both to New Spain with their families. See AGI Indif. General 2055; Contratación 5222.

34. See ARCG 511-2284-8, for Hortún's will. Although some of the family names—Becerra, Bote—that appear in Hortún's will commonly were associated with hidalgos, I was unable to find any relation between Hortún and the hidalgo Becerras or Botes. His illiteracy, the name of his first wife, his wives' modest dowries, and the fact that, with the exception of one son who was to receive half the mill in Tamuja, his property was to be divided equally among heirs, all suggest he was a commoner.

35. See Weisser, *Peasants of the Montes*, 38–44 for analysis of landholding in Navalmoral in 1583 for comparison. In 1561 Hortún was assessed 244 maravedís in taxes (see AGS Exped. Hacienda 189–56), which would place him well within the middle to upper-middle group of the town. Clearly he had sufficient property to produce a commercial surplus and employ others to work his land.

36. AMT 1584:IX-8.

37. AGI Justicia 1070, no. 8, 9. Juan de Muñoz was a native of Na-

valsaz but lived in and owned property in Trujillo before going to Peru. He took his sons Pedro de Bibanco, Alonso de Bibanco, and Francisco Muñoz with him, leaving behind two others, Juan and Diego de Bibanco. Alonso de Bibanco returned to Trujillo, but Pedro died in Peru. Since he had supported Gonzalo Pizarro's rebellion, his properties were confiscated, which is why the inventory of the family's possessions was taken in 1550. Francisco Muñoz was not mentioned in the division of property and he must have died in Peru also.

38. LeFlem, "Cáceres, Plasencia y Trujillo," p. 269.

39. AGS Exped. Hacienda 189-56.

40. AGS Exped. Hacienda 66.

41. AMT Actas 1558.

42. AMC Libros de Acuerdo 1575, 1576.

43. AHPC Pedro González 3831.

44. AGI Indif. General 2059.

45. See AGS Exped. Hacienda 66 for the 1557 padrón of the calle de Caleros.

46. For Casar, see AGS Exped. Hacienda 66; see 902 for El Campo, and 189-56 for Santa Cruz.

47. See AGS Exped. Hacienda 189-56 for Ibahernando and AGS Exped. Hacienda 66 for Sierra de Fuentes. Doubtless there were residents of Ibahernando who had no vineyard at all but belonged to the middle group. Nevertheless ownership of a medium-sized vineyard seems to have correlated with a basic holding in livestock, since virtually everyone in the group had one or two oxen, a cow or two, and small numbers of other livestock (pigs, sheep, goats) and draft animals.

48. AGS Exped. Hacienda 66. The small lugar of Sierra de Fuentes apparently had very little access to land, which would explain the large number of wage laborers there.

49. AHPC Diego Pacheco 4100 (see year of 1551). Sancho de Figueroa was a returnee from the Indies.

50. Francisca Picón, the mother of Dr. Francisco de Sande, in 1572 rented out a garden behind the monastery of San Francisco for four years for 17 ducados (6375 maravedís) a year plus various products, including nuts, onions, garlic, melons, pomegranates, and plums; AHPC Alonso Pacheco 4102.

51. The couple was required to build a hut in the huerta during the next four years if the royal magistrate of Cáceres granted permission, and to keep the garden "well tilled and cultivated and planted with trees." AHPC Alonso Pacheco 4104.

52. AMT 1-1-30.

53. See AGI Indif. General 2080.

54. AHPC Pedro de Grajos 3923.

55. Rodríguez Sánchez, *Cáceres*, 35.

56. AHPC Pedro González 3829.

57. AHPC Pedro González 3827 (1570) and Alonso Pacheco 4103 (1575).

58. AGI Indif. General 2079.

59. For example, a locally made dark cloth called "catorzen" sold for 210 maravedís per yard in 1553 and berbi for 83 maravedís a yard in 1544; see AHPC Pedro de Grajos 3924, 3923. In contrast, in 1535 Valencia cloth sold for 800 maravedís per yard and *velarte* (a fine broadcloth) for 1000 maravedís a yard in 1553; see AHPC Hernando Conde 3712, Pedro de Grajos 3924.

60. AHPC Pedro de Grajos 3923.

61. Solís Rodríguez, "Francisco Becerra," 301.

62. The accounts of the construction work, expenditures, and money received from Dr. Ovando are in ACC-HO leg. 8, no. 101. Carrasco's account book was dated June 1565, soon after Ovando's death.

63. Solís Rodríguez, "Francisco Becerra," 366, 372.

64. Santos and Alonso García were both sons of Teresa Alvarez; Santos García's father, Juan García, was a locksmith. Santos was eighteen or nineteen and Alonso twenty-five or twenty-six years old when they went to Peru. In 1576 Trujillo's council appointed Santos García "sellador" of iron and of weights and measures. In the same year Francisco González, one of the stonecutters who helped finish the entranceway of the dehesa, was appointed inspector of work, AMT leg. 1-1-30. See Solís Rodríguez, "Francisco Becerra," 330–333 for the construction of the entranceway, and *Catálogo*, 3, no. 2447 and AGI Indif. General 2078. Pero Gómez built the choir stalls of the church of Santiago in the late 1550s; he made the contract in December 1557 and was to complete the job by February 1559. He received a total of 450 ducados for the job, paid in installments of 50 ducados every two months and the balance upon completion. Gómez also worked on the house built by the returnee from Peru, Francisco de Godoy; see AHPC Diego Pacheco 4100, 4113.

65. See Vassberg, *Land and Society*, 160 for the continued use of oxen in Extremadura. Mules in the 1560s and 1570s sold for around 35 to 40 ducados (see AHPC Alonso Pacheco 4103), three or more times the price of an ox or donkey and twice that of a horse.

66. AHPC Hernando Conde 3712.

67. AHPC Diego Pacheco 4113, Alonso Pacheco 4102, 4103, Pedro de Grajos 3926.

68. AHPC Diego Pacheco 4113.

69. AHPC Pedro de Grajos 3926.

70. AHPC Pedro González 3829.

71. AHPC Alonso Pacheco 4104.

72. Dyers of Cáceres frequently bought *pastel* (a dye) from people from Seville, and "tratantes de aceite" (oil vendors) also came from Seville. In 1571 Francisco Rodríguez of Trujillo bought some cloth from a merchant from Seville while in Cáceres; see AHPC Martín de Cabrera 3636.

73. AHPC Pedro González 3829.

74. AHPC Pedro de Grajos 3924. Sotoval said that if his wife did not remarry, account should not be made of her gains in the business.

75. AHPC Pedro de Grajos 3924.

76. In 1558 Diego del Saz and his son Francisco del Saz and Felipe Díaz rented a part of the tithes of the church of Coria; AMT García de Sanabria A-1-3. For Luis del Saz, regidor, see Acedo, "Linajes," Vargas, 48ᵃ¹⁴ and Altamirano, 91; see also AMT Pedro de Carmona A-1-1-9. For Diego del Saz, see the 1544 will of Juan de la Huerta of Cáceres, who owed Diego del Saz 6000 maravedís, AHPC Pedro de Grajos 3923. See AMT García de Sanabria A-1-1 for sale to vecinos of Benalcazar of 70,540 maravedís of cloth, García de Sanabria A-1-2-1 for purchase of cloth from Córdoba (1556), and Francisco Enríquez A-1-5-1 for poder of Diego and Luis del Saz to merchants in Segovia in 1561. See García de Sanabria A-1-3 for money owed by Alvaro de Loaysa and Pedro de Carmona A-1-9 for Cristóbal Pizarro's power of attorney.

77. Vicente Navarro del Castillo, *La epopeya de la raza extremeña en Indias* (Mérida, 1978), 427; AGI Contratación 5237. Luis del Saz took his criado Mateo Jiménez of Trujillo with him.

78. Luis de Camargo's heirs appeared together in September 1551; AMT García de Sanabria A-1-1. For purchase of dehesa, see ACC-AT leg. 8, nos. 33, 47. For the claim against Luis de Camargo, see AGI Justicia 1176, no. 2, ramo 3. This suit included a power of attorney of 1535 that Luis de Camargo, along with his son-in-law Vicente Enríquez and son Diego de Camargo, gave to a Trujillo merchant named Duarte López; witnesses were three other Trujillo merchants, Juan de Limosin, Juan López, and Juan de San Pedro.

79. See AMT 1-1-30. Alvaro Pizarro de Camargo in 1578 rented stores across from his main house for two years to Lope Hernández, tendero; AMT Pedro de Carmona B-1-23. Juan de Camargo, son of Luis de Camargo, owned mills on the Almonte and Magasca rivers and a dehesa near Montánchez; see AMT García de Sanabria A-1-1. He probably died in the 1550s, since there is no later record of him; likely Luis del Saz, mayorazgo, was his son.

80. For Vicente Enríquez, see AMT García de Sanabria A-1-1, Pedro de Carmona A-1-9, and note 78 above. In 1551 he bought a vineyard for

33,000 maravedís from Beatriz Alvarez, widow of Francisco González and mother of Licenciado Diego González Altamirano, oidor of Lima; see AMT García de Sanabria A-1-1; Acedo, "Linajes," Altamirano, 91.

81. For Juan de Camargo, regidor, see Acedo, "Linajes," Calderón, 295. Vasco Calderón Enríquez married Juana de San Juan. Vasco Calderón paid a dowry of 400 ducados for his sister Beatriz de Camargo to enter the convent of Santa Clara, and in 1593 he and his wife arranged for one of their daughters to enter the convent of the Magdalena of Aldeanueva del Barco for 500 ducados; see Acedo, "Linajes," Calderón, 334[a12,a33,a41].

82. For Alonso de Camargo, see Boyd-Bowman, *Indice*, 2, no. 3118 and Navarro del Castillo, *La epopeya*, 388. For Alonso Enríquez, see *Catálogo*, 5, no. 1737 and AGI Contratación 5221 (testimony for Licenciado Diego González Altamirano). For Vicente Enríquez, see AMT Pedro de Carmona B-1-23. For Alvaro de Camargo, see *Catálogo* vol. 5, no. 4315; there is no evidence that Alvaro de Camargo was part of the family, other than the names, which are fairly convincing. Juan de Camargo, the son of Alvaro de Camargo and Juana González de Orellana (grandson of Luis de Camargo and Beatriz Alvarez), went to Peru as the criado of Luis de Herrera, AGI Contratación 5235.

83. The power of attorney to his son and guardianship of don Gonzalo de Hinojosa are in AMT Francisco Enríquez A-1-5-1; for the censo and association with Juan Alvarez, see García de Sanabria A-1-1. Juan Alvarez was in Lima in May 1559; see AGI Justicia 418. Diego González went to "Tierra Firme and Peru" in 1559, possibly as his father's factor; see *Catálogo*, 3, no. 4006; he was called "maestre" in the asientos. For Alonso Alvarez de Altamirano, see AGI Indif. General 2092. They might have been related to the family of Licenciado Diego González Altamirano, twice oidor of the audiencia of Lima.

84. The following were on the 1580 list: García de Alarcón and his son Hernando de Alarcón (one horse); Cristóbal de Alarcón and Lucas de Alarcón (one horse); Martín Alonso de Alarcón (to share a horse with Pedro Carrasco); and Diego de Alarcón, widower (to share a horse with Diego de Melo). Melo also was probably a merchant, a relative of Francisco Sánchez de Melo, a Sevillian merchant (native of Trujillo) who sent two brothers from Trujillo (doubtless his relatives) to Peru as his factors in 1557 and 1559. García de Alarcón went to Tierra Firme as a merchant in 1557, the same year Pedro de Melo went (see *Catálogo*, 3, no. 3556). An Hernando de Alarcón and a Juan de Alarcón were in Peru at the end of the sixteenth century; see Acedo, "Linajes," Calderón, 334[a59-60].

85. AGI Contratación 5235, 5237.

86. Naranjo Alonso, *Trujillo y su tierra*, 2: 224.

87. Dr. Felipe Díaz de Orellana of Trujillo was for a time the bene-

ficiado of Alcollarín, Gaspar Gómez of Trujillo was beneficiado of Aldeanueva in 1575 (AGI Contratación 5222), and Bachiller Francisco Carrasco
of Trujillo was "teniente de cura" of Madroñera in 1577 (AGI Indif. General 2089).

88. In 1561 he agreed to instruct Alonso Pizarro until he was ordained
a "clérigo de misa"; see AHPC Diego Pacheco 4113. The city council of
Trujillo hired Bachiller Ojalvo in January 1558 for two years at 100
ducados a year; he also was given lodging, AMT Actas 1558. In October
1570 doña Francisca de Torres, widow of Diego de Ovando de Cáceres,
gave her power of attorney to Bachiller Diego Ojalvo and Bartolomé
Serrano, clérigos presbíteros, to make an inventory of her late husband's
country house at Arguijuela. She also gave her power of attorney to the
merchant Diego Pérez de Herrera and another man for the same purpose,
AHPC Pedro González 3827.

89. Acedo, "Linajes," Escobar, 384.

90. For Cristóbal de Solís, see AGI Indif. General 2084, where he
stated he was the son of Alvar García de Solis, clérigo and Catalina Alvarez,
soltera. One of the witnesses was Solís's brother Miguel Hernández de
Solís, who was thirty years old in 1577. For Alvar García de Solís, see AMT
Pedro de Carmona A-1-9 (1565) and García de Sanabria A-1-1-3 (1558).

91. ACC-HO leg. 5, no. 34.

92. Isabel de Paredes's son, Licenciado Alvaro de Paredes Salinas,
reopened his mother's case against the cofradía de la Cruz in 1599; see
ACC-HO leg. 8, no. 24. Following Licenciado Paredes's death, his son
Melchior de Salinas Paredes left for the Indies in 1615; see ACC-HO leg.
7, no. 14.

93. The priests counted for the years 1534–1537 were all identified in
AHPC Hernando Conde 3712. In 1537 nineteen priests signed a petition
protesting the excommunication (for unknown reasons) of a priest named
Hernando Rodríguez Sanabria. Using the tax and census records in
Simancas, LeFlem, "Cáceres, Plasencia y Trujillo," 280 compiled the
following figures for the clergy in Cáceres: twenty-eight in 1557, forty-two
in 1561 and 1584, thirty-nine in 1586, and fifty-five in 1595. The incompleteness of these censuses has already been discussed. The figures and
records for Trujillo are even less complete.

94. Galíndez's will and inventory appear in AHPC Pedro González
3829; his nephew Juan Mogollón de Acosta's application for license to
leave for Peru is in AGI Indif. General 2085.

95. AMC Libros de Acuerdo 1554, 1571, 1570; AMT 1-20-70-35 and 1-
20-70-33. Salaries and length of contracts varied considerably.

96. For Licenciado Lorenzo Bernáldez of Plasencia and Francisco Bernáldez, *natural* (native) of Medellín and vecino of Plasencia, see AGI

Contratación 5218. Francisco and his wife Isabel Rodríguez were both thirty-five years of age when they emigrated.

97. AHPC Pedro de Grajos 3923, 3924, 3926. Bernáldez bought the oven from Macías de Vita (who was acting for his brother Pedro de Vita, in Peru), Vita's sister Catalina González and her husband Pedro Cano (brother of Juan Cano, encomendero of Mexico), and another couple.

98. AHPC Pedro de Grajos 3923, 3924.

99. AHPC Pedro de Grajos 3923, 3924, 3925. Bernáldez's contract with Pérez also provided that Pérez cover one-fourth of the loss if they did not make good on their investment. The evidence regarding the wood-cutting business is that Bernáldez hired two men in 1544 to cut and transport wood, and in 1546 he sold two "tablas de nogal" for 15 reales; AHPC Pedro de Grajos 3923.

100. AHPC Pedro de Grajos 3924, 3925; see AMC Libros de Acuerdo 1555 for the summons from the bishop of Badajoz.

101. There was an aljama of Moors in fifteenth-century Trujillo (see Beinart, *Trujillo*, 15, 60), but sixteenth-century sources do not mention the existence of such a neighborhood.

102. For the figures on the expulsion, see Bernard Vincent, "L'expulsion des morisques de royaume de Grenade et leur repartition en Castille," *Mélanges de la Casa de Velázquez* 6 (1970): 224–226. An epidemic of typhus affected the deportees to Extremadura in particular; the overall mortality rate among deportees was lower, 20.7 percent (see p. 226).

103. AMC Libros de Acuerdo 1571.

104. Vincent, "L'expulsion des morisques," 234. Rodríguez Sánchez's suggestion (*Cáceres*, 147) that the deportees were actually enslaved cannot be substantiated; the confusion may result from the coincidental arrival of slaves taken in the Granada war in the city.

105. Julio Fernández Nieva, "Un censo de moriscos extremeños de la inquisición de Llerena (año 1594)," *Revista de Estudios Extremeños* 29 (1973): 165, 167, 175. For the numbers of moriscos living in Extremadura at the time of the expulsion, see Vicente Navarro del Castillo, "El problema de la rebelión de los moriscos granadinos y sus repercusiones en Extremadura, principalmente en la comarca emeritense (1570–1604)," *Revista de Estudios Extremeños* 26 (1970): 569, app. III.

106. The letter appears in Mercedes García-Arenal, *Los moriscos* (Madrid, 1975), 263–265. Don Jerónimo de Loaysa was the grandnephew of the archbishop of Lima, Fray Jerónimo de Loaysa. His father Alonso de Loaysa went to Peru in the 1530s, where he married doña María de Ayala; they both returned to Trujillo in the 1560s (see Boyd-Bowman, *Indice*, 2, no. 3173); probably some or all of their children were born in Peru. See also Acedo, "Linajes," Loaysa, p. 222[a3].

107. AHPC Diego Pacheco 4101.

108. ACC-AT leg. 3, no. 2. Sancho de Paredes's mother, Catalina, actually belonged to Corajo, which meant that Corajo also owned his cousin Sancho, whom he freed in his will. Corajo also asked that Sancho de Paredes marry Mari Jiménez, the daughter of his nephew Juan Corajo, if he succeeded to his entail.

109. AHPC Pedro de Grajos 3925 (1557) and Pedro González 3828.

110. AGI Contratación 5221; AMT Pedro de Carmona B-1-23.

111. ACC-HO leg. 1, no. 16.

IV. Family, Kinship, and Society

1. The series of letters spanning almost two decades (1590 to 1608) from Alvaro de Paredes to his brother in Cáceres are in AMG Fondo Barrantes Ms. B/3, as are the letters from Juan Tejado to the same. Paredes's mother, doña Estevanía de Paredes, conceivably was a member of the Paredes family of Trujillo; in one letter Alvaro referred to "our cousin Juan Barrantes," who might have been the son and heir of the returnee Pedro Barrantes and his wife, doña Juana de Paredes. The preservation of such a series of private letters is certainly out of the ordinary. They eventually came into the possession of the nineteenth-century bibliographer Vicente Barrantes, who left his private collection to the archive of the monastery of Guadalupe.

2. See AHPC Pedro González 3830.

3. The *padrones* (tax lists) of the towns in Trujillo's district (see AGS EH 189-56) sometimes note that someone owned half or part of a house.

4. One such case was that of Hernán González, who petitioned to go to New Spain in 1575 with his brother and his family. González's wife, Mari Hernández, was from Plasencia. Witnesses said they were poor and had lived with her parents in Plasencia after they married and then later came to Trujillo, where they lived with his parents; see AGI Indif. Gen. 2056.

5. Demographic reality, of course, also limited the possibilities for multigenerational households, since children might lose one or both parents fairly young.

6. Rodríguez Sánchez, *Cáceres*, 194.

7. Ibid., 234. He found that in eighteen cases of marriages of tailors' daughters, the average age at marriage was seventeen; and in ten cases of marriages of the daughters of shoemakers, the average age was eighteen.

8. AGI Contratación 5222. They were on their way to New Spain with Teresa González's father in 1575 (see chap. 5).

9. AGI Contratación 5221. This is based on information given in 1569 when Licenciado Altamirano was on his way back to Peru. At that time he was fifty, doña Leonor was forty, and their eldest son around fifteen years old.

10. AGI Indif. Gen. 2083.

11. AGI Contratación 5227.

12. AGI Contratación 5234B.

13. AGI Contratación 5228.

14. AGI Contratación 5227. Another example of the considerable age range in children was the family of Juan González, age forty-five, and his wife Juana González, forty, who in 1591 were taking their eight children to Peru. The oldest was a daughter, aged twenty; there were two boys, fourteen and ten; three daughters, all named María, aged nine, eight, and seven; another daughter of five; and a baby boy aged $1\frac{1}{2}$ years.

15. See Lawrence Stone, *The Family, Sex and Marriage in England, 1500–1800* (New York, 1977), 63, 64, who points out that the lengthening of the birth intervals might have been due to decreasing fertility with age, contraceptive practices, or both.

16. Rodríguez Sánchez, *Cáceres*, 217, 219, and Stone, *Family*, 64.

17. ACC-HO leg. 5, pt. 2, no. 10.

18. ACC-HO leg. 8, no. 101; J. M. Lodo de Mayoralgo, *Viejos linajes,* 208. See also Rodríguez Sánchez, *Cáceres*, 83–84, note 64.

19. AGI Contratación 5221.

20. AGI Justicia 1176, no. 2, ramo 1.

21. See Lockhart, *Men of Cajamarca*, 168–189 for Juan and Gonzalo's upbringing. For Blas de Soto's letters to his sister Isabel and Señora Inés Rodríguez de Aguilar, see AGI Justicia 1070, no. 9.

22. The "Open Lineage Family" that Stone, *Family, Sex and Marriage*, 4, 86 describes for sixteenth-century England characterized the upper classes above all. He writes (p. 5) that marrige "among the upper and middling ranks . . . was primarily a means of tying together two kinship groups, of obtaining collective economic advantages and securing useful political alliances. Among peasants, artisans and labourers, it was an economic necessity for partnership and division of labour in the shop or in the fields." Stone's data for the upper class, however, are much more extensive than for other groups, and in fact the differences probably were not as considerable as he suggests.

23. See Solís Rodríguez, "El arquitecto Francisco Becerra," 304, 315.

24. For her acquaintance with Pablo Vicencio (known in Trujillo as Francisco Pérez), see AGI Justicia 1176, no. 2, ramo 8. In 1549, when she testified, Inés Rodríguez was fifty years old and literate (she signed eas-

ily). The evidence that she was in Seville in 1534 when Hernando Pizarro left for the Indies comes from the will made by Martín de Chaves in October 1534, before his own departure; Inés was a witness; see AGI Justicia 1176, no. 2, ramo 1. Doña Graciana's will is in AMT García de Sanabria A-1-1. Inés Rodríguez's father, Gonzalo Pizarro, also made her one of the executors of his estate, along with her brother Hernando and aunt Estefanía de Vargas (see Gonzalo's will in Luisa Cuesta, "Una documentación interesante sobre la familia del conquistador del Peru," *Revista de Indias* 8, 30 (1947): 869. It is interesting to note that Estefanía de Vargas also had been effective head of the household during the years of Gonzalo Pizarro's absence.

25. For the details of Isabel Corvacho's properties, see Altman, "Emigrants, Returnees and Society," 99–100 and AHPC A. Pacheco 4102, 4104. Despite the donation to her sons, she still possessed considerable means. In 1584 she bought 3086 $\frac{1}{2}$ maravedís of winter rental in a dehesa for 115,743 maravedís; see ACC-HO leg. 4, no. 2.

26. See Altman, "Emigrants and Society."

27. Muñoz de San Pedro, *Crónicas trujillanas*, Chaves, 189, 192. Gerbet, *La noblesse*, 316.

28. Boys from age fourteen and girls from twelve years could make their own wills, however.

29. AGI Justicia 1176, no. 2, ramo 1.

30. See AGI Contratación 5227.

31. AGI Contratación 5222.

32. AGI Patronato 112, ramo 2 (probanza of doña Isabel de Aguilar, 1564). The other sister was Mencía de Montenegro. Fray Alonso de Montenegro died in Cartagena, en route back to Spain.

33. In the testimony regarding settlement of the estate and debts of Alvaro de Ovando after his death in 1549 (he had two children, both minors), Cristóbal de Ovando, a regidor, stated he was second cousin to Alvaro de Ovando; another regidor, Francisco de Ovando, testified he was related to the children in the fourth degree; AHPC Pedro Grajos 3923. It may be a mistake to assume that commoners did not keep track of and look to a wide kinship network; we simply lack the documentary evidence. In 1591, for example, Diego de Alarcón testified for Francisco López de Castro, who was leaving Trujillo for Peru. He stated that they were related "but very little, in the fourth degree"; see AGI Contratación 5237.

34. AHPC Pedro González 3828.

35. See Gerbet, *La noblesse*, 175–177.

36. AHPC Pedro de Grajos 3923. If the entail did not go to the direct descendants of Francisco de Saavedra and doña Marina Gutiérrez de

Carvajal, then her share of the estate would go first to her brothers and their descendants, and then to whoever succeeded to her husband's entail.

37. See Altman, "Spanish Hidalgos," genealogical charts following p. 344.

38. Of course there was a more distant connection through the paternal line, since doña Juana de Acuna and her husband, Luis de Chaves, were cousins; see Muñoz de San Pedro, *Crónicas trujillanas*, Chaves, 189–192.

39. Muñoz de San Pedro, *La Extremadura del siglo XV*, 169 and *Crónicas trujillanas*, Hinojosa, 146.

40. See note 14 above.

41. AGI Indif. General 2094.

42. Francisco Rodríguez was an escribano; he went to Peru with his wife and two children, to join his parents, in 1574; see AGI Indif. General 2087. At the age of fifty he testified in December 1591 in Trujillo on behalf of Juan de Camargo, who was going to Peru; AGI Contratación 5235.

43. AHPC Pedro de Grajos 3923.

44. AHPC Pedro de Grajos 3923; Luis de Roa y Ursúa, *El reyno de Chile, 1535–1860* (Valladolid, 1945), 167; and AGS Expec. Hacienda 66 (padrón of Aldea del Cano).

45. For Juan de Vita y Moraga, see AGI Indif. General 2055; for Pedro de Vita, see AHPC Diego Pacheco 4100. For Bernardino de Moraga, see AHPC Alonso Pacheco 4102 and Roa y Ursúa, *Chile*, no. 1829.

46. AGI Justicia 1176, no. 2, ramo 1.

47. Acedo, "Linajes," Vargas, 48[a72].

48. AGI Indif. General 2049.

49. AGI Indif. General 2083.

50. AMT 1584: IX-8 (see also note 90 below).

51. AGI Justicia 1154, no. 5, ramo 1. Juan de Hinojosa de Torres sent Bartolomé Pérez, who lived in Santa Cruz (although he might have been a vecino of Trujillo). Pérez's son Juan de Alvarado also went to Peru. Pérez died there in the late 1560s; AGI Indif. General 2086.

52. ARCG 508-1987-8.

53. ARCG 3ª-599-3.

54. AHPC Pedro de Grajos 3923. Payment was made in 1548.

55. AGI Justicia 1176, no. 2, ramo 1.

56. AHPC Pedro González 3827.

57. AMT García de Sanabria A-1-1. On disinheritance, see Dillard, *Daughters of the Reconquest*, 29–30.

58. Cristóbal's will (1602) and codicil (1618) are in ACC-HO leg. 1, no. 21. Cristóbal de Ovando Paredes's oldest son, don Cosme, was named the heir of his great-uncle Juan de Paredes de la Rocha in his will of 1593 (ACC-HO leg. 1, no. 20), but since this bequest came long before Cristóbal made

his will, clearly it did not influence his plans at the outset. For don Cosme's attempts to reclaim the entail, see ACC-HO leg. 7, no. 22.

59. Muñoz de San Pedro, *Diego García de Paredes*, 359–361.

60. AHPC Pedro González 3828.

61. When two daughters of Cosme de Ovando and doña Beatriz de Paredes entered San Pablo in 1557, their father pledged a dowry of 4,400 maravedís of "renta de yerba" in the dehesa of Torrejón de Arriba and 11,593 $\frac{1}{2}$ maravedís of rents in the dehesa of Arenal. He also agreed to give them each 1,000 maravedís a year; AHPC Diego Pacheco 4100.

62. See the 1602 will of Cristóbal de Ovando Paredes, ACC-HO leg. 1, no. 21.

63. For example, in 1556 Gonzalo de Saavedra paid 77,509 $\frac{1}{2}$ maravedís in cash (about 200 ducados) and 110 fanegas of wheat to Santa María in Cáceres for the time two orphan daughters of Gabriel de Saavedra lived there; AHPC Pedro de Grajos 3925.

64. AHPC Pedro de Grajos 3925.

65. See AMG Fondo Barantes Ms. B/3, fol 94.

66. AGS Exped. Hacienda 189-56.

67. AGS Exped. Hacienda 189-56.

68. AGI Contratación 5220, 5227.

69. Muñoz de San Pedro, *Diego García de Paredes*, 45–46, 88–89, 275, and ACC Asuntos de Trujillo, leg. 3, no. 2.

70. See Lockhart, *Men of Cajamarca*, 137–139.

71. Probably this continued to hold true in the working classes. Gabriel Calderón and his wife María González, both thirty-seven years old in 1591 when they asked for a license to go to Peru with their four daughters, were both illegitimate children of parents who apparently never married; see AGI Contratación 5237. Both gave the names of their parents. Gabriel Calderón's mother was in service to Hernando Calderón de Chaves, probably the source of his surname.

72. AGI Indif. General 2049.

73. ACC-HO leg. 1, no. 7 (will of 1530).

74. Angel Rodríguez Sánchez, "La natalidad ilegítima en Cáceres en el siglo XVI" (Badajoz, 1979), 26, 27, 31. As one example, Sebastiana, the slave of Licenciado Espadero (probably the brother of Alvaro de Paredes in Mexico) gave birth to Antonio (January 1580), Francisco (January 1583), and Pablo (May 1586), all of father unknown.

75. AHPC Pedro González 3829.

76. Don Juan de Sande's will of 1571 is in AHPC Pedro González 3828. He named as his heirs "Diego y Jerónimo mis hijos naturales que al presente tengo en casa de mis padres." When Sande's mother died shortly after he did, the children became the wards of his uncle, don Sancho de

Sande, tesorero of Plasencia. Jerónimo de Sande went to the Indies in 1591 at the age of 21; AGI Contratación 5234A.

77. AHPC Pedro de Grajos 3923, 3924.

78. AHPC Pedro González 3830, Pedro de Grajos 3926.

79. AHPC Pedro González 3830.

80. AHPC Pedro de Grajos 3925.

81. After his death María would inherit 20,000 maravedís at the age of sixteen; if she died before then, her brother Alonso would inherit. If Nuño Gutiérrez died before María was sixteen and she decided to live with her mother, than Alonso García, a silversmith, would administer the 20,000 maravedís until María reached the age of twenty or married; see AMT García de Sanabria A-1-1.

82. AHPC Pedro de Grajos 3925; Pedro González 3828. In a similar case Antonio de Sotomayor, a regidor of Cáceres, freed his slave Mateo, the son of Domingo Pérez. Pérez had been the *mayoral* (foreman) of the comendador de Piedra Blanco, Sotomayor's uncle (whom he called "mi señor"). Pérez had had the child by a mulatta slave who belonged to the comendador. At the time of his death Pérez had asked that Sotomayor free Mateo, which he did in 1563; AHPC Diego Pacheco 4102.

83. AGI Indif. General 2059.

84. AHPC Pedro González 3827. Diego Cano subsequently changed his mind about the house he donated, deciding he needed it for his servants, and instead offered Ana Sánchez 26 reales a year to rent another. After Ana married Francisco Sánchez, in October 1570 they said they had received the thirty fanegas of wheat from Diego Cano.

85. See his información of 1577 when he petitioned to go to Peru; AGI Indif. General 2084.

86. AHPC Diego Pacheco 4113.

87. *Catálogo*, 4, no. 2780; and the biography by Muñoz de San Pedro and Nectario María, *El gobernador y maestre de campo Diego García de Paredes*.

88. See Nader, *Mendozas*, 112. By this method of calculation, the heir to the "tercio y quinto" received 46.7 percent of the total legacy. David S. Reher has suggested that there was another way of figuring the share, by which the "quinto" was set aside "de libre disposición" before any division was made. Added to the "tercio," this would yield 53.3 percent for the designated heir, while the remaining heirs would receive equal portions of the other 46.7 percent. I have not been able to determine which method of calculation was used in sixteenth-century Extremadura; in any case, the difference is not great.

89. Gómez de Solís and Juan de Hinojosa, in Peru in 1559, renounced their inheritance in favor of their brother Francisco de Ulloa Solís, heir of

the family entail, in Cáceres; see AHPC Alonso Pacheco 4104; the donation was listed in the inventory prepared in 1579 after the death of the fourth brother, Lorenzo de Ulloa Solís.

90. Alonso Bravo, the native of Búrdalo who took up residence in Trujillo, had no children. In his will of 1584 he made provisions for various nieces and nephews, but his second wife, Francisca Nuñez, received the largest inheritance—his best pair of oxen, forty pigs, twenty-four fanegas of wheat, half of the house (she owned the other half), all the furnishings in the house, 50 ducados, and the income from a mill; see AMT 1584: IX-8. All the rest of his property was to be sold to buy censos to found an obra pía to marry "an orphan, the closest relative in my lineage who is an honorable woman" (or a relative of his first or second wife).

91. AMT Pedro de Carmona A-1-9. He also made her curador of their children unless she remarried, in which case Pedro Barrantes, another returnee, would become curador. It seems very likely that García López de Aviles himself was in the Indies, although the evidence is entirely circumstantial—his close association with other returnees, and the fact that he had juros in Seville, as did many other returnees.

92. Hernando Corajo in his will of 1513 said his wife Beatriz de Contreras was to live in the house in the "villa" of Trujillo and have everything in the house except the slaves and things his uncle Alvaro de Paredes had sent from Italy; she was also to enjoy the income from the rents; see ACC-AT leg. 3, no 2. Legally a spouse could not inherit outright unless there was no relative within the seventh degree who could inherit; see Gerbet, *La noblesse*, 171.

93. AMT Pedro de Carmona B-1-27. Gonzalo's sons, Captain Martín, Gonzalo, and don Francisco, were in the Indies when the partition of his property was made in 1580.

94. AHPC Pedro González 3830.

95. ACC-HO leg. 4, no. 4 and AHPC Alonso Pacheco 4103. According to Bartolomé Clavero, *Mayorazgo: propiedad feudal en Castilla, 1369–1836* (Madrid, 1974), 235 a woman could found an entail without her husband's permission only in her will.

96. See, for example, the joint entail founded by Francisco de Solís and doña Juana de Hinojosa in 1535, AHPC Pedro de Grajos 3924. Doña Juana de Hinojosa's properties in Trujillo were to go to her Trujillo relatives in default of the direct male line.

97. Clavero, *Mayorazgo*, 222, writes "la voluntad del fundador es la ley fundamental del mayorazgo."

98. AHPC Pedro de Grajos 3924.

99. ACC-HO leg. 1, no. 21 (will of 1534); see Altman, "Spanish Hidalgos," 336–338.

100. AHPC Pedro de Grajos 3923.

101. ACC-AT leg. 3, no. 2.

102. AHPC Alonso Pacheco 4103. Such conditions were not limited to entails. Sancho Solano in 1551 made his daughter Isabel his universal heir if she would marry his cousin's son, Juan Solano; if not she would inherit only one-fourth of his estate, with half going to his brother Juan Solano in Rome and the other fourth to his cousin Alonso Solano as a dowry for the latter's daughter; AMT García de Sanabria A-1-1. Solano does not seem to have been quite acceptable as a surname for a woman (the same was true for other surnames ending in "o," such as Ramiro, Cornejo, etc.). Sancho first referred to his daughter as Isabel Solano but later as Isabel Alvarez la Solana (Alvarez was from his mother's side of the family). Around the same time Solano arranged to give Mari Sánchez, another daughter of his cousin Alonso Solano, 50,000 maravedís for her dowry on behalf of this brother Juan Solano.

103. AHPC Pedro de Grajos 3923 (1546 and 1547).

104. ACC-HO leg. 1, no. 16 (1564).

105. See AMT Pedro de Carmona B-1-27.

106. AHPC Pedro Pérez 4123; Alonso Pacheco 4104.

107. AGI Justicia 1062, no. 1, ramo 2; Acedo, "Linajes," Calderón, 334[a31].

108. AHPC Diego Pacheco 4113, Pedro González 3828.

109. AHPC Alonso Pacheco 4103.

110. AHPC Pedro González 3828.

111. AHPC Pedro González 3829. Don Francisco de Torres's grandmother doña Teresa Rol was from a noble family of Alcántara, the only daughter of Pedro Rol. Martín Rol was her father's first cousin and the comendador of Almorchón and Cabeza del Buey. He founded an entail for doña Teresa in 1506, which was her dowry when she married Diego de Ovando de Cáceres. See AHPC Diego Pacheco 4101 and Gerbet, *La noblesse*, 218, 243.

112. Acedo, "Linajes," Orellana, 92–93, 107.

113. AHPC Pedro de Grajos 3924. Doña Francisca de Ulloa had only one brother, so clearly her father effected a simple division of all his property between his two children. Antonio C. Floriano in *Estudios*, 1:125 writes that in 1170 a member of one of the Leonese contingents involved in the reconquest of the area established an estate between the valleys of the Ayala and Salor rivers, known then as the "aldea de Pedro Cervero" and later as La Cervera.

114. Doña Francisca's second marriage was to a leading noble of Cáceres, Alonso de Ribera, himself a widower, who created an entail for their daughter doña Catalina de Ribera when she married in 1583. Two of

Alonso de Ribera's sons by his first marriage—Juan Pantoja de Ribera and Rodrigo de Chaves—went to the Indies; Juan Pantoja remained in Honduras and Rodrigo de Chaves returned to Cáceres. His oldest son by this marriage, Alvaro de Ribera, received the entail he founded in 1531 (see ACC Mayorazgo de Ribera leg. 1, no. 16); his daughter doña María de Ribera married the wealthy returnee, Trujillo councilman and Pizarro ally, Juan Cortés. Doña Catalina de Ribera, Alonso de Ribera's daughter by doña Francisca de Ulloa, married Pedro Rol de Ovando, the oldest son of Francisco de Ovando, one of the three heirs of Francisco de Ovando, el rico.

115. In the codicil to his will (1577) Pedro de Grajos said his daughter Isabel García la Romera received a dowry of 350 ducados when she married Alonso de Solís. When his daughter Elvira Díaz married Gil Delgado, Grajos and his wife, together with son Gabriel de Grajos and sons-in-law Solís and Francisco Cotrina, endowed her with 500 ducados. Solís also contributed to the dowry of another daughter, Catalina García la Romera. AHPC Alonso Pacheco 4103.

116. AHPC Pedro Gonzalez 3829, 3830.

117. Although this pattern is closely associated with the nobility, its influence extended beyond that group, as can be seen in the Enríquez-Camargo mercantile family. Vicente Enríquez and his wife Leonor Alvarez created an entail for their son Vasco Calderón Enríquez; another son, Juan de Camargo, was a regidor of Trujillo and must have come into a good inheritance also. But son Alonso Enríquez went to Chile, Diego de Camargo became a priest, and one daughter entered the convent of Santa Clara; see Acedo, "Linajes," Calderón, 295, 334[a12,33,41].

V. The Movement to the New World

1. The term "emigrants" generally refers to individuals who intended to leave Spain, regardless of whether they reached their destinations in the Indies, since it may be impossible to prove if someone who planned to emigrate actually did so. The figures are based on a number of sources. The most important published sources are Peter Boyd-Bowman, *Indice geobiográfico de cuarenta mil pobladores españoles de América en el siglo XVI*, 2 vols. (Bogota, 1964; Mexico, 1968) and the *Catálogo de pasajeros a Indias durante los siglos XVI, XVII y XVIII*, 5 vols. (Seville, 1940–1946, 1980). Vicente Navarro del Castillo, *La epopeya de la raza extremeña en Indias* (Merida, 1978) is useful but contains many errors and must be utilized with caution. Material from the following archives supplied additional names of emigrants: Archivo General de Indias (AGI), Archivo Histórico Provincial de Cáceres (AHPC), Archivo Municipal de

Trujillo (AMT), and the Archivo del Conde de Canilleros (ACC). James Lockhart gave me access to his files for Spaniards in early Peru, which yielded another group of emigrants.

2. The figures for Trujillo's jurisdiction include villages that, strictly speaking, were no longer under its jurisdiction by the middle of the sixteenth century. Berzocana and Cañamero, with fourteen and nine emigrants respectively, had removed themselves from Trujillo's jurisdiction early in the sixteenth century but continued to be closely tied to the city thereafter. They furnished soldiers for military levies raised in Trujillo's district, and people from Berzocana at least continued to refer to themselves as being from "tierra de Trujillo" well into the sixteenth century. Similarly Orellana la Vieja, although it was never part of Trujillo's district as such, for centuries belonged to one of the city's leading families and as a result was closely associated with the city.

3. The incompleteness of the passenger lists is evidenced by the number of emigrants found in local archives or other sources not found in the registers in Seville. For the gaps in the passenger lists see Auke Pieter Jacobs, "Pasajeros y polizones: Algunas observaciones sobre la emigración española a las Indias durante el siglo XVI," *Revista de Indias* 172 (1983): 440. The concentration of Boyd-Bowman's published work in the first half of the sixteenth century means that information for that period is much better than for the second half. In addition, there exists the possibility that local notarial records, which yielded a number of names of emigrants or returnees, have a certain bias toward the upper and middle classes of society, which had greater means and necessity of going before notaries. The representativeness of these sources may be somewhat skewed as a result.

4. The capitulaciones were dated July 26, 1529. See Tena Fernández, *Trujillo histórico*, 344–345.

5. See Peter Boyd-Bowman, *Patterns of Spanish Emigration to the New World (1493–1580)* (Buffalo, N.Y., 1973), 28.

6. AGS Expedientes Hacienda 189-56 (averiguación del padrón de Madroñera, 1558). In 1558 Alonso Ruiz, a man who had been at Cajamarca and returned to Spain to marry the sister of his partner in Peru, Lucas Martínez Vegaso (from Trujillo) and become a vecino and regidor of Trujillo, became señor of Madroñera.

7. See información of Francisco Jiménez, zapatero, vecino of Trujillo, who petitioned for a license in 1574 to go to the Indies with his wife and children; AGI Indif. General 2055. In the same year Andrés Hernández, herrero, of Trujillo asked to go to Peru and, if not there, to Mexico or "el reyno nuevo," AGI Indif. General 2087.

8. Society in the New World being what it was, and Spaniards there as mobile (or even more so) as ever, settling in one area hardly precluded contacts with people in another or moving once or twice in the same region. See chap. 6 for discussion of activities in the Indies.

9. For the career of Frey Nicolás de Ovando, see Ernest Schäfer, *El consejo real y supremo de las Indias* (Seville, 1935 and 1947), 1: 31; and Troy Floyd, *The Columbus Dynasty in the Caribbean, 1493–1526* (Albuquerque, 1973), 51–54. See also Ursula Lamb, *Frey Nicolás de Ovando, Gobernador de Indies (1501–1509)* (Madrid, 1956). For the Ovando family see Altman, "Spanish Hidalgos," Cáceres": 323–344.

10. In the documents I found only one use of the term "indiano" in Trujillo, in testimony of 1549 by Juan de la Jara, who had a brother-in-law living in Peru. AGI Justicia 1176, no. 2, ramo 8.

11. Informaciones of Hernán González (1575) and another Hernán González (1547), both of Trujillo, in AGI Indif. Gen. 2056 and 2055.

12. A witness for Alonso Mellado—vecino of Santa Cruz de la Sierra who petitioned to go to Peru in 1579 as the page of a priest named Domingo Rodríguez (also of Santa Cruz)—said Mellado "is not a relative or relation of the Pizarros but rather is a labrador," AGI Contratación 5227. See also información of Francisco Rodríguez, AGI Indif. Gen. 2087 (1574–1575).

13. See *Catálogo*, 3, nos. 1100–1579 for these listings.

14. AGI Indif. Gen. 2048.

15. *Catálogo*, 5, no. 4877. He went as criado of Alonso Gutiérrez de Toledo.

16. AGI Contratación 5224; *Catálogo*, 5, no. 4168.

17. For Costanza Rodríguez, see *Catálogo*, 3, no. 2977, and AGI Indif. Gen. 2093. For Diego de Trujillo's biography, see Lockhart, *Men of Cajamarca*, 362–365. Trujillo dictated a chronicle late in life, in 1571, which has been published, with biographical notes, by Raul Porras Barrenechea, *Los cronistas del Perú (1528–1650)* (Lima, 1962); and Miguel Muñoz de San Pedro, ed., *Tres testigos de la conquista del Perú*, 3d. ed. (Madrid, 1964).

18. Cosme de Ovando Paredes, who later succeeded to his father's entail at the death of his older brother, was accompanied by his first cousin Cristóbal de Ovando; Francisco Gutiérrez (who might also have been a relative, since his father was a Diego de Ovando); and Lorenzo de Ulloa "el mozo," younger brother of the encomendero Lorenzo de Ulloa; see *Catálogo*, 3, no. 2952. For the members of the family in the Indies, see Altman, "Spanish Hidalgos."

19. *Catálogo*, 2, no. 3632; and Navarro del Castillo, *La epopeya*, 155.

20. Boyd-Bowman, *Indice*, 2, no. 3124; *Catálogo*, 4, no. 897; Robert T. Himmerich, "The Encomenderos of New Spain, 1521–1555" (Ph.D. diss. UCLA, 1984), 239. Gonzalo de las Casas's daughters stayed and married in Trujillo. One married a son of Juan de Herrera, a returnee from Peru and regidor of Trujillo, and another a son of Juan de Escobar, brother of Fray Diego de Chaves (confessor of Philip II) and brother-in-law of the famous captain in Peru, Pedro Alonso de Hinojosa (Muñoz de San Pedro, *Crónicas trujillanas*, 273, 267, from manuscrito de don Esteban de Tapia). His eldest son Francisco inherited the encomienda.

21. Navarro del Castillo, *La epopeya*, 401; AGI Indif. Gen. 2060.

22. See Solís Rodríguez, "Francisco Becerra," 335–336.

23. Nodera's father, also named Diego de Nodera and a maestro de cantería, was a long-time resident of Mexico City. He had died in Mexico by 1573, when his widow Catalina Alonso testified in Francisco Becerra's información; Solís Rodriguez, "Francisco Becerra," 304. Nodera (the father) had a long-term business partnership with a Sevillian merchant named Luis de Córdoba, and he returned to Spain from Mexico on business at least once. Córdoba mentioned Nodera in a letter to his wife written from Puebla in 1566; see Enrique Otte, "Cartas privadas de Puebla del siglo XVI," *Jahrbuch für Geschichte von Staat, Wirtschaft und Gesellschaft Lateinamerikas*, 3 (1966): 31–36. Diego de Nodera was twenty-three years old in 1573 when he requested a license to go to Mexico to collect his father's estate and money that Luis de Córdoba still owed him; his petition apparently was rejected. AGI Indif. Gen. 2056.

24. For Alvaro Rodríguez Chacón, see AGI Indif. Gen. 2054, 2055, and 2056; and *Catálogo*, 5, no. 3507. For Cristóbal Hernández Tripa and his wife Teresa González, see AGI Contrat. 5222, Indif. Gen. 2056, and *Catálogo* 5, no. 3843. For Hernán González, see AGI Indif. Gen. 2056. He described his brother in these terms: "tiene comodo y posibilidad para nos aprovechar y remediar . . . con su hacienda."

25. AGI Indif. Gen. 2059.

26. Eleven of the men were from Trujillo, three from Santa Cruz, two from Orellana, and one each from Garciaz and Herguijuela.

27. The recruits for Florida are listed in AGI Contrat. 5220.

28. Francisco Medrano went to the Philippines in 1575 under a bond of 200,000 maravedís to stay eight years, taking two criados from Cáceres; see AGI Contrat. 5222, and *Catálogo*, 5, no. 3659. Don Jerónimo de Ocampo made his will in the same year before departing for the Philippines (AHPC Pedro González 3829). Alonso and Hernando de Ovando, sons of Pedro de Ovando de Saavedra, also left that year, taking a criado from Cáceres and another from Medellín (AHPC Pedro González 3830, and *Catálogo*, 5, nos. 3656 and 3657).

29. The document with the cédulas authorizing recruitment and listing the expedition members is in AGI Contrat. 5227.

30. Information on recruitment for the expedition is in AHPC Pedro González 3830.

31. Ocana sent twenty-two recruits (four married), Escalona fourteen (one married), Ciudad Real thirteen (four married), Valladolid ten (two married), and Segovia, Ciudad Rodrigo, and Maqueda six each. Córdoba, with sixteen recruits (four married) was the only city in Andalusia to contribute more than four people.

32. In 1578 their father was trying to collect the estate of his two sons, Alonso and Hernando de Ovando; see AHPC Pedro González 3830.

33. Fray Gaspar de Carvajal, *Relación del nuevo descubrimiento del famoso río grande que por el nombre del capitán que le descubrió se llamó el río de Orellana,* introd. by Jose Toribio Medina (Cáceres, 1952), 101, n. 116.

34. Carvajal, *Relación,* 148, 167.

35. Muñoz de San Pedro y Nectario Marío, *El gobernador y maestre de campo Diego García de Paredes,* 286.

36. See Nicholas L. Scrattish, "New Perspectives on Castilian Migration to the Audiencias of Mexico and Lima, 1540–1580" (Ph.D. diss., University of California, San Diego, 1975), 120–121. It is difficult to say what the costs of passage meant for prospective emigrants from different levels of society, although Scrattish is probably correct in suggesting that for many workers and artisans the expense was a deterrent to making the trip. He notes (p. 122) that dockyard workers in Seville in 1556 earned 5 reales (170 maravedís) a day, which means that in a year of steady employment they might earn 50,000–60,000 maravedís. Unskilled laborers and even skilled workers and artisans in smaller towns and cities earned much less than that. It is reasonable to assume, then, that workers and tradesmen usually could not make the trip without some form of assistance. What the cost of passage meant for hidalgos, especially young unmarried men, is less clear. Prior to departure these young bachelors probably lived in the households of fathers, relatives, or other nobles; thus whatever income they had was above and beyond the expenses of daily life (food, shelter) and could be invested in passage to the New World much more readily than the salary of a worker or artisan.

For a vivid picture of passengers' experience at sea, see Carla Rahn Phillips, *Six Galleons for the King of Spain* (Baltimore, 1986), chap. 7: "Shipboard Life."

37. Inés González, a single woman of thirty, who went to Tierra Firme in 1579 as a criada of Diego Hernández de Aguilar, had lived with her

aunt since her mother's death. Her aunt said "now she has sold what little she had to go to the Indies"; see AGI Contrat. 5227.

38. AHPC Diego Pacheco 4101.

39. Cotrina's mother Isabel González mentions the sum in her will of 1579; see AHPC Alonso Pacheco 4103. For Cotrina's second trip, see *Catálogo*, 5, no. 1693.

40. Navarro del Castillo, *La epopeya*, 151; and AHPC Pedro de Grajos 3925.

41. AGI Indif. Gen. 2049. Letters of 1559 from Antonio and Andrés Pérez to their brother Francisco Gutiérrez appear in Otte, "Cartas privadas," 28–31.

42. AGI Indif. Gen. 2093.

43. AGI Indif. Gen. 2083.

44. AHPC Pedro de Grajos 3926.

45. AGI Indif. Gen. 2085.

46. See Schäfer, *El consejo de Indias*, 2: 287–288, for the Comisarios de Perpetuidad. The *Catálogo*, 4, nos. 468–475, 483, and 485–487, lists Diego de Vargas Carvajal's criados and his two sons, don Diego and don Lorenzo de Carvajal.

47. See *Catálogo*, 5, nos. 2826–2828, 2830, and 2831; and AGI Indif. Gen. 2088.

48. AGI Indif. Gen. 2048, 2091.

49. Witnesses testified that Mateo Jiménez, a twenty-four-year-old bachelor from Trujillo who accompanied Luis del Saz to Peru in 1592, had been in Saz's service ("le ha servido y sirve de ordinario"). Jiménez was living with his mother. AGI Contratación 5237.

50. AHPC Pedro González 3829. This might have been the same Diego Martín Barquero who was apprenticed in 1571 to a shoemaker for two and a half years for eight ducados, in return for room, board, and shoes. The timing is right, since if he had been apprenticed in 1571, by 1576 he would have been an *oficial*, perhaps in his late teens or around twenty, the age when many young men emigrated.

51. AGI Justicia 215, no. 1. I have not been able to clarify the reference to the "tierra nueva." Possibly it was New Granada ("nuevo reino de Granada").

52. For Jerónimo Holguín, see, for example, AHPC Pedro de Grajos 3926 and Alonso Pacheco 4101.

53. AMT García de Sanabria A-1-1 (1551).

54. AHPC Pedro González 3829. Martín de Chaves of Trujillo also made a will, in Seville, in 1534 before leaving for Peru; see AGI Justicia 1176, no. 2, ramo 1.

55. AMT García de Sanabria A-1-1. At one point Valencia referred to

Amaro de Torres's wife, Mayor Martínez, as his sister and at other times called Torres his brother. If the relationship was close, people might use the terms brother and brother-in-law interchangeably, so Torres might have been his brother-in-law. Gonzalo de Valencia was going to Peru to work for the encomendero Lucas Martínez. Gonzalo's father, Martín de Valencia, had been sent by Alonso Ruiz to Peru to work for Martínez in the 1540s, which would explain Valencia's connection with Ruiz. See Efraim Trelles Arestegui, *Lucas Martínez Vegaso: Funcionamiento de una encomienda peruana inicial* (Lima, 1982), 175.

56. AGI Indif. Gen. 2084.

57. AGI Indif. Gen. 2089.

58. AGI Indif. Gen. 2090; informaciones of García de Escobar and Juan Martín, sillero.

59. AGI Indif. Gen. 2082. In Justicia 405, no. 2, ramo 2, Pedro Alonso Carrasco gave his poder to his brother Florencio Carrasco and his son Bartolomé González Carrasco and other vecinos of Zorita.

60. AHPC Diego Pacheco 4103, Pedro González 3827. One also sees, of course, the opposite process in effect; some emigrants feared to leave their dependents behind. Domingo Rodríguez, clérigo presbítero of Santa Cruz, in 1578 asked to take his twelve-year-old nephew Pedro Alonso with him to Peru "because he is an orphan and leaving him in this country he would suffer toil and need as a resulted of being . . . abandoned" (AGI Indif. Gen. 2090). Another priest, Bachiller Gaspar González from Trujillo who also went to Peru in 1579, took with him two sisters and a brother and his five-year-old niece, all of whom were "orphans and poor and under my authority . . . and I support them" (see AGI Contrat. 5227 and Indif. Gen. 2090).

61. The actual percentage of hidalgos is probably higher, but ambiguous cases were not counted. In dealing with relatively small cities where certain surnames are associated with noble lineages—such as Calderón, Orellana, Chaves, Vargas in Trujillo, or Ovando, Ulloa, or Golfín (Holguín) in Cáceres—it is tempting but not accurate to count everyone with these *apellidos* as hidalgos. Although even in the sixteenth century there still was a close relationship between surname and kinship group—one occasionally sees a statement to the effect that all the Carrascos of Trujillo and Zorita are hidalgos, for example (see testimony of Francisco Regodón for Alonso Carrasco, AGI Justicia 418, 1559)—in most cases hidalgos did not have exclusive claim to an apellido.

62. Gerbet, *La noblesse*, 151–152 (and table 1, p. 150), compares the figures for some cities in Extremadura. She arrives at an estimate of 17 percent (percentage of adult male population who were nobles) for Cáceres, compared to 4 percent for Plasencia or 5 percent for Mérida. The

strength and consolidation of the provincial nobility in Cáceres compared to Plasencia or Mérida might have been due at least in part to the absence of great señors dominating the city (Plasencia was under the bishop and Mérida under the Order of Santiago). In his chapter "La sociedad" in *Historia de Extremadura*, 3: 550, Julio Fernández Nieva estimates that hidalgos formed 15 percent of Cáceres's population in the late sixteenth century and 12.6 percent of Trujillo's.

63. Gerbet, *La noblesse*, 151–153.

64. See, for example, references to Antonio de Ulloa, Lorenzo de Aldana, and Gómez de Solís in Pérez de Tudela, ed., *Documentos relativos a don Pedro de la Gasca*, 1: 80 (letter from Gonzalo Pizarro to Francisco de Carvajal, February 1546), and to Lorenzo de Aldana and Gómez de Solís in a letter of April 1547 from Gonzalo to Francisco Hernández Girón, 2: 46.

65. See Altman, "Spanish Hidalgos."

66. AHPC Pedro González 3829.

67. For Hernando de Moraga, see Navarro del Castillo, *La epopeya*, 161; and Roa y Ursúa, *El reino de Chile*, no. 151.

68. For the mayorazgo, see AHPC Pedro de Grajos 3924; the codicil to the will of Solís's father, Francisco de Solís, is in AHPC Pedro de Grajos 3925 (1556); the donation of their inheritance that Solís and his brother Juan de Hinojosa made to their brother Francisco de Ulloa Solís was executed in La Plata in 1559 (see inventory of bienes of another brother in Cáceres, Lorenzo de Ulloa Solís, 1579, AHPC Alonso Pacheco 4104).

69. Andrés Calderón Puertocarrero was listed as "mercader" when he went to Tierra Firme in 1562; see *Catálogo*, 4, no. 2281. For testimony regarding the murder in Peru of Gonzalo Almonte, a merchant from Guadalcanal, see AGI Justicia 1062, no. 1, ramo 2.

70. Altman, "Spanish Hidalgos."

71. AHPC Pedro González 3830. Pedro de Ovando de Saavedra actually died several years later, in 1584.

72. AHPC Alonso Pacheco 4102; Roa y Ursúa, *El reyno de Chile*, no. 1829.

73. See his will in AGI Justicia 1176, no. 2, ramo 1.

74. AGI Indif. Gen. 2091.

75. Doubtless Juan de Vita y Moraga was referring to Hernando de Moraga Galíndez y Gómez, who had been in Peru in the 1540s but by the 1570s probably was in Chile; see n. 67 above. Juan de Vita's información is in AGI Indif. Gen. 2055.

76. References to Pedro de Vita are in AHPC Diego Pacheco 4100 and Pedro de Grajos 3924 and 3926. There are a number of other such cases.

Juan Altamirano de Hinojosa was twenty-three years old and Alonso de Carvajal twenty-two when they went to Popayán in 1563 as criados of Diego García de Paredes; both were hidalgos and their fathers deceased (see *Catálogo*, 4, nos. 2781 and 2782, and AGI Contrat. 5220).

77. AGI Indif. Gen. 2059. Their brother was called the "hijo bastardo" of Alonso García, tailor; probably all three were his children. The quote regarding the sisters' economic situation is: "son tan pobres que si no es usando mal de sus personas o poniendo taverna o bodega o algun mesón no se podrán sustentar porque para servir a nadie son ya mayores."

78. AGI Indif. Gen. 2059. Alonso said his relative Martín Blanco was "canónigo en la iglesia de Mexico." Fritz Schwaller has told me that there was no such canon in Mexico in the 1570s.

79. AGI Indif. Gen. 2089 (1577). He was described as "pobre y necesitado y tanto que con otros oficiales anda a coser para ganar de comer."

80. AGI Indif. Gen. 2058.

81. AGI Indif. Gen. 2094.

82. AGI Indif. Gen. 2087.

83. AGI Indif. Gen. 2085.

84. For Francisco de Orellana, see *Catálogo*, 4, no. 4027; and AGI Indif. Gen. 2081. For his father, Rodrigo de Orellana, see Navarro del Castillo, *La epopeya*, 335. Rodrigo's sister doña Beatriz de Orellana and her husband García Ruiz de Orellana went to Peru in 1559, taking as their criado Luis de Orellana, probably a relative, all vecinos of Orellana; see *Catálogo*, 3, no. 4293.

85. For Francisco González de Castro, see *Catálogo*, 3, no. 1210, and the información of his nephew Juan de Castro in AGI Indif. Gen. 2083. For Pedro de Castro, see *Catálogo*, 5, no. 1381, and AGI Indif. Gen. 2083; he said he was over forty in 1568. For Juan de Castro see *Catálogo*, 3, no. 2481. A Diego de Castro went to Popayán in 1574; see AGI Indif. Gen. 2087. All are mentioned in testimony in AGI Indif. Gen. 2083. For Alonso de Castro, see AGI Contratación 5227.

86. *Catálogo*, 3, no. 2509, and AGI Indif. Gen. 2083.

87. See Altman, "Spanish Hidalgos" and "Emigrants and Society."

88. AGI Indif. Gen. 2084, información of Rodrigo Alonso de Boroa.

89. Cristóbal de Solís's información appears in AGI Indif. General 2089. For his father see AMT Pedro de Carmona A-1-9 and García de Sanabria A-1-1-3. Sancho Casco, clérigo presbítero, went to Peru in 1571; see AGI Indif. Gen. 2085. Nothing is known about Juan Casco other than Solís's reference to him in his información.

90. Seville was about 250 kilometers from Cáceres or Trujillo. José Luis Martín Martín writes in "Las funciones urbanas en la Transierra occidental" in *La ciudad hispánica*, 1: 405, that the medieval traveler

could easily cover 50 km a day, even on foot. Thus the trip from Alta Extremadura to Seville would take about five days.

91. Testimony about Alonso Delvás appears in the información of his brother Francisco Delvás, a silversmith, who wanted to go join him in New Granada in 1568 taking his wife and three children; see AGI Indif. Gen. 2083.

92. AMT García de Sanabria A-1-1.

93. AGI Contratación 5220, 5224. For Andrada's family in Cáceres, see Lodo de Mayoralgo, *Viejos linajes*, 48.

94. See *Catálogo*, 3, no. 4183, and 4, no. 766, for Baltasar de Melo. For Pedro de Melo, see *Catálogo*, 3, no. 3557; AGI Indif. Gen. 2162A; and Acedo, "Linajes," Vargas, 48[a49], for donation to Ana de Melo. The last also refers to the poder that Ana de Melo gave to her husband in 1581 to settle accounts with her uncle Francisco Sánchez de Melo. Diego de Trujillo's letter appears in AGI Indif. Gen. 2084 (información of his nephew Baltasar Alvarez). For the poder of 1565, see AMT Pedro de Carmona A-1-9-1.

95. AHPC Diego Pacheco 4113.

96. AMT Pedro de Carmona B-1-23.

97. This process is described by Auke Pieter Jacobs in an article entitled "Emigration from Seville, 1550–1650" that will appear in a forthcoming volume edited by Ida Altman and James Horn, *"To Make America": European Emigration in the Early Modern Period*.

98. AGI Contrat. 5218, Indif. Gen. 2082.

99. Inés Alonso Cervera wrote a letter in 1578 to her son García de Escobar from Lima to this effect; see AGI Indif. Gen. 2090.

VI. Extremeños in the New World

1. See Lockhart, *Men of Cajamarca*, 27–31, 40, 77.

2. Pedro Cieza de Leon, *Obras Completas*, ed. Carmelo Saez de Santa María (Madrid, 1985), 2: 11. The translation is mine. Perhaps Aldana's father participated in a military campaign with Hernando Pizarro's father, Captain Gonzalo Pizarro.

3. For Aldana's will of 1562, see Jose Rafael Zarama, "Reseña histórica," app. 1, 189–196 (Pasto, 1942) (my thanks to Leon Helguera for sending me a copy of this offprint). For Aldana's daughter, see Lockhart, *Spanish Peru*, 167. Aldana's nephew of the same name was the son of his brother Alvaro de Aldana; he went to Peru in 1557 (see Navarro del Castillo, *La epopeya*, 147; and also AHPC Diego Pacheco 4100, in which

Lorenzo and his brother Francisco sold 2500 maravedís of censo al quitar in January 1557, at which time their parents were both deceased).

4. Note, for example, what Eugene Lyon, *The Enterprise of Florida. Pedro Menéndez de Avilés and the Spanish Conquest of 1565–1568* (Gainesville, 1976), 74–75, writes about the organization of that enterprise:

What was most remarkable about Menéndez's men was the closeknit nature of their interrelationships. Almost without exception, the men who shared the confidence of Pedro Menéndez and were scheduled to hold the posts of responsibility in Florida belonged to a number of Asturian families which were tied together by complex kinship links. Scores of rank-and-file soldiers and sailors from the same families also participated in the Florida enterprise. It was a family affair, or rather the affair of a small number of closely connected families from the north of Spain.

I would suggest, however, that this form of organization was more standard than "remarkable" in the Indies.

5. For a discussion of how factors of timing and connections affected emigrants from one family, see Altman, "Spanish Hidalgos."

6. AMG Fondo Barrantes MS B/3.

7. AGI Indif. General 2060.

8. AGI Indif. General 2078.

9. For Alonso Ramiro, see *Catálogo*, 5, no. 3819, AGI Contratación 5222, and AGI Indif. General 2055. For Juan Ramiro see AGI Indif. General 2058. See Otte, "Cartas privadas," 56–58, for a copy of the letter from Alonso Morales to Juan Ramiro, and 60–61, for a letter from Alonso Ramiro to his brother-in-law Pedro Alonso in Cabañas de la Peña.

10. *Catálogo*, 3, no. 881.

11. *Catálogo*, 5, tomo 1, no. 2827, tomo 2, no. 4868; AGI Indif. General 2162A, 2089.

12. See AGI Indif. General 2089, 2090.

13. AGI Indif. General 2090.

14. In June 1574 Francisco Calderón de Loaysa and his wife took 150,000 maravedís at censo from Sancho Casco, clérigo in Peru (Acedo, "Linajes," Calderón, 333[a6]). Sancho de Vargas and his two daughters in 1578 sold a censo to the priest Tomé García Calderón (in Peru) for 400 ducados (Acedo, "Linajes," Vargas, 48[a43]).

15. Pedro de Valencia probably was the nephew of the oidor Licenciado Diego González Altamirano (see AMT Pedro de Carmona B-1-23). He is mentioned in testimony regarding the 1570 will of Captain Francisco de Chaves; he succeeded to Chaves's encomienda in Peru (AMT 1585:I-7). For Francisco González de Castro, see AGI Indif. General 2083 (información of his nephew Juan de Castro); for Juan Rodríguez de Ocampo, see Acedo, "Linajes," Vargas, p. 48[a37], and Altamirano, 32).

16. Navarro del Castillo, *La epopeya*, 167–168; Schäfer, *El consejo de Indias*, 2: 114, 452, 463, 473.

17. Schäfer, *El consejo de Indias*, 2: 473, 503, 511, 512.

18. For Licenciado García de Valverde's reports on the state of the encomiendas and proposed measures for reform, see AGI Guatemala 10. George Lovell brought this material to my attention.

19. Emma Helen Blair and James A. Robertson, eds., *The Philippine Islands, 1493–1803* (Cleveland, 1903–1909), 4: 174–176, 219.

20. AGI Indif. General 2092.

21. AGI Justicia 215, no. 1.

22. AGI Justicia 1053, no. 5.

23. AGI Justicia 1061, no. 1, ramo 1.

24. For Carrasco's activities, see AGI Justicia 418 (suit between Alonso Carrasco and Alonso Pizarro de la Rua of Trujillo over the encomienda of Jayanca, jurisdiction of Trujillo, Peru). A witness in Zorita in 1576 testified that he had heard of Carrasco's death from one of Carrasco's factors and another merchant from Trujillo (Peru); see AGI Indif. General 2088, información of Juan Holgado of Orellana, a second cousin of Alonso Carrasco who was sent by Carrasco's brother to recover his property in Peru.

25. See Martínez's biography in Lockhart, *Men of Cajamarca*, 300–305.

26. Robert Keith, *Conquest and Agrarian Change: The Emergence of the Hacienda System on the Peruvian Coast* (Cambridge, Mass., 1976), 73.

27. See información of Nodera's son, Diego de Nodera, in AGI Indif. General 2056, and letter from Luis de Córdoba to his wife Isabel Carrera in Seville (May 1566), in Otte, "Cartas privadas," 31–36.

28. AGI Indif. General 2089.

29. A. Millares Carlo and J. I. Mantecón, *Indice y extractos de los protocolos del Archivo de Notarías de México, D.F.* (Mexico, 1945–1946), no. 2558.

30. See AMG Fondo Barrantes, MS B/3, fol. 270 (without date), for the claim made by Juan Pantoja's sister doña María de Ribera and nephews against his widow.

31. See información of Juan de Campo, husband of Diego Martín's daughter Ana de Aguiilar, in AGI Indif. General 2050.

32. Francisco A. de Icaza, *Conquistadores y pobladores de la Nueva España* (Madrid, 1923), 196; Boyd-Bowman, *Indice*, 2, no. 2778.

33. AMG Fondo Barrantes MS B/3, fol. 270.

34. AGI Justicia 215, no. 1.

35. Troy Floyd, *The Columbus Dynasty in the Caribbean, 1492–1526* (Albuquerque, 1973), 64, 76.

36. Eduardo Sánchez-Arjona, "De las personas que pasaron a esta Nueva España," *Revista de Archivos, Bibliotecas y Museos* 39 (1918): 98.

37. Icaza, *Conquistadores y pobladores*, 1: 166.
38. AGI Justicia 405, no. 2, ramo 2. Witnesses in Cuzco said that because of the protests of Carrasco and other vecinos of Cuzco, Francisco Pizarro was about to return Carrasco's encomienda to him when he died. The grant then passed into the hands of Licenciado Antonio de la Gama, who was succeeded by his daughter. On her death Antonio Vaca de Castro, the son of governor Licenciado Cristóbal Vaca de Castro, got the encomienda.
39. Lockhart, *Men of Cajamarca*, 302; Efraim Trelles Arestegui, *Lucas Martínez Vegazo: Funcionamiento de una encomienda peruana inicial* (Pontificia Universidad Católica del Peru, 1982), 47, says that Martínez offered the viceroy 12,000 pesos and Dr. Cuenca another 6000 pesos.
40. Lockhart, *Spanish Peru*, 16.
41. For Ulloa's suit for the return of his encomienda, see AGI Patronato 117, ramo 7, and AGI Justicia 430; for reassignment of Aldana's encomienda, see AGI Indif. General 2086. For discussion of Lorenzo de Ulloa and his brothers, see Altman, "Spanish Hidalgos," 329–333.
42. Hernando Pizarro's career and management of family properties are discussed in the biography in Lockhart, *Men of Cajamarca*, 157–168, and other references throughout. See also Varón Gabai and Jacobs, "Peruvian Wealth." For the illegal sale of encomiendas, see Lockhart, *Spanish Peru*, 20.
43. Himmerich, "The Encomenderos of New Spain," 239, 499, 327.
44. See AMT 1585:I-7. Chaves's encomienda of Viracomachaqui was in the valley of Condesuyo. It was alleged that Chaves failed to provide his Indians with a priest and therefore died owing them money.
45. Diego de Torres of Trujillo married the widow of the conquistador Cristóbal de Ortega and became an encomendero in Mexico, and Francisco de Torres, also of Trujillo, became an encomendero by his second marriage; see Boyd-Bowman, *Indice*, 2, nos. 3240, 3242.
46. The quote is from the información of Alonso Carrasco in AGI Justicia 418; for his death, see AGI Indif. General 2088.
47. See above, n. 38.
48. AGI Justicia 418.
49. See the biographies in Lockhart, *Men of Cajamarca*, 300–305 (Lucas Martínez) and 343–346 (Alonso Ruiz). Most of the discussion of Martínez's activities is drawn from Lockhart and from Trelles Arestegui, *Lucas Martínez Vegazo*.
50. Trelles, *Lucas Martínez Vegazo*, 38, 40.
51. Trelles, *Lucas Martínez Vegazo*, 199, 203, 207, 210, 213, 108.
52. Trelles, *Lucas Martínez Vegazo*, 112, 129.
53. AMT García de Sanabria A-1-1; Trelles, *Lucas Martínez Vegazo*, 174–177. In 1551 Pedro Alonso de Valencia's widow in Trujillo gave her

power of attorney to Gaspar Hernández, a cacereño living in Arequipa, to recover her husband's property (AMT García de Sanabria A-1-1).

54. Lockhart, *Men of Cajamarca*, 302–303. Trelles, *Lucas Martínez Vegazo*, 135, says that Martínez's marriage essentially was a sale of the encomienda, since Lucas received 16,000 pesos. Alonso Ruiz left at least one illegitimate child in Peru, a daughter named Isabel Ruiz whom he had with a criada named Francisca Miranda; he donated 1000 pesos to her before leaving Peru (see Trelles, *Lucas Martínez Vegazo*, 39).

55. Trelles, *Lucas Martínez Vegazo*, 123, 131.

56. AGI Indif. Gen. 2090.

57. AMG Fondo Barrantes MS B/3.

58. AGI Indif. Gen. 2083.

59. AGI Indif. Gen. 2089.

60. AGI Indif. Gen. 2090.

61. See Altman, "Spanish Hidalgos," 331–332, and AGI Patronato 100, ramo 9, for Diego de Ovando's probanza of 1557.

62. AGI Indif. Gen. 2086, letters of Lorenzo Gutiérrez and his son Cristóbal González.

63. AGI Indif. Gen. 2049.

64. AGI Indif. Gen. 2090.

65. See Boyd-Bowman, *Indice*, 2, no. 2744; Harkness Collection, Library of Congress, no. 260; Raul Porras Barrenechea, ed., *Cedulario del Peru* (Lima, 1944–1948), 2, no. 373; AGI Contratación 2723, no. 2; AGI Patronato 106, ramo 7. Alonso Guerra was mentioned as being in the Indies in the 1532 will of Juan de la Huerta of Cáceres (AHPC Pedro de Grajos 3923).

66. AGI Patronato 106, ramo 7.

67. See Altman, "Spanish Hidalgos," 329–334.

68. AMG Fondo Barrantes MS B/3.

69. See AGI Indif. Gen. 2082, testimony of Francisco de Loaysa of Trujillo, who said his brother Diego de Orellana wrote from Cuzco saying that Martín "had drowned in a river . . . and that an illegitimate daughter of his had inherited the goods that had remained and she had married Hernando Caballero . . . native of this city."

70. See Lockhart, *Spanish Peru*, 44, 158.

71. Pérez de Tudela, *Documentos relativos a la Gasca*, 2: 154.

72. In 1548 Gasca suggested sending a mestiza daughter of Juan Pizarro, and Gonzalo Pizarro's son and daughter, to Spain to live with an aunt in Trujillo (see Pérez de Tudela, *Documentos relativos a la Gasca*, 2: 272). Francisco Pizarro's son and daughter went to Spain, but only doña Francisca married and had children.

73. ACC-HO leg. 7, no. 31; leg. 1, no. 21.

74. Millares Carlo and Mantecón, *Indice y extractos*, no. 1331. Sanabria's brother, Hernando de Sanabria, was a priest in Cáceres who might have been excommunicated in the 1530s (AHPC Hernando Conde 3712). The cacereños in Mexico were entrepreneur Juan de Cáceres Delgado and Gonzalo Durán.

75. Pérez de Tudela, *Documentos relativos a la Gasca*, 2: 267.

76. AGI Indif. Gen. 2085.

77. Don Pedro Puertocarrero's nephew, Andrés Calderón Puertocarrero, in the late 1590s initiated a suit over properties in Medellín that don Pedro's mestizo son had inherited; see ARCG 3ª-599-3.

78. Millares Carlo and Mantecón, *Indice y extractos*, 1, no. 445. It is not clear whether Francisco de Gaete, the son of Hernando de Gaete and Catalina Calderón, both deceased, was in Mexico or not.

79. See Acedo, "Linajes," Hinojosa, p. 366[a13].

80. AGI Indif. Gen. 2093 and ARCG 3ª-599-3.

81. AGI Indif. Gen. 2049.

82. AGI Indif. Gen. 2050.

83. AGI Justicia 1176, no. 2, ramo 1.

84. AMG Fondo Barrantes MS B/3.

85. See AGI Indif. Gen. 2055, información of Gómez's niece Leonor Gómez and her husband, Hernán González, herrador.

86. In 1553 returnee from Peru Juan de Monroy said he had lived in the house of Juan Ramiro and his wife in Lima and had been there when Ramiro died. The other returnees who testified they had been with Ramiro in Lima were Melchor Hernández, Pedro Alonso, Pedro Jara, Alonso Cervantes, Alonso de Bibanco, and Juan Pizarro (AGI Indif. Gen. 2078).

87. See AGI Indif. Gen. 2089 for información of Andrés Gómez (Pedro Gómez's son) and AGI Indif. General 2084 for información of Rodrigo Alonso de Boroa, son of Felipe Rodríguez. See AGI Indif. Gen. 2083 for testimony regarding Francisco González de Castro.

88. See Lorenzo de Aldana's will in Zarama, "Reseña histórica," 191.

89. ACC-HO leg. 7, no. 103.

90. See Gibson, *Aztecs*, 377–378; and Colin A. Palmer, *Slaves of the White God: Blacks in Mexico, 1570–1650* (Cambridge, Mass., 1976), 133.

91. Lockhart, *Men of Cajamarca*, 29.

92. For the rebellion, see Lockhart, *Men of Cajamarca*, 183–189.

93. Pérez de Tudela, *Documentos relativos a la Gasca*, 1: 356.

94. Ibid., 2: 97.

95. Ibid., 2: 41.

96. Lockhart, *Men of Cajamarca*, 213. Perhaps ironically Hernando de Aldana and his brother Alonso made Gómez de Solís, a strong Pizarro partisan, their heir; see AHPC Pedro de Grajos 3923.

97. AGI Justicia 1126, no. 4, ramo 1.

98. Pérez de Tudela, *Documentos relativos a la Gasca*, 2: 46.

99. Ibid., 2: 303–307, 317.

100. Ibid., 1: 471.

101. The 1000 ducados that Blas de Soto donated to his sister had been willed by Juan Pizarro to his maternal siblings; see the two letters from Soto to Señora Inés Rodríguez de Aguilar in AGI Justicia 1070, no. 9.

102. AGI Justicia 1074, no. 4.

103. AGI Justicia 1126, no. 4, ramo 1.

104. AHPC Pedro de Grajos 3925.

105. AHPC Alonso Pacheco 4103.

106. AHPC Alonso Pacheco 4104.

107. See for example, letters 4, 7, 13 in Lockhart and Otte, *Letters and People*.

108. AGI Indif. Gen. 2090.

109. AHPC Pedro González 3831, Alonso Pacheco 4104.

110. AGI Justicia 1126, no. 2, ramo 2.

111. AGI Indif. Gen. 2054; AHPC Alonso Pacheco 4104, Deigo Pacheco 4113.

112. AHPC Alonso Pacheco 4102.

113. AHPC Diego Pacheco 4113, Alonso Pacheco 4103.

114. AGI Indif. Gen. 2083.

115. AGI Indif. Gen. 2084.

116. AGI Indif. Gen. 2094. Juan Rubio's will was dated April 1580.

117. AGI Indif. Gen. 2078.

118. AGI Indif. Gen. 2085. In 1572 returnee Alonso Pizarro testified that he had run into Licenciado Altamirano en route to Peru when he was on his way back to Spain.

119. For the agreement made between Juan Velázquez and Juan de Toro and Marina Ruiz, see AMT García de Sanabria A-1-1. Marina Ruiz and Juan de Toro claimed that they, and Alonso de Toro, were the children of Alejo Bocanegra and Catalina Rodríguez. Alonso de Toro himself, however, named Alonso de Toro and Inés Durán as his parents in AGI Justicia 117, no. 1, ramo 3; see Lockhart's biography and notes in *Men of Cajamarca*, 357–359.

120. AHPC Pedro González 3830.

VII. Return Migration

1. See Theopolis Fair, "The Indiano during the Spanish Golden Age from 1550–1650" (Ph.D. diss., Temple University, 1972), 11, 75.

2. In sixteenth-century Cáceres and Trujillo the term "perulero" is used almost invariably for returnees, occurring not only in informal usage but in legal documents as well, often appended to an individual's name much as occupational designations were. I have seen only one instance of the use of the term "indiano," in testimony of 1549 in Trujillo; Juan de la Jara referred to people who had come from the Indies as "tales indianos," in AGI Justicia 1176, no. 2, ramo 8.

3. See Lockhart, *Men of Cajamarca*, 44–52, 63–64, and also his "Letters and People to Spain," in Chiapelli, *First Images of America*, 2: 790–791. Lockhart specifically discusses the returnees to Trujillo who had been at Cajamarca.

4. For their stories, see Altman, "Spanish Hidalgos," 335–343.

5. Pérez de Tudela, *Documentos relativos a la Gasca*, 1: 567 (letter from Pedro de Valdivia to Hernando Pizarro, September 1545).

6. Casco and the members of the entourage accompanying Gasca appear in the testimony for Pedro Jara and Alonso de Bibanco, AGI Justicia 1126, no. 4, ramo 1.

7. See *Catálogo*, 3, no. 2447; García testified he was thirty-nine in 1547 (AGI Indif. Gen. 2055), but the exact date of his return is not known.

8. For Ribera see *Catálogo*, 5, no. 2248, and testimony in AGI Indif. Gen. 2083, 2089. For Andrés Calderón, see *Catálogo*, 4, no. 2281, and AGI Justicia 1062, no. 2, ramo 1.

9. *Catálogo*, 4, nos. 483, 486, 1278; Acedo, "Linajes," Vargas, 48[a13-14].

10. AGI Contratación 5218.

11. AGI Indif. Gen. 2094.

12. AGI Lima 199.

13. See Miguel Muñoz de San Pedro, *Doña Isabel de Moctezuma, la novia de Extremadura* (Madrid, 1965), 28, 31, 33, and AHPC Alonso Pacheco 4103.

14. For Francisco Sánchez de Melo, see Archivo Histórico de Arequipa Gaspar Hernández, 22 December 1551, 22 July 1553, and letter from Diego de Trujillo, Cuzco, January 1564 in AGI Indif. General 2084. For the Melo brothers, see *Catálogo*, 3, nos. 3557, 4183. For Pedro's return, see AGI Indif. General 2162A; and Acedo, "Linajes," Vargas, 48[a49].

15. AGI Indif. Gen. 2162A.

16. AGI Indif. Gen. 2086.

17. Doña Gracia de Medina, the daughter of Diego Jiménez "perulero," married García de Vargas Carvajal, who was the brother of doña María de Carvajal, the wife of returnee Andrés Calderón Puertocarrero (Acedo, "Linajes," Carvajal, 110[a10]).

18. ACC-HO leg. 4, no. 18; leg. 5, pt. 2, no. 20.

19. In 1603 don Pedro Cano Moctezuma y Toledo, the son of don Juan

Cano Moctezuma and his wife doña Elvira de Paredes Toledo, was a regidor in Toledo and sold 19,609 maravedís of rents for winter pasturage in dehesas in Cáceres's jurisdiction to his uncle Alonso Cano Saavedra, a vecino of Cáceres (ACC-HO leg. 4, no. 39).

20. Lodo de Maryoralgo, *Viejos linajes*, 122; Boyd-Bowman, *Indice*, 2, no. 2741; Lockhart, *Men of Cajamarca*, 213 (note); AHPC Diego Pacheco 4113.

21. See Lockhart, *Spanish Peru*, 20.

22. Godoy's will is in AHPC Diego Pacheco 4113; see also Roa y Ursua, *El reyno de Chile*, 8–9.

23. He purchased the regimiento from his nephew by marriage, Benito Moraga y Nidos, who was the husband of doña Marina de Carvajal, the daughter of doña Marta Martínez de Orellana (Godoy's sister) and Francisco de Carvajal. Their son Gaspar Moraga y Nidos emigrated to New Spain, probably in 1570.

24. See Lockhart's biography of Morgovejo in *Men of Cajamarca*, 230–232.

25. AHPC Diego Pacheco 4101 contains the accounting Godoy made in 1558 at the request of Francisco Morgovejo's grandmother and uncle of expenditures made for his ward.

26. AHPC Diego Pacheco 4100.

27. ACC-HO leg. 4, no. 47.

28. AHPC Diego Pacheco 4113, 4101.

29. AHPC Diego Pacheco 4113, Pedro González 3827.

30. AHPC Pedro González 3829.

31. Lodo de Mayoralgo, *Viejos linajes*, 122. Doña Leonor de Godoy, the daughter of Rodrigo de Godoy and doña Teresa Rol de la Cerda (hence the granddaughter of Francisco de Godoy) in 1558, at the age of fifteen, married another very successful and wealthy returnee, Cristóbal de Ovando Paredes (ACC-HO leg. 7, no. 17).

32. See Lockhart's biography in *Men of Cajamarca*, 343–345; Tena Fernández, *Trujillo histórico*, 227; AGS Exped. Hacienda 311.

33. Lockhart, *Men of Cajamarca*, 288–289; AGI Indif. General 2078; AMT García de Sanabria A-1-1, A-1-2.

34. AMT Pedro de Carmona B-1-27.

35. AGI Justicia 1053, no. 5, Lima 565; AMT García de Sanabria A-1-1, A-1-2. Diego de Carvajal bought the censo from the merchants Juan de Camargo and Juan González de Victoria, who had connections with the Pizarros and with the Indies.

36. AGS Exped. Hacienda 189-56.

37. See ARCG Hidalguía 301-55-21, and the discussion of the suit for

hidalguía in chap. 2. Hernando de Sande's will is in AHPC Pedro González 3830. See also Altman, "Emigrants and Society."

38. Miguel Muñoz de San Pedro, "Aventuras y desventuras del tercer Diego García de Paredes," *Revista de Estudios Extremeños* 13 (1957): 17–32.

39. See AGI Justicia 1126, no. 4, ramo 1.

40. AGI Justicia 1067, no. 5, ramo 2. In 1565 the priest Francisco de Rodas had a benefice in Santa María (AMT Pedro de Carmona A-1-1-9).

41. *Catálogo*, 3, no. 3199; AGI Indif. General 2085 (información of Francisco Cervantes).

42. AGI Indif. Gen. 2055 (return to Spain in 1574), AGI Contratación 5222 (return to New Spain). See AGI Justicia 215, no. 1, for his activities in New Spain.

43. AGI Patronato 117, ramo 7, and 100, and Justicia 430. See also Altman, "Spanish Hidalgos," 331–332.

44. AGI Justicia 1061, no. 1, ramo 1.

45. For Aldana see Raul Porras Barrenechea, ed., *Cedulario del Peru* (Lima, 1944–1948), 2: 127; for Nidos see Porras Barrenechea, *Cedulario*, 2: 217, and Roa y Ursua, *El reyno de Chile*, 9, 210.

46. AGI Indif. Gen. 2093 and ARCG 3ª-599-3.

47. AGI Contratación 5220, 5224, and Lodo de Mayoralgo, *Viejos linajes*, 48.

48. See *Catálogo*, 5, nos. 3507, 3843; AGI Indif. Gen. 2054, 2056; AGI Contratación 5222.

49. *Catálogo*, 3, no. 2977; AGI Indif. General 2093.

50. AGI Indif. Gen. 2090.

51. AGI Contratación 5227; the criado was Alonso Donaire (see also Navarro del Castillo, *La epopeya*, 394, 416).

52. Schäfer, *El consejo de Indias*, 2: 151, 482, 487, 492, 516. Blas Altamirano probably had been in Peru in the 1570s with his parents.

53. *Catálogo*, 5, nos. 1381, 1451; AGI Indif. General 2083.

54. All the documents relating to the transactions between Benito de la Peña and Pedro de Vita, as well as Vita's power of attorney made in Cáceres in October 1546, are in AHPC Diego Pacheco 4100. Peña was one of that large group of young men who left Cáceres in 1535, ostensibly for Santo Domingo, although most of them ended up in Peru (Boyd-Bowman, *Indice*, 2, no. 2776).

55. AGI Indif. Gen. 2085, 2087.

56. AHPC Pedro de Grajos 3925; Gómez de Solís paid the money the following year.

57. AHPC Pedro González 3830.

58. AGI Justicia 1126, no. 4, ramo 1.

59. Lockhart, *Men of Cajamarca*, 220–221, 295; AGI Justicia 1053, no. 5 (for the suit). Juan Cortés had fought in Navarre with Hernando Pizarro (see Justicia 1176, no. 2, ramo 1). Also see Justicia 1176, no. 2, ramo 8, for testimony about the enmity between Cortés and Herrera.

60. AGI Justicia 1176, no. 2, ramo 8. The account of this episode comes mainly from testimony of 1549 taken from Juan de Herrera, who clearly was embittered and seeking any opportunity to get even with Cortés (by this time the incident in which Cortés's criados had wounded Herrera's brother also had occurred), so Herrera might have been a less than wholly credible witness. Nevertheless, although no other witness recounted the incident in such detail, neither did anyone else contradict Herrera's version, and the details sound authentic.

61. ACC-HO leg. 5, pt. 2, no. 20.

62. AMT Pedro de Carmona B-1-23. The regidores were Hernando de Orellana, Juan Casco, Gonzalo Rodríguez de Ocampo, and Melchior González, the last two very likely returnees.

63. AMT Pedro de Carmona B-1-27. Navarro del Castillo, *La epopeya*, 413. Captain Gonzalo de Olmos's brother Juan de Olmos also was in Peru, at least through the 1540s.

64. AGI Indif. Gen. 2090 (informaciones of Cristóbal de Ribera and Juan de Tapia).

65. ARCG 3ª-599-3; Boyd-Bowman, *Indice*, 2, no. 3173; Acedo, "Linajes," Loaysa, 222ª³⁻¹⁵. Don Gaspar de Ayala was thirty in 1596 when he returned from Peru; his brothers don Jerónimo de Loaysa and don Lorenzo de Loaysa Figueroa were thirty-four and twenty-five. They all could have been born in Trujillo in the 1560s, since their mother might have been fairly young when she came to Trujillo. She married a second time in Trujillo, to Diego García Barrantes, son of returnee Pedro Barrantes, and died in 1581 (AMT Pedro de Carmona B-1-23).

66. Icaza, *Conquistadores*, 1: 31; Muñoz de San Pedro, *Doña Isabel*, 28, 31, 33; Gibson, *Aztecs*, 92, 424–426.

67. AHPC Pedro González 3829, ACC-HO leg. 4, no. 39.

Conclusion

1. See, for example, Gibson, *Aztecs*; Nancy Farriss, *Maya Society under Colonial Rule* (Princeton, 1984); James Lockhart, "Some Nahua Concepts in Postcolonial Guise," *History of European Ideas* 6 (1985): 465–482.

2. See Elliott, *The Old World and the New*; Chiappelli, ed., *First*

Images; Alfred W. Crosby, *The Columbian Exchange* (Westwood, Conn., 1972).

3. AGI Justicia 1176, no. 2, ramo 8. The statement was made by Alvaro de Hinojosa, husband of doña Graciana, youngest daughter of Captain Gonzalo Pizarro.

4. See the discussion of the term in Julian A. Pitt-Rivers, *The People of the Sierra*, 2d ed. (Chicago, 1971), 7, 30–31. He compares the word "pueblo" to the term "polis." For use of "pueblo" in reference to Trujillo, see testimony by Juan Vicioso and Juan de la Jara in AGI Justicia 1176, no. 2, ramo 8.

5. Lockhart, *Men of Cajamarca*, 318–320.

6. See, for example, Bernard Bailyn, *Voyagers to the West: A Passage in the Peopling of America on the Eve of the Revolution* (New York, 1986); Mildred Campbell, "English Emigration on the Eve of the American Revolution," *American Historical Review* 61 (1955): 1–20; David Cressy, *Coming Over: Migration and Communication between England and New England in the Seventeenth Century* (Cambridge, 1987); James Horn, "Servant Emigration to the Chesapeake in the Seventeenth Century," in *The Chesapeake in the Seventeenth Century: Essays on Anglo-American Society*, ed. Thad W. Tate and David Ammerman (Chapel Hill, 1979), 51–95. These are only some of the studies of English emigration; work has also been done on Scottish and Irish emigration.

Glossary

alarife:	mason, master builder
albañil:	mason
alcabala:	sales tax
alcacer:	barley field
alcalde:	magistrate
alcalde de la hermandad:	militia official
aldea:	hamlet
alférez:	ensign
alguacil:	constable
alhóndiga:	public granary
aljama:	community of Jews or Moors
almojarifazgo:	customs duties
aparejador:	builder
arcediano:	archdeacon
arcipreste:	archpriest
arriero:	muleteer
arroba:	weight of twenty-five pounds
asiento:	entry in a registry; site

audiencia:	high court
ayuntamiento:	city or town council
bachiller:	holder of a bachelor's degree
baldío:	uncultivated land
bando:	faction, party
barbecho:	harvest
bellota:	acorns
berbí:	cloth made from uncombed wool
berrocal:	rocky land
bodegonero:	tavern keeper
cabildo:	council
cahiz:	twelve fanegas
calero:	lime burner
calle:	street
cantero:	stonecutter
cañada:	sheep walk
capellán:	chaplain
capellanía:	chantry, chaplaincy
capilla:	chapel
capitulaciones:	charters, licenses
carnero:	sheep
carretero:	carter
casado:	married person
casas principales:	town house, urban palace
casilla:	hut
cédula:	royal ordinance
censo al quitar:	redeemable mortgage

censo enfitéutico:	lease (of agricultural land)
cerrajero:	locksmith
ciudad:	city
clérigo:	cleric, priest
clérigo presbítero:	priest ordained to say mass
clérigo vicario:	vicar
cofradía:	confraternity, lay brotherhood
colegio:	college, academy
colmenar:	apiary, hives
comendador:	member of a military order
contador:	accountant
coro:	choir stalls
corona:	350 maravedís
corredor:	gallery, arcade, corridor
corregidor:	royal municipal administrator, magistrate
criadero:	nursery, stockbreeding farm
criado:	servant, retainer
cura:	parish priest
curador:	guardian
chancillería:	royal chancery court
chantre:	cantor
charca:	pond
dehesa:	pasture
depositario general:	treasurer, trustee
deudo:	relative
doctor:	holder of a doctorate
ducado:	375 maravedís

ejido:	municipal commons, grazing lands
encabezamiento:	sales tax assessment
encomienda:	grant of right to tribute from Indians of a designated area or jurisdiction
encomendero:	holder of an encomienda
escribano:	notary
escudero:	squire
escudo:	400 maravedís
fanega:	bushel
fanegada:	*measure of land (about* $1\frac{1}{2}$ *acres); bushel*
fiador:	guarantor
fiel ejecutor:	inspector
fiscal:	treasurer or public prosecutor
fuero:	set of privileges, town charter
hacienda:	wealth, estate; treasury
heredad:	estate
herrador:	farrier, horseshoer
herrero:	blacksmith
hidalgo:	member of privileged, tax-exempt class
hidalguía:	privileged status
hijo natural:	illegitimate child
hipoteca:	mortgage
hortelano:	gardener
huerta, huerto:	garden, orchard
información:	testimonial
jornalero:	day laborer (rural)
juez del rey:	royal judge

juro:	annuity on certain taxes or revenues
justicia real:	royal magistrate
labrador:	farmer
ladino:	Spanish speaking
lavadero:	place for washing wool
letrado:	lawyer
licenciado:	holder of a master's degree
lugar:	hamlet, small village
macho:	mule
maestrazgo:	lands under the jurisdiction of one of the military orders
maravedí:	basic unit of Spanish currency
mayoral:	foreman
mayorazgo:	entail; also heir to an entail
mayordomo:	steward
médico:	physician
mercader:	merchant
merced:	grant (of money, annuities, privileges)
mesón:	inn
mestizo:	person of Spanish and Indian parentage
molino:	mill
montes:	woodlands, low mountains
morisco:	Spaniard of Moorish descent
mozo:	lad, youth
obra pía:	endowed charity
oficial:	artisan
oidor:	judge

olivar:	olive grove
oposición:	competitive examination
padrinos:	godparents
padrón:	census list of taxpayers
palomar:	dovecote
pastor:	shepherd
pechero:	taxpayer
pelaire:	wool carder
pellejero:	wineskin maker
peón:	laborer
peso:	unit of currency in the Indies of varying value ("peso de oro" around 400 maravedís, "peso de plata" around 270 maravedís)
portada:	entranceway
portales:	arcades (of a plaza)
portero:	doorkeeper
preceptor de gramática:	Latin instructor
predicador:	preacher
probanza:	proof (evidence or testimony relating to a person's antecedents, activities, etc.)
procurador de causas:	untitled lawyer
procurador general:	solicitor, representative
propios:	property held by a municipality
provisor:	vicar general
pueblo:	village, town
quintal:	weight of 100 pounds
rastrojo:	stubble
real:	34 maravedís

recuero:	driver
regidor:	councilman
regimiento:	office of councilman
relator:	secretary
religioso:	member of a religious order
renta de yerba:	rents of pasturage
repartimiento de indios:	synonym for encomienda in Spanish America
repostero:	wall hanging with coat of arms
república:	commonwealth
retablo:	altarpiece
ribera:	riverside
señorío:	lordship, jurisdiction
sesmero:	representative
solar:	foundation or lot
soltero:	unmarried person
tendero:	shopkeeper
teniente de corregidor:	deputy of the corregidor
tercio y quinto:	"third and fifth"; the major portion of an estate
término:	jurisdiction or district
tierra:	usually a city and its jurisdiction
tierra baldía:	uncultivated land, crown land
tintorero:	cloth dyer
tratante:	trader, peddler
tundidor:	cloth shearer
vecino:	citizen
veedor:	inspector

velarte:	broadcloth
vicario:	vicar
villa:	town, city
viña:	vineyard
zapatería:	shoemaker's shop or trade
zapatero:	shoemaker
zurrador:	leather currier

Bibliography

Note on Archival Sources

Research for the book was conducted in a number of archives in Spain. The Contratación and Indiferente General sections of the Archivo General de Indias both contain information relating to emigrants and returnees; Patronato and Justicia were particularly useful for the activities of extremeños in the Indies. The local archives in Extremadura, however, in a sense constitute the real core of the study. The material they provided on emigrants, returnees, and their families is solid evidence of the impact of the Indies on local society. Notarial records from the present-day province of Cáceres in principle have been collected in the Archivo Histórico Provincial of the capital. For the sixteenth century the *protocolos* are organized chronologically and by notary but not otherwise catalogued. Cáceres's municipal archive also is uncatalogued for the sixteenth century. Trujillo did not transfer its protocolos to the provincial archive, and the notarial records that remain are still housed in the city's municipal archive, which is extensive and recently has been recatalogued. Unfortunately, most of the protocolos for the sixteenth century are missing. There is nothing before 1550 and very little until 1570; only after 1580 are the records more complete. The third local archive used, the private collection of the late Conde de Canilleros in Cáceres, has excellent material on Cáceres and Trujillo, especially on noble families, and it is well organized and catalogued.

Other archives also provided some important material. The Expedientes Hacienda section of the Archivo General de Simancas contains the censuses and tax lists of the towns prepared in the 1550s and 1560s; they are a very important source of information on local society in Extremadura in the period. The Fondo Barrantes, donated to the archive of the monastery of Guadalupe by the nineteenth-century bibliographer Vicente Barrantes, is strongest for the nineteenth century; but it includes some interesting sixteenth-century material, especially the unusual series of private letters from Alvaro de Paredes in Mexico. As the high court of appeals for the region, the records from the chancillería in Granada contain much information on local conflicts between towns and cities over jurisdiction and similar disputes. Some of the suits for hidalguía proved very useful.

Archivo General de Indias, Seville (AGI)
    Contratación, Indiferente General, Patronato, Justicia
Archivo General de Simancas (AGS)
    Expedientes Hacienda
Archivo Municipal de Trujillo (AMT)
    Municipal and notarial records
Archivo Municipal de Cáceres (AMC)
    City council records
Archivo Histórico Provincial de Cáceres (AHPC)
    Notarial records
Archivo del Conde de Canilleros, Cáceres (ACC)
    Casa de Hernando de Ovando, Asuntos de Trujillo
Archivo de la Real Chancillería de Granada (ARCG)
Archivo del Monasterio de Guadalupe (AMG)
    Fondo Barrante

Acedo Trigo, Federico. "Linajes de Trujillo." Undated ms., Archivo Municipal de Trujillo.
Actas del VI Congreso de Estudios Extremeños. Diputaciones Culturales de Cáceres y Badajoz. Cáceres, 1981.
Altman, Ida. "Emigrants, Returnees and Society in Sixteenth Century Cáceres." Ph.D. diss., Johns Hopkins University, 1981.
———. "Emigrants and Society: An Approach to the Background of Colonial Spanish America." *Comparative Studies in Society and History* 30, 1 (January 1988): 170–190.
———. "Spanish Hidalgos and America: The Ovandos of Cáceres." *The Americas* 43, 3 (1987): 323–344.

Beinart, Haim. *Trujillo. A Jewish Community in Extremadura on the Eve of the Expulsion from Spain*. Jerusalem: The Magnes Press, 1980.

Bermúdez Aznar, Agustín. *El corregidor en Castilla durante la Baja Edad Media (1348–1474)*. Murcia: Sucesores de Nogués, 1974.

Blair, Emma Helen, and James Alexander Robertson, eds. *The Philippine Islands, 1493–1803*. 55 volumes. Cleveland: A. H. Clark Company, 1903–1909.

Bovenkirk, Frank. *The Sociology of Return Migration: A Bibliographic Essay*. Publications of the Research Group for European Migration Problems, 20. The Hague, 1974.

Boxoyo, Simón Benito. *Historia de Cáceres y su patrona*. Biblioteca Extremeña, 6. Cáceres, 1952.

Boyd-Bowman, Peter. *Indice geobiográfico de cuarenta mil pobladores españoles de América en el siglo XVI*. 2 vols. Vol. 1, Bogota, 1964; vol. 2, Mexico, 1968.

———. "Patterns of Spanish Emigration to the Indies until 1600." *Hispanic American Historical Review* 56 (1976): 580–604.

———. *Patterns of Spanish Emigration to the New World (1493–1580)*. Council on International Studies, SUNY at Buffalo, Special Studies no. 34. Buffalo, N.Y., 1973.

Callejo, Carlos. *Cáceres monumental*. 3d ed. Madrid: Editorial Plus-Ultra, 1975.

Caro Baroja, Julio. *El señor inquisidor y otras vidas por oficio*. 2d ed. Madrid: Alianza Editorial, 1970.

Carvajal, Fray Gaspar de. *Relación del nuevo descubrimiento del famoso río grande que por el nombre del capitán que le descubrió se llamó el río de Orellana*. Introd. by Jose Toribio Medina. Biblioteca Extremeña, 8. Cáceres, 1952.

Catálogo de pasajeros a Indias durante los siglos XVI, XVII y XVIII. Vols. 1–3, compiled by Cristóbal Bermúdez Plata; Seville: Imprenta editorial de la Gavida, 1940–1946. Vols. 4–5, compiled by Luis Romero Iruela and María del Carmen Galbis Díez; Seville, 1980.

Christian, William. *Local Religion in Sixteenth-Century Spain*. Princeton: Princeton University Press, 1981.

Cieza de León, Pedro. *Obras completas*, ed. Carmelo Saenz de Santa María. 2 vols. Madrid: C.S.I.C., 1984–1985.

La ciudad hispánica durante los siglos XIII al XVI. Vol. 1. Madrid: Editorial de la Universidad Complutense, 1985.

Clavero, Bartolomé. *Mayorazgo: Propiedad feudal en Castilla, 1369–1836*. Madrid: Siglo Veintiuno de España Editores, S.A., 1974.

Dillard, Heath. *Daughters of the Reconquest: Women in Castilian Town Society, 1100–1300*. Cambridge: Cambridge University Press, 1984.

Domínguez Ortiz, Antonio and Bernard Vincent. *Historia de los moriscos: Vida y tragedia de una minoría*. Madrid: Editorial Revista de Occidente, 1978.

Elliott, John H. *The Old World and the New, 1492–1650*. Cambridge: Cambridge University Press, 1970.

Fair, Theopolis. "The *Indiano* during the Spanish Golden Age from 1550–1650." Ph.D. diss., Temple University, 1972.

Fernández Nieva, Julio. "Un censo de moriscos extremeños de la Inquisición de Llerena (año 1594)." *Revista de Estudios Extremeños* 29 (1973): 149–176.

Floriano Cumbreño, Antonio C. "Cáceres ante la historia: El problema medieval de la propiedad de la tierra." *Revista de Estudios Extremeños* 5 (1949): 3–29.

———. *Estudios de historia de Cáceres*. 2 vols. Vol. 1: *Desde los orígenes a la reconquista*. Vol. 2: *El fuero y la vida medieval, siglo XIII*. Oviedo, 1959.

———. *Guía histórico-artística de Cáceres*. 2d ed. Cáceres: Diputación Provincial, Servicios Culturales, 1952.

———. *La villa de Cáceres y la Reina Católica. Ordenanzas que a Cáceres dio la Reina Doña Isabel Primera de Castilla*. Cáceres, 1917.

Floyd, Troy S. *The Columbus Dynasty in the Caribbean, 1492–1526*. Albuquerque: University of New Mexico Press, 1973.

Foglietta, Huberto. *Vida de Don Alvaro de Sande*. Edited and with notes by Miguel Angel Orti Belmonte. Madrid, 1962.

Foster, George. *Culture and Conquest: America's Spanish Heritage*. Chicago: Quadrangle Books, 1960.

García Arenal, Mercedes. *Los moriscos*. Madrid: Editora Nacional, 1975.

García Zanza, Eugenio. *Evolución, estructura y otros aspectos de la población cacereña*. Badajoz, Diputación Provincial, 1977.

Gerbet, Marie-Claude. "Les confréres religieuses à Cáceres de 1467 a 1523." *Mélanges de la Casa de Velázquez* 7 (1971): 75–114.

———. *La noblesse dans le royaume de Castille: Etude sur ses structures sociales en Estrémadure (1454–1516)*. Paris: Publications de la Sorbonne, 1979.

Gibson, Charles. *The Aztecs under Spanish Rule: A History of the Indians of the Valley of Mexico, 1519–1810*. Stanford: Stanford University Press, 1964.

Góngora, Mario. *Los grupos de conquistadores en Tierra Firme (1509–1530)*. Santiago: Universidad de Chile, 1962.

———. "Régimen señorial y rural en la Extremadura de la Orden de Santiago en el momento de la emigración a Indias." *Jahrbuch für*

Geschichte von Staat, Wirtschaft und Gesellschaft Lateinamerikas 2 (1965): 1–29.

Gutiérrez, Costancio. *Españoles en Trento*. Valladolid: C.S.I.C., 1951.

Himmerich, Robert T. "The Encomenderos of New Spain, 1521–1555." Ph.D. diss., University of California, Los Angeles, 1984.

Historia de Extremadura. 9 vols. (various authors). Badajoz: Universitas Editorial, 1985.

Hurtado, Publio. *Ayuntamiento y familias cacerenses*. Cáceres: L. Jiménez Merino, 1918.

———. *Indianos cacereños*. Barcelona: Tipolitografía de L. Tasso, 1892.

Icaza, Francisco de. *Conquistadores y pobladores de Nueva España*. 2 vols. Madrid: "El Adelantado de Segovia," 1923.

Jacobs, Auke Pieter. "Pasajeros y polizones: Algunas observaciones sobre la emigración española a las Indias durante el siglo XVI." *Revista de Indias* 172 (1983): 439–479.

Kagan, Richard L. *Students and Society in Early Modern Spain*. Baltimore: Johns Hopkins University Press, 1974.

Keith, Robert G. *Conquest and Agrarian Change: The Emergence of the Hacienda System on the Peruvian Coast*. Cambridge, Mass.: Harvard University Press, 1976.

Klein, Julius. *The Mesta: A Study in Spanish Economic History, 1273–1836*. Cambridge, Mass.: Harvard University Press, 1920.

Konetzke, Richard. "Legislación sobre inmigración de extranjeros en America durante la época colonial." *Revista Internacional de Sociología* 3 (1945): 269–299.

Lafaye, Jacques. *Quetzalcoatl y Guadalupe: La formación de la conciencia nacional en México*. Mexico: Fondo de Cultura Ecónomica, 1977.

Lamb, Ursula. *Frey Nicolás de Ovando: Gobernador de Indias (1501–1509)*. Madrid: C.S.I.C., 1956.

LeFlem, Jean-Paul. "Cáceres, Plasencia y Trujillo en la segunda mitad del siglo XVI (1557–1596)." *Cuadernos de Historia de España* 45–46 (1967): 248–299.

Lockhart, James. *The Men of Cajamarca: A Social and Biographical Study of the First Conquerors of Peru*. Austin: University of Texas Press, 1972.

———. *Spanish Peru, 1532–1560*. Madison: University of Wisconsin Press, 1968.

Lodo de Mayoralgo, J. M. *Viejos linajes de Cáceres*. Cáceres: Caja de Ahorras y Monte de Piedad, 1971.

Lohmann Villena, Guillermo. *Los americanos en las órdenes nobiliarias (1529–1900)*. 2 vols. Madrid, 1947.

Lyon, Eugene. *The Enterprise of Florida: Pedro Menéndez de Avilés and the Spanish Conquest of 1565–1568*. Gainesville: University Presses of Florida, 1976.

Madoz, Pascual. *Diccionario geográfico–estadístico–histórico de España y sus posesiones de Ultramar*. 16 vols. 3d ed. Madrid: Est. tip. de P. Madoz y L. Sagasti, 1848–1850.

Maravall, Jose Antonio. *El mundo social de "La Celestina."* Madrid: Editorial Gredos, S.A., 1968.

Martínez, Gonzalo. *Las comunidades de villa y tierra de la Extremeña Castellana*. Madrid: Editora Nacional, 1983.

Martínez, José Luis. *Pasajeros de Indias: Viajes transatlánticos en el siglo XVI*. Madrid: Alianza Editorial, 1983.

Martínez, Santiago. *Fundadores de Arequipa*. Arequipa: Tip. La Luz, 1936.

Martínez-Quesada, Juan. "Documentación de la capellanía y enterramiento del presidente D. Juan de Ovando." *Revista de Estudios Extremeños* 14 (1958): 145–158.

Millares Carlo, A., and J. I. Mantecón. *Indice y extractos de los Protocolos del Archivo de Notarías de México, D.F.* 2 vols. Mexico: Colegio de México, 1945–1946.

Molinié-Bertrand, Annie. *Au siècle d'or: L'Espagne et ses hommes. La population du royaume de Castille au XVIe siècle*. Paris: Economica, 1985.

———. "Contribution à l'étude de la société rurale dans la province de Trujillo au XVIe siècle." In *Mélanges offerts a Charles Vincent Aubrun*, vol. 2. Paris: Editions Hispaniques, 1975.

Muñoz de San Pedro, Miguel. "Aventuras y desventuras del tercer Diego García de Paredes." *Revista de Estudios Extremeños* 13 (1957): 5–93.

———. ed. *Crónicas trujillanas del siglo XVI*. Cáceres: Biblioteca Pública y Archivo Histórico de Cáceres, 1952.

———. *Diego García de Paredes: Hércules y Sansón de España*. Madrid: Espasa-Calpe, 1946.

———. "Don Alvaro de Sande, cronista del desastre de los Gelves." *Revista de Estudios Extremeños* 10 (1954): 467–509.

———. *Doña Isabel de Moctezuma, la novia de Extremadura*. Madrid. 1965.

———. *Extremadura: La tierra en la que nacían los dioses*. Madrid: Espasa-Calpe, 1961.

———. *La Extremadura del siglo XV en tres de sus paladines*. Madrid, 1964.

———, and H. Nectario María. *El gobernador y maestre de campo*

Diego García de Paredes, fundador de Trujillo de Venezuela. Madrid: C.S.I.C., 1957.

————. "Las últimas disposiciones del último Pizarro de la Conquista." *Boletín de la Real Academia de Historia* 126 (1950): 387–425; 127 (1950): 527–560.

Nader, Helen. *The Mendoza Family in the Spanish Renaissance, 1350 to 1550*. New Brunswick, N.J.: Rutgers University Press, 1979.

Naranjo Alonso, Clodoaldo. *Solar de conquistadores: Trujillo, sus hijos y monumentos*. 3d ed. Madrid: Espasa-Calpe, S.A., 1983.

————. *Trujillo y su tierra: Historia, monumentos e hijos ilustres*. 2 vols. Trujillo: Sobrino de B. Peña, 1924.

Navarro del Castillo, Vicente. *La epopeya de la raza extremeña en Indias*. Mérida, 1978.

Orti Belmonte, Miguel Angel. "Cáceres bajo la Reina Católica y su camarero Sancho Paredes Golfín." *Revista de Estudios Extremeños* 10 (1954): 193–328.

————. *La vida en Cáceres en los siglos XIII y XVI al XVIII*. Cáceres, 1949.

Otte, Enrique. "Cartas privadas de Puebla del siglo XVI." *Jahrbuch für Geschichte von Staat, Wirtschaft und Gesellschaft Lateinamerikas* 3 (1966): 10–87.

Parker, Noel Geoffrey. *Philip II*. Boston: Little, Brown and Company, 1978.

Pereira Iglesias, Jose Luis. "Atraso económico, régimen señorial y economía deficitaria en Cáceres durante el siglo XVI." M.A. thesis, University of Extremadura, 1977.

Pérez Moreda, Vicente. "El crecimiento demográfico español en el siglo XVI." In *Jerónimo Zurita: Su época y su escuela*. Zaragoza, 1986.

Pérez de Tudela, Juan. *Documentos relativos a don Pedro de la Gasca y a Gonzalo Pizarro*. 2 vols. Madrid: Real Academia de la Historia, 1964.

Peristiany, J. G., ed. *El concepto de honor en la sociedad mediterránea*. Barcelona: Editorial Labor, 1968. In English, *Honour and Shame: The Values of Mediterranean Society*. Chicago: University of Chicago Press, 1966.

Phillips, Carla Rahn. *Six Galleons for the King of Spain: Imperial Defense in the Early Seventeenth Century*. Baltimore: Johns Hopkins University Press, 1986.

Pike, Ruth. *Aristocrats and Traders: Sevillian Society in the Sixteenth Century*. Ithaca: Cornell University Press, 1972.

Porras Barrenechea, Raul, ed. *Cedulario del Peru*. 2 vols. Lima: Depto. de relaciones culturales del Ministerio de relaciones exteriores del Peru, 1944–1948.

———. "El testamento de Pizarro de 1539." *Revista de Indias* 2, 3 (1941): 39–70.

Ramírez-Horton, Susan. "Land Tenure and the Economics of Power in Colonial Peru." Ph.D. diss., University of Wisconsin, 1977.

Roa y Ursua, Luis de. *El reyno de Chile, 1535–1810.* Valladolid: Talleres Tipográficos "Cuesta," 1945.

Rodríguez Becerra, Salvador. *Encomienda y conquista. Los inicios de la colonización en Guatemala.* Vol. 14. University of Seville, Publicaciones del Seminario de Antropología Americana, 1977.

Rodríguez Sánchez, Angel. *Cáceres: Población y comportamientos demográficos en el siglo XVI.* Cáceres: Editorial Extremadura, 1977.

———. "La natalidad ilegítima en Cáceres en el siglo XVI." Separata, Diputación Provincial de Badajoz, 1979.

Rubio-Muñoz Bocanegra, Angel. "La emigración extremeña a Indias, siglo XVI. Aportación documental para un fichero de emigrantes extremeños del mismo siglo." *Revista del Centro de Estudios Extremeños* 4 (1930): 35–94, 243–259, 309–325; 5 (1931): 67–83, 273–289; 6 (1932): 57–73, 226–243.

Rubio Rojas, Antonio. *Las disposiciones de Don Francisco Carvajal, arcediano de Plasencia y Mecenas de Cáceres, su villa natal.* Cáceres: T. Rodríguez Santano, 1975.

Sánchez Arjona, Eduardo. "De las personas que pasaron a esta Nueva España." *Revista de Archivos, Bibliotecas y Museos* (Madrid) 36, 1 (1917): 419–430; 37, 2 (1917): 111–127; 39, 2 (1918): 89–99.

Sánchez Ochoa, Pilar. *Los hidalgos de Guatemala: Realidad y apariencia en su sistema de valores.* Vol. 13. University of Seville, Publicaciones del Seminario de Antropología Americana, 1976.

Schäfer, Ernest. *El Consejo Real y Supremo de las Indias.* 2 vols. Seville: Centro de Historia de America, 1935–1947.

Scrattish, Nicholas L. "New Perspectives on Castilian Migration to the *Audiencias* of Mexico and Lima, 1540–1580." Ph.D. diss., University of California, San Diego, 1975.

Solís Rodríguez, Carmelo. "El arquitecto Francisco Becerra: Su etapa extremeña." *Revista de Estudios Extremeños* 29 (1973): 287–383.

———. "La plaza mayor de Trujillo." In *Actas del VI Congreso de Estudios Extremeños.* Vol. 1, 277–299. Cáceres, 1981.

Stone, Lawrence. *The Family, Sex and Marriage in England, 1500–1800.* New York: Harper and Row, 1977.

Tena Fernández, Juan. *Trujillo histórico y monumental.* Trujillo, 1967.

Trelles Arestegui, Efraim. *Lucas Martínez Vegazo: Funcionamiento de una encomienda peruana inicial.* Pontificia Universidad Católica del Peru, Fondo Editorial, 1982.

Trujillo, Diego de. *Relación del descubrimiento del reyno del Peru*. Edited and with notes by Raul Porras Barrenechea. Seville: Escuela de Estudios Hispano-Americanos, 1948.

Ulloa Golfín, Pedro. *Privilegios y documentos relativos a la ciudad de Cáceres*. 18 ?. Biblioteca Nacional, Madrid, ms. 430.

Varón Gabai, Rafael, and Auke Pieter Jacobs. "Peruvian Wealth and Spanish Investments: The Pizarro Family during the Sixteenth Century." *Hispanic American Historical Review* 67, 4 (November 1987): 657–695.

Vassberg, David E. "La coyuntura socioeconómica de la ciudad de Trujillo durante la época de la conquista de América." Separata, Publicaciones de la Diputación Provincial de Badajoz, 1979.

———. *Land and Society in Golden Age Castile*. Cambridge: Cambridge University Press, 1984.

Villuga, Pero Juan. *Reportorio de todos los caminos de España (1546)*. Madrid, 1950.

Vincent, Bernard. "L'expulsion des morisques du royaume de Grenade et leur repartition en Castille (1570–1571)." *Mélanges de la Casa de Velázquez* 6 (1970): 211–246.

Weisser, Michael. *The Peasants of the Montes*. Chicago: University of Chicago Press, 1976.

Zarana, Jose Rafael. *Reseña Histórica*. App. 1: "Testamento de Don Lorenzo de Aldana." Pasto, 1942.

Zárate, Agustín. *Historia del descubrimiento y conquista del Peru*. Introd. and notes by Dorothy McMahon. University of Buenos Aires, 1965.

Index

Index

198, 222, 236, 237–238, 242, 266, 267, 281
Solís, doña Juana de, 139
Soria, Rodrigo de, 243–244
Soto, Blas de, 134, 238
Soto, Hernando de, 210
Soto, Isabel de, 134, 218, 238–239, 260
Sotomayor, Alonso de, 83, 139
Sotomayor, doña Beatriz de, 129, 130
Suárez de Toledo, Pedro, 78

Tajo (river), 15
Tamuja (river), 32, 98
Tapia, Juan de, 133
Taxation, 88
Tejado, Juan, 129–130, 131
Tierra, definition and usage of term, 23, 236
Tierra Firme, emigrants to, 100, 150, 155, 168, 172, 235
Toledo, 69, 82; merchants from, 111; population of, 26
Tomás, Maestre Manuel, 223, 234
Toro, Alonso de, 245
Torrecillas, 60; purchase of, 56
Torreorgaz, 32, 97, 159; sale of, 27
Torrequemada, 56, 59, 97, 153
Torres, Alonso de, 190–191
Torres, don Francisco de, 138, 152, 161–162, 197
Torres, Bachiller Gonzalo de, priest, 205, 216, 218, 265
Torres, doña Leonor de, 132, 134, 260
Torres Altamirano, Don Blas de, 265
Torres Hinojosa, Diego de, 60
Trujillo, Diego de, 96, 174–175, 201, 206, 211, 225, 232, 242, 244, 247, 249, 262, 264, 266, 271, 283
Trujillo (city): census of, 100; construction of houses in, 56–57; district of, 16, 23–24, 26; emigration from, 5, 13, 166; expansion of, 18, 57; military levy of 1580 in, 94–95; parishes of, 117; population of, 25; reconquest of, 16, 17; sales of towns of, 26–27
Trujillo (Peru), 139, 219, 229, 262
Trujillo city council of: activities of, 26; agreement with Jaraicejo, 24; appointment of Latin instructor, 35–36; killing locusts, 28; membership of, 34, 86–87, 226, 259, 270; ordinances regulating, 20; properties of, 62; returnees on, 43; treatment of paupers by, 101; use of montes, 69

Ulloa, Alvaro Sánchez de, 153
Ulloa, Antonio de, 23, 197, 251, 255
Ulloa, doña Francisca de, 162
Ulloa, Gonzalo de, 112
Ulloa, Lorenzo de, 139, 199, 222, 223, 231, 240, 262
Ulloa, doña Mencía de, 146
Ulloa Carvajal, don Juan de, 70
Ulloa Solís, Francisco de, 266, 267
Ulloa Solís, Lorenzo de, 81, 117, 242

Vaca de Castro, Licenciado, 224
Valdivia, Pedro de, 230
Valencia, Gonzalo de, 193, 227
Valencia, Martín de, 227
Valencia, Pedro Alonso de, 227
Valencia, Pedro de, 217, 223
Valencia de Alcántara, 15, 192
Valladolid, 21, 25, 93, 107; population of, 26; university of, 120
Valle, Juan del, 191
Valverde, Baltasar de, 85, 162
Valverde, Licenciado Diego García de, 53, 85, 179, 190, 234; career in Indies of, 217
Vargas, doña Beatriz de, 139; entail of, 64, 145
Vargas, Pedro Calderón de, 145, 161
Vargas Carvajal, Diego de: city council seats of, 86; as Comisario de Perpetuidad, 45, 191; purchase of Puerto de Santa Cruz by, 55–56; sons of, 139, 252. See also doña Beatriz de Vargas
Vargas Carvajal, Juan de, 114
Vargas Figueroa, Diego de, 81
Vargas Ocampo, García de, 87
Vazquez de Ayllón, Lucas (the younger), 186, 264
Vega, Andrés, 142
Velázquez, Diego, 115, 228
Velázquez, Juan, 245
Venezuela, 155, 188, 210
Veracruz, 189, 234–235
Vera de Mendoza, Juan de, 143
Villacastín, 66, 68
Villalobos Carvajal, Francisco de, 93
Vineyards, 28, 32; in Ibahernando, 103; sales of, 62
Vita, Juan de, 73
Vita, Macías de, 142
Vita, Pedro de, 142, 199–200, 266
Vita y Moraga, Juan de, 142, 199

Wages and salaries, 124; in agriculture, 103; in construction, 108–109; of Latin instructors, 35–36; of mayordomos (in Peru), 227; of municipal employees, 35; of professionals, 120

Wheat, prices of, 28; table 1, 29–31

Wills and inheritance, 144, 148, 153, 258; disinheritance, 146; before emigration, 192–193; of emigrants, 244; main discussion of, 156–160. *See also* Entails

Women: as bakers and cheese vendors, 109; in business, 112; in censuses, 100; as criadas, 71, 112, 124, 150; as emigrants, 178, 194, 200, 201, 202; as farmers, 103; as gardeners, 104; as heads of household, 135–136; in Indies, 213, 223–224, 229–230, 232; legal protections for, 145–146; main discussion of, 147–150; as mothers of illegitimate chil-

dren, 154; working in construction, 107. *See also* Dowries; Wills and inheritance

Wool: export of, 21, 65; manufacture of, 21; prices in Cáceres, 67 (table 4); sales of, 112

Yucatan, 171

Yuste (monastery), 15; connection to Guadalupe, 20

Zángano, 26

Zarza, 32; hidalgos in, 54; Pizarros in, 56

Zorita, 23, 190, 194, 219, 224, 225, 240, 245, 263; hidalgos in, 54–55, 149; poor in, 100

Designer:	U.C. Press Staff
Compositor:	Huron Valley Graphics, Inc.
Text:	11/13 Caledonia
Display:	Caledonia
Printer:	Edwards Bros.
Binder:	Edwards Bros.